The Best
of
Pulitzer Prize
News Writing

The Best
of
Pulitzer Prize
News Writing

**Wm. David Sloan, Valarie McCrary
and Johanna Cleary**

Publishing Horizons, Inc.
Columbus, Ohio

Copyright 1986, PUBLISHING HORIZONS, INC.
2950 North High Street
P.O. Box 02190
Columbus, Ohio 43202

Printed in the United States.

1 2 3 4 7 6 5 4

Library of Congress Cataloging in Publication Data
Main entry under title:

The Best of Pulitzer Prize news writing.

    1. Journalism—United States. 2. Pulitzer prizes.
I. Sloan, W. David (William David), 1947-   . II. McCrary, Valarie, 1960- . III. Cleary, Johanna, 1961- .
PN4726.B383 1986   071'.3   85-19410
ISBN 0-942280-14-8

CONTENTS

Part II
INVESTIGATIVE WRITING

Part III
PROFILE WRITING

Part IV
DESCRIPTIVE WRITING

Part V
ANALYTICAL WRITING

Preface

Why an anthology of news stories?

The answer is simple. It is a truism that what one reads is reflected in how one writes. That concept is accepted in "literature" — "The way to learn to write," would-be authors are told, "is to read" — and aspiring novelists, poets, and essayists are encouraged to read good writing. What works in the literary genres is no less practicable in journalism. If a journalist wants to turn out ordinary writing, he or she should read ordinary news stories. If the goal is to produce superior writing, the journalist should read examples of superior news writing.

There is the reason for this anthology. Few better sources of superior writing exist than those news stories which have won the Pulitzer Prize. The editors hope this volume of selected winners will provide a source of models of news writing for the journalist who wishes to be good.

The first Pulitzer Prizes were awarded in 1917. For each of the first twelve years only one award for reporting was given. Since 1929 the categories have been increased, and more than two hundred reporters have been recognized with Pulitzer Prizes for "distinguished" reporting. Certainly the most prestigious awards in the field of journalism, the Pulitzers each year attract scores of entries from newspapers, ranging from weeklies to metropolitan dailies. To be selected for a Pulitzer instantly bestows professional distinction on a reporter.

Most awards have been given for the reporting effort that went into stories, rather than for writing quality. To be sure, though, a multitude of winners have been marked by excellent writing style. Collected in this anthology are more than seventy of the articles that impress the editors as exemplars of superior writing. A few of these stories have appeared in other collections, either in part or in full. The editors of this anthology chose to reprint all selections in their entirety to do justice to the writing skills of the authors.

The stories that follow were selected from the approximately 2,000 articles included in the entries by the winning reporters. Each provides, we think, a lesson in news writing style which will benefit the reporter concerned about writing well. Lest the reader think that good writing requires sloppy journalism, we should note that each article not only reads well but is based on thorough reporting and adheres to the journalistic tenets of accuracy, fairness, and completeness. Good news writing must begin with good reporting, and all articles in this anthology more than satisfy that requirement.

Because one purpose of this anthology is to provide a guide for good writing, the articles are arranged to emphasize approaches to writing. They are organized into categories by stylistic and structural techniques rather than subject matter (such as crime or war or politics). Certainly, all stories involve more than one technique, but the reader will find stories grouped by narrative structure, investigative and analytical exposition, characterization, and descriptive writing. These groupings are made to some extent for convenience, and the reader studying them for writing principles should not assume that the only device used in a story in the narrative category, for instance, is narration. A single story might provide examples of many stylistic and structural techniques.

A book of this nature could not be done by one person or even by three editors alone. It requires the help of many, and we wish to thank the numerous individuals who assisted us.

We are especially grateful for the gracious assistance of Pulitzer Prize winners Abe Rosenthal, Nan Robertson, Seymour Hersh, and Vance Trimble; and of members of the staff of the Pulitzer Prize administrative offices: Robin H. Kuzen, assistant administrator, Pulitzer Prizes; Wade A. Doares, librarian, Graduate School of Journalism, Columbia University; E. M. Kliment, administrative assistant, Pulitzer Prizes; and Robert C. Christopher, administrator of the prizes.

A number of individuals provided us invaluable assistance in obtaining material from newspaper files and permission to reprint articles. At the risk of failing to mention some, we wish to thank the following: John V. R. Bull, assistant to the executive editor, Gene Roberts, executive editor, and Gerald Jordan, Philadelphia *Inquirer*; Richard H. Leonard, editor and senior vice-president, Milwaukee *Journal*; David Stolberg, assistant general editorial manager, and James H. Wagner, editorial promotion director, Scripps Howard Newspapers; Shiela L. Hylton-Adkins, manager, Newspaper Products, Bell & Howell; Sherman Dye, Baker & Hostetler, Counselors at Law; Edward M. Storin, assistant managing editor, and Horacio Aguirre, editor, Miami *Herald*; Scott Bosley, managing editor, and Joe Stroud, editor, Detroit *Free Press*; Katherine W. Fanning, editor, and Patricia A. Anderson, *Christian Science Monitor*; Stewart Spencer, editor, and Patricia Olds, Fort Wayne (Ind.) *News-Sentinel*; Joseph Dill, editor, Fargo (N. D.) *Forum*; John M. Lemmon, managing editor, Baltimore *Evening Sun*; James I. Houck, managing editor, and Reg Murphy, president and publisher, Baltimore *Sun*; Richard Thieriot, editor, and Susan Griffin, San Francisco *Chronicle*; James D. Squires, editor, Chicago *Tribune*; Michelle Arnot, editor, International Herald Tribune Corporation; Robert E. Page, president and publisher, Chicago *Sun-Times*; Murray B. Light, editor and senior vice-president, Buffalo *News*; John G. Craig, Jr., editor, Pittsburgh *Post Gazette*; Keith Fuller, president and general manager, and Dan Perkes, assistant general manager, Associated Press; Roger Wood, executive editor, and Peter Faris, editorial manager, New York *Post*; Eugene Patterson, editor, St. Petersburg *Times*; James B. King, editor, and June A. Almquist, assistant managing editor, Seattle *Times*; A. Paul Hogan, managing editor, Tampa *Tribune*; James G. Wieghart, editor, and Robert M. Lane, assistant to the editor, New York *Daily News*; Rose Cervino and Marjorie Langley, New York *Times*; James D. Squires, editor, and Kevin D. Dabe, public service officer, Chicago *Tribune*; Ben Bradlee, executive editor, and Elsie Carper, assistant managing editor, Washington *Post*; Richard H. Sugarman, deputy general counsel, the Hearst Corporation; William F. Thomas, editor, and Cheryl Preston, permissions coordinator, Los Angeles *Times*; Sidney Goldberg, vice-president and director, International Newspaper Operations, United Media; and Leonard Pardue, acting executive editor, and Joanne Heumann, manager of news administration, Louisville *Times* and *Courier-Journal*.

And last we thank someone we could name first: Debbie Wilkinson, a journalism student at the University of Alabama who worked tirelessly in the numerous tedious jobs involved in putting the manuscript together.

News Writing That Wins Prizes

News writing must be dull.

That is an unwritten rule. It is not stated in so many words; reporters are not instructed by editors to be dull, and newspapers do not set dullness as their most desired goal. But dullness is the standard nevertheless. It is caused by slavish adherence to practices which in and of themselves may be good—stylebook rules, conciseness, objectivity, and so forth. The problem results not from the rules but from reporters and editors assuming that the rules themselves account for good writing.

News writing can be good. It can be excellent. But news writing must be thought of in the same way as any other writing: it must be based on what works, not on rules alone. In this volume of prize-winning news stories, the reader will find many examples of writing that works. The articles have been selected from approximately 2,000 that have been included in winning entries in the news and feature categories of the annual Pulitzer Prize awards. While the Pulitzer Prize awards are based primarily on the reporting efforts behind the written articles, the selection of the stories for publication in this anthology is based on writing quality. We do not mean to slight reporting efforts, for good news gathering is mandatory for reporting. But good news gathering is not confined to dull articles. The reporting efforts behind the articles in this anthology are models of news gathering. Reporters may spend hundreds of hours to gather information for thoughtful stories. Thorough, time-consuming reporting can be wasted, however, if its results are not presented to the reader in an interesting manner. If the writing does not keep the reader's attention, all the work expended in gathering the information is futile. This book presents news stories that not only are based on good reporting efforts, but which present the findings in a way that keeps the reader's attention.

Why a collection of Pulitzer Prize news stories? The authors believe that journalists should be more aware of good writing—of the fact that news writing can be exceptional, that it can make interesting, absorbing reading. Writing is the journalist's tool, just as the hammer is the carpenter's. And as the carpenter must know how to use the hammer well, the journalist must know how to write well. The best way a writer can learn to write well is to read good writing. This anthology is intended to provide examples of good writing. Often, journalists turn out dull writing simply because they neglect the fact that news stories can be interesting. On a daily basis they read only typical stories—and the typical news story is bland. It leaves no impression. If it keeps the reader's attention, it does so because of the information it contains, not because of its writing style. Continual acquaintance with such writing magnifies the journalist's impression that such is how news writing is supposed to be and must be. Continual reading of well-written stories should create the opposite impression—that journalistic writing not only can but must be good. The editors hope this anthology will have such an effect, that journalists who read it will believe that news writing can and should be good.

What is "good" news writing?

It is, simply stated, writing that achieves its purpose, that does what it is supposed to do. News writing should do two things: it should inform the reader, and it should interest the reader. Because the role of journalism to provide information is accepted, there is general agreement that news writing should inform. The information function underlies most approaches to journalistic writing. Most rules are aimed at ensuring that news writing presents material clearly, that it is easily understandable to most readers. Conciseness, short sentences, simple words—all these characteristics of journalism have one primary goal: to provide information clearly. Because so much attention has been devoted to clarity, it may be said of journalistic writing that it has one of the most easily understood styles of all types of writing. By emphasizing the basic rules of news writing, college journalism departments find it possible to turn out hundreds of graduates every semester who are able, more or less, to present information easily understood by the typical reader with an average tenth-grade education. Of the requirements for good writing, then, journalism excels in one. It is admirable for its ability to inform, to present information with exceptional clarity.

Clarity alone, however, does not make writing good. To be superior, writing also must interest the reader. Without being interesting, clear writing by itself is deadening. An account of the most interesting event, the most absorbing information, can lose the reader's attention if it is not presented in a style that can carry the interest. A reader may never get past the halfway mark of a story if the writing is dull. The emphasis on rules for clarity may be adequate to train thousands of journalism students how to present information, but adherence only to those rules and an emphasis only on presenting information do little to make that information absorbing for the reader. They make writing simply mechanical. The writer must be concerned with story structure and presentation if the story is to have real interest for the reader. Good journalistic writing is not one-dimensional. That is, it does not present information only. The best journalistic writing appeals to the senses; it gives the reader the feeling of "being there," of experiencing what happened. It makes news events and information come alive.

But being interesting does not mean that writing is to be ostentatious. Good writing does not draw attention to itself. It absorbs the reader in the content being presented; writing fails if it makes the reader aware of the writing itself. Good writing focuses attention on what is being said, not on how it is said. Good writing is unobtrusive. It is not superficial or artificial or pretentious. It is natural and real.

Perhaps the best way to determine whether news writing is good is to examine one's response to a story after having read it. Good writing leaves an impression. Even though the reader may not be aware of the style as he is reading, he has a response upon finishing an article. Effective writing carries the impact of the content by focusing the reader's attention on the story being told. While the reader should be oblivious to the writing style, it is the style that makes possible the wallop that the event inherently contains. Writing is good, then, when it delivers news material in its undiluted strength.

Certain techniques seem most effective in making news writing good. The observant reader will notice these techniques in the Pulitzer Prize winning articles in this anthology. For purposes of discussion, the techniques illustrated by the articles can be divided into two broad categories: those that ensure unity and those that contribute to intensity. Unity in a news story is achieved when all parts contribute to a central idea. All aspects are cohesive. They fit together; they all have their place in the story; extraneous and irrevelant details are omitted.

Good news writing has unity

The most obvious and important concept in the area of unity is *thematic unity*. It requires that the news story be structured around one central idea, or theme. A news story works best when it has a point. Without a unifying theme, a story falls apart. If it is no more than a collection of details or an odd, unintegrated assortment of pieces of information, it works poorly or does not work at all. To have an impact, a news story must do more than pull together a group of facts, quotes, dates, places, names, and other bits of "news." All of its parts must work together as a unified whole. News writing is especially prone to thematic disintegration. At best, news stories normally tend to focus simply around a topic—usually an event, although sometimes around an issue—rather than around a theme. As opposed to a topic, a theme is a central "point" or "meaning." The topic of Ernie Pyle's article on Capt. Henry Waskow, for example, is the death of a soldier; the theme is that the dead captain was dearly loved by men of his company. A topic is a subject; a theme is a statement. All of the best Pulitzer Prize news stories have themes. Too many newspaper stories are routine because they have only topics.

Thematic unity also requires that a news story have only one theme. If it has more, its focus will be diffused; its strength will be diluted. Stories with more than one theme tend to confuse readers. When stories leap from one theme or one point to another, they risk losing readers. A news story needs one central theme and needs to stick with it. Wandering off from that central theme achieves nothing. Staying with it builds a story into a whole.

Reporters tend to wander for two reasons. The first is that they normally do not think in terms of thematic unity. They think in terms of details and pieces of information related to a situation involving a topic. A city council meeting, for example, is the situation, the topic. Things that occur at the meeting are the details. A convenience-store robbery is a situation; when the robbery occurred and how much money was taken are details. To provide a theme, the reporter needs to look for the point—or meaning, if you will—behind the event. He needs to find the idea that unifies the details of the event. The theme in the robbery story could be that a clerk acted calmly in a threatening situation. The story then would be built—details selected and narrated—so that the characters in action are related to the governing idea. The second reason causing reporters to wander is that they frequently assume that all information gathered from a situation is newsworthy. They tend to include all details without asking whether the details are relevant to the point of the story. News stories tend to become hodgepodges of information. The reporter should ask whether details are relevant and necessary. What is the theme, the central idea? Does a particular detail relate directly to that idea? Does including it help build the theme? The rule for including or excluding a detail is this: if it contributes to the theme, include the detail; if it dilutes the theme, leave it out.

Unity also requires that a news story have a logical organization. Parts should be arranged so that each has its appropriate place and seems to follow naturally the part that preceded it. The organization most often used in news writing is the "inverted pyramid" arrangement, in which information is placed in descending order of importance. The most important material comes first in the story, and the least important last. The logic behind the inverted pyramid is sound for the purposes it is intended to serve: the reader may stop reading at any point and still have obtained the most important information, while editors may eliminate paragraphs from the bottom up if limited printing space requires that part of a story be cut. Neither reason for the inverted pyramid approach is based primarily on writing quality. While the inverted pyramid may be adequate for brief stories and announcements, it tends to encourage haphazard arrangement of lengthier, fuller stories. It may work well for stories the reporter does not wish to develop beyond the routine, but it normally results in little more than a stringing together of actions, quotes, and facts. To make news writing good, parts of a story (either individual paragraphs or blocks of paragraphs) should be put together cohesively and coherently. They should fit together, and the fit should make sense to the reader.

Reporters are particularly prone to string together material without evident plan when they work with quotations. Large blocks of stories tend to be made up of direct quote after quote introduced and divided from one another only by the perfunctory "(the source) said." Such quotation and attribution can be boring, and they often lead to confusion as to the significance and meaning of the quotes. When quotation is used to provide information—as opposed to developing a character—it should be introduced with an explanation: what is the point it is illustrating? A quote itself should elaborate on a point explained by the reporter. Strings of direct quotes should be interrupted occasionally for the reporter to provide perspective. When a story is composed of extensive quotation, the reporter serves as little more than a stenographer. The reporter must serve as guide for the reader, pointing out the contours of an issue or explaining the highpoints of an event.

When moving from one part of a story to the next, the reporter needs to signal the reader that a change is being made. The device used to give the signal is *transition.* If the new part is parallel or similar to the previous one, a transition word such as "similarly" or "likewise" might be used. If the subsequent part contrasts with the previous one, then a word such as "however" or "although" can be used. If one part stands out or is more important, its significance can be made clear with "primarily" or "mainly" or a similar transition. If parts are related by logic or time, words such as "therefore" or "then" can be tried. Transitional words should be used, however, with restraint. At times, the change in the thought or from one part of the story to another will be evident without the reporter signaling the reader. In such instances, transitional words read awkwardly and slow down the reading. Transitions should not be used unnecessarily or repetitiously. They should be used but only as necessary to make the structure of a story clear.

Unity is indispensable for good news writing. Stories need to be planned. Although reporters are trained to write under pressure and turn out pages of copy—or VDT screensful of characters—under hurried conditions, thought must be given to a story's overall structure and to its logical development. The reporter should know where a story is to end before the writing begins. When a reporter gets midway into a story and does not know where to go with it from there, as frequently happens, the problem is that the story's development has not been planned. The solution is to determine the theme and then to decide the direction the story is to head, the structure it is to take, before the first word is typed into the VDT. Unity gives structural meaning to a story and makes an impact on the reader more likely.

Good news writing has intensity

Intensity increases the impact. Intensity may be achieved through a number of devices. The most obvious is subject matter. Treated with routine writing style, however, even a subject with great inherent intensity can seem flaccid to the reader. Too many stories which have won the Pulitzer Prize for news writing provide convincing evidence of that fact. Fires, floods, military battles, murders, gambling, and government corruption have made the dullest of stories. Numerous Pulitzer Prize winners have been selected for their coverage of major news and not for writing quality. It is a truism that the best assurance of a good story is good material, but dead style can slay even the liveliest of events and personalities. The reader of this anthology is spared the boredom offered by several hundred Pulitzer Prize stories that won on subject matter alone. The unfortunate fact about most of them is that the reporters, because they had paid little attention to writing quality, lost wonderful opportunities to write intensely absorbing stories. Many features of writing contribute to intensity. A few are suggested here.

Style should be natural, not artificial. The reporter should write in a style that suits him naturally, rather than in one determined by mechanical rules. An effective style must be one's own style; otherwise articles sound as if they were written mechanically. A personal style may be considered by some journalists to be the antithesis of what news writing should be: objective, cold, detached, impersonal. But news writing should be honest, and to attempt to make stories which were written by living reporters sound as if they were all written by the same machine is the utmost in reader deceit. A personal style does not mean necessarily a "subjective style"; it means that a reporter does not write like a robot. The reporter should be freed from the belief that a few style rules learned in news writing textbooks are absolutes.

A natural style also suggests that the reporter responds to news subjects as human beings. A good effective style begins inside a human, not in a typewriter keyboard or the circuitry of a VDT. Reporters are people writing stories which often involve people. People subjects should not be written about as if they are objects. They are not governed by laws of science or mathematical formulas or other "objective measures." If they are in news situations containing emotion, that emotion should be allowed into a news story. Subjects are people; reporters are people. Subjects should be allowed to act like people in news stories. Reporters should write like people.

News stories should include concrete details. The most effective news writing style uses concrete details. Nearly all of the best Pulitzer Prize news stories have done so. Without concrete details, stories seem vague and general. Concreteness makes them specific and particular. Physical descriptions of people help readers grasp characteristics better; hard details of scenes help readers visualize where and how actions took place. Without concrete details, stories remain hazy, action and characters indistinct. Details bring them alive and make them real. They help readers to "see" what the reporter is writing about, to smell it, or to hear it.

Using concrete detail in writing requires that the reporter be able to provide an eyewitness account. It is ideal when the reporter has seen the action or event firsthand. The reporters' presence at scenes of battle, tragedy, or heroism is one of the main reasons so many news stories from America's wars stand out among Pulitzer Prize winners. The reporters were able to include story details that they observed themselves. Such reporting is more likely to be possible in war coverage, because a reporter travels with the action. In most other types of coverage, whether a reporter is present at a news event depends on luck as much as anything else. A journalist is unlikely to know beforehand if, for example, an explosion will ignite a nightclub fire. If he does not witness an event himself, the reporter must rely on others for accounts of the action and descriptions of the scene and people involved. Working under such restrictions, the reporter should attempt to gather as much concrete detail as possible. Even though secondhand, the detail will make the account more vivid and help the event come alive for the reader. Descriptions gathered from witnesses must be more than general accounts. The reporter's story must be more than a collection of hazy descriptions introduced with the ubiquitous "he said." The job of gathering details must be so thorough that the reporter knows exactly what happened, and is able to see, hear, feel, and smell specific actions, events, and characters—and is able to reconstruct them in such a minute degree that the reader can visualize the event.

Effective style evokes mood. Good news writing can create atmosphere, and one measure of good writing is whether the reader senses an atmosphere, or mood, surrounding the events and people in a story. Mood is not, however, a particular aspect of style. It is a result of all other features of writing. Mood is not created artificially but through theme, action, details, characterization, and other factors of a news story. Mood can be used as an indicator of whether news writing is effective. If the writing is good, it often will evoke mood.

Reporters should tell stories. Not all news accounts lend themselves to storytelling; some require exposition. Many of the most effective news stories, however, have a narrative structure. Some lend themselves to plot development, characterization, conflict, rhythm of pacing, and denouement. When an event offers the opportunity for narrative, the reporter should tell a story, introducing the situation and characters, building the action, and reaching the climax.

Even when a news account would not be served well by narrative storytelling, the reporter can make use of shorter stories within the overall article. Anecdotes and examples may be used to illustrate points of exposition. They not only explain; they add a human dimension and make reading livelier and more interesting. Because of the secondary place they play in a large story, anecdotes and examples must be brief (no more than a few paragraphs) and should focus on a single point. The insightful reporter may, within a pithy example, reveal character, capture the essence of an event or situation, or create a sense of place or action.

Effective writing reveals character. News is important primarily because of one reason: people. It involves people, and it affects people. The most inanimate topic takes on importance when and usually only if it has an effect on people. Even atomic energy, a major news topic today, has little news value in and of itself. It becomes of critical importance because of its potentially tremendous impact on people. People are the reason for news. The human angle in news writing should be explored by every reporter. News stories can offer two types of treatment of people. One involves the event, action, or issue that has the potential for affecting large numbers of people. Such a story can gain heightened intensity by examining the effects in human terms. The other involves only one person or a small number of people who serve as representatives of larger numbers or of humanity in general. By examining the individual, the news story captures in one person's life significance that extends to others. The more a reporter writes about people, the more interesting and important a news story becomes to the reader. People are more interesting than inanimate facts. Reader response is aroused more easily by human subjects. Focusing on an individual in a news story helps the reader comprehend the totality of an issue or event.

To write effectively about people, the reporter must think in terms of characterization and should make use of a number of principles. A character in a news story whether the subject of just one paragraph or of an entire article, must seem real to the reader. The characterization, therefore, must be based on concrete detail. Character is revealed through physical characteristics (features such as eyes, facial details, and skin texture), typical gestures and movements, details of the person's surroundings (decoration of the office or tidiness of the home, for example), and dress (which may reveal pride, economic class, taste, or another characteristic). What a person says and how he says it, if noted accurately by the reporter, will make the characterization come alive. Quoting of speech should be used for more than information in news stories; it should reveal character. The reporter should be especially alert to words, quotes, conversation, and dialogue that will help the reader understand the speaker as a real person. Attributions should do more than indicate the source of a quote. They should add to characterization. The word "said," while impersonal and "objective," should be omitted in favor of more revealing words such as "argued" or "vowed" or "snapped" when the reporter's intent is to show character through tone of speech. Most important in revealing character, however, is action. How does a person act or react in a real situation or at a crucial moment? How does he behave when facing a major decision? Character revelation can be strengthened when the reporter has done enough research and alert observation to be able to analyze the motives behind actions. Readers understand character better when they are shown not only the actions taken by a person but also the reasons behind the actions. Despite its importance to effective news writing, characterization is not often done. The reason: it is not easy to do. It takes a reporter who is observant of exact features and alert to the minutest details. If done well, it can add a fuller dimension to news writing.

News writing must be clear. News stories must be easily understandable to the average reader. All types of writing should be clear, but clarity in news writing is especially important because of the attitude which people bring to newspaper reading. Newspaper readers—unlike readers of novels, or scientific reports, or poems—do not expect or wish to have to analyze writing. News writing which is not clear—which is not easily understood on a first read—loses power. The reader should not be confused by vagueness of words or sentences, of points or ideas, of logic or article structure. The reporter should use simple, strong words and sentences instead of complex or complicated or indecipherable ones. He should eliminate jargon, abstruseness, and fancy phrases. Effective news writing is direct. Its logic and meaning are plain.

Various stylistic devices may intensify news writing. While some techniques of effective writing pertain to overall story structure, reporters may employ a number of devices relating solely to word usage and style to intensify their writing. The techniques are common to all types of good writing and are practiced by good journalists.

(1) Reporters should write with precision. Words should be chosen for their exact meaning. Writing should not ramble in the reporter's search to state, finally, the point. The right word should not be left to hope or chance. Obtuse writing is not forceful writing.

(2) Effective writing is economical. Journalists are prone to use the description "concise" for lean wording. While conciseness normally refers, in journalistic usage, to the use of one or a few words instead of many, economical writing suggests not only conciseness, but short words when they are best, short sentences when they are effective, simplicity of phrasing, and exact word choice. Reporters should not be slaves to rules requiring that sentences average only twenty words or so, but they should not use words needlessly. If an effective sentence can be stated in no less than fifty words, fifty words should be used;

but two words should not be used when one makes the point just as well.

(3) Nouns and verbs should outnumber adjectives and adverbs. Adjectives and adverbs only qualify; nouns and verbs provide the substance and the action. Modifiers may be used occasionally to color and brighten, but the strength of writing bursts from things and people on whom others are acting. Strength, decisiveness, power, and intensity come from verbs that act. Passive verbs should be used for victims. Active verbs suggest vigor, movement, action, life.

(4) Writing should use variety. Without it, writing becomes monotonous. Sentence structures should differ; word choice should vary. Sentence length and rhythm should change. Some sentences should have subordinate or coordinate clauses; others should not. Subjects and verbs should be placed at different points in sentences. Some sentences should begin with introductory phrases; others should not. Variety lends emphasis to words and ideas. Variety omitted, writing loses its spice.

No rules can assure great writing. Understanding principles, though, can help the reporter write good news stories more consistently. Reading and studying outstanding examples of good news writing also can help. Not only can they help; they are essential for the reporter who wishes to write well. If people are, as has been said, what they eat, then writers are what they read. Continual exposure to ordinary news stories will encourage ordinary writing. Exposure to effective stories will encourage effective writing. Among the best news stories one may find are the Pulitzer Prize winners in this anthology. While none may be free from flaw, they offer examples of the techniques that make for superior news writing. And while the critic may insist that some are too colorful or personal to be "objective journalism," the editors think they abide by the most fundamental rules of journalism. Besides being interesting to read, they are accurate, fair, and complete in providing information. They are models of responsible, thorough, correct reporting. They not only inform, as is the duty of journalism; they also provide reading that is absorbing to today's journalists, years after the people, events, and issues have lost most of their interest. They are sparkling pieces of writing. They prove that news writing does not have to be dull.

The Best
of
Pulitzer Prize
News Writing

Part I.

NARRATIVE WRITING

One of the oldest styles of journalistic writing is the narrative account. Like a well-written piece of fiction, the narrative should entertain the reader while telling an interesting story.

Many of the techniques used in short story writing also apply to narratives. First, the reader should be drawn in by a lively lead that demands attention. Once attracted, the reader should find some substance within the story's body to maintain that interest. Finally, the conclusion should wrap up loose ends and help establish perspective for the reader.

Often a narrative piece actually includes a number of stories, all sharing common threads woven together by the writer. Reporters frequently must write a single story or series based on a set of wide-ranging events. By placing these various occurrences into a polished story framework, the writer can serve an important function through the narrative format.

1. The Unknown Soldier Is Laid to Rest

Kirke Simpson's account of the burial of the Unknown Soldier is one of the classics of journalism. In dignified, moving prose appropriate for the occasion, he provides not only an account of the ceremonies but a poignant eulogy on America's war dead. Through careful use of details and apt comment, Simpson creates a mood which pervades the account and leaves an unforgettable impression with the reader. *(Pulitzer Prize for Reporting, 1922)*

Bugles Sound Taps for Warrior's Requiem
Kirke L. Simpson
Associated Press
November 11, 1921

Under the wide and starry skies of his own homeland America's unknown dead from France sleeps tonight, a soldier home from the wars.

Alone, he lies in the narrow cell of stone that guards his body; but his soul has entered into the spirit that is America. Wherever liberty is held close in men's hearts, the honor and the glory and the pledge of high endeavor poured out over this nameless one of fame will be told and sung by Americans for all time.

Scrolled across the marble arch of the memorial raised to American soldier and sailor dead, everywhere, which stands like a monument behind his tomb, runs this legend: "We here highly resolve that these dead shall not have died in vain."

The words were spoken by the martyred Lincoln over the dead at Gettysburg. And today with voice strong with determination and ringing with deep emotion, another President echoed that high resolve over the coffin of the soldier who died for the flag in France.

Great men in the world's affairs heard that high purpose reiterated by the man who stands at the head of the American people. Tomorrow they will gather in the city that stands almost in the shadow of the new American shrine of liberty dedicated today. They will talk of peace; of the curbing of the havoc of war.

They will speak of the war in France, that robbed this soldier of life and name and brought death to comrades of all nations by the hundreds of thousands. And in their ears when they meet must ring President Harding's declaration today beside that flag-wrapped, honor-laden bier:

"There must be, there shall be, the commanding voice of a conscious civilization against armed warfare."

Far across the seas, other unknown dead, hallowed in memory by their countrymen, as this American soldier is enshrined in the heart of America, sleep their last. He, in whose veins ran the blood of British forebears, lies beneath a great stone in ancient Westminster Abbey; he of France, beneath the Arc de Triomphe, and he of Italy under the altar of the fatherland in Rome.

And it seemed today that they, too, must be here among the Potomac hills to greet an American comrade come to join their glorious company, to testify their approval of the high words of hope spoken by America's President. All day long the nation poured out its heart in pride and glory for the nameless American. Before the first crash of the minute guns roared its knell for the dead from the shadow of Washington Monument, the people who claim him as their own were trooping out to do him honor. They lined the long road from the Capitol to the hillside where he sleeps tonight; they flowed like a tide over the slopes about his burial place; they choked the bridges that lead across the river to the fields of the brave, in which he is the last comer.

As he was carried past through the banks of humanity that lined Pennsylvania Avenue a solemn, reverent hush held the living walls. Yet there was not so much of sorrow as of high pride in it all, a pride beyond the reach of shouting and the clamor that marks less sacred moments in life.

Out there in the broad avenue was a simple soldier, dead for honor of the flag. He was nameless. No man knew what part in the great life of the nation he had filled when he passed over his home soil. But in France he had died as Americans always have been ready to die, for the flag and what it means. They read the message of the pageant clear, these silent thousands along the way. They stood in almost holy awe to take their own part in what was theirs, the glory of the American people, honored here in the honors showered on America's nameless son from France.

Soldiers, sailors, and marines—all played their part in the thrilling spectacles as the cortege rolled along. And just behind the casket, with its faded French flowers on the draped flag, walked the President, the chosen leader of a hundred million, in whose name he was chief mourner at his bier. Beside him strode the man under whom the fallen hero had lived and died in France, General Pershing, wearing only the single medal of Victory that every American soldier might wear as his only decoration.

Then, row on row, came the men who lead the nation today or have guided its destinies before. They were all there, walking proudly, with age and frailties of the flesh forgotten. Judges, Senators, Representatives, highest officers of every military arm of government, and a trudging little group of the nation's most valorous sons, the Medal of Honor men. Some were gray and bent and drooping with old wounds; some trim and erect as the day they won their way to fame. All walked gladly in this nameless comrade's last parade.

Behind these came the carriage in which rode Woodrow Wilson, also stricken down by infirmities as he served in the highest place in the nation, just as the humble private riding in such state ahead had gone down before a shell or bullet. For that dead man's sake, the former President had put aside his dread of seeming to parade his physical weakness and risked health, perhaps life, to appear among the mourners for the fallen.

There was handclapping and a cheer here and there for the man in the carriage, a tribute to the spirit that brought him to honor the nation's nameless hero, whose commander-in-chief he had been.

After President Harding and most of the high dignitaries of the government had turned aside at the White House, the procession, headed by its solid blocks of soldiery and the battalions of sailor comrades, moved on with Pershing, now flanked by Secretaries Weeks and Denby, for the long road to the tomb. It marched on, always between the human borders of the way of victory the nation had made for itself of the great avenue; on over the old bridge that spans the Potomac, on up the long hill to Fort Myer, and at last to the great cemetery beyond, where soldier and sailor folk sleep by the thousands. There the lumbering guns of the artillary swung aside, the cavalry drew their horses out of the long line and left to the foot soldiers and the sailors and marines the last stage of the journey.

Ahead, the white marble of the amphitheater gleamed through the trees. It stands crowning the slope of the hills that sweep upward from the river, and just across was Washington, its clustered buildings and monuments to great dead who have gone before, a moving picture in the autumn haze.

People in thousands were moving about the great circle of the ampitheater. The great ones to whom places had been given in the sacred enclosure and the plain folk who had trudged the long way just to glimpse the pageant from afar, were finding their places. Everywhere within the pillared enclosure bright uniforms of foreign soldiers appeared. They were laden with the jeweled order of rank to honor an American private soldier, great in the majesty of his sacrifices, in the tribute his honors paid to all Americans who died.

Down below the platform placed for the casket, in a stone vault, lay wreaths and garlands brought from England's King and guarded by British soldiers. To them came the British Ambassador in the full uniform of his rank to bid them keep safe against that hour.

Above the platform gathered men whose names ring through history—Briand, Foch, Beatty, Balfour, Jacques, Diaz, and others—in a brilliant array of place and power. They were followed by others, Baron Kato from Japan, the Italian statesmen and officers, by the notables from all countries gathered here for tomorrow's conference, and by some of the older figures in American life too old to walk beside the approaching funeral train.

Down around the circling pillars the marbled box filled with distinguished men and women, with a cluster of shattered men from army hospitals, accompanied by uniformed nurses. A surpliced choir took its place to wait the dead.

Faint and distant, the silvery strains of a military band stole into the big white bowl of the ampitheater. The slow cadences and mourning notes of a funeral march grew clearer amid the roll and mutter of the muffled drums.

At the arch where the choir awaited the heroic dead, comrades lifted his casket down and, followed by the generals and the admirals, who had walked beside him from the Capitol, he was carried to the place of honor. Ahead moved the white-robed singers, chanting solemnly. Carefully, the casket was placed above the banked flowers, and the Marine Band played sacred melodies until the moment the President and Mrs. Harding stepped to their places beside the casket; then the crashing, triumphant chorus of *The Star Spangled Banner* swept the gathering to its feet again.

A prayer, carried out over the crowd by amplifiers so that no word was missed, took a moment or two, then the sharp, clear call of the bugle rang "Attention!" and for two minutes the nation stood at pause for the dead, just at high noon. No sound broke the quiet as all stood with bowed heads. It was much as though a mighty hand had checked the world in full course. Then the band sounded, and in a mighty chorus rolled up the words of America from the hosts within and without the great open hall of valor.

President Harding stepped forward beside the coffin to say for America the thing that today was nearest to the nation's heart, that sacrifices such as this nameless man, fallen in battle, might perhaps be made unnecessary down through the coming years. Every word that President Harding spoke reached every person through the amplifiers and reached other thousands upon thousands in New York and San Francisco.

Mr. Harding showed strong emotion as his lips formed the last words of the address. He paused, then with raised hand and head bowed, went on in the measured, rolling periods of the Lord's Prayer. The response that came back to him from the thousands he faced, from the other thousands out over the slopes beyond, perhaps from still other thousands away near the Pacific, or close-packed in the heart of the nation's greatest city, arose like a chant. The marble arches hummed with a solemn sound.

Then the foreign officers who stand highest among the soldiers or sailors of their flags came one by one to the bier to place gold and jeweled emblems for the brave above the breast of the sleeper. Already, as the great prayer ended, the President had set the American seal of admiration for the valiant, the nation's love for brave deeds and the courage that defies death, upon the casket.

Side by side he laid the Medal of Honor and the Distinguished Service Cross. And below, set in place with reverent hands, grew the long line of foreign honors, the Victoria Cross, never before laid on the breast of any but those who had served the British flag; all the highest honors of France and Belgium and Italy and Rumania and Czechoslovakia and Poland.

To General Jacques of Belgium it remained to add his own touch to these honors. He tore from the breast of his own tunic the medal of valor pinned there by the Belgian King, tore it with a sweeping gesture, and tenderly bestowed it on the unknown American warrior.

Through the religious services that followed, and prayers, the swelling crowd sat motionless until it rose to join in the old, consoling *Rock of Ages*, and the last rite for the dead was at hand. Lifted by his hero-bearers from the stage, the unknown was carried in his flag-wrapped, simple coffin out to the wide sweep of the terrace. The bearers laid the sleeper down above the crypt, on which had been placed a little of the soil of France. The dust his blood helped redeem from alien hands will mingle with his dust as time marches by.

The simple words of the burial ritual were said by Bishop Brent; flowers from war mothers of America and England were laid in place.

For the Indians of America Chief Plenty Coos came to call upon the

Great Spirit of the Red Men, with gesture and chant and tribal tongue, that the dead should not have died in vain, that war might end, peace be purchased by such blood as this. Upon the casket he laid the coupstick of his tribal office and the feathered war bonnet from his own head. Then the casket, with its weight of honors, was lowered into the crypt.

A rocking blast of gunfire rang from the woods. The glittering circle of bayonets stiffened to a salute to the dead. Again the guns shouted their message of honor and farewell. Again they boomed out; a loyal comrade was being laid to his last, long rest.

High and clear and true in the echoes of the guns, a bugle lifted the old, old notes of taps, the lullaby for the living soldier, in death his requiem. Long ago some forgotten soldier-poet caught its meaning clear and set it down that soldiers everywhere might know its message as they sink to rest:

Fades the light;
And afar
Goeth day, cometh night,
And a star,
Leadeth all, speedeth all,
To their rest.

The guns roared out again in the national salute. He was home, The Unknown, to sleep forever among his own.

Reprinted by permission of the Associated Press.

2. A Lynch Mob's "Swift and Terrible" Retribution

Royce Brier's story of the lynching of two jail inmates was written after eleven hours of strenuous reporting and dangerous work. Even gripping fiction can hardly compare with his straight report of human beings obsessed with lynch fever and victims terrified by a lynch mob. By selecting vigorous verbs and revealing detail, Brier conveys the realism and emotion of the event. (*Pulitzer Prize for Reporting, 1934*)

Murderers Meet Violent Death at Hands of a Mob
Royce Brier
San Francisco *Chronicle*
November 27, 1933

SAN JOSE, Calif.—Lynch law wrote the last grim chapter in the Brooke Hart kidnaping here tonight. Twelve hours after the mutilated body of the son of Alex J. Hart, wealthy San Jose merchant, was recovered from San Francisco Bay a mob of ten thousand infuriated men and women stormed the Santa Clara County Jail, dragged John M. Holmes and Thomas H. Thurmond from their cells, and hanged them in historic St. James Park.

Swift, and terrible to behold, was the retribution meted out to the confessed kidnapers and slayers. As the pair were drawn up, threshing in the throes of death, a mob of thousands of men and women and children screamed anathemas at them.

The siege of the County Jail, a three-hour whirling, howling drama of lynch law, was accomplished without serious injury either to the seizers or the thirty-five officers who vainly sought to defend the citadel.

The defense of the jail failed because Sheriff Emig and his forces ran out of tear-gas bombs. Bombs kept the determined mob off for several hours.

Help from San Francisco and Oakland officers arrived too late to save the Hart slayers.

"Don't string me up, boys. God, don't string me up," was the last cry of Holmes as the noose was put about his neck in the light of flash lamps.

Thurmond was virtually unconscious with terror as the mob hustled him from the jail, down the alley, and across the street to his doom.

Great cheers from the crowd of onlookers accompanied the hoisting of the two slayers. Some women fainted, some were shielded from the sight by their escorts, but the gamut of human nature was here in the park. Old women with graying hair and benign faces expressed satisfaction at the quick end of the murderers, and young women with hardened faces broke down and wept.

King Mob was in the saddle and he was an inexorable ruler.

And here was a sovereign whose rise in invincible power stunned San Jose and will stun the nation and the world.

Brooke Hart's torn body was found in the water this morning. Barricades went up before the County Jail, and the crowd gathered and stayed all the day. It was a good-natured crowd. It knew the deputies and the police and the state highway patrolmen who stood guard. It bandied words with them.

There had been talk of an organized mob, and as the crowd grew in the evening there was no organization. There was shouting, and good nature still ruled.

"This crowd won't do anything," was the constant reiteration of Sheriff Emig's deputies.

Yet as their words of confidence were being spoken there flashed, like a prairie fire, the word through San Jose—eleven o'clock! Eleven o'clock!

The constant bombardment of that hour on the ear was monotonous and ominous.

Indeed, when that hour came the mob was well on its way to its prey, and they were dangling from limbs before midnight.

It was shortly before nine o'clock that the front line at the barricade made its first move of violence. Ten or fifteen patrolmen and deputies were against the barricade, which was not more than thirty feet from the jail door.

There was some pushing from behind, and the good-natured jeering, which had prevailed for almost an hour, took on a deeper tone of muttering. Strangely enough, there was little shouting of "lynch them" at this critical stage. It was a growl which was not unlike the throaty shouting in an African film.

Newspapermen stood behind the barriers, a few deputies stood about. Cameramen snapped flashlights.

Suddenly that front line lunged.

The police locked arms to hold them back. There were fifteen police and a hundred men exerting pressure against them. They swayed for a moment, locked in one another's embrace.

The police shouted orders, but they were mere shrill nothings as the mob behind began a deep rumble, dreadful in its menace.

Out of this twinkling of struggle, while the men behind the barriers held their breath, came a blast like that of a gun. The mob was temporarily quelled and uncertain, staggering back. "Shooting! Shooting!" went up the cry.

But it was a tear-gas bomb which had exploded.

The police suddenly gave way, taking one officer who had been burned back into the jail. The mob, after a moment of uncertainty, surged forward but was still a little cautious.

Out of the jail poured five or six deputies armed with tear-gas sticks. Again the leaders of the mob, those who bear the brunt, staggered back.

But even as they staggered they jeered, and the first shouts of "lynch 'em," stabbed through the tumult.

"We'll get 'em now boys....Bring 'em out....Bring 'em out...." And another dreadful cry went up, a kind of chant which lasted but a minute: "Brooke Hart—Brooke Hart—Brooke Hart—Brooke Hart."

This chant, all of these shouts and screams were choked off in an instant as the the first tear-gas bombs were fired.

"Boom—boom—boom," went the bombs. Again smoke, blue and lazy, drifted in the night air of the besieged jail, as lazy in the arc light as cigar smoke before a hearth.

The crowd broke and ran, women and children went screaming out beside the courthouse, handkerchiefs went to eyes everywhere, and the jail for a moment stood deserted, a grim old fortress which seemed in that moment impregnable.

"That's the end of it," everyone said, deputies, newspapermen, everyone.

And everyone, unable to plumb the depth of fury which has swayed San Jose for seventeen days, was wrong.

This was about nine o'clock.

The women and children had run, but there were hardy spirits who stayed. They were the leaders, they were the men who ultimately hanged Holmes and Thurmond.

They couldn't get in close to the jail. The lazy smoke burned their eyes. But they could stand off and throw rocks, and throw rocks they did.

The first rock came soon after the gas started to dissipate. A new post office building is being built near by.

There was tile aplenty about and bricks. There was also a vantage point from which to throw.

Sixty seconds after the first stone came, a steady shower was beating a tattoo on the stone wall of the jail, clanking against the steel door, making musical tinkles as it struck the bars.

Every rat-a-tat on stone or steel brought cheers from the crowd, and when a window in the jail fell the cheers were redoubled. The sound of a smashing window seemed by some alchemy to get them all, and they roared at the tops of their two hundred voices.

The alleyway before the jail door was now wholly untenable for human beings.

The scene in so far as concerned the pavement was not unlike the front steps of a church during the World War. Debris was everywhere. It was no man's land—no mistaking that.

Now not all of the officers on guard were besieged in the County Jail. Across the alley in Sheriff Emig's office were ten or twelve San Jose police officers, also armed with tear gas.

The situation was complicated by the splitting of forces in this manner, but once accomplished, nothing could be done about it.

The officers fired out the side windows and even sent a bomb out the front window of the courthouse, but the crowd seemed to survive this gas, and went about choking.

The leaders in the front-line trenches, so to speak, most of them boys between eighteen and twenty-three, were not dispersed by any of these bombs.

They stuck. There was some grim and terrible determination in them to get Holmes and Thurmond. There were scarcely more than fifty of them.

After about an hour of this rain of missles at the jail, the leaders seemed to realize that they were getting nowhere. You can't knock a jail down with bricks.

It was then, about ten o'clock or shortly afterward, that the first settled attack was made on the steel door.

From the post-office construction job came a nine-inch iron pipe, weighing several hundred pounds, but there were willing hands to lift it.

Into the lazy smoke went fifteen or twenty men, charging from the crowd across the no-man's land straight for the ancient steel doors of this jail, which had stood unbreeched since 1866.

"Boom," went the great pipe against the doors.

"Yeeoweeeeeeh," went a strange animal cry from the throats of the onlookers.

"Bang—bang—bang," went the tear-gas bombs from the second story of the jail.

"Ping," went a rock through the arc light at the corner of the jail, and the greatest cheer of all rent the air.

An eerie gloom swam in the courthouse alleys. It was like a stage set for the deepest of blue lights, and here was transpiring a drama the like of which has seldom been seen in America—a drama of a life brutally ended and two more to end.

There was no mistaking this mob now. It was out for Thurmond and Holmes, and nothing short of an army would stop it.

Who held that first iron pipe doesn't matter. They are known in San Jose, but ask someone who was there.

Here was the darkness and here was the mob out in the street. A policeman at the corner tooted his whistle. He was directing traffic. If the courthouse had blown up, if the sky had fallen, that policeman would still toot his whistle, directing traffic at the corner of St. James and First Streets.

He kept on sending 'em down First Street by the courthouse. Traffic was in a terrible snarl. All about the courthouse, about St. James Park to the east, wandered thousands, youngsters and their girls, women with children in their arms, men and their wives, nice old ladies with their daughters.

They milled about, went up as close to the howling front-line boys as possible, wandered away, wondering if they would get them or if they wouldn't get them.

It was a carnival, nothing less, and, after all, you couldn't drum up a straw of sympathy for Jack Holmes and Thomas Thurmond in this valley city.

But what was going on in the front lines? Darkness like a blanket wrapped the alleyway and the boxlike old prison.

Out of the darkness leaped another sound, the ominous sound the iron-pipe battering ram made on the steel door. Cheers, cheers, cheers, and more blasting of tear gas bombs, more staggering back by the men who held the ram.

Somebody said help is coming. San Francisco's and Oakland's inexhaustible supply of peace officers were speeding this way in automobiles and on motorcycles.

Armed with gas, more gas, and more gas, armed with riot guns.

It must have got about by telepathy, traveled to the front lines as surely as though an army had phones hooked up to the bombproofs.

"Get 'em! Get 'em! The cops are coming!" galvanized the mob and the leaders to more strenuous efforts. Still the bricks beat like an interminable tropic rain on the jail walls and bars and the steel door. Still the scene was plunged in darkness, blue darkness in which the slowly drifting smoke of the tear gas seemed to take the reflection from the very sky.

The third ram went into action. The leaders leaned as they strained at the great pipe, and in the darkness lunged at the door again. This time the double door gave way. It gave way with a tremendous crash, which stirred an entire block to frenzy.

Into the front corridor went the leaders with their ram. Screaming madly for vengeance, they had come to close quarters with the defenders, men they had known all their lives.

Across the corridor is a heavy barred grating, with a door. This door was open. The ram went through the grating, tearing it from its moorings. On went the ram to the brick wall behind, where it stopped.

In the darkness below, in the no man's land of a few minutes before, surged the mob, sending up yells in waves like the ocean surf. It was a steady drum of sound, in which words were indistinguishable.

In the second-story window at this moment appeared two of the leaders. "We're getting 'em.... We're bringing 'em down."

If it was possible the sound from below rose to a greater volume. Those below could not get into the jail. There wasn't room for them in the narrow corridors and cells.

And while the crowd screamed, here was the scene inside a jail occupied by men who had stood by valiantly, whatever may be said, against overwhelming odds.

They all knew one another—remember that—the mob and the officers. This was not a masked job.

Howard Buffington, veteran jailer, wept. He knew he was helpless before those men. They ran up the stairways, through the jail. No one could shoot them down. What is the law? No one had been hurt yet. Joe Walsh and Felix Cordray, all of them veterans, were helpless.

The mob knew where their prisoners were, and there was little chance of mistake. The mob leaders knew Thurmond and Holmes personally.

They went to Thurmond's cell on the third floor, the old northeast cell of David Lamson. Buffington went along with the leaders. They took the keys from Buffington. Thurmond, in mortal terror, was clinging to the grating in the toilet of his cell.

Then there occurred a scene probably never enacted before in a lynching in the history of America.

The leaders prayed for Thurmond's soul.

They knelt in that jail cell, five or six of them, in the midst of the turmoil and the shouting, and they prayed to God Almighty for the man who was soon to meet that God.

They arose with the whimpering prisoner, arms grasping him on either side, and he stumbled down the stairs. He stumbled along tongue-tied with his last great terror.

The scene in the Holmes cell on the second floor of the prison was a different one. No one prayed for Holmes, the so-called leader of the Brooke Hart slaying.

Holmes was also concealed in the washroom off his cell, and when the crowd went in he denied he was Holmes.

With a last bravado he shouted: "I'm not Holmes."

But his destroyers laughed in his face. Too many of them knew him well. One man struck him in the face.

"By God you are!" shouted the men jammed in his cell. He fell to the floor. Grasping him by the feet they dragged him down the steps and out into the open, where Thurmond had just arrived.

For a moment there was bedlam about the jail. A few on the out-skirts of the crowd shouted that one was the wrong man. There was some doubt at first that two men had been taken. But those next to the men knew whom they had.

There had been some howling in the jail for Tony Serpa, a youth recently convicted of manslaughter, when he had been charged with murder. It was a short-lived cry. The mob leaders were not to be diverted from their purpose.

The snarling mob with the half-unconscious prisoners did not tarry before the jail. They moved with a kind of mindless precision down the alley beside the courthouse to First Street, and across that street to St. James Park.

That movement across First Street seemed instantaneous. One moment the men were in the jail alley; there was yet a ray of hope for them, even though policemen were wandering away in a bewildered manner. The next moment the mob had the prisoners in the park, and their end had come.

A great murmuring went up from the thousands who had thus far taken little part in the actual seizure of Holmes and Thurmond. These spectators, men, women, and children, streamed like a mighty surf toward the park.

They climbed the statue of William McKinley, and they milled about, gorging the entire west side of the big park.

There was not the remotest doubt where sympathy of these people lay.

"String 'em up!" came from a thousand throats, from grammar-school boys, from businessmen with spectacles, and from workingmen in rough garb.

There was some delay in getting a rope, some impatience from the crowd. Several men started climbing trees, and every man was given a cheer. The light was dim in the park, but there were a couple of arc lights and hundreds of flashlights.

After a delay of almost fifteen minutes, ropes were produced, and Thurmond, who was at the south end of the park, was the first man to be hanged. He was benumbed with fear, and his crazed mutterings were without meaning.

Thurmond was hanged to a low limb. As his body was hoisted, the crowd broke into frantic cheering. Someone in that crowd must have had the technique of hangman's knots. Thurmond thrashed as he hung there, swaying to and fro, seeming to bend his body at the hips in a last spasm of life.

For perhaps three minutes he swayed there, his face blackening slowly, his tongue extended, although he was obviously unconscious.

"Brookie Hart—Brookie Hart," cried his executioners to the man who could no longer hear them.

The taunts went on as the man's body dangled at the end of the rope, slowly turning, now this way and now that, as though some mocking power were giving all a full view of him.

The crowd ran hither and thither, children scampering through the crowd to get the best view. Some children in arms were held twenty-five feet from the dangling man as the mob of onlookers milled about and gave vent to cries of triumph.

Holmes' execution followed that of Thurmond by a few minutes. In a despairing voice, which was nevertheless clear, he kept denying that he was Holmes, but the crowd knew better and those immediately about him did not bother to fling his words back at him.

Holmes, his bloody face turned on his captors, took death with more stamina than did Thurmond. As the rope was let down from a limb, he begged:

"Don't string me up, boys....Don't string me up."

"Yes, I'm Holmes," he gasped, and held his head up, and in the next instant the noose dropped over it, and with a cheer his body was flung into the air.

Holmes did not struggle as long as did Thurmond. It seemed that that last relinquishment of hope had taken the life from him. The rope about his neck, too, seemed to have left him nothing but reflexes to cause motion.

There was a report that both nooses were the hangman's knots which crush into the skull behind the ear, and destroy consciousness.

While Thurmond still dangled, his feet even with the faces of the crowd, Holmes was thrown far into the air. The crowd gasped for a moment as it observed that his body was stark-naked.

Now, as the men swung there, both playthings of the winds and the twisted ropes, many who had cried for their execution turned away. Several women fainted in the crowd, but there were thousands who did not faint; there were hundreds who looked on with smiles.

And the burden of all the talk was:

"Well, there won't be any kidnapping in this county for a long time."

The dead men swung there. Some of the more violent spirits were for cutting them down and burning them with gasoline. Thurmond's trousers were stripped from him, and some of the mob set fire to his rubber coat, which burned for a few minutes.

The bodies hung in the park for almost an hour. Shortly before midnight came squads of San Francisco police officers. The crowd ran. These were the police for whom Sheriff Emig called when he ran out of tear gas about half an hour before his prisoners were seized. They were too late to save anything but the dead clay of the murderers.

3.   *A Funeral Pyre in Germany*

Frederick Birchall's story of the burning of books in the early years of Nazi Germany was intended not only to inform American readers, but to ridicule the "childishness" of the action. The college youth who led the burning in an attempt to purify German literature and thought are made to look ludicrous, although Birchall perhaps did not recognize the seriousness of the threat posed by the Nazi attitude. Still, the story is an effective use of concrete details and narrative to help the reader experience an event, and today it provides a lesson for both the reporter interested in good writing and the reader interested in learning about history from an eyewitness. *(Pulitzer Prize for Reporting, 1934)*

Nazi Book-Burning Fails To Stir Berlin
Frederick T. Birchall
New York *Times*
May 11, 1933

In most of the German university towns tonight the enthusiastic student-hoods are ceremoniously burning "the un-German spirit" as exemplified in literature, pamphlet, correspondence and record. It is all being done to the accompaniment of torchlight parades, martial music and much patriot speechifying—the British Guy Fawkes Day intensified a thousandfold. There are some thirty universities in Gemany, at least one to each State. Each was to have had its bonfire, but the celebrations in Cologne, Heidelberg and other places were postponed until next week.

The celebrations held varied somewhat, but more in degree than in kind. Berlin naturally had the largest, and what happened here was more or less typical of the celebrations elsewhere. Probably 40,000 persons assembled in the great square between the opera house and the university and stood in a drizzle to watch the show. Perhaps as many more gathered along the five miles of streets through which the torchbearing parade of students escorted the borrowed trucks and private cars containing the books and pamphlets to be burned. But to the uninspired observer it savored strongly of the childish.

Five thousand students, young men and young women together, marched in the parade. All the student corps were represented—red caps and green caps, purple and blue, with a chosen band of officers of the dueling corps in plush tam o'shanters, white breeches, blue tunics and high boots—with spurs. Bearing banners and singing Nazi songs and college melodies, they arrived. It was toward midnight when they reached the great square. There, on a granite block of pavement protected by a thick covering of sand, had been built up a funeral pyre of crossed logs some twelve feet square and five feet high. Until the parade appeared a Nazi band had striven to keep up enthusiasm. Finally the head of the procession arrived. It passed the piled logs and formed within the great space reserved for it.

As they passed, the paraders tossed upon the logs the stumps of lighted torches that they had carried, until from end to end the mass was aflame. Then came the books and pamphlets. The cars carrying them stopped at a distance, and each group of students brought an armful and tossed it into the fire. A draft caught up the embers, bearing them far and wide. First the crowds cheered each new contribution, but they soon tired. Then the students' president, Gutjahr, in a Nazi uniform, made a speech. He and his fellows had gathered, he said, to consign to the flames "un-German" books and documents that threatened to disintegrate the national movement. They took joy in it. Henceforth there must be purity in German literature.

It was a boy's speech, and it was received with boyish enthusiasm— by the students. The crowd seemed disappointed. To work up enthusiasm when fresh consignments reached the fire a student barker began to name the authors: "Sigmund Freud—for falsifying our history and degrading its great figures." The crowd cheered. "Emil Ludwig—burned for literary rascality and high treason against Germany!" Loud cheers!

Then Erich Maria Remarque—"for degrading the German language and the highest patriotic ideal"; Alfred Kerr, late dramatic critic of the Tageblatt, denounced as "a dishonest literary adventurer"; Theodor Wolff, former editor of the Tageblatt, pilloried as "anti-German"; and Georg Bernhard, former editor of the Vossische Zeitung. For these last there were available for burning only a few copies of their respective newspapers and a few magazine articles. So it went until there appeared, amid Nazi salutes and protected by uniformed satellites, the attraction of the evening, Dr. Paul Joseph Goebbels, the Minister of Propaganda, himself. Mounted on a tiny swastika-draped rostrum, he spoke.

"Jewish intellectualism is dead," he declared. "National socialism has hewn the way. The German folk soul can again express itself. These flames do not only illuminate the final end of the old era; they also light up the new. Never before have the young men had so good a right to clean up the debris of the past. If the old men do not understand what is going on, let them grasp that we young (Dr. Goebbels is under 40) men have gone and done it. The old goes up in flames; the new shall be fashioned from the flame in our hearts."

Much more, but all like that. Then the song "The Nation to Arms" and the Horst Wessel Song. More literature on the fire. And more student singing. But the crowd disintegrated until it became a dreary duty to burn what literature was left. It was not so large in quantity, because today a papermill offered a small price for all it could get and the offer was accepted on condition that the student representatives should supervise the actual destruction. The proceeds will pay for the torches and the bands.

As to what went into the ceremonial bonfires tonight and will be included in the reconversion into raw material by the papermills at the rate of one mark for 100 kilograms (currently about 27.5 cents for 220 pounds), the destruction is not quite so all-embracing as was at first threatened. There is good reason to believe that the ripples of arousement that went through the outside world over the first rush of student enthusiasm had some effect on the older and wiser university heads. German propaganda authorities themselves, who recently had seen the effect of making Germany ridiculous as well as censurable, may even have been heard from. At any rate, not everything under

attack went into the discard. For several days whole truckloads of
books, both seized and voluntarily offered for immolation, have been
arriving at the students' house in Oranienburgerstrasse, but these
have undergone a weeding-out-process. Students have been busy night
and day going through the piles to insure that especially valuable
books or others not on the German index expurgatorius should escape.
Such of these as were found are to be returned to the libraries.

Nevertheless, plenty has been left that elsewhere in the world would
be deemed innocuous if not positively beneficial, or at worst capable of
carrying its own condemnation. In the pink-faced, healthy student-
hood between the ages of 18 and 22 is found boundless enthusiasm,
but not overmuch discretion. In this instance the enthusiasm had
virtually free rein.

About such pictures and pamphlets as were gathered in from Dr.
Magnus Hirschfeld's so-called Institute of Sexual Science the other
day—which, with all the correspondence from outsiders who had taken
the place seriously, went into the flames tonight—there could be little
question. But there was so much more. Take this formula, laid down in
one of the students' appeals for sacrificial material and note its
comprehensiveness: "Anything that works subversively on family life,
married life or love or the ethics of our youth or our future or strikes at
the roots of German thought, the German home and the driving forces
in our people; any works of those who would subordinate the soul to
the material, anything that serves the purpose of lies."

Almost anything could be understood by this student enthusiast to
be covered by that. And so with "the seeping poison that hides under
the mask of pacifism," to say nothing of the ban on all literature
emanating from Jewish thinkers, all of which—although the works of
Heine are strangely enough not among the sacrificed—are included in
this comprehensive student anathema. "The Jew, who is powerful in
intellect, but weak in blood and without home and fireside, remains
without understanding in the presence of German thought, fails to
dignify it and, therefore, is bound to injure the German spirit."

Inevitably the bonfire piles became large. World distinction and
world praise had not counted in assembling them. Nobel Prize winners
and all went into the auto da fe. There was, for example, one of the first
pacifist novels ever written. Bertha von Suttner got the Nobel Prize
for "Lay Down Your Arms" in 1905, but it has now become "un-
German" and was burned. The works of Thomas Mann, a later Nobel
Prize winner, went into the flames en bloc. What saved Sinclair Lewis
may never be revealed, but many other 3,000,000-volume sellers
became sacrifices, beginning with Erich Maria Remarque's "All Quiet

on the Western Front." The victims even included Count Coudenhove-Kalergi, the Japanese-Viennese author, who dreams of Pan-Europa. He falls under the ban because it is not a Prussian Pan-Europa and, moreover, might be suspected of having a Socialist tint.

For Berlin the first list alone—supplemented later—comprised four long typewritten pages containing the names of 160 authors, many of them almost unheard of before. It almost seemed as if any German student browsing in a second-hand bookstore, encountering a volume that he privately regarded as spicy, had been privileged to name a candidate. Among the Americans, Helen Keller's "How I Became a Socialist" got into the fire. She had for company Upton Sinclair, Judge Ben Lindsey, Jack London and Morris Hillquit, among others. Judge Lindsey got there because he is regarded as assailing the marriage system. Robert Carr was burned in the shape of his "Wild-Blooming Youth," which might have been expected to be unknown to fame in Berlin but evidently isn't.

Socialist and Communist authors naturally figured largely. Karl Marx, Friedrich Engels, Lassalle, Bebel, Liebknecht, Bernstein and Hilferding among the Germans and Austrians, Lenin, Stalin, Zinovieff, Lunacharsky and Bukharin among the Russians, and Henry Lichtenberger, French philosopher who wrote on Franco-German relations, all went up in smoke as "un-German." In the domain of belles lettres Heinrich Mann is included with Thomas Mann, and then comes a long list including Emil Ludwig, who writes about Germany for *The New York Times*; Lion Feuchtwanger, Arthur Schnitzler, Jakob Wassermann, Arnold and Stephan Zweig, Walther Rathenau, the German Foreign Minister who was assassinated by Nationalist gangsters; Hugo Preuss, who wrote the Weimar Constitution for the republic and spent the rest of his time expounding it; and countless others.

The bonfires are still burning as this is being written, and there is going up in smoke more than college boy prejudice and enthusiasm. A lot of the old German liberalism—if any was left—was burned tonight.

4.   An Emergency Appendectomy Under Enemy Waters

George Weller's story of an appendectomy performed by a pharmacist's mate in a submarine is vivid and detailed, certainly not your everyday account of such an operation. Intertwined with the seriousness of the operation is a comical twist, and the story is brought fully to life through a minute-by-minute narrative. There's not a dull sentence or detail in the entire story. *(Pulitzer Prize for Reporting, 1943)*

Improvised Surgery Saves Sailor's Life
George Weller
Chicago *Daily News*
December 14, 1942

SOMEWHERE IN AUSTRALIA—"They are giving him ether now," was what they said back in the aft torpedo rooms.

"He's gone under, and they're ready to cut him open," the crew whispered, sitting on their pipe bunks cramped between torpedoes.

One man went forward and put his arm quietly around the shoulder of another man who was handling the bow diving planes.

"Keep her steady, Jake," he said. "They've just made the first cut. They're feeling around for it now."

"They" were a little group of anxious-faced men with their arms thrust into reversed white pajama coats. Gauze bandages hid all their expressions except the tensity in their eyes.

"It" was an acute appendix inside Dean Rector of Chautauqua, Kansas. The stabbing pains had become unendurable the day before, which was Rector's first birthday at sea. He was nineteen years old.

The big depth gauge that looks like a factory clock and stands beside the "Christmas tree" of red and green gauges regulating the flooding chambers showed where they were. They were below the surface. And above them were enemy waters crossed and recrossed by whirring propellers of Japanese destroyers and transports.

The nearest naval surgeon competent to operate on the nineteen-year-old seaman was thousands of miles and days away. There was just one way to prevent the appendix from bursting, and that was for the crew to operate upon their shipmate themselves.

And that's what they did; they operated upon him. It was probably one of the largest operations in number of participants that ever occurred.

"He says he's ready to take his chance," the gobs whispered from bulkhead to bulkhead.

"That guy's regular"—the word traveled back bow planes to propeller and back again.

They "kept her steady."

The chief surgeon was a twenty-three-year-old pharmacist's mate wearing a blue blouse with white-taped collar and squashy white duck cap. His name was Wheeler B. Lipes. He came from Newcastle near Roanoke, Virginia, and had taken the Navy hospital course in San Diego, thereafter serving three years in the naval hospital at Philadelphia, where his wife lives.

Lipes' specialty as laboratory technician was in operating a machine that registers heartbeats. He was classified as an electrocardiographer. But he had seen Navy doctors take out one or two appendixes and thought he could do it. Under the sea, he was given his first chance to operate.

There was difficulty about the ether. When below the surface the pressure inside a boat is above the atmospheric pressure. More ether is absorbed under pressure. The submariners did not know how long their operation would last.

They did not know how long it would take to find the appendix. They did not know whether there would be enough ether to keep the patient under throughout the operation.

They didn't want the patient waking up before they were finished.

They decided to operate on the table in the officers' wardroom. In the newest and roomiest American submarine the wardroom is approximately the size of a Pullman-car drawing room. It is flanked by bench seats attached to the wall, and a table occupies the whole room—you enter with your knees already crooked to sit down. The only way anyone can be upright in the wardroom is by kneeling.

The operating room was just long enough so that the patient's head and feet reached the two ends without hanging over.

First they got out a medical book and read up on the appendix, while Rector, his face pale with pain, lay in the narrow bunk. It was probably the most democratic surgical operation ever performed. Everybody from boxplane to the cook in the galley knew his role.

The cook provided the ether mask. It was an inverted tea strainer.

They covered it with gauze.

The twenty-three-year-old "surgeon" had, as his staff of fellow "physicians," all men his senior in age and rank. His anesthetist was Communications Officer Lieutenant Franz Hoskins of Tacoma, Washington.

Before they carried Rector to the wardroom, the submarine Captain, Lieutenant Commander W.B. Ferrall of Pittsburrgh, asked Lipes as the "surgeon" to have a talk with the patient.

"Look, Dean, I never did anything like this before," Lipes said. "You don't have much chance to pull through, anyhow. What do you say?"

"I know just how it is, Doc."

It was the first time in his life that anybody had called Lipes "Doc." But there was in him, added to the steadliness that goes with a sub-mariner's profession, a new calmness.

The operating staff adjusted gauze masks while members of the engine-room crew pulled tight their reversed pajama coats over their arms. The tools were laid out. They were far from perfect or complete for a major operation. The scapel had no handle.

But submariners are used to "rigging" things. The medicine chest had plenty of hemostats, which are small pincers used for closing blood vessels. The machinist "rigged" a handle for the scapel from a hemostat.

When you are going to have an operation, you must have some kind of antiseptic agent. Rummaging in the medicine chest, they found sulfanilamide tablets and ground them into powder. One thing was lacking: there was no means of holding open the wound after the in-cision had been made. Surgical tools used for this are called "muscular retractors." What would they use for retractors? There was nothing in the medicine chest that gave the answer, so they went as usual to the cook's galley.

In the galley they found tablespoons made of Monel metal. They bent these at right angles and had their retractors.

Sterilizers? They went to one of the greasy copper-colored torpedoes waiting beside the tubes. They milked alcohol from the torpedo mechanism and used it as well as boiling water.

The light in the wardroom seemed insufficient; operating rooms always have big lamps. So they brought one of the big floods used for night loading and rigged it inside the wardroom's sloping ceiling.

The moment for the operation had come. Rector, very pale and stripped, stretched himself out on the wardroom table under the glare of the lamps.

Rubber gloves dipped in torpedo alcohol were drawn upon the youthful "Doc's" hands. The fingers were too long. The rubber ends dribbled limply over.

"You look like Mickey Mouse, Doc," said one onlooker.

Lipes grinned behind the gauze.

Rector on the wardroom table wet his lips, glancing a side look at the tea-strainer ether mask.

With his superior officers as his subordinates, Lipes looked into their eyes, nodded, and Hoskins put the tea mask down over Rector's face. No words were spoken; Hoskins already knew from the book that he should watch Rector's eye pupils dilate.

The twenty-three-year-old surgeon, following the ancient hand rule, put his little finger on Rector's subsiding umbilicus, his thumb on the point of the hipbone, and, by dropping his index finger straight down, found the point where he intended to cut. At his side stood Lieutenant Norvell Ward of Indian Head, Maryland, who was his assistant surgeon.

"I chose him for his coolness and dependability," said the Doc afterward of his superior officer. "He acted as my third and fourth hands."

Lieutenant Ward's job was to place tablespoons in Rector's side as Lipes cut through successive layers of muscles.

Engineering Officer Lieutenant S. Manning of Cheraw, South Carolina, took the job which in a normal operating room is known as "circulating nurse." His job was to see that packets of sterile dressings kept coming and that the torpedo alcohol and boiling water arrived regularly from the galley.

They had what is called an "instrument passer" in Chief Yeoman H.F. Wieg of Sheldon, North Dakota, whose job was to keep the tablespoons coming and coming clean. Submarine Skipper Ferrall too had his part. They made him "recorder." It was his job to keep count of the sponges that went into Rector. A double count of tablespoons used as retractors was kept: one by the Skipper and one by the cook, who was himself passing them out from the galley.

It took Lipes in his flap-finger rubber gloves nearly twenty minutes to find the appendix.

"I have tied one side of the caecum," he whispered after the first minutes. "Now I'm trying the other."

Whispered bulletins seeped back into the engine room and the crew's quarters.

"The Doc has tried one side of something and now is trying the other side."

After more search, Lipes finally whispered, "I think I've got it. It's curled way into the blind gut."

Lipes was using the classical McBurney's incision. Now was the time when his shipmate's life was completely in his hands.

"Two more spoons." They passed the word to Lieutenant Ward.

"Two spoons at 14.45 hours (2:45 p.m.)," wrote Skipper Ferrall on his note pad.

"More flashlights. And another battle lantern," demanded Lipes.

The patient's face, lathered with white petrolatum, began to grimace.

"Give him more ether," ordered the Doc.

Hoskins looked doubtfully at the original five pounds of ether now shrunk to hardly three quarters of one can, but once again the tea strainer was soaked in ether. The fumes mounted up, thickening the wardroom air and making the operating staff giddy.

"Want those blowers speeded up?" the Captain asked the Doc.

The blowers began to whir louder. Suddenly came the moment when the Doc reached out his hand, pointing toward the needle threaded with twenty-day chromic catgut.

One by one the sponges came out. One by one the tablespoons bent into right angles were withdrawn and returned to the galley. At the end it was the skipper who nudged Lipes and pointed to the talley of bent tablespoons. One was missing. Lipes reached into the incision for the last time and withdrew the wishboned spoon and closed the incision.

They even had the tool ready to cut off the thread. It was a pair of fingernail scissors, well scalded in water and torpedo juice.

At that moment the last can of ether went dry. They lifted up Rector and carried him into the bunk of Lieutenant Charles K. Miller of Williamsport, Pennsylvania. Lieutenant Miller alone had had control of the ship as diving officer during the operation.

It was half an hour after the last tablespoon had been withdrawn that Rector opened his eyes. His first words were, "I'm still in there pitching."

By that time the sweat-drenched officers were hanging up their pajamas to dry. It had taken the amateurs about two and a half hours for an operation ordinarily requiring forty-five minutes.

"It wasn't one of those 'snappy valve' appendixes," murmured Lipes apologetically as he felt the first handclasps upon his shoulders.

Within a few hours, the bow and stern planesmen, who, under Lieutenant Miller's direction, had kept the submarine from varying more than half a degree vertically in the 150 minutes below the stormy sea, came around to receive Rector's winks of thanks. Rector's only remark was, "Gee, I wish Earl was here to see this job." His brother Earl, a seaman on the Navy submarine tender *Pigeon*, is among the list of missing at Corregidor, probably captured.

When the submarine surfaced that night, the ether-drunk submarine crewmen found themselves grabbing the sides of the conning tower and swaying unsteadily on their feet. Thirteen days later Rector, fully recovered, was at his battle station, manning the phones. In a bottle vibrating on the submarine's shelves was the prize exhibit of surgeon Lipes—the first appendix ever known to have been recovered below enemy waters.

Reprinted by permission of the Chicago *Sun-Times*.

5.   *American Soldiers Face Japanese Willing To Die*

Ira Wolfert's accounts of the battles of the Solomon Islands in the early stages of World War II provide clear analysis through a clean, forceful narrative. The telling of events that occurred on a massive scale is made cohesive through the stories' unified thematic structure. All parts fit neatly within an overall story plan. Although Wolfert gives the reader an understanding of the perspective and significance of the battles within the larger context of the entire war, the following story helps the reader visualize the battles themselves. Its success at doing that lies in its narrative anecdotes and concrete scenes, with the story told in an informal tone. *(Pulitzer Prize for Telegraphic Reporting, International, 1943)*

G.I.s Lick Japs in Solomons
Ira Wolfert
North American Newspaper Alliance, Inc.
November 1942

In the five battles of the Solomons, the least we have done is to keep the Japs from winning—which is victory, in a military sense when a long, hard war is still in its preliminary stages—and in our biggest successes, in the fourth and fifth battles, we not only have kept the Japs from winning, but have made them pay heavily for trying to win.

We've licked the Japs on land, on sea, and in the air. We've shown that we have more military brains than they have, are better at war, all kinds of war, from strangling and knife-fighting and dead-trampling on up into the complicated mechanized operations of modern battle. The Solomons haven't shown yet that we can outproduce the Japs, but we think that's true, that we can make as good material as anybody and can make more of it than the Japs, and can replace it faster than they can.

But there's one thing that nobody in the world can be better at than the Japs, and that's in the guts department. They have more guts than the Germans have. At least, they have shown thus far in the Solomons deal, which is the first deal where they've had to hold their chins out and take it, that they have more guts. The Germans have said "Kamerad" in the past and may be relied on to say it in the future. But the Japs have never surrendered, never en masse, and only rarely as individuals. We have not yet taken a single officer alive on Guadalcanal, although we have tried in every way we know how. And the great majority of the few soldier prisoners we have taken have been wounded and in a condition where their minds have not been up to par.

Every day I was there, the Jap gave new evidence of his intense willingness to go to any lengths to win, or, if unable to win, to go on fighting until his breath stopped.

Under the heading of going to any lengths to win, the following incident may be cited as an illustration. The Jap seems to think it useful in land fighting to put snipers in our rear to harass us. Once, early in November, our fellows, working their way west of the Matanikou River, were held up for a day and one-half along a narrow sector. They drove the Japs out of that sector about dawn of a Wednesday and held there all that day and the next day. Toward five o'clock Thursday afternoon, a Marine, deciding to dig in for the night, found some soft-looking dirt on the edge of a tree and with the first poke of his shovel hit a Jap body. The Jap was covered over very lightly with a sprinkle of dirt, but his uniform had made him look only like some leaves and rotting twigs lying amid the dirt. The Marine uncovered the Jap, and through the whole brushing-off process the Jap did not move except as pushed and jostled. But nobody who knows anything takes chances with the Japs any more. So the Marine picked up this Jap's arm and let it drop. It dropped limply, and the face remained motionless and emotionless as in death. The Marine did it again, half-heartedly this time, very sure that this was a dead Jap. But the Jap, who had performed the superhuman task of lying under our feet feigning death for a day and a half just in order to get behind our lines and snipe at us, proved to have a human touch around his eyes. This second time he couldn't stand it any more, and one eyelid twitched nervously.

Under the heading of willingness to go on fighting, this story may be told. I haven't my notes with me, and I can't remember this Marine captain's name, but everybody called him Wimpy. Wimpy was out on patrol and ran into some Japs holed up in a native hut. Quite a hot little brush followed, and after about fifteen minutes our side got no more answering fire.

Wimpy crawled up close and saw that all the Japs were dead except one, who seemed badly wounded. This one was lying on the floor of the hut in a corner farthest from the door. He was bleeding from the mouth and stared solemnly at Wimpy, and Wimpy decided to try taking him prisoner.

For twenty minutes, Wimpy cajoled and begged and tried everything he knew, waving a handkerchief as a flag of truce, offering "pogie bait," as the Marines call candy, as a bribe. The Jap did not answer. The blood flowed steadily from his mouth and his face occasionally broke under pain, but he just stared solemnly at Wimpy.

So the Marine captain decided to go in after the man. He went in the door, holding his revolver in his hand, and stood there pointing the revolver. He stood as far away as he could because wounded Japs, so hurt they could not throw a grenade, have been known to pull the pin as somebody comes near them and blow up the reckless one as well as themselves.

So Wimpy stayed as far away as possible and pointed his gun. The Jap lifted himself to his hands and knees and began to crawl toward a dead Jap officer who was wearing a sword. "Don't do that!" cried Wimpy. "I'll have to shoot you." Wimpy didn't dare go near the man. All he could do was point his gun and shout. The Jap kept crawling slowly for the sword and took out the sword, and Wimpy stamped his foot and shouted, "You damn fool! Oh, you damn damn fool! I'll have to kill you." Then the Jap lifted himself to his feet and lifted the sword over his head and started for Wimpy, and Wimpy had to shoot him dead.

These are not exceptional cases. They are typical. So there can be no question of our being better fighters than the Japs. The best anybody can possibly do is be as good and rely on our superiority in all other departments of war to give us the victory in the long run.

It's not easy to be as good. And it's important that we should be, because if we aren't we're going to lose this war, or, if not lose it, make a compromise peace which will turn over to the next generation the job of winning it. Our fellows fighting have to be as tough; and the people back home have to be able to stand the losses, stand all the terrible sorrow and misery that the dead leave in their wake, and have to be able to feel that the dead husband and dead lover and dead son have not died for something that we could do without, but have swapped their lives for something worth the price. And they have to be able to keep on feeling it steadily every day for all the time it will take to win.

Our losses have been very small thus far. That is because we have been on the defensive in the Solomons since the day we took the place. The Japs have had to come after us. Soon we'll have to start north and go in after them. Then our losses are very likely to increase. There are a lot of people better able than I am to guess how the people back home are going to stand under that. What I can say is how our fighting fellows are going to stand up under it because I've seen them do it.

In every battle I've watched out here, our side turns up with quite a few heroes, fellows who do more than they are supposed to do.

But heroes don't win wars. They help, just as everything else that's good helps. But the heroes are the exception; and it's the ordinary, run-of-the-mill guy who doesn't feel tempted to do more than his share who has to be relied on to win for our side. This doesn't sound glamorous, but I think it's accurate. So all the words that follow will be devoted to the ordinary fighting man on our side and how he measures up to this most difficult job in our history—being as tough, man for man, as the Japs.

As I have noted previously, our fellows look very calm in battle. The look of them is very provocative because, as I know from personal experience, a part of the mind seems to run away during battle and keeps trying to make the rest of the mind run away with it. The conscious mind, which is the part of the mind that knows all the things it has been taught, wants to stay and do the job it's supposed to do, and this other part of the mind, the subconscious part, doesn't want to know from nothing and just wants to get the hell away from there. The subconscious mind can't go off all by itself. It has to take you along with it. And to a fellow in this position, particularly when the battle is long and the struggle in himself is prolonged, it actually feels as if the subconscious mind is laying rough hands on the rest of him and pulling, hauling, and screaming at him. And I know in my own case whenever I have been in an action there has always been this uproar in my head, this steady, wild-eyed, wild-haired screaming, making it very difficult to think about the work I had to do there.

But our fellows, filled inside with this demented uproar and hemmed in all around outside by the uproar of battle, just stay there and do the work they have to do. They don't look like actors being brave. They look mostly like fellows working.

Nobody looks young in a fight. I've seen lots of twenty-year-olds out there in the middle of all that stuff flying around and some eighteen-year-olds, but I never saw anybody who looked much under forty while the fight was going on. That's one way our fellows show what they're up against. The blood in their young faces gets watered with a kind of liquid of fear and takes on that blued-over color of watery milk. Their skin looks clothlike, with the texture of a rough, wrinkled cloth.

Then, when things get really thick, like when fellows start getting hit and dropping and crying out with pain all around you, and you can't pay any attention to that, but just have to keep on working your little gadget, pressing that little button or turning that little wheel or adding up that little set of figures, whatever it is—well, when it gets like that, still the faces of our fellows don't show what an actor's would.

Sometimes the flesh around their mouths starts to shake as if they were whimpering, and their eyes...you can see their eyes coated over with a hot shine as if they were crying. But they go right on doing what they have to do. The bombardiers keep right on figuring with their pencils on little white scratch-pads of paper, right in the middle of all that's going on, marking down figures and adding them up or subtracting or dividing and checking the answers, just like in school, looking—except maybe for the crying in their eyes and the whimpering around their mouths—all puckered up with the thought, too, like earnest students in a school. And the gunners and radio operators, all the technicians and specialists, the plumbers, mechanics, cooks, the skilled laborers, doing the work of war—they're the same.

6.   *Nagasaki Annihilated*

Though decades have familiarized the world's people with the effect of the atomic bomb, William Laurence's article on the bombing of Nagasaki, Japan, still leaves the reader awe-struck. The concrete detail of the narrative helps the reader live the experience of being on the bombing mission, feeling the drama and tension as the bomber nears its target, with each paragraph building the anticipation of the devastation that ultimately will occur. Laurence's description of the explosion leaves the reader with the indelible picture of a monumental fury. *(Pulitzer Prize for Reporting, 1946)*

Reporter Saw Atomic Bomb Dropped on Nagasaki
William L. Laurence
New York *Times*
September 9, 1945

WITH THE ATOMIC-BOMB MISSION TO JAPAN, AUGUST 9 (Delayed)—We are on our way to bomb the mainland of Japan. Our flying contingent consists of three specially designed B-29 Superforts, and two of these carry no bombs. But our lead plane is on its way with another atomic bomb, the second in three days, concentrating in its active substance an explosive energy equivalent to twenty thousand and, under favorable conditions, forty thousand tons of TNT.

We have several chosen targets. One of these is the great industrial and shipping center of Nagasaki, on the western shore of Kyushu, one of the main islands of the Japanese homeland.

I watched the assembly of this man-made meteor during the past two days and was among the small group of scientists and Army and Navy representatives privileged to be present at the ritual of its loading in the Superfort last night, against a background of threatening black skies torn open at intervals by great lightning flashes.

It is a thing of beauty to behold, this "gadget." Into its design went millions of man-hours of what is without doubt the most concentrated intellectual effort in history. Never before had so much brain power been focused on a single problem.

This atomic bomb is different from the bomb used three days ago with such devastating results on Hiroshima.

I saw the atomic substance before it was placed inside the bomb. By itself it is not at all dangerous to handle. It is only under certain conditions, produced in the bomb assembly, that it can be made to yield up its energy, and even then it gives only a small fraction of its total contents—a fraction, however, large enough to produce the greatest explosion on earth.

The briefing at midnight revealed the extreme care and the tremendous amount of preparation that had been made to take care of every detail of the mission, to make certain that the atomic bomb fully served the purpose for which it was intended. Each target in turn was shown in detailed maps and in aerial photographs. Every detail of the course was rehearsed—navigation, altitude, weather, where to land in emergencies. It came out that the Navy had submarines and rescue craft, known as Dumbos and Superdumbos, stationed at various strategic points in the vicinity of the targets, ready to rescue the fliers in case they were forced to bail out.

The briefing period ended with a moving prayer by the chaplain. We then proceeded to the mess hall for the traditional early-morning breakfast before departure on a bombing mission.

A convoy of trucks took us to the supply building for the special equipment carried on combat missions. This included the Mae West, a parachute, a lifeboat, an oxygen mask, a flak suit, and a survival vest. We still had a few hours before take-off time, but we all went to the flying field and stood around in little groups or sat in jeeps talking rather casually about our mission to the Empire, as the Japanese home islands are known hereabouts.

In command of our mission is Major Charles W. Sweeney, twenty-five, of 124 Hamilton Avenue, North Quincy, Massachusetts. His flagship, carrying the atomic bomb, is named *The Great Artiste*, but the name does not appear on the body of the great silver ship, with its unusually long, four-bladed, orange-tipped propellers. Instead, it carries the number 77, and someone remarks that it was "Red" Grange's winning number on the gridiron.

We took off at 3:50 this morning and headed northwest on a straight line for the Empire. The night was cloudy and threatening, with only a few stars here and there breaking through the overcast. The weather report had predicted storms ahead part of the way but clear sailing for the final and climactic stages of our odyssey.

We were about an hour away from our base when the storm broke.

Our great ship took some heavy dips through the abysmal darkness around us, but it took these dips much more gracefully than a large commercial airliner, producing a sensation more in the nature of a glide than a "bump," like a great ocean liner riding the waves except that in this case the air waves were much higher and the rhythmic tempo of the glide was much faster.

I noticed a strange eerie light coming through the window high above the navigator's cabin, and as I peered through the dark all around us I saw a startling phenomenon. The whirling giant propellers had somehow become great luminous disks of blue flame. The same luminous blue flame appeared on the plexiglas window in the nose of the ship and on the tips of the giant wings. It looked as though we were riding the whirlwind through space on a chariot of blue fire.

It was, I surmised, a surcharge of static electricity that had accumulated on the tips of the propellers and on the di-electric material of the plastic windows. One's thoughts dwelt anxiously on the precious cargo in the invisible ship ahead of us. Was there any likelihood of danger that this heavy electric tension in the atmosphere all about us might set it off?

I expressed my fears to Captain Bock, who seemed nonchalant and unperturbed at the controls. He quickly reassured me.

"It is a familiar phenomenon seen often on ships. I have seen it many times on bombing missions. It is known as St. Elmo's fire."

On we went through the night. We soon rode out the storm, and our ship was once again sailing on a smooth course straight ahead, on a direct line to the Empire.

Our altimeter showed that we were traveling through space at a height of seventeen thousand feet. The thermometer registered an outside temperature of thirty-three degrees below zero Centigrade, about thirty below Fahrenheit. Inside our pressurized cabin the temperature was that of a comfortable air-conditioned room and a pressure corresponding to an altitude of eight thousand feet. Captain Bock cautioned me, however, to keep my oxygen mask handy in case of emergency. This, he explained, might mean either something going wrong with the pressure equipment inside the ship or a hole through the cabin by flak.

The first signs of dawn came shortly after five o'clock. Sergeant Curry, of Hoopeston, Illinois, who had been listening steadily on his earphones for radio reports, while maintaining a strict radio silence himself, greeted it by rising to his feet and gazing out the window.

"It's good to see the day," he told me. "I get a feeling of claustrophobia hemmed in in this cabin at night."

He is a typical American youth, looking even younger than his twenty years. It takes no mind reader to read his thoughts.

"It's a long way from Hoopeston," I found myself remarking.

"Yep," he replies, as he busies himself decoding a message from outer space.

"Think this atomic bomb will end the war?" he asks hopefully.

"There is a very good chance that this one may do the trick," I assured him, "but if not, then the next one or two surely will. Its power is such that no nation can stand up against it very long." This was not my own view. I had heard it expressed all around a few hours earlier, before we took off. To anyone who had seen this manmade fireball in action, as I had less than a month ago in the desert of New Mexico, this view did not sound over-optimistic.

By 5:50 it was really light outside. We had lost our lead ship, but Lieutenant Godfrey, our navigator, informs me that we had arranged for that contingency. We have an assembly point in the sky above the little island of Yakushima, southeast of Kyushu, at 9:10. We are to circle there and wait for the rest of our formation.

Our genial bombardier, Lieutenant Levy, comes over to invite me to take his front-row seat in the transparent nose of the ship, and I accept eagerly. From that vantage point in space, seventeen thousand feet above the Pacific, one gets a view of hundreds of miles on all sides, horizontally and vertically. At that height the vast ocean below and the sky above seem to merge into one great sphere.

I was on the inside of that firmament, riding above the giant mountains of white cumulus clouds, letting myself be suspended in infinite space. One hears the whirl of the motors behind one, but it soon becomes insignificant against the immensity all around and is before long swallowed by it. There comes a point where space also swallows time and one lives through eternal moments filled with an oppressive loneliness, as though all life had suddenly vanished from the earth and you are the only one left, a lone survivor traveling endlessly through interplanetary space.

My mind soon returns to the mission I am on. Somewhere beyond these vast mountains of white clouds ahead of me there lies Japan, the land of our enemy. In about four hours from now one of its cities, making weapons of war for use against us, will be wiped off the map by the greatest weapon ever made by man: in one-tenth of a millioneth of a second, a fraction of time immeasurable by any clock, a whirlwind from the skies will pulverize thousands of its buildings and tens of thousands of its inhabitants.

But at this moment no one yet knows which one of the several cities chosen as targets is to be annihilated. The final choice lies with destiny. The winds over Japan will make the decision. If they carry heavy clouds over our primary target, that city will be saved, at least for the time being. None of its inhabitants will ever know that the wind of a benevolent destiny had passed over their heads. But that same wind will doom another city.

Our weather planes ahead of us are on their way to find out where the wind blows. Half an hour before target time we will know what the winds have decided.

Does one feel any pity or compassion for the poor devils about to die? Not when one thinks of Pearl Harbor and of the Death March on Bataan.

Captain Bock informs me that we are about to start our climb to bombing altitude.

He manipulates a few knobs on his control panel to the right of him, and I alternately watch the white clouds and ocean below me and the altimeter on the bombardier's panel. We were then over Japanese waters, close to their mainland. Lieutenant Godfrey motioned to me to look through his radar scope. Before me was the outline of our assembly point. We shall soon meet our lead ship and proceed to the final stage of our journey.

We reached Yakushima at 9:12; and there, about four thousand feet ahead of us, was *The Great Artiste* with its precious load. I saw Lieutenant Godfrey and Sergeant Curry strap on their parachutes, and I decided to do likewise.

We started circling. We saw little towns on the coastline, heedless of our presence. We kept on circling, waiting for the third ship in our formation.

It was 9:56 when we began heading for the coastline. Our weather scouts had sent us code messages, deciphered by Sergeant Curry, informing us that both the target as well as the secondary were clearly visible.

The winds of destiny seemed to favor certain Japanese cities that must remain nameless. We circled about them again and found no opening in the thick umbrella of clouds that covered them. Destiny chose Nagasaki as the ultimate target.

We had been circling for some time when we noticed black puffs of smoke coming through the white clouds directly at us. There were fifteen bursts of flak, right up to our altitude, but by this time were too far to the left.

We flew southward down the channel and at 11:33 crossed the coastline and headed straight for Nagasaki, about one hundred miles to the west. Here again we circled until we found an opening in the clouds. It was 12:01, and the goal of our mission had arrived.

We heard the prearranged signal on our radio, put on our arc welder's glasses, and watched tensely the maneuverings of the strike ship about half a mile in front of us.

"There she goes!" someone said.

Out of the belly of *The Great Artiste* what looked like a black object went downward.

Captain Bock swung around to get out of range; but even though we were turning away in the opposite direction, and despite the fact that it was broad daylight in our cabin, all of us became aware of a giant flash that broke through the dark barrier of our arc welder's lenses and flooded our cabin with intense light.

We removed our glasses after the first flash, but the light still lingered on, a bluish-green light that illuminated the entire sky all around. A tremendous blast wave struck our ship and made it tremble from nose to tail. This was followed by four more blasts in rapid succession, each resounding like the boom of cannon fire hitting our plane from all directions.

Observers in the tail of our ship saw a giant ball of fire arise as though from the bowels of the earth, belching forth enormous white smoke rings. Next they saw a giant pillar of purple fire, ten thousand feet high, shooting skyward with enormous speed.

By the time our ship had made another turn in the direction of the atomic explosion the pillar of purple fire had reached the level of our altitude. Only about forty-five seconds had passed. Awe-struck, we watched it shoot upward like a meteor coming from the earth instead of from outer space, becoming ever more alive as it climbed skyward through the white clouds. It was no longer smoke, or dust, or even a cloud of fire. It was a living thing, a new species of being, born right before our incredulous eyes.

At one stage of its evolution, covering millions of years in terms of seconds, the entity assumed the form of a giant square totem pole, with its base about three miles long, tapering off to about a mile at the top. Its bottom was brown, its center was amber, its top white. But it was a living totem pole, carved with many grotesque masks grimacing at the earth.

Then, just when it appeared as though the thing had settled down into a state of permanence, there came shooting out of the top a giant mushroom that increased the height of the pillar to a total of forty-five thousand feet. The mushroom top was even more alive than the pillar, seething and boiling in a white fury of creamy foam, sizzling upward and then descending earthward, a thousand Old Faithful geysers rolled into one.

It kept struggling in an elemental fury, like a creature in the act of breaking the bonds that held it down. In a few seconds it had freed itself from its gigantic stem and floated upward with tremendous speed, its momentum carrying it into the stratosphere to a height of about sixty thousand feet.

But no sooner did this happen when another mushroom, smaller in size than the first one, began emerging out of the pillar. It was as though the decapitated monster was growing a new head.

As the first mushroom floated off into the blue it changed its shape into a flowerlike form, its giant petals curving downward, creamy white outside, rose-colored inside. It still retained that shape when we last gazed at it from a distance of about two hundred miles. The boiling pillar of many colors could also be seen at that distance, a giant mountain of jumbled rainbows, in travail. Much living substance had gone into those rainbows. The quivering top of the pillar was protruding to a great height through the white clouds, giving the appearance of a monstrous prehistoric creature with a ruff around its neck, a fleecy ruff extending in all directions, as far as the eye could see.

7. *A Hate Organization*

Columbians, Inc., was a Nazi-style group operating out of Atlanta, Georgia, whose goal was to be more racist than the Ku Klux Klan. To reveal the character of the Columbians, Edward Folliard began a series of reports by showing the rituals that took place in their meetings. The story that follows gives a vivid description of the kind of people who attended the meetings, including "...a squalling baby in its mother's arms to stooped old men leaning on canes." In simple, clear language Folliard tells the story of what happened in the meetings, relates effects, and gives background on the organization. *(Pulitzer Prize for National Reporting, 1947)*

Columbians, Like Hitler, Play Up to 'Little People'
Edward T. Folliard
Washington *Post*
December 3, 1946

A mass meeting of the Columbians, Inc., starts off with martial music. Then comes the Lord's Prayer, and after that a verbal flogging of Negroes, Jews, Communists and the rich.

At the end, of course, there is the appeal for money; for "quarters, half dollars, dollars—anything you can spare to help in our fight for the white race."

The rally Thanksgiving night was the last the Columbians will hold in the hall of the AFL Plumbers and Steamfitters, the union having notified the Nazi-like outfit that their rental contract has been canceled.

It was not very impressive, this particular rally. The music, Sousa's "Washington Post March," "Stars and Stripes Forever," and other martial pieces—came from a cheap phonograph. The chaplain, a man with a hunched back, talked too long. Not content to intone the Lord's Prayer, he went on to recite the Columbians' creed and to elaborate on it with some hate talk of his own. After him came the orator of the evening—Home Loomis, jr., No. 2 man of the Columbians.

Approximately 200 persons made up the audience. They were of all ages, from a squalling baby in its mother's arms to stooped old men leaning on canes. One woman, built like a barn, wore a sky-blue uniform and an overseas cap to match. On her arm was the thunderbolt insigne of the Columbians.

The men, except for the younger ones in storm-trooper attire, nearly all wore odd coats and trousers. Once during the proceedings a dirty-looking fellow got noisy and quarrelsome, and was dragged out by two Atlanta policemen. He was blind drunk. Another drunk, seeing this, wobbled out under his own steam.

Who were these people who were being asked to pay $3 to join the Columbians and $2 for "The Thunderbolt"?

Homer Loomis, in a hair-down talk with me earlier, had explained that the Columbians were out to enroll the "little people."

"Any mass movement has to use mass tactics," he said, his eyes afire. "Hitler appealed to the little people. The Communists appealed—no, no, strike that out...Our movement appeals to the little people.

"Most of them lead dull lives—work, sleep, maybe an occasional beer. We're giving them something new, something exciting. We're satisfying their lust for power. We're building up their egos, making them feel that they will have a part in the victory if only they're willing to sacrifice."

At one point in this particular interview Loomis grew cynical. He said that the little people were at heart "animals and capitalists"— that they had no desire to share anything with anybody.

"Of course," he said, "we don't say the same thing at our meetings that I'm saying to you here."

Atlanta's newspaper editors are not nearly as harsh as that in their judgment of Columbian audiences.

Ralph McGill, editor of the Atlanta Constitution, wrote a column the other day in which he asked: "Why do these things always come to roost in Georgia?" The inevitable answer was, he said, that the ringleaders thought they could succeed.

"Therein," wrote McGill, "have we all failed and therein are we all to blame."

"Their audiences are almost entirely good, plain persons of little or no education, of little working skills, in a very low income group. The spellbinders, their fingers itching to get those $3 initiation fees, talk to them with a certain logic.

"They talk to people whose lives are dreary at best. They work on people in the poorest, most squalid slum areas and to a person unable to read or write, or to one with no more than a third or fourth-grade education, the appeal has logic.

"No person likes to admit his own failure and this technique explains satisfactorily to a failure, why he or she is a failure. It removes any personal responsibility. It places the blame on something else...."

To get back to the Thanksgiving night rally, it did not seem to be a howling success. Loomis, the Princeton-trained New Yorker, was not very good with his phony Southern accent. The whining Emory Burke, president of the Columbians and a born rabble-rouser, doubtless would have done better. It was explained, however, that he was tied up that night with the Columbians' lawyers.

At any rate, only about a third of the audience moved forward to contribute money for the battle for "white supremacy."

It should be understood, however, that there is a good deal more to the Columbians than those mass meetings. They have set out, as Hitler did long ago, to organize people in neighborhoods or blocks. To get them interested they perform certain services.

For example:

One day recently a Negro couple, Mr. and Mrs. Frank Jones, arrived in Garibaldi St. with a truck loaded down with bedding and furniture. They had bought a house there after being told that it was a Negro neighborhood.

They found a Columbian placard tacked to the door. On it was the red thunderbolt insigne and the words "White Community Only." (Actually it was a mixed neighborhood.)

A number of Columbians, in storm-trooper outfits, paráded up and down in front of the house. One of them was the block leader for that neighborhood, R.L. Whitman. He had with him his 16-month-old daughter, Marian Helen, and she, too, had a thunderbolt patch on her shoulder.

The Columbians warned Mr. and Mrs. Jones not to go in their new house.

Jones later told this story:

"I was living in two rooms on Davis St. My son, Eddie, came home from the Army and he moved his wife and baby in with me. I had to have more room and the real estate people told me this house was all right and we wouldn't be bothered here."

Mrs. Jones agreed with her husband, saying that they never would have bought the house if "the real estate-man hadn't told us all these houses were colored."

Police Chief M. A. Hornsby and Captain of Detective Buck Weaver, having received a tip, arrived in Garibaldi St. just as the Columbians were badgering the Negro couple.

Chief Hornsby spoke to one of the uniformed Columbians, Jack Price.

"What are you doing here?" he asked.

"Protecting white families," said Price.

"What business is that of yours?"

"We got some phone calls."

Chief Hornsby turned to Captain Weaver and said:

"Lock 'em up."

Thereupon four of the Columbians were taken in on a charge of inciting to riot.

The Negro, Jones, said tentatively:

"Well, if I don't bother nobody around here..."

Chief Hornsby told him to go ahead and move in. He reserved his opinion of the real estate man.

Reprinted by permission of the Washington *Post.*

8. *A Neighborhood in a Killer's Path*

The following story by Meyer Berger chronicling a veteran's killing spree on his city block gains its power through narrative structure and detailed news gathering. The narrative provides a step-by-step, minute-by-minute account of the actions of the killer, his victims, and his neighbors. It is made possible by Berger's gathering of a multitude of exact and concrete details. The writing is free from psychological analysis and opinion, leaving the facts alone to provide the impact of the event. Particularly noticeable is the avoidance of repetition of the attributive phrase "(the source) said...." Berger's exacting and detailed gathering of information allows him to reconstruct the morning of the killings without having to state continually that his material came from quotes by witnesses. *(Pulitzer Prize for Reporting, 1950)*

Berserk Gunman Kills 12
Meyer Berger
New York *Times*
September 7, 1949

Howard B. Unruh, 28 years old, a mild, soft-spoken veteran of many armored artillery battles in Italy, France, Austria, Belgium and Germany, killed twelve persons with a war souvenir Luger pistol in his home block in East Camden this morning. He wounded four others.

Unruh, a slender, hollow-cheeked six-footer paradoxically devoted to scripture reading and to constant practice with firearms, had no previous history of mental illness but specialists indicated tonight that there was no doubt that he was a psychiatric case and that he had secretly nursed a persecution complex for two years or more.

The veteran was shot in the left thigh by a local tavern keeper, but he kept that fact secret, too, while policemen and Mitchell Cohen, Camden County prosecutor, questioned him at police headquarters for more than two hours immediately after tear gas bombs had forced him out of his bedroom to surrender.

Blood betrays his wound

The blood stain he left on the seat he occupied during the questioning betrayed his wound. When it was discovered, he was taken to Cooper Hospital in Camden, a prisoner charged with murder.

He was as calm under questioning as he was during the twenty minutes that he was shooting men, women and children. Only occasionally excessive brightness of his eyes indicated that he was anything other than normal.

He told the prosecutor that he had been building up resentment against neighbors and neighborhood shopkeepers for a long time. "They have been making derogatory remarks about my character," he said. His resentment seemed most strongly concentrated against Mr. and Mrs. Maurice Cohen, who lived next door to him. They are among the dead.

Mr. Cohen was a druggist with a shop at 3202 River Road in East Camden. He and his wife had had frequent sharp exchanges over the Unruhs' use of a gate that separates their back yard from the Cohens'. Mrs. Cohen had also complained of young Unruh's keeping his bedroom radio turned high into the late night hours. None of the other victims had ever had trouble with him.

Unruh, a graduate of Woodrow Wilson High School here, had started a GI course in pharmacy at Temple University in Philadelphia some time after he was honorably discharged from the service in 1945, but had stayed with it only three months. In recent months he had been unemployed, and apparently was not even looking for work.

Mother separated from husband

His mother, Mrs. Rita Unruh, 50, is separated from her husband. She works as a packer in the Evanson Soap Company in Camden, and hers was virtually the only family income. James Unruh, 25 years old, her younger son, is married and lives in Haddon Heights, N.J. He works for the Curtis Publishing Company.

On Monday night, Howard Unruh left the house alone. He spent the night at the Family Theatre on Market Street in Philadelphia to sit through several showings of the double feature motion picture there— "I Cheated the Law" and "The Lady Gambles." It was past 3 o'clock this morning when he got home.

Prosecutor Cohen said that Unruh told him later that before he fell asleep this morning he had made up his mind to shoot the persons who had "talked about me," that he had even figured out that 9:30 a.m. would be the time to begin because most of the stores in his block would be open at that hour.

His mother, leaving her ironing when he got up, prepared his breakfast in their drab little three-room apartment in the shabby gray two-story stucco house at the corner of River Road and Thirty-Second Street. After breakfast he loaded one clip of bullets into his Luger, slipped another clip into his pocket, and carried sixteen loose cartridges in addition. He also carried a tear-gas pen with six shells and a sharp six-inch knife.

He took one last look around his bedroom before he left the house. On the peeling walls he had crossed pistols, crossed German bayonets, pictures of armored artillery in action. Scattered about the chamber were matches, a Roy Rogers pistol, ash trays made of German shells, clips of 30-30 cartridges for his use and a host of varied war souvenirs.

Mrs. Unruh had left the house several minutes before, to call on Mrs. Caroline Pinner, a friend in the next block. Mrs. Unruh had sensed, apparently, that her son's smoldering resentments were coming to a head. She had pleaded with Elias Pinner, her friend's husband, to put a little gate in the Unruhs' back yard so that Howard need not use the Cohen gate again. Mr. Pinner finished the gate early Monday evening after Howard had gone to Philadelphia.

At the Pinners' house at 9 o'clock this morning, Mrs. Unruh had murmered something about Howard's eyes; how strange they looked and how worried she was about him.

A few minutes later River Road echoed and reechoed to pistol fire. Howard Unruh was on the rampage. His mother, who had left the Pinners' little white house only a few seconds before, turned back. She hurried through the door.

She cried, "Oh, Howard, oh, Howard, they're to blame for this." She rushed past Mrs. Pinner, a kindly gray-haired woman of 70. She said, "I've got to use the phone; may I use the phone?"

But before she had crossed the living room to reach for it she fell on the faded carpet in a dead faint. The Pinners lifted her onto a couch in the next room. Mrs. Pinner applied aromatic spirits to revive her.

Panic grips entire block

While his mother writhed on the couch in her house dress and worn, old sweater, coming back to consciousness, Howard Unruh was walking from shop to shop in the "3200 block" with deadly calm, spurting Luger in hand. Children screamed as they tumbled over one another to get out of his way. Men and women dodged into open shops, the women shrill with panic, men hoarse with fear. No one could quite understand for a time what had been turned loose in the block.

Unruh first walked into John Pilarchik's shoe repair shop near the north end of his own side of the street. The cobbler, a 27-year-old man who lives in Pennsauken Township, looked up open-mouthed as Unruh came to within a yard of him. The cobbler started up from his bench but went down with a bullet in his stomach. A little boy who was in the shop ran behind the counter and crouched there in terror. Unruh walked out into the sunlit street.

"I shot them in the chest first," he told the prosecutor later, in meticulous detail, "and then I aimed for the head." He had won marksmanship and sharpshooters' ratings in the service, and he practiced with his Luger all the time on a target set up in the cellar of his home.

Unruh told the prosecutor afterward that he had Cohen the druggist, the neighborhood barber, the neighborhood cobbler and the neighborhood tailor on his mental list of persons who had "talked about him." He went methodically about wiping them out. Oddly enough, he did not start with the druggist, against whom he seemed to have the sharpest feelings, but left him almost for last.

Newlywed wife shot dead

From the cobbler's he went into the little tailor shop at 3214 River Road. The tailor was out. Helga Zagrino, 28 years old, the tailor's wife, was there alone. The couple, incidentally, had been married only one month. She screamed when Unruh walked in with his Luger in hand. Some people across the street heard her. Then the gun blasted again and Mrs. Zagrino pitched over, dead. Unruh walked into the sunlight again.

All this was only a matter of seconds and still only a few persons had begun to understand what was afoot. Down the street at 3210 River Road is Clark Hoover's little country barber shop. In the center was a white-painted carousel-type horse for children customers. Orris Smith, a blond boy only 6 years old, was in it, with a bib around his neck, submitting to a shearing. His mother, Mrs. Catherine Smith, 42, sat on a chair against the wall and watched.

She looked up. Clark Hoover turned from his work, to see the six-footer, gaunt and tense, but silent, standing in the doorway with the Luger. Unruh's brown tropical worsted suit was barred with awning shadow. The sun lay bright in his crew-cut brown hair. He wore no hat. Mrs. Smith could not understand what was about to happen.

Unruh walked to "Brux"—that is Mrs. Smith's nickname for her little boy—and put the Luger to the child's chest. The shot echoed and reverberated in the little 12 by 12 shop. The little boy's head pitched toward the wound, his hair, half-cut, stained with red. Unruh said never a word. He put the Luger close to the shaking barber's hand. Before the horrified mother, Unruh leaned over and fired another shot into Hoover.

The veteran made no attempt to kill Mrs. Smith. He did not seem to hear her screams. He turned his back and stalked out, unhurried, a few doors north. Cominick Latela, who runs a little restaurant, had come to his shop window to learn what the shooting was about. He saw Unruh cross the street toward Frank Engel's tavern. Then he saw Mrs. Smith stagger out with her pitiful burden. Her boy's head lolled over the crook of her right arm.

Mrs. Smith screamed, "My boy is dead. I know he's dead." She stared about her, looking in vain for aid. No one but Howard Unruh was in sight, and he was concentrating on the tavern. Latela rushed out, but first he shouted to his wife, Dora, who was in the restaurant with their daughter, Eleanor, 6 years old. He hollered, "I'm going out. Lock the door behind me." He ran for his car and drove it down toward Mrs. Smith as she stood on the pavement with her son.

Latela took the child from her arms and placed him on the car's front seat. He pushed the mother into the rear seat, slammed the doors and headed for Cooper Hospital. Howard Unruh had not turned. Engel, the tavern keeper, had locked his own door. His customers, the bartender, and a porter made a concerted rush for the rear of the saloon. The bullets tore through the tavern door panelling. Engel rushed upstairs and got out his .38 caliber pistol, then rushed to the street window of his apartment.

Unruh was back in the center of the street. He fired a shot at an apartment window at 3208 River Road. Tommy Hamilton, 2 years old, fell back with a bullet in his head. Unruh went north again to Latela's place. He fired a shot at the door and kicked in the lower glass panel. Mrs Latela crouched behind the counter with her daughter. She heard the bullets, but neither she nor her child was touched. Unruh walked back toward Thirty-second Street, reloading the Luger.

Now the little street—a small block with only five buildings on one side, three one-story stores on the other—was shrill wih women's and children's panicky outcries. A group of six or seven little boys or girls fled past Unruh. They screamed, "Crazy man!" and unintelligible sentences. Unruh did not seem to hear, or see, them.

Autoist goes to his death

Alvin Day, a television repair man who lives in nearby Mantua, had heard the shooting, but driving into the street he was not aware of what had happened. Unruh walked up to the car window as Day rolled by and fired once through the window, with a deadly aim. The repair man fell against the steering wheel. The car seemed to wabble. The front wheels hit the opposite curb and stalled. Day was dead.

Frank Engel had thrown open his second-floor apartment window. He saw Unruh pause for a moment in a narrow alley between the cobbler's shop and a little two-story house. He aimed and fired. Unruh stopped for just a second. The bullet had hit, but he did not seem to mind, after the initial brief shock. He headed toward the corner drug store, and Engel did not fire again.

"I wish I had," he said later. "I could have killed him then. I could have put a half-dozen shots into him. I don't know why I didn't do it."

Cohen, the druggist, a heavy man of 40, had run into the street shouting "What's going on here? What's going on here?" but at the sight of Unruh hurried back into his shop. James J. Hutton, 45, an insurance agent from Westmont, N.J., started out of the drug shop to see what the shooting was about.Like so many others he had figured at first that it was some car backfiring. He came face to face with Unruh.

Unruh said quietly, "Excuse me, sir," and started to push past him. Later Unruh told the police; "That man didn't act fast enough. He didn't get out of my way." He fired into Hutton's head and body. The insurance man pitched onto the sidewalk and lay still.

Cohen had run to his upstairs apartment and had tried to warn Minnie Cohen, 63, his mother, and Rose, his wife, 38, to hide. His son Charles, 14, was in the apartment, too. Mrs. Cohen shoved the boy into a clothes closet and leaped into another closet herself. She pulled the door to. The druggist, meanwhile, had leaped from the window onto a porch roof. Unruh, a gaunt figure at the window behind him, fired into the druggist's back. The druggist, still running, bounded off the roof and lay dead in Thirty-second Street.

Unruh fired into the closet where Mrs. Cohen was hidden. She fell dead behind the closed door, and he did not bother to open it. Mrs. Minnie Cohen tried to get to the telephone in an adjoining bedroom to call the police. Unruh fired shots into her head and body, and she sprawled dead on the bed. Unruh walked down the stairs with the Luger reloaded and came out into the street again.

A couple had stopped at River Road, obeying a red light. The passengers obviously had no idea of what was loose in East Camden, and no one had a chance to tell them. Unruh walked up to the car, and, though it was filled with total strangers, fired deliberately at them, one by one, through the windshield. He killed the two women passengers, Mrs. Helen Matlack Wilson, 43, of Pennsauken, who was driving, and her mother, Mrs. Emma Matlack, 66. Mrs. Wilson's son

John, 12, was badly wounded. A bullet pierced his neck, just below the jawbone.

Several take refuge in grocery

Earl Horner, clerk in the American Stores Company, a grocery opposite the drugstore, had locked his front door after several passing men, women and children had tumbled breathlessly into the shop panting "crazy man...killing people..." Unruh came up to the door and fired two shots through the wood panelling. Horner, his customers, the refugees from the veteran's merciless gunfire, crouched, trembling, behind the counter. None there was hurt.

"He tried the door before he shot in here," Horner related afterward. "He just stood there, stony-faced and grim, and rattled the knob, before he started to fire. Then he turned away."

Charlie Petersen, 18, son of a Camden fireman, came driving down the street with two friends when Unruh turned from the grocery. The three boys got out to stare at Hutton's body lying unattended on the sidewalk. They did not know who had shot the insurance man, or why and, like the women in the car, had no warning that Howard Unruh was on the loose. The veteran brought his Luger to sight and fired several times. Young Petersen fell with bullets in his legs. His friends tore pell-mell down the street to safety.

Mrs. Helen Harris of 1250 North Twenty-eighth Street with her daughter, Helen, a 6-year-old blonde child, and a Mrs. Horowitz with her daughter, Linda, 5, turned into Thirty-second Street. They had heard the shooting from a distance but thought it was auto backfire.

Unruh passed them in Thirty-second Street and walked up the sagging four steps of a little yellow dwelling back of his own house. Mrs. Madeline Harrie, a woman in her late thirties, and two sons, Armand, 16, and Leroy, 15, were in the house. A third son, Wilson, 14, was barricaded in the grocery with other customers.

Unruh threw open the front door and, gun in hand, walked into the dark little parlor. He fired two shots at Mrs. Harrie. They went wild and entered the wall. A third shot caught her in the left arm. She screamed. Armand leaped at Unruh, to tackle him. The veteran used the Luger butt to drop the boy, then fired two shots into his arms. Upstairs Leroy heard the shooting and the screams. He hid under a bed.

By this time, answering a flood of hysterical telephone calls from various parts of East Camden, police radio cars swarmed into River Road with sirens wide open. Emergency crews brought machine guns, shotguns and tear gas bombs.

Sergeant Earl Wright, one of the first to leap to the sidewalk, saw Charles Cohen, the druggist's son. The boy was half out the second-floor apartment window, just above where his father lay dead. He was screaming, "He's going to kill me. He's killing everybody." The boy was hysterical.

Wright bounded up the stairs to the druggist's apartment. He saw the dead woman on the bed, and tried to soothe the druggist's son. He brought him downstairs and turned him over to other policemen, then joined the men who had surrounded the two-story stucco house where Unruh lived. Unruh, meanwhile, had fired about thirty shots. He was out of ammunition. Leaving the Harrie house, he had also heard the police sirens. He had run through the back gate to his own rear bedroom.

Guns trained on window

Edward Jozlin, a motorcycle policeman, scrambled to the porch roof under Unruh's window. He tossed a tear gas grenade through a pane of glass. Other policemen, hoarsely calling on Unruh to surrender, took positions with their machine guns and shotguns. They trained them on Unruh's window.

Meanwhile, a curious interlude had taken place. Philip W. Buxton, an assistant city editor on the Camden Evening Courier, had looked Unruh's name up in the telephone book. He called the number, Camden 4-2490W. It was just after 10 a.m., and Unruh had just returned to his room. To Mr. Buxton's astonishment, Unruh answered. He said hello in a calm, clear voice.

"This is Howard?" Mr. Buxton asked.

"Yes, this is Howard. What's the last name of the party you want?"

"Unruh."

The veteran asked what Mr. Buxton wanted.

"I'm a friend," the newspaper man said. "I want to know what they're doing to you down there."

Unruh thought a moment. He said, "They haven't done anything to me—yet. I'm doing plenty to them." His voice was still steady without a trace of hysteria.

Mr. Buxton asked how many persons Unruh had killed.

The veteran answered: "I don't know. I haven't counted. Looks like a pretty good score."

"Why are you killing people?"

"I don't know," came the frank answer. "I can't answer that yet. I'll have to talk to you later. I'm too busy now."

The telephone banged down.

Unruh was busy. The tear gas was taking effect, and police bullets were thudding at the walls around him. During a halt in the firing the police saw the white curtains move, and the gaunt killer came into plain view.

"Okay," he shouted. "I give up. I'm coming down."

"Where's the gun?" a sergeant yelled.

"It's on my desk, up here in the room," Unruh called down quietly. "I'm coming down."

Thirty guns were trained on the shabby little back door. A few seconds later the door opened and Unruh stepped into the light, his hands up. Sergeant Wright came across the morning glory and aster beds in the yard and snapped handcuffs on Unruh's wrists.

"What's the matter with you," a policeman demanded hotly. "You a psycho?"

Unruh stared into the policeman's eyes—a level, steady stare. He said, "I'm no psycho. I have a good mind."

Word of the capture brought the whole East Camden populace pouring into the streets. Men and women screamed at Unruh and cursed him in shrill accents and in hoarse anger. Someone cried "lynch him," but there was no movement. Sergeant Wright's men walked Unruh to a police car and started for headquarters.

Shouting and pushing men and women started after the car, but dropped back after a few paces. They stood in excited little groups discussing the shootings and the character of Howard Unruh. Little by little the original anger, born of fear, that had moved the crowd, began to die.

Men conceded that he probably was not in his right mind. Those who knew Unruh kept repeating how closed-mouthed he was, and how soft spoken. How he took his mother to church, and how he marked scripture passages, especially the prophecies.

"He was a quiet one, that guy," a man told a crowd in front of the tavern. "He was all the time figuring to do this thing. You gotta watch them quiet ones."

But all day River Road and the side streets talked of nothing else. The shock was great. Men and women kept saying: "We can't understand it. Just don't get it."

9. *Marines in Korea: Suffering and Valor*

Writing about military actions in a way that is more than isolated play-by-play is a challenge to war correspondents. In the early days of the Korean conflict, the Chicago *Daily News'* Keyes Beech met the challenge by covering the war from the front in vivid and precise terms. He combined his own first-hand observations with pertinent quotes from soldiers to make for informative and forceful stories. As is the case with most well-written stories, the one below is loaded with detail. Beech writes of the agony of intense frostbite and cold for American Marines. He describes the ferocity of the Chinese attack and demonstrates the deep pride of the Marines in their refusal to admit defeat. The story, told with brevity and an economy of words, is an impressive accomplishment. *(Pulitzer Prize for International Reporting, 1951)*

"We About-Faced and Attacked"
Keyes Beech
Chicago *Daily News*
December 11, 1950

YONPO AIRSTRIP, KOREA—"Remember," drawled Colonel Lewis B. "Chesty" Puller, "whatever you write, that this was no retreat. All that happened was we found more Chinese behind us than in front of us. So we about-faced and attacked."

I said "so-long" to Puller after three snowbound days with the 1st Marine Division, 4,000 feet above sea level in the sub-zero weather of Changjin Reservoir. I climbed aboard a waiting C-47 at Koto Airstrip and looked around.

Sixteen shivering Marine casualties—noses and eyes dripping from cold—huddled in their bucket seats. They were the last of more than 2,500 Marine casualties to be evacuated by the U.S. Air Force under conditions flatly impossible.

Whatever this campaign was—retreat, withdrawal, or defeat—one thing can be said with certainty. Not in the Marine Corps' long and bloody history has there been anything like it. And if you'll pardon a personal recollection, not at Tarawa or Iwo Jima, where casualties were much greater, did I see men suffer as much.

The wonder isn't that they fought their way out against overwhelming odds but that they were able to survive the cold and fight at all. So far as the Marines themselves are concerned, they ask that two things be recorded:

1. They didn't break. They came out of Changjin Reservoir as an organized unit with most of their equipment.

2. They brought out all their wounded. They brought out many of their dead. And most of those they didn't bring out they buried.

It was not always easy to separate dead from wounded among the frozen figures that lay strapped to radiators of jeeps and trucks. I know because I watched them come in from Yudam to Hagary, 18 miles of icy hell, five days ago.

That same day I stood in the darkened corner of a wind-whipped tent and listened to a Marine officer brief his men for the march to Koto the following day. I have known him for a long time but in the semidarkness, with my face half-covered by my parka, he didn't recognize me. When he did the meeting broke up. When we were alone, he cried. After that he was all right.

I hope he won't mind my reporting he cried, because he's a very large Marine and a very tough guy.

He cried because he had to have some sort of emotional release; because all his men were heroes and wonderful people; because the next day he was going to have to submit them to another phase in the trial by blood and ice. Besides, he wasn't the only one who cried.

In the Marines' twelve-day, forty-mile trek from Yudam to the "bottom of the hill," strange and terrible things happened.

Thousands of Chinese troops—the Marines identified at least six divisions totalling 60,000 men—boiled from every canyon and rained fire from every ridge. Sometimes they came close enough to throw grenades into trucks, jeeps and ambulances.

Whistles sounded and Chinese ran up to throw grenades into Marine foxholes. Another whistle and the Chinese ran back.

Then mortar shells began to fall. The 3d Battalion of the 5th Marine Regiment was reduced to less than two companies but still was ordered to attack "regardless of cost."

"We had to do it," said Lt. Col. Joe Stewart, of Montgomery, Ala. "It was the only way out."

Fox Company, 7th Regiment, was isolated for three or four days—nobody seems to remember dates or days—but held at terrible cost.

One company killed so many Chinese the Marines used their frozen bodies as a parapet. But for every Chinese they killed there were five, ten, or twenty to take his place.

"What'n hell's the use of killing them," said one Marine. "They breed faster'n we can knock 'em off."

The Chinese had blown bridges and culverts behind the Americans. The Marines rebuilt them or established bypasses under fire.

No part of a division escaped, including headquarters sections composed of file clerks, cooks, and bakers. Bullets plowed through a Korean house in Hagaru occupied by General O. H. P. Smith.

Always the infantry had to take high ground on each side of the road to protect the train of vehicles that sometimes stretched ten miles.

When the Chinese attacked a train the artillerymen unhooked their guns from their vehicles and fired muzzle bursts from between trucks at the onrushing foe. This was effective, but rather rough on Marine machine gunners who had set up their guns on the railroad tracks fifteen or twenty yards in front of the artillery.

If there was an occasional respite from the enemy there was none from the cold. It numbed fingers, froze feet, sifted through layers of clothing, and crept into the marrow of your bones. Feet sweated by day and froze in their socks by night. Men pulled off their socks—and the soles of their feet with them.

Among the men of the 5th Marines, Lieutenant Commander Chester M. Lessenden Jr., of Lawrence, Kansas, a Navy doctor, became a hero.

"Lessenden is the most saintly, Godlike man I've ever known," said Stewart. "He never seemed to sleep. He was always on his feet. He never said it can't be done. And yet he was suffering from frostbite worse than most of the men he treated."

In their struggle to keep from freezing, the Marines wrapped their feet in gunnysacks or pieces of old cloth scrounged from the countryside. When they could, they built fires but this wasn't often because fire gave away their positions.

When they came at Koto before the final breakthrough to the sea they made tents of varicolored parachutes used by the Air Force to drop supplies. The red, white, and green tents looked like Indian wigwams.

Some covered themselves with Japanese quilts dropped from the air. But they were warmest when they were fighting. Combat was almost welcome because they forgot about the cold.

The cold did strange things to their equipment. Because of the subzero temperatures artillery rounds landed as much as 2,000 yards short. Machine guns froze up. Men tugged frantically at their frozen bolts. The M-1 rifle generally held up but the Marines cursed the lighter carbine.

Communications gear broke down because equipment, like men, can stand only so much. Canteens burst as water froze inside them.

Despite all these things, the Marines who walked down from Changjin Reservoir still could laugh.

"It was impossible for us to get out because we were surrounded, encircled, and cut off," said one lieutenant. "But we never got the word so we came out. That's us—we never get the word."

Reprinted by permission of the Chicago *Sun-Times*.

10. *Korean Village Collapses Under Communism*

Relman Morin, covering a variety of topics for the Associated Press, won the Pulitzer Prize twice during the 1950s. The following story, looking at the animosity between Communist and non-Communist villagers, was one of a series of his stories that won the prize for 1951. In his story, Morin explained graphically what had happened in one relatively unimportant village, dramatizing the mood throughout the country. By mixing his skillful narrative with quotes from the villagers, Morin produced a memorable story about the collapse of a community. *(Pulitzer Prize for International Reporting, 1951)*

Hatred to Stay
Relman Morin
Associated Press
September 25, 1950

Long after the last shot is fired, the weeds of hatred will be flourishing in Korea, nourished by blood and bitter memories.

This is the heritage of the short weeks during which most of South Korea was learning Communism.

Only weeks ago in the region around Seoul and Inchon, people were being killed, dispossessed of land and homes, left to starve, or driven away from all they held dear—because they were not Communists and refused to act like Communists.

Expect to remain Red

Today, in that same region, the same things are still happening—because some Koreans are Communists and propose to remain so.

Hidden in the hills a mile off the road to Seoul, there is a village of twenty-four mud-stone huts with thatched roofs. The people raise rice and corn. Once they had a few cattle.

There were no rich here and, by Korean standards, no poor either.

Even before the North Korean military invasion last June, nine of the men in the village were Communists.

The headman didn't know why. He simply said they belonged to a Red organization, and frequently went to meetings in Inchon at night.

They talked of the division of land and goods.

"It made trouble," the headman told an American intelligence officer through an interpreter.

She says the lectures talked about life in Russia, how things are done there, and how good everything is. She says it was convincing, and people believed what they heard.

"But she is not a Communist. She went because she was hungry."

Beat the Communists

As a result, the headman said, some of the other villagers banded together and beat the Communists.

"There was always trouble and fighting," said the headman, "and we talked of driving the Reds away."

Then the North Korean army swept southward over this little village. The nine Communists suddenly appeared in uniforms.

They killed some of their neighbors and caused others to be put in jail at Inchon. The headman himself fled to safety in the south. One of the villagers went with him.

"He did not want to go," said the headman. "He was to be married. The girl stayed here. She is 18 and a grown woman, but she did not know what to do."

Back in the village the nine Communists began putting theory into practice. First they confiscated all land. Then they summoned landless tenant farmers from nearby villages and told them the land would be given to them if they became Communists.

Conformed to get land

"The farmers are ignorant of these things," the headman said. "They were very glad, and they accepted the land and said they were Communists."

Next the nine Reds went to the homes of all the men who had fought with them before.

"They took away all the furniture, even the pots and kettles, and put all these things into one house," the headman related. "Then they said the people who were Communists could come and take whatever they wanted.

"Even the people who were robbed in this way were permitted to come. If they agreed to be Communists they could take back some of their things. Most of them did that."

The parents of the engaged girl were among those who fled. She stayed. Maybe she was waiting for the man who escaped to the south with the headman.

Promised food by Reds

"She was hungry most of the time," the headman said. "The Communists told her that if she would attend some cultural classes they would give her food."   So she went to the school.

Then, ten days ago, the Americans attacked Inchon. Before the Communists left they herded thirty-three men into a large cell in the Inchon jail and locked the doors. Then the thirty-three were shot to death.

As soon as possible the headman came back to his village. Soon the man who had fled with him came back too.

The landowners took back their own fields and furniture. Some of the newly made "Communists" were bewildered, and tried to resist. Some were injured.

The American officer asked: "What would you do if the nine Communists came back?"

The headman and the others listening burst into hearty laughter.

"Kill them, naturally," the headman said.

11.   *The Integration of Central High*

Relman Morin used an effective chronological narrative approach in reconstructing the integration of Little Rock's Central High School. The structure is not elaborate, but the story is built on scenes that are connected by narrative transitions. The reader's sense of the event is heightened by his use of descriptive adjectives to depict the setting and by his selection of direct quotes. The quotes help to construct the characterization of the people in the story and to crystallize their emotions and attitudes. The art of handling quotes comes from the reporter's knowing when to use quotes, when to paraphrase, and when to omit quotes altogether. *(Pulitzer Prize for National Reporting, 1958)*

Howling Crowd Greets Black Students
Relman Morin
Associated Press
September 23, 1957

LITTLE ROCK, ARK.—A howling, shrieking crowd of men and women outside Central High School, and disorderly students inside, forced authorities to withdraw eight Negro students from the school Monday, three and one-half hours after they entered it.

At noon, Mayor Woodrow Wilson Mann radioed police officers on the scene, telling them to tell the crowd: "The Negro students have been withdrawn."

Almost immediately, the three Negro boys and the five girls left the school under heavy police escort. The officers took them away in police cars.

Crowds clustered at both ends of the school set up a storm of fierce howling and surged toward the lines of police and state troopers. They were beaten back.

The explosive climax came after the school had been under siege since 8:45 a.m., when the Negroes walked quietly through the doors. Police, armed with riot guns and tear gas, had kept the crowd under control.

Inside, meanwhile, students reported seeing Negroes with blood on their clothes. And some whites who came out—to protest against integration—pictured wild disorder, with policemen chasing white students through the halls, and attacks on Negroes in the building.

The break came shortly before noon.

Virgil Blossom, school superintendent, said he asked Gene Smith, assistant chief of police at the scene, if he thought it would be best to pull out the Negroes. Smith said he did.

Mann's announcement, ordering the police to notify the crowd, came minutes afterward.

Three newspapermen were beaten by the crowd before the sudden turn in the situation. They were Paul Welch, a reporter, and Gray Villette and Francis Miller, photographers. All three are employed by *Life* magazine. A man smashed Miller in the face while he was carrying an armful of camera equipment. Miller fell, bleeding profusely.

Even after the Negroes left the school, the crowds remained. Teenagers in two automobiles cruised on the outskirts yelling, "Which way did the niggers go?"

During the hours while the Negroes were in the school an estimated thirty to fifty white students left. The crowd yelled, cheered, and clapped each time a white student left the school. "Don't stay in there with the niggers," people yelled.

Four Negroes were beaten and some arrests were made before the eight students went into the school.

The initial violence outside the school was a frightening sight. Women burst into tears, and a man, hoisted up on a wooden barricade, roared, "Who's going through?"

"We all are," the crowd shouted. But they didn't.

The drama-packed climax of three weeks of integration struggle in Little Rock came just after the buzzer sounded inside the 2,000-pupil high school at 8:45, signaling the start of classes.

Suddenly on a street leading toward the school, the crowd spotted four Negro adults, marching in twos, down the center of the street. A man yelled, "Look, here come the niggers."

They were not the students. One appeared to be a newspaperman. He had a card in his hat and was bearing a camera.

I jumped into a glass-windowed telephone booth on the corner to dictate the story. As the crowd surged toward the four Negroes they broke and ran.

They were caught on the lawn of a home nearby. Whites jumped the man with the camera from behind and rode him to the ground, kicking and beating him. They smashed the camera.

This, obviously, was a planned diversionary movement to draw the crowd's attention away from the school. While I was dictating, someone yelled, "Look! They're going into the school!"

At that instant, the eight Negroes—the three boys and five girls— were crossing the schoolyard toward a side door at the south end of the school. The girls were in bobby sox and the boys dressed in shirts open at the neck. All were carrying books.

They were not running, not even walking fast. They simply strolled toward the steps, went up and were inside before all but a few of the 200 people at that end of the street knew it.

"They're gone in," a man roared. "Oh, God, the niggers are in the school."

A woman screamed, "Did they get in? Did you see them go in?"

"They're in now," some other men yelled.

"Oh, my God," the woman screamed. She burst into tears and tore at her hair. Hysteria swept the crowd. Other women began weeping and screaming.

At that moment a tall, gray-haired man in a brown hunting shirt jumped on the barricade. He yelled, waving his arms: "Who's going through?"

"We all are," the people shouted.

They broke over and around the wooden barricades, rushing the policemen. Almost a dozen police were at that corner of the street. They raised their billy clubs.

Some grabbed men and women and hurled them back. Two chased a dark-haired man who slipped through their line, like a football player. They caught him on the schoolyard, whipped his coat down his arms, pinning them, and hustled him out of the yard.

Another man, wearing a construction worker's hard hat, suddenly raised his hands high in front of a policeman. It was only a dozen yards or so in front of the phone booth.

I couldn't see whether the officer had a gun in the man's stomach, but he stopped running abruptly and went back. Two men were arrested.

Meanwhile a cavalcade of cars carrying state troopers, in their broad-brimmed campaign hats and Sam Browne belts, wheeled into the street from both ends. They came inside the barricades, and order was restored for a moment.

The weeping and screaming went on among the women. A man said, "I'm going in there and get my kid out."

An officer said, "You're not going anywhere."

Suddenly another roar—and cheering and clapping—came from the crowd. A white student, carrying his books, came down the front steps. He was followed by two girls wearing bobby sox. In the next few minutes, other students came out. Between fifteen and twenty left the school within the next half hour.

Each time they appeared, the people clapped and cheered. "Come on out," they yelled. "Don't stay in there with the niggers. Go back and tell all of them to come out."

Inside, it was reported, the eight Negro students were in the office of the principal. A moment later, two policemen suddenly raced into the building through the north door. When they came out, they were holding a girl by both arms, rushing her forcibly toward a police prisoner's wagon.

For an instant it looked as though the crowd would try to break the police lines again to rescue her. But the police put her in the car and drove swiftly down the street. Screams, cat-calls, and more yelling broke out as the car raced down the street.

A man, distraught, came sprinting after it. "That's my kid in there," he yelled. "Help me get my kid out."

But the car was gone. Soon afterward four white students ran down the steps of the school and across the street. Policemen were chasing them.

One of the boys said they had caught a Negro boy outside the principal's office in the school. "We walked him half the length of the building, and we were going to get him out of there," they said. They refused to give their names.

Meanwhile, on the streets, at both ends of the school, clusters of troopers took up their stations, reinforcing the police. The crowd heckled them, hurling insults and some obscenity.

"How you going to feel tonight when you face your neighbors?" a man shouted.

The people called the police "nigger lovers" and insulted them. The officers stood, poker-faced, making no response.

Then the crowd, lacking any other object, turned on the newspapermen and photographers. A boy jumped up, caught the telephone wire leading from one of the three booths to the main wire and swung on it, trying to break it. The booth swayed and nearly toppled to the street.

Someone said, "We ought to wipe up the street with these Yankee reporters."

"Let's do it right now," another replied.

But it was only words. Nothing happened. The same woman who had burst into tears first buttonholed a reporter and said, "Why don't you tell the truth about us? Why don't you tell them we are peaceful people who won't stand to have our kids sitting next to niggers?"

People in the crowd reported gleefully—and shouted it at the other officers—that one policeman had torn off his badge and thrown it on the ground.

"There's one white man on the police force," a burly slick-haired youth in a tee shirt yelled at the policeman in front of him.

Sporadic tussles broke out, from time to time, when men tried to pass the police and trooper lines. The police wrestled one man to the street and then, taking him by the hands and arms, hauled him into the squad car and drove off.

A number of plainsclothesmen—some reported to be FBI agents— kept circulating up and down in front of the school.

Inside there was no sign that this was different from any other school day. Students who came out at the 10:30 recess said that, in one class of thirty students, only one stayed in the classroom when a Negro entered.

Reprinted by permission of the Associated Press.

12. The Death of an Opera Star

The majority of obituary stories are monotonous. Routineness is the rule for them more than perhaps for any other type of story. Yet, obituaries offer the writer the opportunity for forceful, moving stories. The following story on the death on stage of Metropolitan Opera star Leonard Warren is an example of what the good writer can do with an obituary. Sanche de Gramont sets the scene skillfully and then takes the reader to the event by using quotations that reveal the characters as real people. He treats the subject's life sympathetically yet factually, integrating pertinent background information into the account of Warren's death. The major strengths of the story lie in its completeness; simple, dignified language; and the drama of the announcement that Warren indeed was dead. Despite the polished product, de Gramont had less than ninety minutes in which to go to the Metropolitan Opera, gather all information, return to his office, and write the story. (Pulitzer Prize for Reporting, 1961)

Leonard Warren Dies at the Met

Sanche de Gramont

New York *Herald Tribune*

March 5, 1960

Leonard Warren, leading baritone of the Metropolitan Opera, died last night on the stage where he had sung for more than twenty years.

The forty-nine-year-old singer collapsed as he was ending the second act of Verdi's "La Forza del Destino." He fell forward as he was making his exit at 10:05 p.m., and twenty-five minutes later the house physician pronounced him dead, victim of a stroke.

There was an awesome moment as the singer fell. The rest of the cast remained paralyzed. Finally someone in the capacity audience called out "For God's sake, bring down the curtain."

The curtain came down, ambulances were called and a member of the cast tried to administer the last rites to the singer, who was a recent convert to Roman Catholicism.

Members of the staff who came from the stage weeping announced that the opera star was dead.

The news was met with hushed consternation by many in the opera house who had come backstage after the curtain was lowered.

In the audience were many critics who came to hear Mr. Warren and Renata Tebaldi, making her first appearance this year. Mr. Warren was acknowledged to be the world's best dramatic baritone. He had a repertoire of twenty-six operatic roles.

A member of the Metropolitan staff said Mr. Warren had appeared in perfect health when he came to sing last night.

At the time he collapsed, Mr. Warren had just finished the aria "O fatal pages of my destiny." He was singing the role of Don Carlo in the opera, set in Italy and Spain, and was dressed in the colorful uniform of a Spanish grenadier. The opera has a tragic ending in which Don Carlo is killed by an erstwhile friend.

The surgeon, in the opera, played by Ronald Reitan, a baritone, sings to Mr. Warren: "E salvo." ("He's well".)

Mr. Warren responds: "E salvo, e salvo, O Gloria." ("He's saved, he's saved, O joy.")

He turned to his left, and prepared to make his exit, which ends the act, and collapsed. Some thought he had tripped. The conductor, Thomas Shippers, froze. Mr. Reitan raced to Mr. Warren's side as the curtain fell. He was followed by Richard Tucker, who was playing Don Alvaro and was watching from the wings.

Mr. Tucker said: "Lennie, Lennie, what is it?"
They turned him over.

Wife in audience

The singer's wife, Mrs. Agatha Leifflen Warren, was watching from a parterre box with her brother, Roy Leifflen, a Washington attorney, and Msgr. Edwin Broderick, of St. Patrick's Cathedral, a friend of the Warrens.

Mrs. Warren saw Mr. Warren's face and gasped. Msgr. Broderick went backstage. Dr. Adrian W. Zorgniotti, the house physician, also went backstage.

Mr. Warren remained unconscious. The physician said he thought the singer suffered a massive cerebral vascular hemorrhage. His respiration stopped two or three minutes after he collapsed. He was pronounced dead at 10:15 p.m.

Half an hour after Mr. Warren collapsed, the warning buzzer sounded in the foyers and lobbies of the packed house. The audience returned to its seats.

The audience chattered until the house lights dimmed, and a moment later the spotlight hit the curtain and Rudolf Bing, general manager of the Metropolitan Opera, stepped out.

With his hands clasped in front of him he announced: "It is one of the saddest days—"

At this point the audience broke into shouts of "Oh, no. Oh no."

Tribute by Bing

Mr. Bing continued, "I ask you to stand..."

The audience again moaned, and whispers went through the audience, "He's gone. He's gone."

"...in tribute," Mr. Bing continued, "to one of our greatest performers; he died as I am sure he would have wanted to die.

"He died in the middle of a peformance."

"Cannot continue"

"I'm sure you will agree that under these circumstances we cannot possibly continue."

Mr. Bing made an about face and returned backstage.

The audience left the theater in visible shock and disbelief.

Ambulances from at least three hospitals and oxygen from a police emergency squad arrived at the opera too late to help.

Audience stunned

The audience emptied into Broadway and stopped momentarily in front of the W. 40th St. exit, its red light flashing. Police blocked the backstage entrance. In the theater, musicians talked quietly among themselves, recalling the singer's career.

Mr. Bing called the singer's last performance "one of his greatest."

A spokesman for the Metropolitan Opera said it was believed to be the first time in the opera house's existence that a star had been fatally stricken on stage in the middle of a role.

Mr. Warren was taken to the dressing room he occupied for many years, and from there to the Abbey Funeral Home, 66th St. and Lexington Ave.

Mr. Warren made his debut at the Metropolitan on Jan. 13, 1939. He was to sing another Verdi role, "Simon Boccanegra," in Philadelphia Tuesday, and had been scheduled for the title part in the company's first production of Verdi's "Nabucco" for the Metropolitan's fall season.

In 600 performances

Mr. Warren had sung a total of more than 600 performances of twenty-two roles, more than a fifth of them as Rigoletto.

Like most top-flight singers he was temperamental. He told other singers how to sing, conductors how to conduct, directors how to direct, photographers how to make pictures, recording engineers how to record and costumers how to costume.

He was forgiven for all this because many regarded him as the greatest baritone in Italian repertory, a "human bellows mounted on matchsticks." He had a fifty-one-inch chest (unexpanded), a size 17 ½ collar, a massive head, almost six feet of height and well over 200 pounds of weight—all supported on thin legs.

At the time he was engaged by the Metropolitan he had seen only one opera in his life, "La Traviata," when he was twenty-two. He had no definite idea of making a career in music, and began his career in his father's fur business.

In 1935, he went to Radio City Music Hall, went backstage, asked for an audition and got it and a job. He stayed at Radio City for three years, spending all of the time in the chorus. He never got a chance for a solo turn.

Mr. Warren went to the Met by way of the "Auditions of the Air" in 1938, when he was dared into entering by fellow chorus members at Radio City. When he auditioned for Wilfrid Pelletier, the conductor thought a ringer had been brought in.

He did not have a single operatic role at that time, and he went to Italy to prepare some repertoire. Working under Giuseppe Pais and

Ricardo Piccozi in Rome and Milan, he learned seven roles in seven months.

Mr. Warren was born in the Bronx and attended Public School 11 and Evander Childs High School. For a year he studied business at night at Columbia University, preparatory to entering his father's fur brokerage business.

As a hobby he began studying music at the Greenwich House Music School and sang lustily while counting muskrats and minks in his father's establishment.

After his audition with the Radio City Music Hall, he studied voice production with Sidney Dietch.

Besides the Metropolitan Opera, Mr. Warren appeared with the San Francisco Opera, the Chicago Opera and the Cincinnati Summer Opera and sang concerts extensively throughout North and South America.

He also appeared often on major radio and television programs, including "Voice of Firestone" and "Toast of the Town." His extensive list of recordings for RCA Victor included a wide variety of music from "Falstaff" to sea chanties and Kipling ballads.

© I.H.T. Corporation. Reprinted by permission.

13. The Death of a Marine Column

Peter Arnett was just one of the Associated Press team covering Vietnam in the 1960s to win a Pulitzer Prize. The vivid imagery Arnett used in his stories set his work apart from many of the routine accounts of offensives and counter-offensives common in war coverage. He was a witness day after day to some of the most intense fighting of the war and was able to translate that experience into language that allowed his readers to understand what he had seen and experienced. Arnett's lead in the following story is simple, yet powerful. It hits the reader with the sense of desperate irony present in battle. His use of simple declarative sentences allows his already dramatic story to tell itself. He writes, "Survivors said the Vietcong rose out of hedge rows and swamps." It is a hauntingly descriptive sentence, typical of his subtle choice of words throughout the story that powerfully brings home the scenes and events for the reader. *(Pulitzer Prize for International Reporting, 1966)*

Supply Column 21 Never Returns
Peter Arnett
Associated Press
August 19, 1965

VAN TUONG, Vietnam—The mission of U.S. Marine Supply Column 21 yesterday was simple: Get to the beachhead, resupply a line company and return to the 7th Fleet mother ship anchored a mile out in the bay.

It never found the line company. And it never returned.

Supply Column 21 was a formidable force made up of five steel-shod amtracks—35-ton amphibious vehicles—to carry food and ammunition—and two M48 tanks to escort them once ashore.

The column packed a total of 287 tons of steel. It was made up of 30 men.

The paths that led to its destruction were paved with confusion.

Failing to locate the designated line company immediately, Column 21 set out to look for it.

But the huge amtraks, once out of water, were unwieldy. They flopped from one rice paddy to another, with their crews calling at one battalion and then the next. No one seemed to pay much attention.

At 11 A.M., Supply Column 21 was about 400 yards ahead of the nearest Marine riflemen. The vehicles were deep in Vietcong territory and, suddenly, were deep in trouble.

Survivors said the Vietcong rose out of hedge rows and swamps.

Lance Corporal Richard Pass of Homewood, Ill., said his amtrak veered aside as explosions erupted around them. The leading tank was hit with an armor-piercing shell. Two men inside were wounded.

The terraced paddies made maneuvering difficult and the supply men were not trained for it. Attempting to get into good firing positions, three of the five amtraks backed into a deep paddy and bogged down.

The other two edged toward the tanks for shelter. One didn't make it. A Vietcong knocked it out by dropping a grenade down its hatch, killing two Americans inside and wounding others.

Mortar fire bounced off the vehicles and cannon put three holes in one tank. The wounded driver squeezed himself through the 18-inch wide escape hatch under his vehicle only to be riddled by bullets.

Corporal Pass saw Vietcong with ammunition bandoliers, black pajama uniforms, and camouflaged steel helmets move right up to an amtrak 30 yards to his left.

He said the doors of the vehicle clanged open as the two drivers tried to make a break to Pass's vehicle. One of the Americans was killed as he leaped out.

The other was plunging through the paddyfield swinging his Marine knife when he went down. When pulled out dead today, he still had the knife clutched in his hand.

Soon after noon, as the hot sun beat down on the scurrying figures and the steel vehicles, the Vietcong knocked out a third amtrak. Survivors massed in the other two.

Corporal Frank Guilford of Philadelphia said machine guns sliced into the guerrillas, but they kept coming.

The men took turns as sharpshooters at peepholes on top of the vehicles. All were wounded in some degree.

"I couldn't maneuver up there," said Pfc. James Reeff of Seattle, who escaped with a slight injury.

A young corporal shouted, "Okay, men, we're Marines. Let's do the job."

He started to climb out of the vehicle but never got his rifle to his shoulder. A bullet hit him between the eyes.

Among those sweltering in the other amtrak was Staff Sgt. Jack Merino of Limita, Calif. He said he almost passed out from heat exhaustion. The men took turns splashing water over each other from resupply cans within the vehicle.

Merino said that in midafternoon he heard a man outside whispering, "Amtrak, amtrak." He proved to be a wounded tank crewman. Merino and others pulled him inside.

"It was a hair-raising moment but we managed it," Merino said.

The Marines continued with the nerve-wracking task of keeping off the attackers. The enemy bodies began piling up.

In late afternoon, air strikes eased the pressure.

By this time, a lieutenant had been killed and another wounded.

Another tank joined the beleaguered group.

At daybreak, a solitary helicopter landed at the scene. It had mistaken the landing zone.

At the drone of the helicopter, the Americans surged from their amtraks like moths to a flame.

Crouched, and with weapons at the ready, the Americans slipped past the bodies of their own and the enemy. They carried the wounded to the helicopter and left the dead.

The helicopter came back once more for wounded.

Ground forces arrived to relieve the others. In the interval they had scoured the nearby paddyfields and brush for Vietcong bodies. They found 18.

Corporal Earle Eberly of Sycamore, Ill., said:

"We don't like being here and killing people and being killed. But this is a job we've been told to do, we have to do it, and we're going to do it."

The fate of Supply Column 21 was sealed at noon.

The men thought the disabled vehicles might be carted off and repaired. But an officer of the relief force told them:

"Take your personal belongings out of the vehicles. We're going to blow them up."

The remains of the amtraks at Van Tuong will be a reminder of Supply Column 21.

Reprinted by permission of the Associated Press.

14. *The Death and Burial of Private Gibson*

In the Pulitzer nomination statement for the following story, John Fetterman's editor wrote, "'Pfc. Gibson Comes Home' is a simple story. It has meaning, however, for every American." Indeed, the narrative account has little noticeable flare in its writing, yet it packs a strong emotional punch because of its painstaking detail and description. Fetterman seemingly keeps himself out of the story, allowing neighbors and family to speak for themselves. His descriptions are understated, and all the more powerful as a result. The story is a good example of how effective restraint in writing can be. *(Pulitzer Prize for Local General Spot News Reporting, 1969)*

Pfc. Gibson Comes Home

John Fetterman
Louisville *Times*
July 1968

It was late on a Wednesday night and most of the people were asleep in Hindman, the county seat of Knott County, when the body of Private First Class James Thurman (Little Duck) Gibson came home from Vietnam.

It was hot. But as the gray hearse arrived bearing the gray Army coffin, a summer rain began to fall. The fat raindrops glistened on the polished hearse and steamed on the street. Hindman was dark and silent. In the distance down the town's main street the red sign on the Square Deal Motor Co. flashed on and off.

Private Gibson's body had been flown from Oakland, California, to Cincinnati and was accompanied by Army Staff Sgt. Raymond A. Ritter, assigned to escort it home. The body was picked up in Cincinnati by John Everage, a partner in the local funeral home, and from that point on it was in the care of people who had known the 24-year-old soldier all his life.

At Hindman, the coffin was lifted out while Sgt. Ritter, who wore a black mourning band on his arm, snapped a salute. One funeral home employee whispered to another: "It's Little Duck. They brought him back."

Most of his life he has been called Little Duck—for so long that many people who knew him well had to pause and reflect to recall his full name.

By Thursday morning there were few people who did not know that Little Duck was home—or almost home. During the morning the family came: his older brother, Herschel, whom they call Big Duck; his sister, Betty Jo; and his wife, Carolyn.

They stood over the glass-shielded body and let their tears fall upon the glass, and people spoke softly in the filling station next door and on the street outside.

The soldier's parents, Mr. and Mrs. Norman Gibson, waited at home, a neat white house up the hollow which shelters Flax Patch Creek, several miles away. Mrs. Gibson had been ill for months, and the family did not let her take the trip to Hindman. Later in the morning, they took Little Duck home.

Sweltering heat choked the hills and valleys as Little Duck was placed back in the hearse and taken home. The cortege had been joined by Maj. Lyle Haldeman, a survival assistance officer, sent, like Sgt. Ritter, to assist the family. It was a long, slow trip—over a high ridge to the south, along Irishman Creek and past the small community of Amburgey.

At Amburgey, the people stood in the sun, women wept and men removed their hats as the hearse went past. Mrs. Nora Amburgey, the postmistress, lowered the flag in front of the tiny fourth-class post office to half-mast and said, "We all thought a lot of Little Duck."

At the point where Flax Patch Creek empties into Irishman Creek, the hearse turned, crossed a small wooden bridge and drove the final mile up Flax Patch Creek to the Gibson home. The parents and other relatives waited in a darkened, silent home.

As the coffin was lifted upon the front porch and through the door into the front living room, the silence was broken by cries of grief. The sounds of anguish swelled and rolled along the hollow. Little Duck was home.

All afternoon and all night they came, some walking, some driving up the dusty road in cars and trucks. They brought flowers and food until the living room was filled with floral tributes and the kitchen was crammed with the food. The people filled the house and yard. They talked in small groups, and members of the family clasped each other in grief.

They went, time and time again, to look down into the coffin and weep.

The mother, a sweet-faced mountain woman, her gray hair brushed back and fastened behind her head, forced back the pangs of her illness and moved, as in a trance, among the crowd as she said:

"His will will be done no matter what we say or do."

The father, a tall, tanned man, his eyes wide and red from weeping, said:

"He didn't want to go to the Army, but he knew it was the right thing to do; so he did his best. He gave all he had. I'm as proud of him as I can be. Now they bring him home like this."

Around midnight the rain returned and the mourners gathered in the house, on the porch and backed against the side of the house under the eaves.

The father talked softly of his son.

"I suppose you wonder why we called him Little Duck. Well, when the boys were little they would go over and play in the creek every chance they got. Somebody said they were like ducks.

"Ever since then Herschel was 'Big Duck' and James was 'Little Duck.'

"You work hard all your life to raise your family. I worked in a 32-inch seam of coal, on my hands and knees, loading coal to give my family what I could.

"There was never a closer family. Little Duck was born here in this house and never wanted to leave."

Other mourners stepped up to volunteer tributes to Little Duck.

"He never was one to drink and run up and down the road at night."

"He took care of his family. He was a good boy."

Little Duck was a big boy. He was 6 feet 5 ½ inches tall and weighed 205 pounds. His size had led him to the basketball team at Combs High School where he met and courted the girl he married last January.

Little Duck was home recently on furlough. Within a month after he went down Flax Patch Creek to return to the Army, he was back home to be buried. He had been married six months, a soldier for seven.

The Army said he was hit by mortar fragments near Saigon, but there were few details of his death.

The father, there in the stillness of early morning, was remembering the day his son went back to the Army.

"He had walked around over the place, looking at everything. He told me, 'Lord, it's good to be home.'

"Then he went down the road. He said, 'Daddy, take care of yourself and don't work too hard.'

"He said, 'I'll be seeing you.' But he can't see me now."

An elderly man, walking with great dignity, approached and said, "Nobody can ever say anything against Little Duck. He was as good a boy as you'll ever see."

Inside the living room, the air heavy with the scent of flowers, Little Duck's mother sat with her son and her grief.

Her hand went out gently, as to comfort a stranger, and she talked as though to herself:

"Why my boy? Why my baby?"

She looked toward the casket, draped in an American flag, and when she turned back she said:

"You'll never know what a flag means until you see one on your own boy."

Then she went back to weep over the casket.

On Friday afternoon Little Duck was taken over to the Providence Regular Baptist Church and placed behind the pulpit. All that night the church lights burned and the people stayed and prayed. The parents spent the night at the church.

"This is his last night," Little Duck's mother explained.

The funeral was at 10 o'clock Saturday morning, and the people began to arrive early. They came from the dozens of hollows and small communities in Letcher, Knott and Perry counties. Some came back from other states. They filled the pews and then filled the aisle with folding chairs. Those who could not crowd inside gathered outside the door or listened beneath the windows.

The sermon was delivered by the Rev. Archie Everage, pastor at Montgomery Baptist Church, which is on Montgomery Creek near Hindman. On the last Sunday that he was home alive, Little Duck attended services there.

The service began with a solo, "Beyond the Sunset," sung by a young girl with a clear, bell-like voice; then there were hymns from the church choir.

Mr. Everage, who had been a friend of Little Duck, had difficulty in keeping his voice from breaking as he got into his final tribute. He spoke of the honor Little Duck had brought to his family, his courage and his dedication. He spoke of Little Duck "following the colors of his country." He said Little Duck died "for a cause for which many of our forefathers fought and died."

The phrase touched off a fresh swell of sobs to fill the church. Many mountain people take great pride in their men who "follow the colors." It is a tradition that goes back to October of 1780, when a lightly regarded band of mountaineers handed disciplined British troops a historic defeat at Kings Mountain in South Carolina and turned the tide of the Revolutionary War.

Shortly before Little Duck was hit in Vietnam, he had written two letters intended for his wife. Actually the soldier was writing a part of his own funeral. Mr. Everage read from one letter:

"Honey, they put me in a company right down on the Delta. From what everybody says that is a rough place, but I've been praying hard for the Lord to help me and take care of me so really I'm not too scared or worried. I think if He wants it to be my time to go that I'm prepared for it. Honey, you don't know really when you are going to face something like this, but I want you to be a good girl and try to live a good life. For if I had things to do over I would have already been prepared for something like this. I guess you are wondering why I'm telling you all of this, but you don't know how hard it's been on me in just a short time. But listen here, if anything happens to me, all I want is for you to live right and then I'll get to see you again."

And from another letter:

"Honey, listen, if anything happens to me I want you to know that I love you very very much and I want you to keep seeing my family the rest of their lives and I want you to know that you are a wonderful wife and that I'm very proud of you. If anything happens I want Big Duck and Betty Joe to know that I loved them very much. If anything happens also tell them not to worry, that I'm prepared for it."

The service lasted two hours and ended only after scores of people, of all ages, filed past the coffin.

Then they took Little Duck to Resthaven Cemetery up on a hill in Perry County. The Army provided six pallbearers, five of whom had served in Vietnam. There was a seven-man firing squad to fire the traditional three volleys over the grave and a bugler to sound taps.

The pallbearers, crisp and polished in summer tans, folded the flag from the coffin and Sgt. Ritter handed it to the young widow, who had wept much, but spoken little, during the past three days.

Then the soldier's widow knelt beside the casket and said softly, "Oh, Little Duck."

Then they buried Little Duck beneath a bit of the land he died for.

The Louisville *Times.* Reprinted with permission.

15. *A Fatal Journey Through the Brain*

In writing about a revolutionary brain operation, Baltimore Evening Sun reporter Jon Franklin tackled a real challenge. He had to explain an extraordinarily complicated medical procedure in layman's terms as well as sustain reader interest through two stories. He managed to do both admirably. Through skillful writing, Franklin captures the tension in the operating room while informing readers about the latest in medical technology. He also makes his subjects—the doctor and patient—real for the readers. It is an impressive example of narrative writing. *(Pulitzer Prize for Feature Writing, 1979)*

Frightening Journey Through Tunnels of the Brain
Jon Franklin
Baltimore *Evening Sun*
December 12, 1978

In the cold hours of a winter morning, Dr. Thomas Barbee Ducker, University Hospital's senior brain surgeon, rises before dawn. His wife serves him waffles but no coffee. Coffee makes his hands shake.

Downtown, on the 12th floor of the hospital, Edna Kelly's husband tells her goodbye.

For 57 years Mrs. Kelly shared her skull with the monster. No more. Today she is frightened but determined.

It is 6:30 a.m.

"I'm not afraid to die," she said as this day approached. "I've lost part of my eyesight. I've gone through all the hemorrhages. A couple of years ago I lost my sense of smell, my taste, I started having seizures. I smell a strange odor and then I start strangling. It started affecting my legs and I'm partially paralyzed.

"Three years ago a doctor told me all I had to look forward to was blindness, paralysis and a remote chance of death. Now I have aneurisms; this monster is causing that. I'm scared to death...but there isn't a day that goes by that I'm not in pain and I'm tired of it. I can't bear the pain. I wouldn't want to live like this much longer." As Dr. Ducker leaves for work, Mrs. Ducker hands him a paper bag containing a peanut butter sandwich, a banana and two fig newtons. Downtown, in Mrs. Kelly's brain, a sedative takes effect. Mrs. Kelly was born with a tangled knot of abnormal blood vessels in the back of her brain. The malformation began small, but in time the vessels ballooned inside the confines of the skull, crowding the healthy brain tissue.

Finally, in 1942, the malformation announced its presence when one of the abnormal arteries, stretched beyond capacity, burst. Mrs. Kelly grabbed her head and collapsed.

After that, the agony never stopped.

Mrs. Kelly, at the time of her first intracranial bleed, was carrying her second child. Despite the pain, she raised her children and cared for her husband. The malformation continued to grow.

She began calling it "the monster."

Now, at 7:15 a.m. in Operating Room 11, a technician checks the brain surgery microscope and the circulating nurse lays out bandages and instruments. Mrs. Kelly lies still on a stainless steel table.

A small sensor has been threaded through her veins and now hangs in the antechamber of her heart. Dr. Jane Matjasko, the anesthesiologist, connects the sensor to a 7-foot-high bank of electronic instruments. Waveforms begin to move rhythmically across a cathode ray tube.

With each heartbeat a loudspeaker produces an audible popping sound. The steady pop, pop, pop, pop isn't loud, but it dominates the operating room.

Dr. Ducker enters the operating room and pauses before the X-ray films that hang on a lighted panel. He carried those brain images to Europe, Canada and Florida in search of advice, and he knows them by heart. Still, he studies them again, eyes focused on the two fragile aneurisms that swell above major arteries. Either may burst on contact.

The one directly behind Mrs. Kelly's eyes is the most dangerous, but also the easiest to reach. That's first.

The surgeon-in-training who will assist Dr. Ducker places Mrs. Kelly's head in a clamp and shaves her hair. Dr. Ducker checks his work. "We can't have a millimeter slip," he says, assuring himself that the three pins of the vise are locked firmly against the skull.

Mrs. Kelly, except for a 6-inch cresent of scalp, is draped with green sheets. A rubber-gloved palm goes out, and Doris Schwabland, the scrub nurse, lays a scapel into it. Hemostats snap over the arteries of the scalp. Blood splatters onto Dr. Ducker's sterile paper booties.

The heartbeat goes pop, pop, pop, 70 pops a minute, steady.

It is 8:25 a.m.

Today Dr. Ducker intends to remove the two aneurisms, which comprise the most immediate threat to Mrs. Kelly's life. Later, he will move directly on the monster.

It is a risky operation, destined to take him to the hazardous frontiers of neurosurgery. Several experts told him he shouldn't do it at all, that he should let Mrs. Kelly die. But the consensus was he had no choice. The choice was Mrs. Kelly's.

"There's one chance of three that we'll end up with a hell of a mess or a dead patient," Dr. Ducker says.

"I reviewed it in my own heart and with other people, and I thought about the patient. You weigh what happens if you do it against what happens if you don't do it. I convinced myself that it should be done."

And Mrs. Kelly said yes.

Now, the decision made, Dr. Ducker pulls back Mrs. Kelly's scalp to reveal the dull ivory of living bone.

The chatter of the half-inch drill fills the room, drowning the rhythmic pop-pop-pop of the heart monitor. It is 9 o'clock when Dr. Ducker hands the 2-by-4-inch triangle of skull to the scrub nurse.

The tough, rubbery covering of the brain is cut free, revealing the soft gray convolutions of the forebrain.

"There it is," says the circulating nurse in a hushed voice. "That's what keeps you working."

It is 9:20.

Eventually, Dr. Ducker steps back, holding his gloved hands high to avoid contamination. While others move the microscope into place over the glistening brain, the neurosurgeon communes once more with the X-ray films.

The heart beats a strong 70 beats a minute, 70 beats a minute, 70 beats a minute.

"We're gonna have a hard time today," the surgeon says, to the X-rays.

Dr. Ducker presses his face against the microscope. His hand goes out for an electrified, tweezer-like instrument. The assistant moves in close, taking his position above the secondary eyepieces.

Dr. Ducker's view is shared by a video camera. Across the room, a color television crackles, displaying a highly magnified landscape of the brain. The polished tips of the tweezers move into view.

It is Dr. Ducker's intention to place tiny, spring-loaded alligator clips across the base of each aneurism. But first he must navigate a tortured path from his incision, above Mrs. Kelly's right eye, to the deeply buried Circle of Willis.

The journey will be immense. Under magnification, the landscape of the minds expands to the size of a room. Dr. Ducker's tiny, blunt-tipped instrument travels in millimeter leaps.

His strategy is to push between the forebrain, where conscious thought occurs, and the thumb-like forward projection of the brain, called the temporal lobe, that extends beneath the temples.

Carefully, Dr. Ducker pulls these two structures apart to form a deep channel. The journey begins at the bottom of this crevasse.

The time is 9:36 a.m.

The gray convolutions of the brain, wet with secretions, sparkle beneath the powerful operating theater spotlights. The microscope landscape heaves and subsides in rhythm to the pop, pop, pop of the heart monitor.

Gently, gently, the blunt probe teases apart the tiny convolutions of gray matter, spreading a tiny tunnel, millimeter by gentle millimeter, into the glistening gray.

Dr. Ducker's progress is impeded by scar tissue. Each time Mrs.

Kelly's monster flooded her brain with blood, scars formed, welding the structures together. To make his tunnel, Dr. Ducker must tease them apart again.

As the neurosurgeon works, he refers to Mrs. Kelly's monster as "the AVM," or arterial-veinous malformation.

Normally, he says, arteries force high-pressure blood into muscle or organ tissue. After the living cells suck out the oxygen and nourishment, the blood drains into low-pressure veins, which carry it back to the heart and lungs.

But in the back of Mrs. Kelly's brain, one set of arteries pumps directly into veins, bypassing the tissue. Over the years the unnatural junction, not designed for such a rapid flow of blood, has swollen and leaked. Hence the scar tissue.

It is 10:58.

Dr. Ducker now begins following the Circle of Willis back into the brain, toward the second, and more difficult, aneurism that swells at the very rear of the circle, tight against the most sensitive and primitive structure in the head. The brainstem. The brainstem controls vital processes, including breathing and heartbeat.

The going becomes steadily more difficult and bloody. Millimeter, millimeter, treacherous millimeter the tweezers burrow a tunnel through Mrs. Kelly's mind. Blood flows, the tweezers buzz, the suction slurps. Push and probe. More blood. Then the tweezers lay quiet.

"I don't recognize anything," the surgeon says. He pushes further and finds a landmark.

Then, exhausted, Dr. Ducker disengages himself, backs away, sits down on a stool and stares straight ahead for a long moment. The brainstem is close, close.

"This is a frightening place to be," whispers the doctor.

In the background the heart monitor goes pop, pop, pop, pop, 70 beats a minute, steady. The smell of ozone and burnt flesh hangs thick in the air.

It is 11:05 a.m.

Tomorrow: The Monster

Surgeon Vs. the Monster

Jon Franklin
Baltimore *Evening Sun*
December 13, 1978

It is 11:05 a.m., the Day of the Monster.

Dr. Thomas Barbee Ducker peers into the neurosurgery microscope, navigating the tunnels of Mrs. Edna Kelly's mind.

A bank of electronic equipment stands above the still patient. Monitor lights flash, oscilloscope waveforms build and break, dials jump and a loudspeaker announces each heartbeat, pop, pop, pop, 70 pops a minute, steady.

The sound, though subdued, dominates the room.

Since 8:25 a.m., when an incision was opened in the patient's scalp above the right eye, University Hospital's chief neurosurgeon has managed to find and clip off one of two deadly aneurisms.

Now as he searches for the second aneurism he momentarily loses his way in the glistening gray tissue. For 57 years the monster has dwelled in Mrs. Kelly's skull, periodically releasing drops of blood and torrents of agony, and in the process it altered the landscape of the brain.

Dr. Ducker stops and ponders, makes a decision and pushes ahead, carefully, carefully, millimeter by treacherous millimeter.

The operating room door opens, and Dr. Michael Salcman, the assistant chief neurosurgeon, enters. He confers briefly with Dr. Ducker and then stands in front of the television monitor.

Thoughtfully, he watches the small tweezer instrument, made huge by the microscope, probe along a throbbing, cream-colored blood vessel.

An aneurism on an artery is like the bump on a tire that is about to blow out, Dr. Salcman says. The weakened wall of the artery balloons outward under the relentless pressure of the heartbeat and, eventually, it bursts. That's death.

He says the aneurisms appeared because of the monster, a large malformation of arteries and veins in the back of the brain. Eventually Dr. Ducker hopes to remove or block off that malformation, but today the objectives are limited to clipping the two aneurisms.

Then, those hair-trigger killers out of the picture, he can plan a frontal assault on the monster itself.

But that will be another day. This day the objectives are the aneurisms, one in front and one in back. The front one is finished. One down, one to go.

The second, however, is the toughest. It pulses dangerously deep, hard against the brain's most sensitive element, the brainstem. That ancient nub of circuitry, the reptilian brain, controls basic functions like breathing and heartbeat.

"I call it the 'pilot light,'" says Dr. Salcman, "because if it goes out...that's it."

Dr. Ducker has a different phrase. It is "a frightening place to be."

Now, as the tweezer probe opens new tunnels toward the second aneurism, the screen of the television monitor fills with blood.

Dr. Ducker responds quickly, snatching the broken end of the tiny artery with the tweezers. There is an electrical bzzzzzzt as he burns the bleeder closed. Progress stops while the red liquid is suctioned out.

"It's nothing to worry about," he says. "It's not much, but when you're looking at one square centimeter, two ounces is a damn lake."

The lake drained, Dr. Ducker presses on, following the artery toward the brainstem. Gently, gently, gently, gently he pushes aside the gray coils. For a moment the optic nerve appears in the background, then vanishes.

The going is even slower. Dr. Ducker is reaching all the way into the center of the brain and his instruments are the length of chopsticks. The danger mounts because, here, many of the vessels feed the pilot light.

The heartbeat goes pop, pop, pop, 70 beats a minute.

Dr. Ducker is lost again in the maze of scars that have obscured the landmarks and welded the structures together.

Dr. Salcman joins his boss at the microscope, peering through the assistant's eyepieces. They debate the options in low tones and technical terms. A decision is made and again the polished tweezers probe along the vessel.

The scar tissues that impede the surgeon's progress offer testimony to the many times over Mrs. Kelly's lifespan that the monster has leaked blood into the brain, a reminder of the constant migraines that have tortured her constantly since 1942, of the pain she'd now rather die than further endure.

Back on course, Dr. Ducker pushes his tunnel ever deeper, gentle, gentle, gentle as the touch of sterile cotton. Finally the gray matter parts.

The neurosurgeon stares intently at the veins, surprised, chagrined, betrayed by the X-rays.

The monster.

The monster, by microscopic standards, lies far away, above and back, in the rear of the head. Dr. Ducker was to face the monster itself on another day, not now. Not here.

But clearly these tangled veins, absent on the X-ray films but very real in Mrs. Kelly's brain, are tentacles of the monster.

Gingerly, the tweezers attempt to push around them.

Pop, pop, pop..pop...pop....pop.....pop...

"It's slowing," warns the anesthesiologist, alarmed.

The tweezers pull away like fingers touching fire.

....pop...pop..pop.pop, pop, pop.

"It's coming back," says the anesthesiologist.

The vessels control blood flow to the brainstem, the pilot light.

Dr. Ducker tries to go around them a different way.

Pop, pop, pop.pop...pop...

And withdraws.

Dr. Salcman stands before the television monitor, arms crossed, frowning. "She can't take much of that," the anesthesiologist says. "The heart will go into arrhythmia and that'll lead to a...call it a heart attack."

Dr. Ducker tries a still different route, probing clear of the area and returning at a different angle. Eventually, at the end of a long, throbbing tunnel of brain tissue, the sought-after aneurism appears.

Pop, pop, pop.pop..pop...pop...

The instruments retract.

"Damn," says the chief neurosurgeon. "I can only work here for a few minutes without the bottom falling out."

The clock says 12:29.

Already, the tissue swells visibly from the repeated attempts to burrow past the tentacles.

Again the tweezers move forward in a different approach and the aneurism reappears. Dr. Ducker tries to reach it by inserting the aneurism clip through a long narrow tunnel. But the pliers that hold the clip obscure the view.

Pop, pop, pop...pop....pop.....

The pliers retract.

"We're on it and we know where we are," complains the neurosurgeon, frustration adding a metalic edge to his voice. "But we're going to have an awful time getting a clip in there. We're so close, but..."

A resident who has been assisting Dr. Ducker collapses on a stool. He stares straight ahead, eyes unfocused, glazed.

"Michael, scrub," Dr. Ducker says to Dr. Salcman. "See what you can do. I'm too cramped."

While the circulating nurse massages Dr. Ducker's shoulder, Dr. Salcman attempts to reach the aneurism with the clip.

Pop, pop, pop.pop..pop...pop...

The clip withdraws.

"That should be the aneurism right there," says Dr. Ducker, taking the place at the microscope again. "Why the hell can't we get to it? We've tried, 10 times."

At 12:53, another approach.

Pop, pop, pop.pop..pop...pop...

Again.

It is 1:06.

And again, and again, and again.

Pop...pop...pop, pop, pop...pop

Pop-pop-pop...

The anesthesiolgist looks up sharply at the dials. A nurse catches her breath and holds it.

"Damn, damn, damn."

Dr. Ducker backs away from the microscope, his gloved hands held before him. For a full minute, he's silent.

"There's an old dictum in medicine," he finally says. "If you can't help, don't do any harm. Let nature take its course. We may have already hurt her. We've slowed down her heart. Too many times." The words carry defeat, exhaustion, anger.

Dr. Ducker stands again before the X-rays. His eyes focus on the rear aneurism, the second one, the one that thwarted him. He examines the film for signs, unseen before, of the monster's descending tentacles. He finds no such indications.

Pop, pop, pop, goes the monitor, steady now, 70 beats a minute.

"Mother nature," a resident surgeon growls, "is a mother."

The retreat begins. Under Dr. Salcman's command, the team prepares to wire the chunk of skull back into place and close the incision.

It ends quickly, without ceremony. Dr. Ducker's gloves snap sharply as a nurse pulls them off.

It is 1:30.

Dr. Ducker walks, alone, down the hall, brown paper bag in his hand. In the lounge he sits on the edge of a hard orange couch and unwraps the peanut butter sandwich. His eyes focus on the opposite wall.

Back in the operating room the anesthesiologist shines a light into each of Mrs. Kelly's eyes. The right pupil, the one under the incision, is dilated and does not respond to the probing beam. It is a grim omen.

If Mrs. Kelly recovers, says Dr. Ducker, he'll go ahead and try to deal with the monster itself. He'll try to block the arteries to it, maybe even take it out. That would be a tough operation, he says, without enthusiasm.

"And that's providing she's in good shape after this."

If she survives. If. If.

"I'm not afraid to die," Mrs. Kelly had said. "I'm scared to death...but...I can't bear the pain. I wouldn't want to live like this much longer."

Her brain was too scarred. The operation, tolerable in a younger person, was too much. Already, where the monster's tentacles hang before the brainstem, the tissue swells, pinching off the source of oxygen.

Mrs. Kelly is dying.

The clock in the lounge, near where Dr. Ducker sits, says 1:40.

"It's hard even to tell what to do. We've been thinking about it for six weeks. But, you know, there are certain things...that's just as far as you can go. I just don't know..."

He lays down the sandwich, the banana and the fig newtons on the table before him, neatly, the way the scrub nurse laid out instruments.

"It was triple jeopardy," he says, finally, staring at his peanut butter sandwich the same way he stared at the X-rays. "It was triple jeopardy."

It is 1:43 and it's over.

Dr. Ducker bites, grimly, into the sandwich.

The monster won.

Reprinted with permission of *The Baltimore Evening Sun.*

16.   *A Cover-up of America's Worst Nuclear Accident*

In news stories of major events, the strongest impressions sometimes are made by smaller, personalized episodes. During the days surrounding the accident at a nuclear plant on Three-Mile Island, which received extensive national coverage, one of the strongest images was drawn by the staff of the Philadelphia *Inquirer* in telling of a secret meeting of a handful of men. While attention from around the world was focused on the dangers created and the questions raised by the accident, two small groups of officers and public relations people for the company which owned the plant met in closed hotel rooms to plan a strategy for making the company look good. Told in narrative form, the *Inquirer's* story uses concrete detail and revealing dialogue to make the episode come alive for the reader. *(Pulitzer Prize for Local General Spot News Reporting, 1980)*

A Secret Utility Meeting about Public Relations
Philadelphia *Inquirer* Staff
April 8, 1979

While beer-drinking conventioneers caroused in the hallways of the Hershey Motor Lodge last Wednesday evening, officials of Metropolitan Edison packed themselves into two small rooms—603 and 605—and worked feverishly into the night.

They were not drawing up plans to bring the nuclear crisis to an end. Nor were they discussing how to tell the public exactly what had happened over the previous eight days. Rather, they were discussing ways to hide from the public and the press and somehow at the same time salvage the company's credibility.

The executives were clearly worried. They did not know how to handle the mounting pressures—not the least of which were hundreds of requests for information from reporters all over the world.

With relief, Metropolitan Edison had stopped answering most questions last weekend, at the NRC's request. Until that moment, listening to statements from the NRC and conflicting reports from Metropolitan Edison had been, for the press and the world, an exercise in confusion.

"We refer everything to the NRC," one top Metropolitan Edison official said in one of a series of private meetings at the Hershey hotel rooms. "That's good for now. But as soon as those national people (NRC officials) get on out of here, we're back in the bucket. We're in the bucket now."

At that meeting, Blaine Fabian, the power company's communications manager, led a discussion among eight people, including two consultants from the Chicago office of a public relations firm, Hill & Knowlton.

Though the meeting was private, the voices of the Metropolitan Edison officials were loud enough to be heard outside the room by *Inquirer* reporters.

Inside the room, the officials discussed several possible strategies to avoid talking directly to the press or public.

They considered distributing telephone numbers to the press as "Met Ed communications numbers," then keeping those phones off the hooks, or keeping the lines busy all the time.

They discussed continuing to refer all or some questions to the NRC.

And they talked about refusing to give interviews, offering instead a "press kit" that would address certain issues and avoid others.

All the officials expressed serious concern about press interviews with Metropolitan Edison's principal executives.

"Interviews are a massive problem," one company official said. "There's no doubt about it."

However, the officials stressed, they had to somehow present information to the public about the nuclear accident at Three Mile Island. "We got to do something," one official said. "We're starting to get editorials all over the country....And do you know what they're saying? They're all saying the same thing: You're not telling us the facts."

Fabian, the power company's top public relations official, said that scores of reporters had been calling him for information—and that he had not been answering their questions.

"As soon as I go—everywhere I go," Fabian said, "they are tracking me down. The trouble is, they have my name as the head honcho. I keep getting nailed by all the reporters and I have to get the hell out of there."

When an *Inquirer* reporter had approached Fabian earlier in the day in the Metropolitan Edison communications trailer directly across the river from Three Mile Island, Fabian had said he had no time to speak to reporters or to answer questions.

He said he was "too busy dealing with the nuclear problem. Our concern is with the public interest—that has to come first."

Minutes after making that comment, Fabian drove to the hotel in Hershey, where he began a series of sessions dealing with the utility's public relations problems. The session lasted until 2 a.m.

During the evening, Metropolitan Edison officials discussed the possibility of holding their own press conference. They said they might open the briefing by saying: "We're in here and you think we're the bad guys, and now we're going to tell you we're the good guys."

After that opening statement, they speculated, the spokesman might say that "nobody was seriously hurt" in the nuclear accident.

"But the problem with that," one official quickly pointed out, "is that the NRC said we won't know for 30 years."

(Low-level radiation of the sort that has escaped or has been released from the plant since the accident causes no immediate illness or injury. However, some scientists believe that it may cause latent cancer or other disorders that do not become apparent for decades.)

Another Metropolitan Edison official suggested that in response to that question an "expert could easily show scientifically that there is no danger."

Another official in the room then worried that "if we have a press conference, somebody's going to ask who was in the operating room (at the nuclear plant) at 4 a. m. Wednesday, March 28 (when the accident began)."

The proposed response to that question was: "We'll just say, 'You'll have to go to the NRC. They've got the logs.'"

The officials also discussed other possible ways of giving out information without having to face unlimited questions by reporters.

For example, one utility official suggested a prepared packet of printed information about Three Mile Island.

"It's a fallback in case somebody says, 'Hey, you guys aren't talking,'" the official said. "We have to have an alternative. It's really difficult to give out information about such a leak."

The officials agreed that they had to prepare their own version of the events of the past week.

"We need a chronology," Fabian said. "The *New York Times* has printed a chronology. The *Wall Street Journal* has one. *Time* has one. Now let's put out ours."

The utility executives debated how to go about preparing a chronology.

"How much do the employees know?" one official asked.

"They seem to know what they read in the papers," another said.

"What makes you think that because we put out a story, they (the employees) will believe it?" one official asked.

By 10:10 p. m., about four hours after the sessions began, as the hotel's conventioneers were getting drunker and more boisterous in the long, narrow, orange-carpeted hallway outside their rooms, the Metropolitan Edison officials called room service for delivery of a large gray plastic container filled with bottles of Molson's Ale and ice.

The waiter had no sooner delivered the beer to Fabian's bedroom

(Room 601) than he was summoned to bring another container to executives in Room 603.

When the waiter arrived at Room 603, he viewed a group of disheartened power company people slouched on a couch and chairs— motel-modern furniture that had been moved in to replace the two double beds that were normally in the room.

In the center of the room, on the same orange carpeting that the hallway had, sat a plastic-topped working table covered with the Sunday *Washington Post, Time* magazine and numerous Metropolitan Edison documents and reports, and a large tray of stale danish pastries remaining from earlier in the day.

Also on the table were the feared links with the outside world—two telephones, one the regular hotel extension (717-533-3311, Room 603) and the other a special line ordered by Metropolitan Edison (717-533-7432).

As the waiter walked out of the room, he said, "It's been a busy night."

The executives continued their intense discussion as they opened their beers.

"When it comes to the bubble bursting," one official said, "when it comes to the people who pay us, when it comes to cutting budgets— the guys out in Reading (Metropolitan Edison's company headquarters) will say, 'Hey, they're over in the Hershey Motor Lodge ordering six packs of beer.' We better get something done."

What they agreed to do, finally, was to prepare "fact sheets" about the company, about the effects of radiation, about the financial impact of the accident. They also decided to send letters to the governor and to the mayors of towns near Three Mile Island.

The fact sheets and the letters would go into the "press kits."

The officials said that the letter to the governor should convey their concern about the people of Pennsylvania.

One official proposed that the letter to Gov. Dick Thornburgh could begin "Dear Governor: Radiation is scaring the s--- out of the people. Dr. Miller, nationally recognized specialist, is here in Hershey and he can explain it."

Near the end of the meeting—which lasted well past midnight—the officials expressed concern about the utility company's image. They worried about how company president Walter Creitz appeared in news photographs.

"What can we do with Walter? Did you see that shot they had of him?" one official asked the others. "It was a full-face shot....The guy looks like a demon.''

17. *The Journey of an Illegal Alien*

John M. Crewdson begins his story of the journey of a Mexican alien with descriptive prose which immediately entices the reader into the story. Throughout the story, he paints for the reader perfect pictures of people, places, and happenings—leaving little to the imagination. He provides an abundance of details of facts and figures. The reader leaves with a thorough understanding of what happened to Don Bernabe Garay, an alien in search of a better life. *(Pulitzer Prize for National Reporting, 1981)*

The Illegal Odyssey of Don Bernabe Garay
John M. Crewdson
New York *Times*
December 14, 1980

WHY, Ariz.—It was the sweetest and gentlest of desert evenings, pitch-black except for a sliver of new moon and the light from a hundred thousand stars. Nearby, a coyote scampered among the stately organ pipe cactuses, its occasional mournful howl slicing the silence like a jagged knife.

Presently the stillness was broken by a softer sound, a brief, two-toned whistle. For half a minute there was nothing, then an identical whistle was heard from beyond the rise, followed by a flash of light and an answering flash, the signal that the way was clear. Within seconds, shadowy figures emerged from the desert. Smiling and talking softly, they gathered in a circle near the little-used highway.

After a moment, Bernabe Garay stepped forward. A dignified, cheerful man with a fondness for battered hats, "Don Berna" had led the others here: by bus, third class, from their cloud-high, stone-poor village in the Sierra Madre; by pickup truck, at danger rates, from the border town of Sononita to the gap in the barbed wire where, a few hours earlier, at nightfall, they had become illegal aliens; on foot, pressing hard, wary of rattlesnakes and border patrols, to a prearranged pickup point here in the Arizona desert. As it would prove, they had yet to face the greatest obstacles in their journey in search of work in the citrus groves around Phoenix.

Driven north by poverty

Like uncounted millions of their countrymen before them, like the millions who will follow their well-worn path, they were driven north by the astounding poverty of rural Mexico, where life reduces to the simplest of equations: work or starve. But there was no work for them in Mexico, and so they were here.

As it was, they were among the last men to leave the village for the United States. The only ones left there now, Don Berna said, "are those that are older than me." Despite his 55 years, Bernabe set the others a rapid pace. They covered the 20 miles from the border in four hours, but they are mountain men from the Mexican village of Ahuacatlan, and for them such a walk is a brisk stroll.

The first leg of their journey was remarkable only for its monotony. As in years past, the 60 men of Ahuacatlan traveled for two days and nights by third-class bus to the Mexican border town of Sonoita; a favored jumping-off place for those seeking to enter the United States illegally. They expected no problems, but this year the crossing proved more nettlesome than usual.

It was near here that 13 from El Salvador died last July, abandoned without water by some of their Mexican guides, unfamiliar with the unforgiving ways of the desert. The discovery of their dehydrated bodies caused some embarrassment to the immigration authorities in Mexico, who are now cracking down on illegal border crossers.

The men of Ahuacatlan are old hands at such crossings—Don Berna has been coming to the United States to work for nearly three decades—and they know enough to walk through the desert in the cool of evening. It was in finding someone to take them to the crossing point that they encountered the problem.

That Monday afternoon, Don Berna, two of his sons and four other men, wearing the straw cowboy hats favored by workers from Mexico, gathered under a bridge over a sluggish creek in Sonoita to plan their route. In a dusty gully littered with red and silver Tecate beer cans, the men huddled over maps, marking the spot 30 miles east of town to which Jose, a man with a truck, had promised to take them for $7 apiece.

Despite his age, Bernabe climbed the creek bank like a mountain goat, walked to a nearby pay telephone and placed a call to a number in Phoenix. The voice on the other end assured him that transportation would be waiting at the pickup point in the Papago Indian Reservation.

But when Bernabe returned, Jose the driver announced his reluctance to make the trip. Anyone caught driving workers in to the desert these days was sure to get in trouble. Jose said, although for $600 he might consider taking a risk. Another conference was held, but the answer was no. "The workers feel that it is too much money," said Bernabe.

As it grew dark, about half of the group, eager to reach Phoenix, decided to set off along the border on foot. But Bernabe and the others, sensing some kind of danger, elected to stay behind in Sonoita. Jose, ever accommodating, sold them tacos filled with beans and a Mexican sausage called chorizo that his wife had prepared for just such an eventuality. The men scouted the area for cardboard boxes to use for mattresses and carried them into the arroyo above the creek.

Agent on aliens' trail

It was not until later that Bernabe and his friends learned how lucky they were. A Border Patrol agent from the tiny station here at Why, riding his horse at dusk, found the tracks left by the splinter group as they came across the border. For six hours the Mexicans walked, the agent hard on their trail. Shortly after midnight, they reached the ranch of a Papago Indian named David, who they hoped could arrange rides to Phoenix for them. But they were met instead by other Border Patrol agents, including one in an airplane.

While their fellow villagers spent Monday night in the Gila Bend jail, Bernabe and the others slept soundly on the ground in Sonoita, and when they awoke the next morning they went again to visit Jose. They had decided, they told him, to pay his price.

Most of Tuesday, Bernabe and the others languished in Sonoita, telling stories and waiting for dark. At noon they bought some chicken from a restaurant for $4 a plateful, an exorbitant price. The chicken, Bernabe said, was "terrible." But the merchants in Mexican border towns like Sonoita know that those who come to cross the border are a long way from home, and take advantage of them accordingly.

At 4:30 P.M., Jose arrived with his truck, collected his money and drove the men to a desolate spot east of Sonoita where crossing the border is as easy as crossing the street. There is almost no border there at all, just a barbed-wire fence strung between red metal poles, its twisted strands filled with holes large enough for a man to climb through.

By 5:30, the group was walking north. There are only five Border Patrol agents assigned to this 3,300 square-mile stretch of desert, and mass arrests like the one at David's ranch are not an everyday occurence. The real danger is from the rattlesnakes that come out to bask in the cool of the desert night. Stepping on one means being bitten, and those who pass through this country tell of the skeletons they see along the way.

Sorry to leave home

The men were traveling very light. Bernabe carried with him only a gallon jug of water and a sack containing two spare shirts and two pairs of trousers.

"We walked very, very fast," Bernabe said later. "We pushed it very hard." They saw no sign of the Border Patrol and only three snakes, which they killed with sticks.

It was 9:30 when they reached the pickup point, a large sand dune just off Arizona 1, which leads directly to the border. The moon had set an hour earlier, but the sky was filled, as someone said, with "cinquente" stars, literally 50 but figuratively "countless." For men from a poor village like Ahuacatlan, 50 of anything—50 cows, 50 shirts, 50 acres of land—is an unimaginable number.

As he stood with the others waiting for a ride, Bernabe spoke about the village he would not see again until the citrus harvest ended next July, and about Pilar, his wife, and the five children he had left behind. He was very sorry not to be home, he said, "but this is the only way I can make money."

$100 for drive to Phoenix

Just then, bouncing across the desert in a rattletrap blue Pontiac, there came a welcome sight, a smiling, 18-year-old alien smuggler named Ricardo, wearing the black leather jacket that is the unofficial badge of his profession. Ricardo—at least that was the name he was using that night—is himself an illegal alien, "from Sinaloa," he said proudly, the Mexican state with a reputation for producing fast operators.

For $100 apiece, Ricardo was to drive the men to Phoenix, seven at a time, two trips that night and two the next. For two days' work, he stood to clear nearly $3,000, the kind of money that has made alien smuggling a booming business. At these prices, Ricardo could afford a much better car. But he developed a taste for junk heaps last year, after the Border Patrol began impounding vehicles used to transport illegal aliens.

His profits are high, but Ricardo also has a lot of idle time. He was here most of the previous night, for example, waiting for the men who had decided to stay in Sonoita. It was just as well. An undercover Customs agent, wearing an outlandish cowboy costume, had been cruising up and down the back roads, stopping and searching every car in sight.

But this Tuesday night, the agent was nowhere to be seen. Bernabe, his three sons and four others piled into Ricardo's car, and Ricardo sped off toward Phoenix, his taillights glowing red against the blackness of the rugged mountains.

Since its founding in the late 16th century, Ahuacatlan has endured 400 years of solitude without complaint. Hidden away in the blue-green Sierra Madre, it is reached by a narrow, twisting roller coaster of a road, high enough in some places that travelers can reach out and touch the clouds. So isolated, so inconsequential a place is it that residents of San Juan del Rio, 100 miles to the south, have never heard its name. But then, Ahuacatlan has known more departures than arrivals.

Seen from a distance, its pastel houses dripping color against the mountainside, it might be mistaken for Shangri-la. Up close, such a mistake is not possible. Few of the houses have electricity, none have plumbing and some are barely standing beneath their thatched roofs. A handful of ill-stocked shops face the plaza where women, their faces hidden behind bright shawls, slowly pass with baskets tottering on their heads. What is there to hurry for in Ahuacatlan?

Like hundreds of villages across central Mexico, Ahuacatlan these days is only half a place, a village without fathers or husbands. A thousand people—the women and children, the old and the idle—live there now and perhaps another thousand, all men, are in the United States.

"I call my parish a widow's parish," Padre Tomas Cano, the earnest, handsome young village priest, said with a sigh as he sat in the rectory of his crumbling church. "Most of the wives are alone here with their children. This is a very big problem for them, the family disintegration."

"The men don't want to work in the fields here. The harvest, it is very bad, and people are so poor that they need money quickly, in order to eat."

And so, each autumn, the men go north, and each summer they return, bringing dresses and gifts and always, money from America. So closely is Ahuacatlan bound to the American economy that the preferred medium of exchange here is not the peso but the dollar.

Summers are a happy time in Ahutacatlan. "But when the money is finished," Father Tomas went on, "the men say, 'Let's go again,' and then the women are not so happy. They come to me and say, 'I have no money, no food, my husband is not here, I don't know what to do.'" Shopkeepers extend credit, and money may be sent home from the United States, but the mails are not reliable and eventually the credit runs out. The winters in Ahuacatlan are long and cold.

When the men come home, they speak of their time in America as a great adventure. But the priest, who hears their confessions, knows the truth. "Up there," he said, "the problems are very terrible for them." But except for the men without families to feed, America is the only choice.

Ahuacatlan means "land of avocados," and its residents agree that avocado trees must have covered these lush hillsides once. But the avocados grow here no longer, and neither does much else. Like Bernabe Garay, many of the men of Ahuacatlan own a few acres of steep mountain land and in the summertime they try to grow some corn and beans. "A lot of work for no money," is what Bernabe says.

Each summer, fewer men return to Ahuacatlan than left the year before, and it is always to Father Tomas that their wives bring the official telegrams for translation. "They go and we know nothing about them. Their wives go to the authorities, nothing. Some of these women, they want to marry again, but they cannot." There is no divorce in Ahuacatlan.

Bass drum, church bells

The village is a patriarchy without patriarchs, and it has not learned to cope with the stresses that brings. The children are growing up without fathers, and each year they seem more restless. "Now they want to go to dances," said Father Tomas, arching his eyebrows as if to ask, "What next?" There are no fathers to tell them no. Ahuacatlan has a school but the children do not want to study hard. "They dream only to go to the United States," Father Tomas said, "to have a good adventure and money."

Nearly everyone over 25 in Ahuacatlan is illiterate, and most residents of all ages are in poor health. "When the kids are born they are not very healthy in their minds," the priest said, "retarded. Their health is very poor." Malnutrition is one reason, but some from

Ahuacatlan have learned that they have been exposed, in the lemon groves of Arizona, to a toxic and now illegal pesticide known as DBCP that can affect human reproduction.

Despite the stunning natural beauty, a visitor to Ahucatlan cannot help wondering why the people cling to its misery. The answer seems to be that the village is all they know. "They think they are safe here, morally speaking."

As twilight came to the village, a man appeared in the plaza with a bass drum and beat it loudly to announce that the cantina was open. Muttering, Father Tomas pulled on his white cassock and hurried off to the answer with a peal of church bells for evening mass. "My people drink too much beer," he said.

The cock crows early in Ahuacatlan, and though it was not yet dawn Pilar Garay had been up for some time, laying a wood fire beneath the grate in her sparse kitchen. Its fragrant pine smoke mingled with that of a hundred other fires as, across the village, water began to boil for porridge and coffee. The Garays' adobe house, which Bernabe built himself a quarter century ago, has electricity. But water for cooking and washing is still hauled up from the river, as it has been for hundreds of years.

Promptly at 8 o'clock Primitivo Perez, an elderly neighbor, dropped by for his morning ration of Pilar's coffee. Lest anyone think him lazy, Mr. Perez explained that he was retired; like nearly all the old men, most of his working life was spent in the United States.

In another corner of the kitchen, near an ancient, pedal-driven sewing machine, sat 15-year-old Rafael Garay. Rafael had finished the sixth grade, all that the village school has to offer, and now he was biding his time, waiting to join his father and older brothers in the Arizona citrus groves. He was ready to go now, he said, and his eagerness made Pilar smile. Perhaps, she replied, next year.

Rafael is the same age as the two sons of Onorio Garcia, who owns what passes for a hardware store in the plaza. Mr. Garcia's sons also dream of going to America, but as students. They are attending an expensive private academy in San Luis Potosi, several miles away. One hopes to be a doctor, the other an architect, and Mr. Garcia, who has a battered yellow truck and a wristwatch, is one of the few in Ahuacatlan who has the money to help his sons realize their dreams. Despite his education, Rafael Garay, for example, knows that the only way he will get to America is as a farmhand.

With a husband and three sons working in America, Pilar said, she hoped she would be able to make ends meet. In the old days, Bernabe alone might manage to save only $50 in an entire harvest. With the beginnings of unionization in the Arizona citrus industry, wages have improved, and last season he sent home $1,200. This year, with Reginaldo, 28, Kiko, 23, and 18-year-old Bernabe Jr. working too, they may save as much as $6,000, but nearly a quarter of that must be set aside for next year's journey.

Is she sad that her husband and sons will not be home for Christmas? "Si," Pilar said, "muy triste." But Bernabe has not been home for the last 29 Christmases, except for 1976, when he fell off a ladder in the grove, broke three ribs and came to Ahuacatlan to recuperate.

It was just north of Ajo, Ariz., that Ricardo the smuggler ran out of gas. As his car rolled to a stop, Bernabe and the other passengers burst out and scrambled up the hill to hide in the brush at the side of the highway. The men watched a policeman arrive, they watched as he spoke over his radio, and they watched the Border Patrol cruiser drive up and take Ricardo away. All night they stayed in the bushes, and they were very quiet.

At dawn Kiko Garay made his way carefully down from the hillside and found a telephone. One call to the efficient underground smuggling network, and another ride was on the way.

Ricardo was permitted, as are most illegal aliens, to return to Mexico "voluntarily," a practice that saves the Immigration and Naturalization Service much time and money. Had he been caught with Bernabe and the others, he almost certainly would have spent a minimum of six months in jail for alien smuggling. But this arrest was a minor inconvenience. The next day Ricardo was back in Phoenix and back in business.

When Bernabe and the others reached Phoenix on Wednesday they went to the ranch where they worked last year. The lemons were not yet ready for picking, so they spent that day, and the next, setting up housekeeping, renewing old friendships and playing cards.

It was not until Thursday night, as the desert air began to chill, that Bernabe remembered the blankets that he left the summer before with his friend, Manuel Diaz. He resolved to get them in the morning.

In past years, the Border Patrol raided the citrus ranches every so often, picking up the workers and sending them back to Mexico. But this year, because of manpower shortages and new regulations, such raids have been very few. Once they reach the ranches the workers are vitually safe from arrest. It is when they venture out that they court danger.

And so it was early that Friday morning, when Bernabe and Kiko went round to Manuel Diaz's to retrieve the blankets. He was not at home, and as they walked away from his house a lime-green Border

Patrol van screeched to a halt in front of them. It was at that point that Don Bernabe Garay, father of nine, a man of respect and influence in Ahuacatlan, secretary general of the struggling Arizona Farm-workers Union, became a statistic.

The next hours were unpleasant ones. Bernabe and Kiko were taken first by the Border Patrol to the station in Phoenix, then to a holding cell in Tucson. At 9 that night they were driven to Nogales, Mexico, and let go.

A week after leaving Ahuacatlan, Bernabe was back in Mexico. On Sunday morning, he and Kiko took the bus to Sonoita and set out again in search of Jose the driver. They finally found him and struck another deal, for $30 apiece, and on Sunday the two men retraced their steps along the border, through the desert and back to Phoenix. Nine days after leaving home, $300 poorer and without having earned a penny to send to Pilar, Bernabe returned to the ranch.

At 8 o'clock Monday morning, Bernabe finally went to work. He worked furiously all day, hauling his heavy canvas bag up and down the stepladders propped against the tall lemon trees. By 5:30, he had filled his bag 82 times and picked 3,690 pounds of lemons, an impressive total for a man half his age. He was paid $41, slightly over a penny a pound but far more money than he could have earned in Mexico in a week if he could have found a job there. Bernabe Garay was a happy man at last.

18.   *What Makes High Tech Fly*

The Boeing Company is extremely important to Seattle's ecomomy. In 1983, the Seattle *Times* assigned reporter Peter Rinearson to tell the "story of 30,000 people making 130,000 pounds of high technology fly." His end product was a seven-part series made up of more than a dozen stories. The following piece, a look at the delivery of the Boeing 757, reads with the suspense of a well-written short story. Rinearson carefully sets the scene at the beginning and concludes by tracing the plane's development through the people who worked on it. His use of a random, one-day time frame in this portion of the story is especially effective. The story also offers an impressive example of how to explain complicated and specialized concepts such as safe-harbor leasing in terms the average reader can understand. The end result is a product of very thorough reporting combined with masterful writing. *(Pulitzer Prize for Feature Writing, 1984)*

Making It Fly: The Delivery
Peter Rinearson
Seattle *Times*
June 19, 1983

It hardly looked like an airplane about to enter commercial service.

Some passenger seats were missing. A rack jammed with electronic equipment was strapped to the floor in the first class section. Technicians and engineers swarmed over the airplane, inside and out.

Seats were pushed forward on their tracks, with carpets rolled back and mechanics climbing in and out of floor recesses. Six technicians were crammed into a cockpit meant for two pilots.

A team of mechanics worked on a recurring problem with the right-wing forward flaps. A heavy-set man looked up at the tail, eyeing the airplane's rudder alignment. A pair of workers used an array of photo-electric cells to aim the airplane's landing lights.

It was Friday, Dec. 17, 1982, and Boeing was late delivering its first 757 to Eastern Airlines. Not contractually late, because the manufacturer had given itself a cushion of extratime. Such buffers, both in projected dates of completion and projected airplane performance, let Boeing almost always point to "better than anticipated" results.

Nevertheless, it already was two weeks past the date Eastern had been told it would receive the first of its silver-and-blue 757 twinjets.

The airline, which had launched the 757 project, was getting impatient. It had anounced plans to begin 757 service Jan. 1 and had purchased television advertising to herald the new jetliner during the Rose Bowl and other New Year's Day football games. Even more important, millions of dollars in safe-harbor-leasing tax benefits were riding on getting delivery before the end of 1982.

On that overcast day a week before Christmas, while technicians scurried and chiefs paced impatiently, Boeing had yet even to acquire Federal Aviation Administration certification which would allow the 757 to be operated commercially.

An engine-icing problem on a test flight a month earlier had sidetracked certification. The engine had been modified, but was yet to be proved in icing conditions.

Deadlines and timetables were being revised continuously. The target had been certification by Nov. 23, but the days and numbers kept changing. Hundreds of Boeing employees were destined to keep working on the program during the traditional long Boeing holiday recess. There was even talk of working Christmas Day.

Things were, in short, a mess.

"Every time you set a number, it slips. I don't even want to set another one," lamented Bill Robison, director of manufacturing on the 757 project.

Robison was standing with Paul Johnstone, then senior vice president of operations for Eastern, since retired. Johnstone is an amiable man, but he was growing perturbed by the delays in delivery of the jetliner.

Johnstone was head of a delegation that had come to Seattle from Eastern's Miami headquarters to look over the new Boeing jet before accepting it. Every Boeing airplane is subjected to such inspections when it is delivered to an airline. Just as a careful car buyer scrutinizes a new automobile carefully before driving it off the lot, an airline examines a $30 million airplane before flying it home.

Eastern's inspection of the 757 program really had begun in 1979, when the airline sent an ex-Boeing engineer, Ben Gay, back to Seattle to be Eastern's on-site representative. Gay had an impossible job, keeping track of an enormous program, but he was assisted by Boeing employees whose sole job is to help represent the interest of airlines.

Gay's mission was to make sure the airplane would meet Eastern's needs—that every light bulb could be replaced easily, that the cockpit would please Eastern's pilots, that the carpets were the right colors.

"You can't see it all," Gay said. "I can go out quite a bit, but I can't cover all of it. Too much for one man."

But one man is enough when Boeing's high level of quality control is considered, Gay said. "If we had doubts about Boeing's ability to build a decent airplane, not only design-wise but quality and work-manship-wise, we'd have people up here. But they've proven to us in the past that they can build a good airplane with good workmanship, and if it isn't right they fix it."

Gay's activities were reaching a high pitch in the closing days of December as the first 757s were being readied.

The particular airplane under inspection on Dec. 17 was No. NA007, the newest of the new 757s. It had flown for the first time only two days earlier.

On that shakedown flight, 39 problems had been detected—not big problems, but typical little first-flight problems: an annoying sound of hissing air around a seat in row 20, an electrical-access panel that fell off the first time the airplane ever landed.

Now Johnstone, Gay and other Eastern personnel waited for a planned 1 p.m. demonstration flight of the airplane which in just two weeks was supposed to carry the first paying Eastern Airlines 757 customers.

Hours ticked by. Mid-day came and went and still the airplane sat outside Plant 2 at Boeing Field. Technical problems kept cropping up. Even the modest 1 p.m. timetable could not be met.

Johnstone recognized the possibility Eastern might not get its first two 757s certified and in service by the end of the month. Every minute seemed precious. "We're down to moving hours out of the schedule, not days or weeks," he said.

Many of Johnstone's thoughts that Friday afternoon were 900 miles south at Edwards Air Force Base near Los Angeles, where another 757 was facing obstacles of a more substantial nature.

It was Boeing 757 No. 3, a flight-test airplane flown by pilot Kenny Higgins. The pilot and his crew were almost desperately trying to build up ice on the airplane's engins to prove that the icing problem had been remedied.

On a routine flight test Nov. 16, both Rolls Royce engines on 757 No. 3 had been damaged when ice built up on their spinner cones, hubs for the forward set of fan blades. The ice had broken off in chunks large enough to bend blades and cause dangerous engine vibration.

After a sometimes-heated debate with Boeing over the cause of the problem, Rolls responded by installing heated spinner cones to prevent ice build-up, and it was presumed the problem was solved. But presumption alone would not win an FAA airworthiness certificate. The "fix" had to be proven.

Boeing and Rolls worked out a strategy in which they would take FAA personnel on a flight through the same sort of supercooled weather conditions that caused the engine damage on Nov. 16. The jetliner would use one engine with a heated spinner and one without—

as a control—for the test. The idea was to damage the unmodified engine as before, while demonstrating the safety of the engine with the heated spinner.

But proof was elusive. Day after day, 757 No. 3 flew across the western United States seeking appropriate weather conditions, and day after day it had no luck.

"We had a week of totally dry weather in this half of the whole United States," said John Hodson, a Rolls Royce vice president.

Finally, Boeing asked the Air Force to help it make ice. At Edwards, a KC-135 tanker was loaded with water. The tanker, a deriviative of the Boeing 707, normally is used to refuel another airplane in flight with an arm-like boom. This time, however, the tanker dispensed water into the freezing air.

The 757 flew about 70 feet behind and the water had turned to ice by the time it hit the airplane and its engines. It was a last-ditch attempt to create icing conditions, prove the engine modification, win certification and get the first two airplanes to Eastern by the end of the year.

Johnstone knew the test was under way as he paced around the 757 on Boeing Field, but he didn't know how it as going to turn out.

He would have been relieved to know that, in fact, over the next few days the test would succeed, certification would be granted, and Eastern would receive its first two 757s before the end of the year.

December's ill winds weren't the first turbulence the 757 program weathered during its five-year flight.

By 1981 the health of the airline industry was fading, and Boeing faced the prospect of canceled orders for the new airliner. Some airlines, such as American, eventually withdrew plans to buy the new and expensive 757. They couldn't afford it.

Eastern President Frank Borman went before Congress in 1981 and 1982 to plead for tax breaks so that his company's "launch" order for the 757 could proceed.

"The performance of the (airline) industry in 1980 and 1981 jeopardized not only Eastern's participation in that (757) program, but the entire Boeing program," Borman told the Senate Finance Committee on March 18, 1982.

Borman told the senators he had been to Seattle in July 1981 attempting to cancel or delay a third of Eastern's order for 757s. Then Congress passed safe-harbor leasing, which improved the situation.

"We went back and did our numbers and found that with the provisions of safe-harbor leasing we could indeed continue the $909 million capital (757) order," Borman testified. "And we went to Boeing and said, 'With the new tax law, it's go,' and Boeing is in fact producing our airplanes. And they are coming down the assembly line, ready or not.''

Safe-harbor leasing was an ingenious, controversial mechanism which allowed unprofitable companies to sell unusable tax breaks to profitable companies. Fortune magazine called it ''an obscure form of tax-avoidance boogie-woogie.'' Here's how it worked:

With or without safe-harbor leasing, a company acquiring capital assets (in this case, airplanes) is entitled to tax breaks such as depreciation. But tax breaks are little good to an unprofitable company which pays no tax anyway. In fact, they can even hurt a money-losing airline.

That's because a profitable airline might get a $10 million tax break on a $30 million Boeing jetliner, making its true cost $20 million, while an unprofitable airline would have to pay the full $30 million for the same airplane.

Under safe-harbor leasing, an unprofitable company could sell its tax breaks to a profitable company for cash. In the hypothetical case of the $30 million jetliner, ABC Airline could sell its $10 million tax break to XYZ Oil Co. for, say, $8 million.

The $8 million in cash for ABC Airline would reduce the true out-of-pocket expense for a $30 million jetliner to $22 million. XYZ Oil, meanwhile, would get a $10 million tax reduction for the $8 million it paid—a quick $2 million profit.

Technically, ABC would temporarily sell the jetliner to XYZ, then lease it back. It is a complicated shuffle of paperwork in which nothing really is exchanged except tax breaks and cash. Both the profitable and unprofitable company are sheltered from taxes in a ''safe harbor.''

No one loses—except the federal treasury, which, in this hypothetical example, would be out the $8 million.

Safe-harbor leasing was pushed through Congress in 1981 by Borman and others, who argued that unprofitable companies like Eastern were suffering and could not afford to buy needed equipment, such as 757s.

By early 1982, however, it was clear that Uncle Sam was being taken to the cleaners.

Alan Greenspan, a conservative economist, labeled safe-harbor leasing ''food stamps for American businss.'' Profitable companies were gobbling up available tax credits from unprofitable companies, and some big profitable companies—including General Electric—used the loophole to pay no taxes at all for 1981.

In February 1982 the mood in Congress was turning against safe-harbor leasing. Senate Finance Committee Chairman Robert Dole called for repeal of the tax loophole.

Borman and leaders of other unprofitable companies returned to Congress. Borman's argument was compelling: Eastern had proceeded with the 757 order only on the promise of safe-harbor leasing, and revoking that promise would be unjust and disastrous.

Congress chose a middle course, eliminating much of safe-harbor leasing but allowing a timed phase-out for several key and depressed industries, including airlines.

The 757 seemed safe again, although as Eastern's financial picture continued to deteriorate there were other doubts whether it would be able to complete the purchase of 757s.

By Dec. 17, when Johnstone was examining the first of the new jetliners, financial packages involving safe-harbor leasing had been assembled. Once the jetliner was ready, Eastern would have money available for transfer to Boeing, Johnstone said.

The actual purchase of a completed Boeing jetliner is conducted in a variety of ways.

Typically about a third of the price has been prepaid to Boeing during the course of manufacture. But increasingly, as airlines have fallen on hard times (or developed shrewdness in such dealings), Boeing itself has provided financing for part of the purchase price and the whole deal has grown more complicated.

In the case of the sale to Eastern, final funds were to be transferred by wire, with telephone conference calls between several cities confirming the movement of funds from one New York bank account to another. The moment the money changed accounts, the airplane changed hands.

For competitive reasons, Boeing and the airlines tend to obscure the details of such financial transactions. But Eastern's 1982 annual report provides some details.

For instance, the report reveals that the British government provided roughly $10 million financing per 757 "at an attractive interest rate" because of the purchase by the airline of Rolls Royce engines. More to the point, the report said Eastern made $12.8 million on the sale of the tax benefits associated with the first two 757s.

The report says Eastern will raise another estimated $130 million through the sale of the tax benefits associated with 13 additional 757s and four Airbus A-300s due for delivery this year.

"We would have had to cancel the (757) program had we not had safe-harbor leasing," Borman said in an interview last month. "There's no question. It's fact."

Eastern Airlines is looking to the 757 as part of the solution to its financial woes. The 757 is the world's most efficient jetliner, on a per-seat basis, and the airline hopes that its position as the only U.S. operator of the airplane for two years will give it some competitive advantage on costs.

"Frank Borman sees it as a vehicle to thwack his competition with," said Alan Smith, a Rolls Royce official.

Boeing has faced lean years recently, too, and also is looking to the 757 to help restore the strong profitability of the past. Announced total orders for the 757 actually have fallen rather than risen during the past two years, but Boeing claims the airplane will be the world's all-time best-seller.

This is a point of speculation and dispute. While Boeing contends the 757 is about the right size to capture a large share of future sales, other aviation-industry forces—notably Europe's Airbus Industrie—believed the still-to-be-built 150-seat airplane will be far more attractive than the 185-seat 757.

The Airbus view, shared by many others, is that the 757 is a technological success but is likely to be a financial failure—the same bittersweet combination that characterized the European Concorde SST.

"The 757 would sell beautifully if it had 150 seats," said Reinhardt Abraham, chief technical executive of Lufthansa German Airlines. "My personal opinion always was that the 757 was too close to the 767 and A-310, and it is meeting its own (Boeing) competition. Only huge airlines will be able to fly both the 757 and 767."

But M.J. Lapensky, president of Northwest Airlines, offered a sharply contrasting view. "I don't know what's magic about 150 seats," he said, adding that the 757 is sized perfectly at 185 seats to fill the gap in capacity between the 140-seat 727s and 290-seat DC-10s.

However, Lapensky added that Northwest won't order any 757s until it becomes apparent which of three available engines (two made by Rolls Royce, one by Pratt & Whitney) offers the best economy.

Wolfgang Demisch, an aerospace analyst for the Wall Street firm of First Boston, takes a middle view.

Demisch suggests that the 757 will be a money-losing burden for Boeing in the short run because the company will sell relatively few in each of the first few years of production.

But he believes that the long run will show Boeing has sized the airplane correctly—that the 185-seat airplane will prove more valuable than the 150-seat airplane, because of the shortage of air-traffic controllers and growing congestion in air space will force airlines to fly fewer flights with larger-capacity airplanes.

And although it is costing Boeing a bundle to build an airplane which isn't yet selling well, it could have cost Boeing much more not to build the 757, Demisch contends.

Airbus elected to build its second jetliner, the A-310, at the same 210-passenger size as the 767—a size where there is a known strong market and where appropriate new-technology engines already were under development.

In Demisch's view, Airbus probably would have sized its airplane smaller, at about 160 seats, if the 757 hadn't already been under development to fill that need.

"I think in essence that the 757 has...rattled Airbus sufficiently by its presence that they didn't launch a competitive entry," Demisch said.

"There was a time when Airbus was feeling pretty bouyant a couple of years back, and if there hadn't been a 757 at that point there would have been a large, gaping hold between 140 seats for the 727 and 210 seats for the 767," he said. The temptation to build an airplane in the middle "would, I think, have been irresistible.

"As it is, that opportunity was preempted, and as it stands now I think Airbus is probably regretting that they didn't go ahead and do it anyhow," Demisch said. "Basically, I think it means Boeing is going to be gaining market share, courtesy of the 757, which protected them at the short-to-medium-haul length."

Successful jetliner models seem to stay in production about 20 years. When a jetliner is retired it generally is because its technology is outmoded, not because it is physically worn out.

By incorporating state-of-the-art technology in the 757, Boeing attempted to create an airplane that would be flying well into next century. In fact, the 757 and 767 share a cockpit design which Boeing calls, ambitiously, the "Century 21 flight deck."

The cockpit can be updated readily by replacing computer software (programs), eliminating the need for challenging or impossible hardware changes. This simplicity and flexibility should add to the longevity of the 757.

But a Boeing airplane design is not static. As long as the 757 is in production it likely will be refined. Derivative versions of the airplane are under study, so one day soon men and women may be creating 757 freighters, or stretched or shortened passenger models.

In Renton and around the world, people continue laboring to make the 757—and make it a success.

The range of human endeavor on any given day is impressive.

On Wednesday, April 20, 1983, a day picked·at random, Barry Buckworth was running a 90-foot-long milling machine at the Hawker de Havilland plant in Bankstown, Australia.

The machine, first of its kind in Australia, was automatically shaping three 757 wing-shear ribs simultaneously. The ribs were destined for the 40th Boeing 757, and Buckworth's job was to monitor a video screen and blow away metal shavings with an air hose.

That same day, in Burbank, Calif., Ken Tuttle was running a similar milling machine, although he was sweeping away the metal shavings rather than blowing them off. Tuttle is an employee at Menasco, another Boeing subcontractor, and his milling machine was simultaneously shaping the outer housings of the left-hand main landing gears of six 757s.

In Derby, England, 20-year-old Martin Spooner squirted lubricating oil onto carbon-hardened steel he was milling for Rolls Royce. Working in oil-laden air, Spooner was creating tooling for the manufacturer of the 757 engines.

In Minneapolis, Richard Butler, a group leader at a Honeywell factory, was looking after a high-technology machine which used ultrasound energy to drill and mill dense glass. The glass would become the heart of a laser-gyro inertial navigation system used on the 757.

At the Boeing plant in Wichita, Kan., Sharon Baily drilled holes and mounted parts of ribs in the nose section of 757 No. 33, while Jessie Biship, Jr. cut out wheel-door panels of graphite, using a concentrated spray of water at 50,000 pounds of cutting pressure per square inch.

At Boeing's Vertol Division in Philadelphia, which mostly makes helicopters, Larry Troutman supervised assembly of the fixed leading-edge structure of the right wing for 757 No. 37. The structure is a 2,100-pound device, 64 feet long and containing 700 parts.

On that day, Art Flock of Delta Airlines was in Everett pondering how his airline wanted its 60 757s painted. And near Boeing Field in Seattle, Rob Wood, chief pilot of Britain's Monarch Airlines, was giving a test to two of his pilots in a 757 full-flight simulator.

At Renton Municipal Airport, Eastern's Ben Gay told Boeing to send 757 No. 6, destined for his airline, back into the point hangar for more polishing.

"My main effort since those early deliveries has been to look for early in-service problems," Gay said. "There's a lot of little things. But overall, you'd give the airplane an excellent grade."

Nearby, top officials of Rolls Royce and Pratt and Whitney laid out for Boeing executives the first glimpse of the "I-2500," a collaborative engine proposed to power a 150-seat airplane Boeing and other manufacturers are considering building.

On that day, April 20, Tom White finished two sketches of a proposed control box that airline personnel could use to load the 757's cargo hold automatically. Late in the day, he and his coworkers began a new project, a theoretical redesign of airplane passenger cabins in which convention is tossed aside and new ideas are given free rein.

In the Renton plant, Ken Baesler climbed from the inside of a 757 wing which he had been checking for leaks with a mixture of pressurized air and ammonia. In another building Paul Duxbury was helping assemble the wings, driving titanium fasteners with a rivet gun.

In the final-assembly hangar at Renton, Bill English installed a wing part, tightening a ¾-inch nut to 100 foot-pounds of pressure. A Boeing inspector, J.J. Johnson, witnessed the operation and then stamped a seal on the nut to signal his approval. The pressure on the nut cannot be altered without breaking his personalized seal.

On the underside of the same 757, Dennis Kitchen spent an hour installing a nose landing gear, pushing the 3,000-pound installation dolly away like Superman when he was finished (the dolly was riding on a cushion of air).

And inside yet another 757 that day, Tanjer Gillard filled a Dixie cup with shiny white acrylic enamel and began to paint the heads of screws in a doorjamb. A finishing touch.

All these men and women, and thousands more, were contributing to the 757 program, an industrial venture of massive proportions— whether measured by the yardstick of economics, technology, politics, utility, or even romance.

All these men and women, and tens of thousands more, were helping to make it fly.

Reprinted by permission of the Seattle *Times*.

19.   "*I Lay Dying*"

In the following story, Nan Robertson provides a precisely detailed narrative of her near-fatal bout with toxic shock syndrome. The autobiography is told in clear, straightforward terms, enabling the reader to experience the pain, fear, and difficulty the author faced. While including much medical explanation of toxic shock, the article's strength comes primarily from the narrative form and from the small stories and anecdotes that make up the overall story. *(Pulitzer Prize for Feature Writing, 1983)*

Toxic Shock

Nan Robertson
The New York Times Magazine
September 19, 1982

I went dancing the night before in a black velvet Paris gown on one of those evenings that was the glamour of New York epitomized. I was blissfully asleep at 3 a.m.

Twenty-four hours later, I lay dying, my fingers and legs darkening with gangrene. I was in shock, had no pulse and my blood pressure was lethally low. The doctors in the Rockford, Ill., emergency room where I had been taken did not know what was wrong with me. They thought at first that I might have consumed some poison that had formed in my food. My sister and brother-in-law, whom I had been visiting, could see them through the open emergency-room door: "They were scurrying around and telephoning, calling for help, because they knew they had something they couldn't handle, that they weren't familiar with," was the instinctive reaction of my brother-in-law, Warren Paetz.

I was awake and aware, although confused and disoriented. The pain in my muscles was excruciating. I could hear the people bent over me, blinding lights behind them, asking me how old I was, when I had stopped menstruating, and, over and over, what I had eaten for Thanksgiving dinner the previous afternoon, Thursday, Nov. 26, 1981, and what I had had the day before.

The identical, delicious restaurant meal my mother, Eve, and I had consumed on Thursday centered on roast turkey with the classic Middle Western bread stuffing seasoned with sage that I had loved since childhood. I had eaten slowly, prudently, because I had had only three hours' sleep the night before, catching an early plane to Chicago to connect with a bus to Rockford, a city of 140,000 in north-central Illinois where all my family lives. Immediately after finishing my

Thanksgiving dinner, I threw it up. It was 4 p.m. at the Clock Tower Inn in Rockford. I thought excitement and fatigue had made me ill. Neither I nor my mother, a gutsy, 90-year-old, was overly concerned.

That was how it began: almost discreetly. I felt drained; my legs were slightly numb. The manager, apologizing all the way, drove us back to my sister's house in the hotel van. I was put to bed in the downstairs den.

I awoke, trancelike, in the middle of the night to find myself crawling and crashing up the stairs to the bathroom. The vomiting and diarrhea were cataclysmic. My only thought was to get to the bathtub to clean myself. I sat transfixed in my filthy nightgown in the empty tub, too weak to turn on the water. Warren and my sister, Jane, awakened by the noise of my passage, carried me back downstairs, with exclamations of horror and disgust at the mess I had created. Warren, an engineer who is strong on detail, remembers it as five minutes before 3 a.m.

As I lay in the darkened den, I could hear their voices, wrangling. Jane said it must be the 24-hour flu: "Let's wait until morning and see how she is." Warren said: "No, I can't find a pulse. It's serious. I'm calling an ambulance. Nan, do you want to go to the hospital now?" "Yes," I said. His choice, of course, was Rockford Memorial—the status Protestant hospital in Rockford where my family's doctor practiced.

The ambulance came within a few minutes in the wake of a sheriff's car and a fire truck. People in uniforms spoke gently, gave me oxygen. Lying in the ambulance, I could feel it surging forward, then beginning to turn right, toward Rockford Memorial, 15 minutes across town. I heard an emergency technician, 18-year-old Anita Powell, cry out: "Left! Left! Go to St. Anthony! She has no pulse! Rockford Memorial is 15 minutes away—she'll be D.O.A. (dead on arrival) if we go there! St. Anthony is three minues from here—she'll have a chance."

"Do what she says," my sister told the driver. We turned left to St. Anthony Hospital, and my life may have been saved for the second time that night, following Warren's decision to call the ambulance.

In the early hours of Friday, Nov. 27, the baffled young medical staff on holiday emergency-room duty telephoned several physicians. One of them was Dr. Thomas E. Root, an infectious-diseases consultant for the Rockford community. He arrived at 7:30 a.m.

Dr. Root was informed about the vomiting, diarrhea, the plummeting blood pressure. By then, a faint rash was also beginning to stipple my body. I did not develop the last of the disease's five classic acute symptoms—a fever of more than 102 degrees—until later. But

Dr. Root is a brilliant diagnostician. And, incredibly, he and his colleagues had treated two similar cases within the previous year. "I think she has toxic shock syndrome," Dr. Root said to his colleagues. "Let's get going."

Most doctors have never seen, or have failed to recognize, a single case of this rare malady. Yet the St. Anthony doctors had treated two before me. The first, an 18-year-old who was hospitalized for six months in 1981, was left with total amnesia regarding the first weeks of her illness, but no other apparent damage. The second, a 17-year-old boy, who had a mild case, was out of the hospital within a week with no lasting damage.

"The most striking thing about you was your terribly ill appearance," Dr. Root recalled later. "Your whole legs and arms were blue—not just the fingers and toes. But the central part of your body, the trunk and your face, were more an ashen color. You were in profound shock. Your blood was not being pumped to your extremities. There was just almost no circulation at all. Your eyes were red, another important clue. But you were 55 years old, and you had not worn tampons since the onset of your menopause 11 years before." Nevertheless, Dr. Root made the diagnostic leap to toxic shock syndrome.

This is the story of how, almost miraculously and with brilliant care, I survived and prevailed over that grisly and still mysterious disease. Almost every major organ of my body, including my heart, lungs and liver, was deeply poisoned. I narrowly escaped brain damage and kidney collapse. The enzyme released into my bloodstream that reflected muscle destruction showed almost inconceivable damage—an abnormally high reading would have been anything over 100 units; I showed 21,000 units. At first, the Rockford doctors thought they would have to amputate my right leg and the toes of my left foot. Because of the treatment, my legs were saved. But the dry gangrene on eight fingers persisted.

The end joints of my fingers were amputated. In all, three operations were performed. The first, at St. Anthony on Jan. 14, 1982, was delayed in a successful effort to save more of each digit. The other operations, involving corrective surgery, took place at the University Hospital in New York at the end of April and again in May. The Illinois doctors theorized that gangrene had not affected my thumbs because the blood vessels in them were larger and nearer to a major artery.

This is also the story of how—with luck and expertise—this life-threatening disease can be avoided or detected, monitored, treated and destroyed before it reaches the acute stage. Yet few physicians know how to test for it or what to do about it once the strain of common bacterium, Straphylococcus aureus, releases its toxins. Toxic shock syndrome strikes healthy people like a tidal wave, without warning. Only two weeks before in New York, my internist of 25 years had said, after my annual physical checkup, which included a gynecological examination: "If you didn't smoke, Nan, you'd be perfect." Later, other doctors told me that smoking constricts blood vessels, further impeding circulation and thereby worsening gangrene when it occurs.

But, "Nobody should die of toxic shock syndrome," says Don Berreth, a spokesman for the United States Public Health Service's Center for Disease Control in Atlanta, "provided one gets prompt treatment and appropriate supportive care." This view is shared by Dr. Kathryn N. Shands, the physician who until last June headed the Federal toxic shock syndrome task force at the C.D.C. and who has studied every case reported to it from January 1980 to last June.

Toxic shock is rooted in the public mind—and in the minds of many doctors as well—as a tampon-related disease. It is true that of menstruating cases, about two-thirds occur in women under the age of 25, almost all of whom are using tampons when the disease strikes. They are at very high risk.

But about 15 per cent of all cases are nonmenstruating women such as myself, men and children. In this group, there has been no recorded case of a recurrence of toxic shock.

Dr. Shands warns, however, that a tristate study—conducted by the Wisconsin, Minnesota and Iowa departments of health—"showed that menstruating women who have had toxic shock syndrome and who have not been treated with an anytistaphylococcal androme and who continue to wear tampons have possibly as high as a 70 per cent chance—horrifyingly high—of getting toxic shock again. Some people have had their second episode six months later; others as soon as one month later." The shockingly high rate of recurrence among menstruating women indicates that most doctors may misdiagnose toxic shock the first time around, or that sufferers may not seek medical aid if the case is relatively mild.

The disease was first given its present name in 1978 by Dr. James K. Todd, an associate professor of pediatrics at the Univesity of Colorado and director of infectious diseases at Denver Children's Hospital. Writing in the British medical publication Lancet, Dr. Todd described seven cases of the devastating malady he called toxic shock syndrome and suggested that staphylococcus bacteria may be the cause. His patients were seven children from 8 to 17 years old: three were boys and four were girls of menstrual age. One boy died with "irreversible shock" on the fourth day after being hospitalized. One girl, aged 15, suffered amputation at the end joints on two toes.

By June 1980, the national Centers for Disease Control had linked toxic shock with tampon use. The findings were based on a study it had conducted after surveys of victims of the disease by the Wisconsin state health department had suggested a correlation. Publicity about the disease ballooned, spreading alarm across the nation, particularly among the estimated 52 million American women who wear tampons.

Also that June, the C.D.C. toxic shock task force invited the major tampon manufacturers to Atlanta to brief them on the results of the studies. Shortly thereafter, the Federal Food and Drug Administration (F.D.A.) issued a ruling requesting tampon manufacturers to include warnings about their products.

As part of its surveillance, the C.D.C. began to take cultures of women patients at family-planning clinics for Staphylococcus aureus—a procedure as simple as obtaining a pap smear to test for cervical cancer. It was found that 10 per cent of the menstruating patients carried the bacterium in their vaginas, a statistic that still holds. "But it is not necessarily the particular strain that causes toxic shock syndrome," Dr. Shands pointed out in a recent telephone interview. Only "about 1 per cent of all menstruating women," she said, "carry the poison-producing strain of the bacterium in their vaginas during their menstrual periods." Infectious-disease experts say that approximately 2 per cent of the general population carry the poison-producing strain of Staphylococcus aureus in the mucous membranes of their noses.

In September 1980, the C.D.C. reported that of 50 toxic shock victims contacted who had become ill during the previous two months, 71 per cent had used superabsorbent Rely tampons. From January through August of 1980, 299 cases had been reported. The death rate was 25 persons, or 8.4 per cent.

Late in September 1980, after the C.D.C. toxic shock task force had met with F.D.A. officials in Washington about the matter, Procter & Gamble announced it would withdraw its Rely tampons from the market. (Other superabsorbent tampons, however, are still being marketed.) The company is now facing about 400 lawsuits from the surviving victims, or the next of kin of those who died. The plaintiffs have won every one of the half-dozen or so cases that have come to trial, and last month Procter & Gamble settled out of court with a woman whose original trial was the first against the company.

In October 1980, Procter & Gamble blitzed the country with advertisements encouraging women to stop using the superabsorbent Rely tampon. Then, both publicity and the number of reported cases among menstruating women fell precipitously in virtually all states.

One of the few exceptions is Minnesota, where the health department has vigorously ridden herd on doctors and hospitals to count and report all toxic shock cases. There, the incidence has remained at about nine cases a year for every 100,000 menstruating women. The severity of the disease can range from mild to fatal: The death rate in cases *reported* in 1981 was 3.3 per cent overall, but the actual count is almost certainly higher, according to experts on the disease.

A National Academy of Sciences advisory panel also warned last June that toxic shock syndrome had not disappeared. Indeed, the academy's experts concluded, the disease is probably under-reported by physicians who don't recognize the symptoms in victims or don't report the cases they do identify to state authorities. State health agencies, however, are still giving notice of about 30 to 50 cases a month to the Centers for Disease Control in Atlanta.

Between 1970 and April 30, 1982, the Centers for Disease Control received word of 1,660 toxic shock cases, including 88 deaths. Although only 492 cases were reported in 1981, down from a high of 867 in 1980, the Institute of Medicine of the National Academy of Sciences estimated that the true number is about 10 times greater, or at least 4,500 a year. That estimate is based on figures from Minnesota.

Last month, the Journal of the American Medical Association carried an article by three doctors from the Yale University School of Medicine that said a review of five toxic shock studies found flaws that could lead to biased conclusions against tampons. However, an editorial in the same issue of the journal, while agreeing that there were deficiencies in the studies (the largest of which found tampon users were up to 18 times more likely than non-users to develop the disease), said that "only substantial new research evidence evoking alternative explanations for the existing observations would be sufficient to negate the association between TSS in menstruating women and tampon use."

In the cases of non-menstruating victims, Staphylococcus aureus can enter the body through a post-surgical wound or boil; is found inside women who have recently given birth; or anywhere on the skin. According to Dr. Root, there is no evidence that it can be sexually transmitted. In my case, among my theories, a tiny sore on the vaginal wall "may have favored the staphylococcus getting there from somewhere on your skin and then growing," according to Dr. Root. The staph was also found in my colon and urinary tract.

I was one of the dangerously ill cases. For at least four days after toxic shock struck me, the Rockford doctors did not believe I would live. Dr. Edward Sharp, a leading surgeon at St. Anthony, who would later perform the first amputation of the ends of my fingers, alternately bullied and coaxed me to fight on, and was "amazed" that I survived. "If ever anybody had a good reason to die, you did," he said later. "Your age alone! If you had been a 15-or 20-year-old, it wouldn't be so unusual. Of course, it just means you're as tough as nails."

It also means the treatment was swift and superlative, once Dr. Root decided I had the syndrome. Afterwards, Dr. Root recalled: "There are two aspects to the therapy. One is the right antibiotic to treat the staphylococcus germ. Almost all staph is resistant to penicillin now." So he prescribed beta-lactamase-resistant antibiotics to inhibit and wipe out Staphylococcus aureus and to prevent recurrences. Last June, the National Academy of Sciences' advisory panel on toxic shock emphasized, however, that, in the disease as it usually appears in menstruation, "evidence is not available to indicate that such treatment ameliorates symptons or shortens the course of the acute illness."

The two-pronged attack on the disease in my case began, as it would in all others, with "vigorous therapy for the cardiovascular collapse, the shock." And what that involves, Dr. Root said, "is massive amounts of intravenous fluid. Your body has to have a certain amount of fluid within the blood vessels, the heart, to be able to pump effectively."

The amount of fluid that flowed from wide-open bottles and flushed through me in the first 24 hours "would stagger the imagination of many physicians," Dr. Root declared. "You got approximately 24 liters, or quarts, of fluids. I think it was because of the 24 liters, 10 of which replaced fluid lost from vomiting and diarrhea before coming to the hospital, that your kidneys managed to make it through without being terribly damaged. You gained, with those fluids, about 40 pounds in the first day. Your body blew up."

At one point, a nurse emerged from the intensive-care cubicle where I lay and blurted out to my sister and brother-in-law: "Your sister has become a conduit."

"But if we hadn't kept that adequate volume of fluid in your blood, then the kidneys would have gone and we would have lost the whole ball game because everything would have collapsed," Dr. Root explained. "The single most important thing in your therapy, in my opinion, was the incredible volume of fluid we put into you, keeping some measure of circulation going. And then, as the effects of the poison weakened, that circulation eventually picked up and was enough to restore you back to normal."

I was left, however, with eight partially dead and gangrenous fingers; bilateral foot-drop, a form of paralysis in both feet caused by lack of blood flow resulting in damaged nerves, which can leave the patient with a permanent limp, and severely poison-damaged muscles all over my body.

"Shock basically means that your legs and arms were getting no circulating blood anymore, that the amount of blood in your body was so depleted because, first of all, you'd lost volumes and volumes of fluid from your diarrhea and vomiting," Dr. Root told me. "Secondly, with toxic shock, the whole body is damaged, so that the blood vessels, instead of holding the fluid that's circulating through them, leak it, and the blood doesn't flow well; it gets too thick. Your body is made so that at all costs it preserves the blood flow into the brain and the kidneys and the heart. When you lose blood pressure, those organs get the blood flow and the legs and arms don't."

About 12 hours into my hospitalization I slipped into a moderate coma, from which I did not emerge for two days. My brother-in-law went to the Rockford retirement home where my mother lives to tell her I might not make it. Forever gallant, she never showed me her grief and dread during the two months I was hospitalized in St. Anthony. Her tears were secret tears. The day before I was transferred to the Institute of Rehabilitation Medicine in New York, my mother confessed, "I have cried more in the last eight weeks than I have in all my 90 years."

In the first hours, a catheter was inserted into my heart so that the doctors could judge how much fluid to give me. Another tube ran from my trachea to a respirator to enable me to breathe.

Within the week, in a profound gift of friendship, Pat Novak, a close friend since college days and a doctor's daughter, came out to Illinois from New Jersey to stay by my side until the worst was over. She kept a daily diary which she later sent to me. These were her first impressions:

"I drove into St. Anthony Hospital and donned the gloves, mask, hat and apron required for the isolation unit. There, lost in a huge white bed, was a small face swathed in tape, with tubes from each nostril. Nan's sister, Jane, was there talking loudly, getting limited response from the brown eyes that opened occasionally as the head nodded, indicating a positive or negative response. A gurgling and hissing came from the respirator pumping oxygen directly into her lungs through the thick plastic tube in her nose.

"After asking permission of the nurses, I reached over to touch Nan. I stroked her tightly stockinged legs. Her eyes were wet with tears of welcome and gratitude. I saw the hands, fingers ending in charred and blackened tips, lifeless and distorted. Her arms were webbed in maroon rashes from her armpits to her wrists, sores and lesions and Band-Aids, wounds of the battle of the past few days.''

Shirley Katzander, another dear old friend who had already become my "information central" back East, arrived from New York for a visit. "Your hands were a mummy's hands," she told me afterward. "The fingers were black and shriveled, with small, perfect black nails. I almost fainted when I saw them. Thank God you were asleep when I walked in, and could not see my face."

It was clear by then that the ends of my fingers would have to be amputated. Both thumbs had been spared from the gangrene, which meant that I could possibly retain 40 per cent of my hand function, using my thumbs and palms only. The day the surgeon told me he would have to amputate, I was filled with horror. I was certain I would never be able to write again. I was still on the respirator, and speechless. My friend and executive editor at the New York Times, Abe Rosenthal, telephoned. Pat Novak broke the news. Abe began to cry. When he had composed himself, he said something that carried me through many of the hardest days: "For Chrissake, tell Nan we don't love her for her typewriter; tell her we love her for her mind."

Then I was swept with rage, rage that fate had once again struck me down, after 10 dark, troubled years following the traumatic death of my husband, Stan Levey, at the age of 56. Through my long struggle and the help of others, I had finally emerged the previous summer onto what Winston Churchill had called the "broad, sunlit uplands" of life.

But now, as soon as they took me off the respirator, I began to heap my anger onto my family, the doctors and the nurses. I reviled everyone who entered the room. I became impetuous, demanding, argumentative, impossible. One day, when my sister materialized at the foot of the bed, I looked at her with hatred. "Go home," I said, icily.

For at least 10 days I was possessed by fury, at everyone. One morning, I awoke and felt for the first time cleansed and filled with hope. "You have everything to live for," I told myself. That morning in late December 1981, my recovery truly began. It has been a long road back.

Among my Illinois doctors, I shall always cherish Dr. Root, the first to diagnose me correctly, and with whom I later had many instructive and comforting talks, and Dr. Sharp, the surgeon who took a risk and decided to wait before operating on my fingers, putting me as soon as possible into physical therapy. I had dry gangrene, akin to frostbite gangrene, not the wet burn gangrene that gets infected and spreads and so must be removed immediately. Day after day until mid-January 1982, as I winced with pain, Dr. Sharp would rip away bits of the hard black sheaths around my fingers to find, triumphantly, healthy pink flesh beneath. Then the physical therapists would pull and bend the joints of my fingers to bring them back to life and flexibility. "We saved an inch of your fingers," he said later—which meant I retained a whole middle joint on each of the eight affected digits.

Waiting to be operated on was agonizing. I longed for it to be over. Finally thay had saved all the tissue they could. Dr. Sharp operated on Jan. 14, 1982, more than six weeks after the onset of toxic shock. I awoke from the anesthesia to find my hands suspended from bedside poles, swathed in bandages like boxing gloves. The healthy thumbs stuck out.

Two days later, Dr. Sharp unwound the bandages. I was afraid. Then I forced myself to look at what my hands had become. I felt a surge of relief and surprise. I rotated the hands, front and back, and told the doctors with a smile: "I can live with this." My truncated fingers did not repel me. Nor did they shock my family and friends. "This is the worst they will ever look," Dr. Sharp said.

Meantime, the doctors and therapists were fighting to save me from foot-drop paralysis. I began to stand and walk in orthopedic shoes, with steel braces up to my knees. I exercised my legs and arms and hands obsessively, in bed and out. Under the sheets, I wore cross-shaped board splints attached to what I called "bunny boots" on my feet. I loathed them because they prevented me from turning on my side to sleep. I kept removing them. "If you don't wear them," Dr. Sharp finally warned me, "you will be a cripple for life." I wore them, after first making an enormous fuss, and was soon walking short distances—without braces, unaided and with only a slight limp when I was tired.

As yet another index of how catastrophic the sweep of toxic shock syndrome can be, I was treated by 14 doctors during the eight weeks at St. Anthony. They ranged from cardiologists and lung specialists to a podiatrist who cut thick crusts from my toes and the soles of my feet. The cost of the eight weeks' hospitalization in Rockford was $35,000, not counting the doctors' fees. Ahead lay additional tens of thousands of dollars in New York, in hospital stays, additional surgery and daily out-patient therapy on my hands, which will continue for months to come.

On Jan. 26, 1982, my brother-in-law and sister put me on a plane, homeward-bound to New York. For weeks, I had wanted to return to the city that was the center of my life and my career, and by then, thanks to my Illinois doctors, I was well enough to make the trip. I had had the good fortune to be accepted by the Institute of Rehabilitation Medicine, of New York University Medical Center, on East 34th

Street, commonly known as the Rusk Institute, after its founder, Dr. Howard A. Rusk, the great father of rehabilitation for the disabled. I went there by ambulance directly from the airport.

It is a place with miracles in every room, with people in wheelchairs crowding the halls like the pilgrims at Loudes. During 17 days there as an inpatient, the beneficiary of some of the most sophisticated physical and occupational therapy available anywhere, I progressed by quantum leaps. It seems incredible to me, considering the vast need, that there are only a half-dozen civilian rehabilitation centers associated with university hospitals around the United States, outside the Veterans Administration network.

I was so rare, as the first and only case of toxic shock seen at the hospital despite its worldwide reputation, that the doctors and nurses looked at me as if I were a piece of the Ark. "They will not believe your medical records from St. Anthony," Dr. Sharp had predicted, and he was right. Dr. Root had also delivered himself of a statement the day before my discharge from the Rockford hospital. "You now know more about toxic shock syndrome," said this expert, "than the majority of physicians in the United States."

For instance, the terrifyingly high rate of recurrence in menstruating victims—70 per cent—indicates that most doctors may misdiagnose toxic shock the first time around, or that the sufferers may not get to a doctor if the case is relatively mild. My gynecologist in New York, Dr. Howard Berk, who has seen several hospitalized toxic shock cases some time after acute onset, said he advises his patients "to call me immediately and urgently if they have sudden high fever, vomiting or diarrhea during their menstrual period—it could point to toxic shock syndrome." Although it is most unlikely that I will ever get the disease again, because I have not menstruated for more than 11 years, Dr. Berk is monitoring me carefully. He now examines me every three months; takes cultures of my nasal mucosa and vagina for Staphylococcus aureus, and immediately after my discharge from Rusk began a program of local estrogen therapy to strengthen the vaginal walls, thus preventing irritation.

Publicity and the performance of the tampon manufacturers in warning users about toxic shock have been spotty since Procter & Gamble took superabsorbent Rely off the market in late 1980. A new F.D.A. ruling issued last June 22—and effective in December—requires a warning on the outside of tampon boxes and a longer explanation of the association between toxic shock and tampons on the leaflet inside the package.

Right now, the major manufacturers of superabsorbent tampons have warning notices on the boxes or on their inside instruction leaflets, or both.

This year, International Platex Inc., which manufactures Playtex superabsorbent tampons, has been running a television commercial that begins: "Brenda Vaccaro for Playtex tampons. If I was a mother of a teen-ager, I'd tell her to buy Playtex tampons..."—thus aiming at the age group that is at the highest risk of getting toxic shock syndrome.

When Walter W. Bregman, president of Playtex, U.S., was asked to comment on that television advertisement, he said: "The objective of the current Brenda Vaccaro commercial is to appeal and communicate to a variety of women, both in terms of age—in other words, those both older and younger than Brenda—and those with and without children. It is not intended to reach only teenagers, and, in fact, Burke day-after recall research indicates this commercial most effectively communicates to women 25 to 34 years of age."

Government research has shown that a blood-filled tampon can provide a place for the growth of Staphylococcus aureus. "What we think probably happens is that the staph either grow better in the presence of menstrual fluid and a tampon, or they produce toxin better in the presence of menstrual fluid and a tampon," said Dr. Shands of the C.D.C toxic shock task force. The bacterium was not found on unused tampons, but could be grown on them. One study showed that the "supers" absorb more fluid, making the vaginal walls dryer and more subject to irritation. Dr. Shands pointed out that the risk of using superabsorbent tampons is greater than the risk of using less absorbent tampons. At least one case of toxic shock in women using sea sponges had also been recorded.

Testing for Staphylococcus aureus might be a good idea in my case, but not in many others, according to Dr. Kathryn Shands. "You could pick up Staph. aureus from someone else at any time," she said, by touching them or from particles of a sneeze. In addition, you could pick it up and carry it in your nose, and you'd certainly never know it, and transfer it to your vagina at any time. So suppose you went to your gynecologist today and said, 'Please do a culture for Staph. aureus,' and he did and said, 'It's negative. There's no Staph. aereus.' There's nothing to pevent your picking up Staph. aereus on Saturday."

She went on: "So in order to have some reasonably high degree of certainty that you will not develop toxic shock syndrome with this menstrual period, you would have to go in the day before your menstrual period and every day during your period and have Staph. aereus cultures done. And you would have to do it for every menstrual period every month. Pretty expensive for you and pretty much a waste of time. And if you multiply it by the millions of menstruating women in the United States, it becomes a ridiculous exercise: the entire health budget could be used up doing just that."

Asked if there is any way a young woman can eliminate the risk of coming down with toxic shock syndrome, Dr. Shands replied: "She could not use tampons." She hastened to add: "What we've tried to do is put the whole thing into perspective. You are more likely to be killed in a car accident than you are to get toxic shock syndrome. Not *die* from toxic shock syndrome, but *get* toxic shock syndrome. And yet people make the choice every day to drive cars. And if you want to take protective measures, you are far likelier to *die* from lung cancer from smoking cigarettes than you are to *get* toxic shock syndrome when using tampons."

From a doctor's point of view, such a perspective is no doubt reasonable. From my point of view, as I continue the torturous process of regaining the use of my hands and right leg, such statistics seem irrelevant.

The day after I was admitted to Rusk, Dr. Krisjan T. Ragnarsson, my chief physician there, did the first evaluation of me based on my Rockford medical records and his own hospital's neurological, muscle and mental tests. My first question on the day was: "Will I ever take notes again?" Dr. Ragnarsson nodded and said "Yes." "Will I ever type again?" I persisted. His rosy face darkened. Then he smiled. "Oh, well, all you newspaper people are hunt-and-peck typists with two fingers, anyway," he responded. I said, "Dr. Ragnarsson, I have been a touch typist, using all 10 digits, since I was 18 years old." He looked somber again. I did not pursue my queries.

For a long, long time, pain was my daily companion. The worst is now over, but Dr. Ragnarsson believes it could be one or two more years, or never, before normal sensation returns to my finger tips and my right foot. The recovery time depends on how far up the toxic shock struck my limbs, since the nerve endings regenerate at the rate of about an inch in a month.

I have been an outpatient at Rusk five mornings a week since my discharge last Feb. 12.

On Feb. 13, back in my own apartment and alone after 10 and a half weeks of being hospitalized, I totally panicked for the first time. Because of the long Lincoln-Washington holiday weekend, I was not immediately able to arrange for a nurse's aide to help me readjust. I could not turn a single knob on any door, or any faucet, or the stereo, or the television set. I could not wash myself, dress or undress myself, pull a zipper, button a button, tie shoelaces. Punching the telephone numbers with one thumb, I called Nancy Sureck, perhaps the most maternal of all my friends, awakening her and her husband, David. "Help," I said. Nancy was at my side within the hour, taking charge. The next week I hired a wonderful nurse's aide for the mornings; afternoons, I was at Rusk; evenings, a half-dozen close women friends took turns coming in to fix dinner and pop me into bed. Harriet Van Horne, another earth mother, always arrived, like Little Red Riding Hood, with a basket of exquisite home-cooked goodies.

It was months before I could open a taxi door on my way to and from the outpatient hand clinic at Rusk. The cabdrivers of New York, with one exception, invariably sprang to my rescue with a gallantry that amazed, amused and touched me. I had decided to try a frontal, self-confident approach to all strangers in this tough city. I would hail a cab, hold up my hands and say with a smile, "I have a bum hand— could you open the door for me?" Without an instant's hesitation, the drivers would leap around to the back door and open it with a flourish. As we approached our destination, I would hand them my wallet, tote bag or purse and they would hold up each bill and coin like a rosary or miraculous medal or baby to be blessed. "This is a dollar bill," they would say. "This is a quarter," and then return the rest of the money to its place. One driver said, "Even my wife won't trust me with her wallet," and another muttered, "Anyone takes advantage of you should be shot."

Once, in bitter cold that turned my fingers purple because I could not bear yet to wear gloves or mittens, or stick my fingers into my pockets, I could not find an unoccupied taxi. An off-duty cabbie finally stopped in the rush-hour crush for my young, beautiful occupational therapist Gail Geronemus, while she explained why he should take me. As we reached one end of my block, we saw a fire engine blocking the other end. A policeman approached the taxi. "Back up," he commanded. "Hey, hey, this lady's come straight from surgery!" cried the driver, lying with that brilliant New York penchant for instant invention. "We've got to get her through to Number 44!" "Back up," the stone-faced cop repeated. The two men exchanged a stream of obscenities. When I had recovered from my laughter, I told the cabbie that I could make it to my apartment in the middle of the block. As usual, he hopped around to open the back door. I got to my lobby, and burst into tears of fatigue and relief.

The one and only stinker cabbie was an elderly man who refused to roll down his window or open the back door for me. I finally asked a woman on the street corner to help; she complained with alacrity and without asking why. "You roll down the window, you get a gun to your head," the driver said. When I had settled inside, he snarled, "You got only one bum hand, why didn't you open the door with the other?" I shrieked back: "Because all the fingers on both my hands have been amputated!" He almost dissolved into a heap of ashes. "I'm sorry, lady," he said, while a surge of gratifying catharsis rolled through me. I reflected later that I had finally expressed my deepest, pent-up resentments for the first time since my rages in St. Anthony.

Every day of my recovery had brought its frustrations and disasters—and triumphs. On March 25 at the Rusk Institute's hand clinic, Gail, my occupational therapist, said, seemingly casually: "Why don't you try out our electric typewriter?" I was stunned with the enormity of her suggestion. I had thought it would be months before I would be able to attempt such a thing. I went to the typewriter. With incredible slowness and apprehension, I pecked out "Now is the time..." As the letters appeared on the paper, I began to sob. Gail and Ellen Ring, my physical therapist, rushed to my side. "Are you in pain?" they chorused. "These are tears of joy," I said.

Almost six weeks after I had begun outpatient therapy at Rusk, Gail wrote this evaluation of me: "Patient tends to protect her hyper-sensitive stumps by using her palms and thumbs instead of her fingers. She self-splints her hands (holds wrists, hands and fingers rigidly upright) by using her palms and thumbs instead of her fingers to complete various tasks." The tasks I could not properly perform then included picking up coins and unscrewing jar lids.

But, day by day, my occupational and physical therapists were bringing my hands back to life and function. Traumatized by toxic shock, gangrene and then surgery, my finger tips—the most sensitive part of the body, I had been told—had stiffened straight out, the opposite of a stroke victim's fingers that often curl into claws. As an outpatient, I began to wear custom-made "splints," which consisted of castlike wrist braces, leather nooses for each finger and rubber bands that passively pulled my fingers down into fists so that I could grasp objects. These splints perform much like braces on a child's teeth, without active effort on the wearer's part.

There were endless, excruciatingly boring but vital exercises at home. At the clinic, I pawed through coffee cans heaped with raw rice, kidney beans, macaroni and gravel to toughen my finger ends: this invariably set my teeth on edge. I hated the touch of metal of any kind, such as the nails I had to pick up and put in the holes. But there is no way to win at physical therapy without working through pain to healing. "There are the survivors, and there are those who would rather take 50 pills and just slip under," a nurse at Rusk told me. "All human beings divide into those two groups. I have even seen babies who do not want to live—who literally pined away and died."

By early May, I was able to open taxi doors with two hands, and the door knob crisis was over. I was buttoning my blouses and dresses in a trice with a button hook, and awkwardly cutting the top off my breakfast soft-boiled egg with a knife encased in a tube of foam that provides a wider gripping surface. By mid-June, I could punch a push-button telephone with my index finger. (I am still having trouble cutting meat.) By late July, my therapists were "thrilled" with my progress in hand strength, dexterity and range of motion.

Just as important, Dr. Barry M. Zide, a skilled young plastic surgeon at University Hospital, with which Rusk is associated, liberated me from much of my pain in two operations on my fingers last April 29 and May 26. One of my doctors at Rusk had run into Dr. Zide, a kind of Alan Alda in M*A*S*H—witty, irreverent and all heart as well as talent—in the hospital corridor just after failing, as had two other doctors, to remove the Illinois surgical stitches from my fingertips without causing me agony. "No problem," said Dr. Zide. "I'll throw a nerve block in her wrists." The next day, painlessly, he took the sutures out, and I fell in love with yet another doctor.

He then told me to brace myself for more surgery. With a sinking heart, I heard him say: "I can see by the way your nails are coming in that you are set up for chronic infection as soon as the nails grow back. In addition, the unpadded skin at the fingertips will never withstand the constant trauma of daily living. The bone below this thin skin is surely going to become exposed and infected."

First on the left hand in April and then on the right in May, Dr. Zide amputated up to half an inch of some fingers, removing the nailbeds and infected bone. The thicker, more resilient skin on the palm side of my fingers was then draped over the newly shaped bone. Within a week, I was making tremendous progress in the use of my hands and becoming increasingly independent in every facet of my daily life.

My story is almost over except for one crucial detail: My deepest fear did not materialize.

I have typed the thousands of words of this article, slowly and with difficulty, once again, able to practice my craft as a reporter. I have written it—at last—with my own hands.

Part II.

INVESTIGATIVE

WRITING

One of the newspaper's most important functions is to serve as a watchdog for the public—to safeguard the people's interests. Corruption and official legal actions that are not performed with the public's best interests in mind would be much more prevalent were it not for the constant scrutiny of newsmen.

The purpose of an investigative article is to explore situations, specifically those concerning government, which may be adverse to public interests.

The investigative story should be based on facts. All sources of information should be tapped and a fair presentation of evidence made. The story does not judge; it simply tells what the situation is and lets the reader form his own judgments.

The basic organization of investigative stories consists of an interesting lead, the sources of information, and the views of those sources.

Investigative reporting requires more patience than most other types of news gathering. Anyone whose actions, if exposed, would be subject to criticism, condemnation, or incrimination is going to try to put every possible obstacle in the way of the reporter seeking information.

20. A Monstrous, Medieval Prison

Harold Littledale made an extensive investigation of the Trenton, New Jersey, prison in 1917. Although Littledale presented his findings as pure facts, he built the facts into a strong indictment. The story uses plain words throughout, which makes it easy for the reader to follow and understand. The repetition of the phrase "it is a fact that..." hammers in the charges made by the story. Each paragraph makes its point directly and economically, without bringing in needless details. The technique presents the evidence in a straightforward manner that brings the reader to a judgment at the end of the story. *(Pulitzer Prize for Reporting, 1918)*

New Jersey State Prison Breeds Crime
Harold A. Littledale
New York *Evening Post*
January 12, 1917

Bad prisons breed crime, and the New Jersey State Prison at Trenton is among the worst in the country. It is bad in its structure, bad in its influence, and bad in its management. By comparison Sing Sing is a cozy corner, for Trenton is monstrous, medieval, unhealthy, and overcrowded.

It is hard to believe that in the twentieth century, one hundred years after Elizabeth Fry visited Newgate and the English convict ships, man's inhumanity to man should express itself as it does express itself at Trenton. It is hard to believe that for infractions of the rules men are placed face to the wall for punishment and deprived of their meals. It is hard to believe that their labor is farmed out to private contractors for a pittance while their families are in want. It is hard to believe that the state's wards are cast into dungeons. It is hard to believe that women are placed with men. It is hard to believe that the insane mingle with the sane, the consumptive with the healthy, the pervert with the pure. But this, and much more, obtains at Trenton; this and much more exists and is sanctioned and is permitted to be.

Here is the indictment:

It is a fact that two, three, and even four men are confined together in the same cell in violation of the law.

It is a fact that dungeons exist and that men are incarcerated therein and given only bread and water twice a day.

It is a fact that men have been chained to the walls of underground dungeons.

It is a fact that every day a man serves in a dungeon is added to his minimum sentence.

It is a fact that women convicts are confined with men, and that cell 55, wing 4, is kept apart for that purpose.

It is a fact that there is no dining hall and that men are fed in their cells or in the corridor.

It is a fact that the cries of convicts protesting against their food have been heard by those who passed through the streets outside.

It is a fact that these wards of the state save the scraps of one meal to eat at the next.

It is a fact that the men have only half an hour's recreation a week and that the recreation yard for fourteen women convicts is larger than the recreation yard for 1200 men.

It is a fact that many cells are dark and ill-ventilated.

It is a fact that in the newest wing seventy cells are so damp that they cannot be used, and that on occasions the corridor is so wet that the keepers have to wear rubbers.

It is a fact that a cell building erected in 1835 is in use today.

It is a fact that the state's wards were confined up to last Monday in an old wing that the State Board of Health had condemned as unfit for human habitation.

It is a fact that consumptives circulate with the well, exposing them to contagion.

It is a fact that the degenerate, the pervert, and the homosexual are placed with other convicts, with what result can well be imagined.

It is a fact that the first offender is thrown with the habitual criminal.

It is a fact that a youth was released in December who came to the prison a boy of thirteen years, wearing short trousers.

It is a fact that men are punished by being put face to the wall and that sometimes they are kept there all day without food.

It is a fact that convicts may not receive fruit.

It is a fact that a commodious bathhouse, with hot-and cold-water supply, is used only two months in the year.

It is a fact that for ten months in the year the convicts are given only a bucket of water once a week in which to bathe, that after bathing they must wash their clothes in this water and then wash out their cells.

It is a fact that the lights in the cells are extinguished at 8:30 P.M., and that on Sunday evenings there is no light at all.

It is a fact that the hospital is too small and its equipment inadequate.

It is a fact that the management of the prison is vested in a Board of Inspectors who meet only once a month, and whose members are from scattered parts of the state.

It is a fact that the Board of Inspectors of six members appointed six committees, a chairmanship for each member, creating so much more interference.

It is a fact that paroles can be granted by two independent bodies—the Board of Inspectors and the Court of Pardons.

It is a fact that a salaried schoolteacher is employed, but that there is no schoolroom or furniture, in violation of the law.

It is a fact that three chaplains are employed, but that the chapel seats only 350 persons, while the prison population is usually in excess of 1300.

It is a fact that the salaried moral instructor is the Reverend Thomas R. Taylor, father of Leon R. Taylor, ex-Speaker of the Assembly, and that he was appointed by his son while Acting Governor of the state.

It is a fact that contract labor exists, if not in violation of the law, certainly against the spirit of it.

It is a fact that some of the shops where convicts are employed by private contractors are ill-ventilated and dark.

It is a fact that one contract shop is in the cellar.

It is a fact that more than one hundred men are employed on a contract in violation of the law.

It is a fact that much space is given over to these private contractors for use as storerooms.

It is a fact that the Board of Inspectors turns the convicts over for work on the public roads at the rate of $1.25 a day, which is paid by the taxpayers, but that the board turns the convicts over to private contractors at thirty-five cents a day.

It is a fact that free light, heat, and power are furnished to the contractors.

It is a fact that goods made in the prison for private contractors are not marked "Manufactured in New Jersey State Prison," and that this is a violation of the law.

It is a fact that while the contract shops are put in operation daily, the shop, equipped at a cost of more than $12,000 to make socks and underwear for inmates of state institutions, is idle and has been idle for some months, and that the salaried instructor has nothing to do.

It is a fact that the graded and meriting system was recommended in 1911 and that nothing was done.

It is a fact that the employment of a dietarian was recommended in 1911 by the State Commissioner of Charities and Corrections and that nothing was done.

It is a fact that the keepers are underpaid and overworked.

It is a fact that the powers of the Principal Keeper (Warden) are little more than those of janitor.

It is a fact that convicts are supposed to be paid 2 ½ cents a day for their work in prison and that they do not get it.

That then, is the New Jersey State Prison at Trenton, where 1300 men are confined at a net cost in 1915 (the last available report) of more than $253,000. That is how the state's wards are kept. That is how they are punished. That is how they are "reformed." That is how society is "protected." That is the state affairs in this year of grace, 1917. It is really one hundred years since Elizabeth Fry found men and women shut together, found them in rags, found them dirty, and inveighed so against the malice and all uncharitableness that the English conscience was stirred and the era of reform begun? In the state of New Jersey today is there no Elizabeth Fry who will come forward and fight this thing? Or is it "mollycoddling" convicts to permit them to see the sun in the day, to give them better food, to give them light in their cells at night that they may read or study as they would, to provide them with dining halls where they might eat like human beings instead of having their food thrust into their cages as if they were wild and dangerous beasts, to end forever the vicious system of contract labor as Chapter 372 of the Laws of 1911 intended it should be ended, to permit them to receive fruit from their friends who wish to bring them fruit, to try to bring them fruit, to try to bring out the good that is in each and every one of them, for good there is in all of them, and it is like pure gold. If this is "mollycoddling" convicts it is best to leave them as they are with midnight in their hearts.

21. *Civil War in the Coal Fields*

John Leary's exposure of an autocratic ruler in the coal fields of Guyan River in West Virginia is full of details and well researched information. It is a good example of mixing background, present issues, and personal stories in a clear way to provide a thorough analysis of a complex situation. Each sentence is well constructed and cogent and keeps the narrative and explanation flowing smoothly. *(Pulitzer Prize for Reporting, 1920)*

Autocrats of Coal Dominate
"No Man's Land" in Guyan Valley
John J. Leary Jr.
New York *World*
December 8, 1919

With the Eastern seaboard depending upon its mines to keep warm and operate its railroads and industrial plants, and the rest of the country crying: "Coal, more coal," something akin to civil war reigns in West Virginia. True, Federal troops, called in here early in November, have been withdrawn, but the peace is only a truce, which Gov. John J. Cornwell, who helped arrange it, fears may be broken any moment.

Consequently, he is prepared as are his associates in the government of the State to again call on the shortest notice for United States regulars. The call itself is ready. Major Gen. Leonard Wood, in charge of the Central Department in which the State lies, is also ready, for he has been advised that it may be sent at any moment.

Meanwhile the State is producing the bulk of the bituminous coal produced in the United States. The nonunion mines are turning it out to capacity plus. Union districts are not as certain a quantity. Since the strike orders were issued, they have been in operation and on strike intermittently. What they will do in the next few days or weeks neither operators nor union leaders dare to prophesy. The operators hope for the best. The union leaders say: "We don't know."

Trouble dates back

Nominally, and so far as the outer world knows, the trouble in the union fields and nervousness and doubt in non-union districts of the State, follow the order for a nation-wide strike on Nov. 1. Actually, the trouble predates even the convention which in September last fixed the strike date and outlined the demands it was calculated to enforce, and has its origin in Logan County, where in the Guyan River field, the old fashioned "coal baron" is making his last stand.

In Guyton, less than twenty-four hours' ride from Brooklyn Bridge, the only law is the will of the Logan Coal Operators' Association. That law is enforced at the point of pistol and rifle in the hands of men supposed to be deputy sheriffs, but admittedly the servants of the operators who pay the Sheriff, one Frank M. Hurst, a lump sum for "protection." How much they pay him, leading members of the Logan Coal Operators' Association say they do not know.

They admit, however, that a tax is laid on every ton of coal produced in the country, and it produces 2 per cent of the national supply and that from this tax the Sheriff is given his share. Only they do not mention the Sheriff. They speak, as does every one else, of doing business with Don Chafin, ex-Sheriff, now County Clerk, Democratic boss of the county and member of the noted Hatfield clan. The Sheriff one never hears mentioned. Always it is Chafin. To all intents and purposes he is czar, commander-in-chief of the army and chief executive. He proclaims himself "boss," and no one disputes his proclamation.

Rules with an iron rod

Under Chafin's rule, no one comes into the Guyan field that is not approved of by the operators. No one stays in it that for any reason is objectionable to the operators: and in all cases the operators get the benefit of any doubt.

This was the rule prior to the rise of Chafin, when mines were few and far between in Logan County. It was made to keep union organizers out and protect the operators from all kinds of outside interference. It has also served to make a safe haven for men driven from or quitting other fields for reasons best known to themselves.

Known to all as a place where shots were fired before questions were asked, and as a place where trouble always lurked, it gradually developed into a sort of no man's land, isolated from the rest of the world and reserved for coal operators and moonshiners.

Moonshining was the ancient industry of the county. Its maintenance made the exclusion of strangers who might be "revenuers" necessary and trained the natives to silence on all things, including the sudden deaths of strangers. "Welcome" was and is a word seldom used toward strangers in that county.

Under the rule, however, the coal industry of the county grew. Men, particularly men with families, were attracted there by tales of high wages and steady work. Once in, they rarely came out. Reports have it that visiting abroad is discouraged almost if not as much as are visitors from abroad. Also reports of long hours, of low pay, of mistreatment reached the outer world.

Sometimes a venturesome, ambitious union official sought to investigate these tales. It is not on record that any made two attempts. The most of these came back bruised and beaten. Others came out unhurt, but telling of pistols put to head or stomach to enforce orders to get out.

Trouble came in Guyan

Consequently, Guyan was pretty much left to itself until in midsummer reports reached the outer world that the unorganized miners in the several camps had begun to strike on their own initiative. These reports were followed by the expulsion from Guyan of a considerable number of men. These came out telling tales of cruelties that, if believed, would make Guyan worse than any field in Pennsylvania in the old days, of Colorado at its worst.

According to these men, they were underpaid, forced to do work for nothing that is paid for in all other fields, were compelled to work more than the nine hours permitted by law in the State, were not paid for all they were supposed to do, compelled to trade in the stores operated by the companies under the name of commissaries and were restricted in their movements.

They further complained of brutality at the hands of the company guards, otherwise known as Deputy Sheriffs, charging that these men not only beat them, while others held revolvers on them, but robbed them as well of whatever they might have on their persons. It was also charged that they were compelled to stand and submit to being searched whenever it struck the fancy of the deputies to search them, while on Election Day, those who did not propose to vote as the guards told them to vote, to wit the straight Democratic ticket were kept away from the polls and their names voted on.

In detail they told of specific cases of abuse—showing bruises and scars to back up their stories. Some of these are unbelievable and have to do with such things as bodies being disposed of by burning in coke ovens. This latter story—it seems to be the one story virtually told— has in no way been corroborated. The stories of assaults and other abuses have, at least to the satisfaction of the miners living outside

Guyan, and to many who are neither miners nor unionists.

All laid to Chafin's men

Don Chafin's men figured in nearly all their stories of brutality. Never does it appear that any one mentioned Sheriff Hurst. It was some difference with mine or petty boss, some charge of advocating unionism, some dispute at the commissary and then an attack of some sort and degree of ferocity on the part of the deputies.

Many of these exiles told of being driven out of the district without an opportunity to get their wages or see their families. They had, they said, been threatened with death if they returned for any purpose.

These men for the most part sought and obtained work in union fields. In these fields they told their stories. To some it has appeared that this was organized propaganda. There is, however, no proof of this as yet, the known facts indicating that in driving these men out, the deputies or guards, however described, simply sent so many missionaries abroad to preach for the time when Guyan would be "cleaned up."

However this may be, it is certain that midsummer found a large number of men going through the union fields in adjoining counties, and in the northern part of Logan County itself, urging that something be done for those left behind.

Those left behind, according to documents held by district officers of the United Mine Workers, were all this time trying to do something for themselves. These documents show secret meetings and appeals signed by a considerable number of men that the union sent in as organizers.

The names on these petitions are for the greater part American names. On the lists there is hardly a name indicating either foreign birth or blood. On one, the soiled appearance of which District President Charles F. Keeney says is due to its having been smuggled out hidden in a shoe, there is not a foreign name.

Secret meetings held

These secret meetings, it further appears, were largely dominated by newly arrived men from union fields and, to a great extent, by men of no union experience freshly discharged from the army. Keeney says none was an organizer in the sense of being detailed by the union.

"It has been found impossible to get organizers in there or for them to work in there," he says. "Certainly I would not detail any man to a job that probably would cost his life, and Guyan is not the place volunteers clamor for permission to work in. These people, driven to desperation, simply took their chances just as they did in the unorganized strikes.

"They first began striking in Guyan a year ago, when the men on two properties quit and sent committees in to ask for organizers. We told them we wouldn't organize them while they were on strike and advised them to return to work. Again in July last they appealed to us.

"Then we decided on action, the District Board deciding on a campaign of education such as was used in the Fairmont Field in June 1918. There was no trouble there, the operators signed up and everything has been all right since. When the strike order was revoked, these men went back to work. This committee was made up of 50 Americans and 2 Italians."

This committee, working with the men within Guyan's confines arranged to hold a mass meeting on Labor Day on the mountain ridge dividing the union field of Coal River from Guyan. Preceding this meeting the union miners held their annual barbecue in Blair, three miles from Sovereign.

To prevent the meeting, a large force of deputies posted themselves on the union side of the hill. Against them were sent scouting parties armed with rifles. The guards, however, paid most attention to dispersing the non-union men and preventing their meeting with the unionists, and there was no shooting. They were not entirely successful and some eighty were taken into the union. Several were arrested and one organizer, who went over the hill, was badly beaten. He also said he had been robbed of $300.

Took them to count

"A few days after this," Keeney says in telling the story, "the men in Guyan who had been beaten up after the event, sent committees in to ask for help. I took eleven of these to see Gov. Cornwell. Five of them frankly said they had had pistols on them. They were natives of the county where gun toting is not uncommon. The Governor asked time to investigate.

"I told the Governor that as we had an organization in there now, if he would allow me to send in men to take care of the needs of the men discharged for unionism, I'd agree that they would do no organizing.

"He would not agree to this. Instead he said he'd see that the men got their jobs back and not be molested, to hold them a few days, and then send them back. I agreed to this. They went back as told. Of them, six were brutally beaten and driven out. They returned here after I had left town."

Then (Sept. 4) the first demonstration that seemed serious began. Four miles from Charleston, at Lynscreek miners from the surrounding country began to assemble for a march on Guyan. They came bringing their rifles, for this is a country of riflemen and rifle clubs. To head them off, Gov. Cornwell wired Kenney, who caught up with the procession at Maumelte, a few miles up the road. Kenney was told to go home and mind his business.

"'We're going to Logan to re-establish the Constitution there,'" they told him.

50,000 men on the march

Keeney returned here, the men meanwhile resuming their march. By this time miners were marching from several points, all converging on Logan, until perhaps 50,000 men, all armed, were on the move. Of this number 700 were service men from overseas, 300 of whom were in uniform and wearing their trench helmets.

After another conference with the Governor, another attempt was made to head the marchers, Kenney this time bearing credentials from the Governor, in whose name he was authorized to promise the remedying of any evil conditions. Fret S. Mooney, Andrew Stanton and other union leaders went on similar errands. The main body, reduced by the falling out of older men to 1,500, reached Danville, twenty miles from Logan, where Kenney finally induced them to board a special train for home. At other points other leaders performed a similar service.

Between them, and with the assistance of Gov. Cornwell, who addressed the marchers at one point, they undoubtedly averted a pitched battle in which there would have been heavy loss of life, for in and about Logan, in narrow passes commanded by hills, the deputies, "Don Chafin's men," were waiting, armed with rifles and, it is said, a few machine guns.

The result of such a battle, considering the calibre of the men on both sides, would easily have made the battles in Colorado's mine war seem tame indeed. In getting the men to desist the best argument was an assurance that a commission would be named to look into the evils said to exist in Guyan and report the necessary remedy.

22. *Justice Hugo Black and the KKK*

Ray Sprigle's account of Supreme Court Justice Hugo Black's membership in the Ku Klux Klan is a superior example of how a reporter can present the findings of a lengthy investigation in readable form. Whereas most investigative stories—including even winners of the Pulitzer Prize—make for tedious reading, Sprigle's story is able to sustain reader interest because of both the subject matter and the writing style. It provides intricate details such as exact dates of Black's KKK membership, his resignation—described as "scrawled in long hand on a sheet of the stationery of the Grand Dragon of the Alabama Klan"—and the precise location of the state Klan meetings in an engaging method. *(Pulitzer Prize for Reporting, 1938)*

Evidence Shows His Membership for Long Period
Ray Sprigle
Pittsburgh *Post-Gazette*
September 13, 1937

BIRMINGHAM, Ala.—Hugo Lafayette Black, Associate Justice of the United States Supreme Court, is a member of the hooded brotherhood that for ten long blood-drenched years ruled the Southland with lash and noose and torch, the Invisible Empire, Knights of the Ku Klux Klan.

He holds his membership in the masked and oath-bound legion as he holds his high office in the Nation's Supreme tribunal—for life.

For Supreme Court Justice Hugo Lafayette Black bears the proud distinction that not a half dozen other men in the United States can claim. The cloaked and hooded Knights of the Klan have bestowed upon him the solid gold engraved Grand Passport that betokens life-membership in the mysterious super-government that once ruled half a continent with terror and violence.

Became member of Klan September 11, 1923
Hugo L. Black, future United States Senator and United States Supreme Court Justice, joined Robert E. Lee Klan No. 1, Invisible Empire, Knights of the Ku Klux Klan, September 11, 1923.

Klansman Black resigned from the Klan July 9, 1925. His

resignation, scrawled in longhand on a sheet of the stationery of the Grand Dragon of the Alabama Klan, was the first move of his campaign for the Democratic nomination for United States Senator from Alabama. Klansman Black and the leaders of the Klan decided it was good political strategy for Black to make the senatorial race unimpeded by Klan membership but backed by the power of the Klan. That resignation, filed for the duration of the campaign but never revealed to the rank and file of the order and held secretly in the records of the Alabama Realm, is reproduced with this series of articles.

Senator-Nominate Hugo L. Black was welcomed back into the Klan at a great state meeting or Klorero of the Klan held in Birmingham Klan headquarters, South Twentieth street, Birmingham, Thursday, September 2, 1926. Imperial Wizard Hiram Wesley Evans and leading Klansmen from other states attended. Klansman Hugo L. Black was at this meeting made a life member of the hooded order and was presented with a gold membership card in the Klan. Klansman Black attributed his election to the support of the Klan, expressed his gratitude for that support and pledged himself to remain loyal to the principles of the Klan.

"I realize," he told his fellow Klansmen, "that I was elected by men who believe in the principles that I have sought to advocate and which are the principles of this oganization."

Proceedings of that meeting were taken by an official Klan stenographer, transcribed and made a part of the records of the Alabama Klan. The accounts of that meeting are taken from that official record, obtained from the official files of the Alabama Klan. Portions of that official record are reproduced with this series of articles.

No record of resignation in files

No record of the resignation of Hugo L. Black from the Knights of the Ku Klux Klan is contained in the files of the Alabama Klan. The gold life-membership card presented to him when he was made a life member of the Klan never has been returned to the officials who had it made and presented it to him, so far as the official files of the Alabama Klan indicate.

It took two great American mass movements, both of them of supreme importance, socially and historically, to make Hugo L. Black what he is today. One of them is the Invisible Empire of the dreaded Klan. The other is the New Deal.

The Klan picked Attorney Hugo L. Black out of the ruck of small-time Alabama politicians and made him a United States Senator. And then President Franklin D. Roosevelt and the New Deal lifted him from that high office and made him a justice of the United States Supreme Court.

Today, throughout the Old South the scattered remnants of the shattered Klan are stirring into new and vigorous life with the realization that a loyal son of the hooded horde has won a place in the highest court in the land.

By grace of the New Deal the Invisible Empire has been born again. Once more the aulic, the royal court of the Imperial Wizard in Atlanta, where Hiram W. Evans, deserted by his Dragons and his Titans and his Terrors, has sat in decaying loneliness these many years, has become the seat of a reborn and growing Empire.

Once more silver-tongued and persuasive Kleagles are proselyting throughout the old South. Old time Klansmen are coming back into the fold, their apostasy forgotten. Converts from a newer generation are being naturalized into the realm of the secret empire of the shadows.

Florida now boasts a Klan membership of 30,000, many of these thousands recruited since the New Deal bestowed upon Hugo L. Black the sombre robes of a Supreme Court Justice to hang beside his Klansman's robes of white in the Black family closet, when the Klansman-Justice is neither klucking nor justicing.

Birmingham Klan swamped with applications

The Birmingham, Alabama, Klan is swamped with applications for membership at each of its regular Thursday night meetings. In Atlanta, Klansmen are flocking back to the standard of the fiery cross by the hundreds. Old time Kleagles throughout the South are wiring and writing to the Imperial Wizard's aulic in Atlanta, sending in their old commissions, creased and smutted with the neglect and dust of the years, begging to have them renewed.

Once more the Klan is proudly on the march, preaching its creed of racial hatred and religious bigotry but this time with a brand new slogan.

"A Klansman sits on the Supreme Court of the United States. Join the Klan."

Hugo L. Black's membership in the Ku Klux Klan is no secret in his home state of Alabama. The leaders of the New Deal were wise men when they steam-rolled the Klansman's confirmation as United States Supreme Court Justice through the Senate in less than a week.

The New Deal had to move fast. It had to gag the handful of protesting Senators who wanted time to look up the Klan record of the first New Deal Supreme Court justice. For what nearly everyone in Alabama already knew, everyone in the United States would know— that when Hugo Lafayette Black took his seat on the Nation's highest tribunal, he wouldn't have to bother to buy himself a black robe. He could save time and money by dyeing his old Klansman's robe.

United States Senator Hugo Lafayette Black was a creation of the Ku Klux Klan. Hugo L. Black's sole contribution to the creation that the Klan built up was a brain and an intelligence much above the average. Everything else the Klan furnished. The Klan took him, a little known but competent Birmingham damage suit lawyer, a former police court judge, a former county prosecutor, and with loving and meticulous care, fashioned him into a United States Senator.

Obstacles used as stepping stones to greater glory

It was 1923 before Attorney Hugo L. Black decided that the time had come for him to join the Klan. The hooded order was sweeping the nation, and especially the South, like a crusade. It had triumphantly surmounted every obstacle that its enemies had placed in its path. More, it had used those obstacles as stepping stones to greater glory. A United States Senatorial investigation in 1921 had turned the Klan inside out, revealing its secrets to the world. And every day that the committee sat and denounced the Klan, the Invisible Empire "naturalized" more thousands, eager to don robe and hood and swear blood-oath of brotherhood.

So, on an evening in September 1923, in the Klavern of Robert E. Lee Klan No. 1, Birmingham, Alabama, Hugo Lafayette Black stood before the white-robed brethren of the Klan, his left hand over his heart, his right hand raised to heaven. Crossed swords lay on the Bible on the altar.

Solemnly Hugo Black intoned the long oath of allegiance to the Klan, swearing never to divulge, not even under threat of death, the secrets of the Invisible Empire. And at last: "I swear that I will most zealously and valiantly shield and preserve by any and all justifiable means and methods...white supremacy.

"All to which I have sworn to by this oath, I will set with my blood, be thou my witness Almighty God, Amen."

Klansman Hugo Lafayette Black proved an ideal member of the hooded brotherhood. He sought no office or preference in the Klan, was willing to serve where he could. In those early days of his membership many of the Klans in the Birmingham district got to know the shrewd young lawyer who appeared before them from time to time to lecture.

But political history was in the making in Alabama. Senator Oscar

W. Underwood, the old warhorse of Southern Democracy, had broken with the Klan, and the Klan had sworn to sweep him out of public life.

They take their politics seriously in Alabama, and as early as the spring of 1925 candidates for the Democratic nomination for United States Senator for the primaries in midsummer of 1926 were bobbing up here and there.

Saw that Klan would name next senator

Probably there was but one man in the entire state of Alabama who in 1925 would have considered seriously the possibility of Klansman-Attorney Hugo L. Black of Birmingham becoming United States Senator from Alabama in 1926. That one man was Hugo L. Black himself.

Klansman Black saw unerringly in 1925 what Alabama political leaders were not to discern until 1926, that the Ku Klux Klan of Alabama was going to name the next United States Senator from Alabama.

More than a year before the 1926 primaries, in July 1925, Klansman Hugo Black laid his dream of a seat in the United States Senate before the rulers of the Invisible Empire in Alabama. He assured them that he did not need or want the Klan to finance his campaign. All he wanted was a pledge of Klan support throughout the length and breadth of the state. He sold his dream to the Grand Dragon and his Great Titans.

And right then and there, July 19, 1925, in the state offices of the Ku Klux Klan, for the Realm of Alabama, in room 505 First National Bank Building in Birmingham, Klansman Hugo L. Black became United States Senator; Hugo L. Black, not to take office, however, until 1927 after the formalities of the Democratic primaries and the general election had been disposed of.

Klansman Hugo L. Black's campaign for United States Senator began before he left Klan headquarters. His first campaign gesture surprisingly enough was to resign as a member of the Klan.

Action seen as grade-A political strategy

That was Grade A political strategy. The Klan had its enemies; that was inevitable and natural. From the beginning the Jewish and Catholic elements among the population had opposed the Klan in self-defense. Negro opposition could be discounted. Negroes don't vote in Alabama. Not many of them in any event. But sentiment against the Klan had developed in other quarters, notably among the women's clubs of the state.

There was no use intensifying that opposition by dressing a Klan candidate up in a robe and hood and mask and sending him out to get votes.

So on a sheet of stationery of the Grand Dragon of the Realm of Alabama, Hugo L. Black wrote out his resignation from the Klan in long hand.

"Mr. J. W. Hamilton, Kligraph" wrote the future associate justice of the United States Supreme Court. And even so erudite and learned a Klansman as Hugo L. Black demonstrated that not even he was wholly familiar with the weird nomenclature of the Klan, for the secretary of a Klan is not a "Kligraph" as future Justice Black wrote it but a "Kligrapp."

"Dear Sir and Klansman," he continued. "Beg to tender you herewith my resignation as a member of the Knights of the Ku Klux Klan, effective from this date on—
                    Yours I.T.S.U.B.,
                    HUGO L. BLACK."

And that cabalistic "Yours I.T.S.U.B." was no mere idle gesture of a departing brother. The brother wasn't actually departing.

"Yours In The Sacred Unfailing Bond" is the translation of those hastily scrawled capitals with which Hugo L. Black closed his letter of "resignation," and the future was to prove that the bond was unfailing even if not exactly sacred.

Resignation never accepted or acted upon

That resignation was to lie unnoted and neglected in the files of the Klan. Kligrapp J. W. Hamilton was never to see it—unless he happens to read this chronicle. It never was accepted or even acted upon.

But Candidate for the United States Senate Hugo L. Black, by virtue of that three-line scribble in a dusty desk drawer in the offices of the Alabama Klan, was able to square his conscience whenever it might prove politically expedient to deny membership in the order.

Resignation or no, in any event, that brief farewell was to become but a worthless scrap of paper on the night of September 2, 1926, when in the great hall of the Invisible Empire in South Twentieth street in Birmingham, before an audience composed of the Dragons and the Titans and the Cyclops of the entire state of Alabama, under the beaming smile of Imperial Wizard of the Invisible Realm Hiram Wesley Evans, Hugo Lafayette Black, victor in a bitter fight for the Democratic nomination for the United States Senator from Alabama (which in that state is equivalent to election), was to be proferred and accept the golden Grand Passport of the Alabama Klan emblematic of his life membership in the hooded legion.

23. *Rent Gougers in Welfare City*

Buffalo *News* reporter Ed May served as a caseworker for six months with the Erie County, New York, Department of Social Welfare to find out what living on welfare was like. The article that follows is one from a fourteen-part series. Told in large part from the point of view of people on welfare, it includes shorter personalized stories within the larger story and places much of the blame for high welfare costs on owners of rental properties. Costs are used understandably and as necessary to document the argument. Concrete and extensive details help the reader "see" and understand the situation. *(Pulitzer Prize for Reporting, No Edition Time, 1961)*

Welfare City Is Landlord's Paradise
Ed May
Buffalo *Evening News*
June 20, 1960

Population: 36,301. This is the second largest city in Erie County.

It has no mayor, no tax rate and no boundary lines. Its name is Welfare City.

Its residents are scattered from the crowded tenements of Buffalo to an occasional ramshackle farmhouse in the outlying towns. And in its center—the tattered pattern of slums—it has its own special characteristics.

Welfare City's colors are gray and rust. The once white houses and yellow houses have succumbed to the brushings of countless rainstorms.

There are the locks on the mailboxes—so no one can steal the welfare check...light bulbs burning feebly in the shadow-filled hallways....The smell of fish (they're inexpensive) cooking on a stove.

"Landlord's Paradise" is what some caseworkers call it.

But in Welfare City, like in any other, there are the neat-as-pin places, too, where a fussy housewife will greet a caseworker with an accusing glare if he should forget to remove his overshoes.

Today to keep a collective roof over Welfare City costs the taxpayers

$7,000,000 a year. The rent bill ranks among the top of welfare's expense list.

In 1958, an Erie County Welfare Department survey showed it was paying $5,800,000 rent a year. Today, officials concede, with a higher caseload and higher rentals, that figure is much larger.

In my own caseload while I served as a caseworker in the Erie County Welfare Department the average rent was $49.68 a month without utilities. If heat, cooking and light are included, the figure rises to $63.80.

"Some of these places aren't worth half the price we're paying for them," more than one welfare official has said.

As an example, take the case of John B., a steelworker and father of seven children. He is receiving supplementary help from the Welfare Department so he can make ends meet.

If it were not for his exorbitant rent he wouldn't be on welfare.

John earns an average of $80 a week. About 10% of it goes to pay for a 4-year-old furniture bill. What he's paying for is already worn out.

He lives in a seven-room, weather-worn flat in the Fruit Belt, and his carefully worded lease says:

"Witnesseth that the landlord leases to the tenant and the tenant hereby hires and takes from the landlord....at the annual rent of one thousand and eighty dollars ($1080)."

For his $90 a month John gets the floors, the walls and the ceilings. Heat, and the gas stove to furnish it, are his responsibility. In the winter his shelter bill is about $130 a month.

If the flat were under rent control, reports the Temporary State Housing Rent Commission, the maximum monthly fair rental figure would be $34.50.

The two-apartment building is assessed at $3090. In two years the owner's gross rent receipts will exceed the assessed valuation.

Less than a mile away, a welfare client, occupying a similar seven-room flat, pays $22.50 a month.

This contrast is one of welfare's prime dilemmas. Only a few months ago Commissioner Paul F. Burke lashed out at slum landlords who are gouging your tax dollars away.

In the high welfare areas, tenement rents often are charged by the week. Anywhere from $20 to $30 is not uncommon.

This leads to tenant arithmetic and landlord arithmetic. The two are different.

In one of my cases, the client, paying $22 a week, was convinced it was $88 a month since you multiply by four. The actual figure (landlord arithmetic) was $95.33 since there are 4 ⅓ weeks in a month.

In a few cases, the unscrupulous have duped the uninformed because they have no understanding of the laws. Take, as an example, Mrs. Harriet F., one of my clients who was on welfare because she injured her foot.

Mrs. F. said she owned the house she was living in and showed bundles of what she considered payment receipts that had been made to the "former" owner. A resource check produced this from the "former" owner's attorney:

"It appears this estate has been and still is paying the taxes on this property. It further appears that Mrs. F. has never paid any rental or other consideration for the use of this property."

In other words, Mrs. F. is paying rent, not making monthly payments toward the purchase of her house as she thinks. But as far as the owner's concerned, he knows nothing about rent or property payments.

On the other side of the picture, some landlords who pride themselves on a "square deal" have refused welfare tenants.

"Too hard to collect the rent. Too much damage to the property," is their complaint.

City and county officials dealing with housing, as well as the banks, know the big-time slum operators by name. A half-dozen, they estimate, own hundreds of buildings alone.

These officials also know the sorry tangle of housing violations that thread their way through Buffalo. About 15,000 multiple dwellings now violate various fire, health and building laws. Since 1956, fewer than 700 have qualified for a certificate of occupancy.

One County Health Department spokesman termed "numerous" the houses which lack even minimum bathroom facilities of a toilet, wash basin and tub or shower.

Serious minimum housing law violations, he said, "run into the thousands" for lack of time and personnel to inspect the dwellings.

In New York City, on the other hand, a Special Sessions Housing Court has fined a steady parade of landlords. Some, who were chalking up fines as "a business expense," were sent to jail.

The County Health Department's court record here looks like this:

In 1959 it took 438 cases to City Court. Because of various adjournments allowed by the courts this required 1110 appearances. Sixteen persons paid fines.

24. *The Truth Behind Batista*

Joseph Martin and Philip Santora began their search for the truth behind the Cuban regime of Fulgencio Batista in March 1958. They exposed to Americans for the first time the real story behind the dictatorship. In the following account, the terror is emphasized through such stylistic techniques as active voice, precise word selection, and strong verbs. The concrete detail of the writing allows the full reality of conditions to be experienced by the reader. *(Pulitzer Prize for International Reporting, 1959)*

Batista Rules by Death, Terror
Joseph Martin and Phil Santora
New York *Daily News*
April 8, 1958

This is a grim rollcall of Fulgencio Batista's chief terrorists—killers so brutal and ruthless than even the man who helped create the monsters seems afraid of trying to control them. These are the men whose names are whispered with fear and hate, whose incredibly sadistic deeds read like pages torn from the records at Dachau.

Maj. Estaban Ventura Nobo dislikes dull evenings. When one comes along, he sends his police out to pick up unfortunates who stray into one of the three police districts technically under his control—actually, he operates throughout Havana. Then he beats a selected victim into insensibility just for the kicks.

Ventura's name has become a lewd epithet throughout Cuba. He is an avid student of torture, having been tutored in the fine points by Angel Borlenghi, who was minister of the interior in Argentina under ex-dictator Juan Peron.

Recently, Ventura used a Borlenghi invention—putting two electrodes on the genitals of a 16-year-old boy and shocking him into what he hoped would be a confession of "his crimes against the state." The electrodes touched, and the boy was electrocuted, cutting short Ventura's fun for the day.

Another Ventura gimmick is a basket made of piano wire which is fastened about the genitals. Two wires draw the basket shut, causing indescribable pain. He has been known to rip the ear off a subject when a beating with fists failed to get results.

Goes to psychiatrist, then reverts to type

Ventura goes under psychiatric care at intervals. But in between treatments he roams the streets of Havana with up to a dozen heavily armed bodyguards, looking for victims to assuage his thirst for torture.

He loves expensive white suits and keeps one or two in each of the precincts under his command. He's also nuts about publicity; and when the photographers show up, Ventura dons a fresh white suit, sprinkles a bit of cologne on his hair and pencil-thin moustache and holds a press conference.

Lean, about 160 pounds, 40 years old, married and the father of two young daughters, he was born in Pinar del Rio Province in the western part of Cuba. Those are the so-called vital statistics.

Ventura has mistresses throughout the area of his command. He can well afford them with the money he gets from businessmen who either get up the monthly assessment or find themselves answering questions in the cellar of a stationhouse.

Batista turns a deaf ear to pleas—and some of these come from his top aids—to remove Ventura from his post. Even the Gerardo Abreu incident failed to sway him from loyalty to the terrorist who swaggers through Havana instilling fear in the most innocent of Cubans.

Gerardo Abreu's death resulted in the only indictment ever handed up against Ventura. Abreu was a 20-year-old pianist-student who was socially popular among young people in Havana.

Ventura ordered him arrested on charges of terrorism—an ironic touch—and sentenced him to jail. He was released on a writ of habeas corpus. Less than a week after his release, he was again arrested by Ventura.

Witness wraps up the grim story

Immediately, there were cries for "justice" from social and student groups. A witness gives the conclusion of the grim story:

"I heard noises on the street in front of the Palace of Justice. Guards from the palace were there, and they were discussing something in loud tones with other men. It was about 11 p.m. A few minutes later, I heard the chatter of a machine gun. I saw three men get into a car and drive off." Abreu's body was found there the next morning. No one dared approach the spot during the night.

Ventura was quoted later as saying: "They wanted justice—and I gave them justice, with interest."

The dreaded, dapper killer is also the author of the phrase, "Here's your habeas corpus." It was uttered when the lifeless body of a suspected terrorist was dumped at the feet of the lawyer who had obtained the writ.

He won his spurs by beating a priest

Ventura was an obscure lieutenant in charge of the 5th Precinct five years ago, before he distinguished himself by working over a priest, the Rev. Ramon O'Farril, who had plotted to have President Batista ambushed on one of his frequent visits to church.

Father O'Farril was so badly beaten that he suffered fractures of two ribs and internal injuries and is permanently deaf in one ear.

In Miami, the exiled priest admitted his part in the plot to have Batista assassinated. "It is high time," he said, "that the UN stepped into the Cuban case. They should step in if for no other reasons than the reasons of humanity. The bloodiest drama in the gory history of Latin America is now taking place in Cuba. There have been thousands of deaths—murders by the Batista regime. There are the countless tortures and humiliations. These and the exiles who have been ousted from their homeland are more than sufficient reasons for international intervention in the Cuban problem.

"Not even the highest prelates of the Roman Catholic Church have escaped terrorist action under the Batista regime. The Cuban people are in immediate need of the help of all the Catholics of the world and also of the moral and physical support of all the upright and wholesome people of the free world."

Ventura's closest rival in the brutality sweepstakes is Capt. Julio Laurent, in charge of naval intelligence. Laurent was an unknown bush-leaguer before he murdered his first Cuban.

The victim was a supporter of ex-President Carlos Pris Socorras. He was arrested in a house in the swank Vedado section, dragged out into the street where Laurent, then a lieutenant, was waiting with a submachine gun in hand.

A medieval touch for the finale

While two men held the suspected terrorist, Laurent pressed the tommygun against his body and cut him almost in half with three long bursts. Then he turned to the crowd of horrified spectators and shouted: "And anyone who accuses me will die a similar death." He was charged with murder, but no witnesses would appear against him.

Along with Ventura, he was accused of the murder of a captain involved in the Cienfuegos uprising last Sept. 8. The captain, Alfredo Gonzales Brito, was brought to Havana after his arrest in Cienfuegos. In the home of the second ranking commander of the Cuban navy, he was beaten and kicked into unconsciousness. Revived, he was tortured with cigars and cigarets that burned holes over more than half of his body.

The finale came when Laurent and Ventura ordered the captain and a close friend taken to a castle tower overlooking the sea. There, the two were gagged, trussed and thrown into the sea.

An incident that has caused the greatest indignation concerns a 50-year-old schoolteacher, Mrs. Esther Milanes. Mrs. Milanes was a teacher in a Catholic school and had a minor part in the underground movement. She was picked up, along with a student from Colombia, South America, by men under the command of Capt. Jose Sosa, another of the sadists who pretend to administer justice in Havana.

The woman was beaten with fists and the flat feet of Sosa and his henchmen in an attempt to make her talk. They threatened to have her raped by a particularly repulsive-looking member of the precinct force. When threats and beatings failed, they took an iron bar and inserted it forcibly into her body.

Mrs. Milanes might never have been released alive had it not been for the Colombian ambassador, who went looking for the student. She and the boy were released in his custody and she was rushed to the hospital. She revealed that they tortured the boy in front of her in an attempt to break her down.

Then there is Col. Manuel Uglade Carrillo, who likes to sit in the third degree room and watch prisoners being given a working over. Uglade, who was the first chief of the SIM (secret police) when Batista came into power, laughs heartily while the grisly torture goes on.

The new chief of police in Havana is Pilar Garcia, who got his reputation by quelling a riot at Matanzas two years ago this month. After the uprising had been put down Garcia made "examples" of 11 rioters. He had them shot.

Equipped to treat people like oxen

There is, in Santiago de Cuba, a lieutenant colonel named Jose Maria

Salas Canizares who, along with his brother, gained notoriety throughout the island for violence.

Canizares, 6-foot, 200-pound thug, likes to lead his men into battle with the visor of his legion-style cap turned up. Sort of a trade mark. He carries an ox goad with which he strikes people during demonstrations.

When he was assigned to Santiago, he promptly ordered a blackout and then riddled a few houses with machine gun bullets so that the "people in this city will know who's boss."

Then he went out to pick up the local leader of Castro's July 26 movement. He picked up two young men. He had an idea that one of them was the real thing but didn't know which one. So he killed them both to make sure.

When the weeping widow of one remonstrated, Canizares laughed and volunteered that he and his men could take care of her sexual wants.

These are the chiefs. But the men under them can be equally brutal. In some instances, they surpass their leaders because they feel that is the way to success and recognition under Batista.

Another killer was Col. Fermin Cowley, who won his spurs in Holguin, in the northern port of Oriente Province on Christmas Day, 1956. On that day, Cowley hanged 14 students, supporters of the Castro movement. One of the victims was the brother of Rep. Eugenio Cusido, who is still in office. On the day the victims were being buried, Cowley showed up and said he didn't like the way the ceremonies were being conducted. He ordered the funerals suspended.

Early last year, rebels stopped a bus on the main road into Oriente. They ordered the passengers out—with their luggage—and then set fire to the bus.

He hanged all four, just to be sure

Cowley demanded that the passengers and driver identify the rebels. They said they couldn't. When four suspects were brought in, Cowley asked the driver to identify them. He said he couldn't because he hadn't seen their faces. Cowley hanged all four, "just in case they were all guilty."

A year ago this month, a World War II paratrooper went to Oriente Province with 27 men. The veteran, Calixto Sanchez, was one of those suspected of having taken part in the March 1957 attack on the presidential palace in Havana.

In mid-April, he was surrounded by government forces and surrendered to a lieutenant who offered him the guarantee of a formal trial. When Cowley learned of the surrender he personally machine-gunned all 28 to death.

The "mad colonel" was married seven times. He had no children, but he collected German-made toys with a sort of psychopathic intensity.

But he's one that castro's men got

His career came to an abrupt halt several weeks later when Fidel Castro sent two men out of the Sierra Maestra with orders to liquidate the colonel. Cowley—traveling confidently with a small bodyguard—showed up at a store one day to buy lightbulbs. The clerk said he didn't have the type on hand and suggested Cowley return the next day.

Cowley came back the following day and was shot to death by the Castro executioners waiting in ambush.

On March 24—two weeks ago—a woman was arrrested in a Havana hospital only two days after bearing a child. The charge was not made clear, and she hasn't been seen since. The baby is still in the hospital.

In the little town of San Juan Martinez, a local magistrate sent his sons off to the movies. The boys, Luis Saiz, 16, and Sergio Saiz, 14, got into an argument with a soldier. He shot them to death.

Turn machine gun on the mourners, too

When the funeral was held the next day, the angry townspeople had words with soldiers and police. The police opened fire and killed eight with machine-gun fire.

These are but a few of the incidents sworn to by Cubans of highest integrity but smothered by the Cuban press, which is firmly under Batista's thumb. And with such things taking place less than an hour's plane ride from Miami—less than 100 miles from United States soil—these Cubans want their democratic neighbors to know.

Copyright 1958 New York News Inc. Reprinted by permission.

25.   How To Help One's Family

Stories on government are frequently mundane and tedious. Vance Trimble's series on Congressional nepotism is an exception. It is lively, interesting and filled with information. When Trimble wrote the series for Scripps Howard in 1959, it represented a breakthrough in national affairs reporting. One of the more notable qualities of Trimble's writing style is the short paragraphs he uses throughout his work. Even though he has packed a lot of information into the story, he prevents it from looking intimidating to the reader. It is a skillful explanation of a complex issue. *(Pulitzer Prize for National Reporting, 1960)*

Nepotism on Capitol Hill
Vance Trimble
Washington *Daily News*
January 5, 1959

When Rep. Hale Boggs (D., La.) leaves for his Congressional office he doesn't kiss his pretty wife, Corrine, goodbye. She goes with him.

Sen. John Sparkman (D., Ala.) also takes along his wife, Ivo.

Likewise to their husbands' offices go the wives of Reps. James Auchincloss (R., N.J.), Ross Bass (D., Tenn.), John F. Shelley (D., Calif.), Henry O. Talle (R., Iowa), Arthur Winstead (D., Miss.), John Dowdy (D., Tex.).

That doesn't begin to be a complete list.

Forty Congressmen have the Mrs. on their staff.

Daughters work, too. Those of Sen. John A. Carroll (D., Colo.), Rep. Overton Brooks (D., La.), Sen. James O. Eastland (D., Miss.), Sen. Sam J. Ervin Jr., (D., N.C.), Rep. Thomas M. Pelly (R., Wash.), and Sen. Francis Case (R., S.D.) also take up posts at telephones, typewriters or executive desks in their fathers' offices.

They are part of the big daily kinfolk parade to Capitol Hill.

In it are brothers, sisters, sons, nephews, nieces, fathers, uncles, assorted in-laws.

All are on the public payroll.

Some are paid as much as $16,300 a year.

Jefferson opposed it

The 86th Congress convenes Wednesday to start grinding out new laws for all of us, but it's a safe bet the legislators will take no action that disturbs their privilege of putting relatives on the Government payroll.

The reason: At least one of every five of the lawmakers has some kinfolk on his staff.

This is called nepotism. Thomas Jefferson was bitterly against it. Periodically a congressional insurgent tries to stop it. He always loses.

One of the last to try was colorful Rep. Usher Burdick (R., N.D.). After a "kickback" pay scandal in the House in 1950, he proposed a full-scale investigation of "abuses of the payroll privileges of members of Congress.

"They killed it off," Mr. Burdick recalled today. "You can't fight nepotism on Capitol Hill. But it isn't right. Congressmen get enough salary these days. They don't have to put their in-laws on the payroll. Even though it is legal, there are some things a Congressman ought not do."

Mr. Burdick is retiring after 20 years in the House.

"Now that I'm going out of Congress," he said, "I can raise hell about it . I couldn't before."

In the Senate, a sub-committee studying "Ethical Standards in Government" proposed Oct. 17, 1951, that "the employment of relatives as members of Congressional staffs, paid at public expense, should be forbidden by law."

That didn't get far. The chairman of the parent committee, Sen. James E. Murray (D., Mont.), and a member, Sen. Irving Ives (R., N.Y.), employ their sons as their $16,300-a-year-administrative assistants. Sen. Ives retires this week.

Another lost voice was that of Rep. John R. Mitchell (D., Tenn.). As soon as he entered Congress in 1931 he introduced an anti-nepotism bill. He couldn't even get a hearing. He kept after it with new bill after new bill. But with no success.

"Public officials," Mr. Mitchell told his colleagues, "should be free from selfishness. Yet at least 100 members of the House and 50 in the Senate have relatives on their staffs.

"It is a fraud against the taxpayers. Many of these don't even come to Washington. Their pay is just a gift."

Where we actually work

That charge was made a quarter of a century ago, but it is still timely. You hear it repeated not infrequently today when nepotism is mentioned in Capitol Hill offices.

The same idea was voiced the other day by the son of one of the leading Congressmen, Rep. John Taber (R., N.Y.). Charles Taber, 39, former furniture manufacturer who is now the $1112.05-a-month chief aide to his father, told me:

"I suppose people don't think much of this—relatives being on the payroll. I don't think they mind, though, where we actually work. Some of them have their wives on the payroll but they don't even show up at the office."

Do you know that personally? Or do you mean that's just the gossip you've heard around?"

"Oh, no," said Charles Taber. "I know it personally—in at least two cases. But, perhaps, I shouldn't have said that."

The monthly payroll of Representatives is open for public inspection in the House Disbursing Office in the Capitol. It shows to the penny to whom a Congressman hands out his clerk-hire funds.

Senators are more secretive. They publish a report showing the names of their workers, but don't list the pay. Even this is outdated by the time it is made public. For instance, the latest available report is dated Jan. 9, 1958, and covers the period fron July 1, 1956 to June 30, 1957.

Several relatives on the House side draw top pay of $1112.05 monthly. The majority get $400 to $800. There are a few low-paid kinfolk. Rep. James Roosevelt (D., Calif.) has his wife, Irene, who formerly was his secretary, on the payroll at $72.24 a month.

Top Senate pay for administrative assistants is $16,300 a year. Workers usually will not divulge their rate of pay and neither will most of their Senator bosses.

Though the lawmakers get an annual salarly of $22,500, plus liberal funds for travel, postage, telephones, telegrams, etc., and extra income tax deductions, some contend that employing members of the family is an economic necessity.

Genial, hard-working Rep. Boggs readily confirmed that he has had his wife on the payroll for years, and then told me candidly:

"I have three children to send through college. I need the money."

Pays for operation

When the office of Rep. Errett P. Scrivner (R., Kan.), defeated in the last election, was asked to identify J. Lorraine Scrivner who is on the payroll at $132 monthly, an aide said:

"That's Mrs. Scrivner. She had a serious operation during the past year with a bad recurrence—cost about $2000. The boss put her on the payroll—last July, I believe—to make it up."

There's a general contention on Capitol Hill that "the folks back home" do not consider it improper for a member of Congress to hire relatives. Rep. Clair Engle (D., Calif.), whose wife Lucretia has been his $572.78-a-month aide for years, has just been promoted by the California voters to the Senate.

For term after term voters in many states have reelected Congressmen whose wives, sons, daughters, or brothers are known to be paid by the public, even while some act as campaign managers.

Senate Majority Leader Lyndon Johnson's (D., Tex.) brother, Sam Houston Johnson, points out that "I guess everybody in Texas knows I work for Lyndon. I've talked on the phone from here to about two-thirds of the editors down there."

"If a call comes in from Texas and Lyndon is out, the office will always say, "The Senator isn't here; will you talk with his brother?"

"I think Lyndon called the reporters in before he put me on and asked if there would be any objection."

Sam Houston Johnson's wife, Mary (formerly Senator Johnson's secretary), also works in the office.

Some work back home

It isn't uncommon for payrolls to list a relative who works "back home." Sen. Richard B. Russell (D., Ga.) has a nephew, Richard B. III, in charge of his district office at Winder, Ga. Sen. Pat McNamara (D., Mich.) hires wife Mary to run his headquarters in Detroit. Rep. Elmer J. Holland (D., Pa.) has a wife Emily on at $945.16 a month in his Pittsburgh office.

Rep. Milton R. Glenn (R., N.J.) leaves his Atlantic City district office to his brother, Alfred. Rep. Frank C. Osmers Jr. (R., N.J.) lets his wife Margaret handle correspondence in their home at Tenafly, N.J. Her salary is $835.32 a month. Rep. Hugh J. Addonizio (D., N.J.) employs his sister, Ida, in his Orange, N.J., office.

There are many others in that category.

Nevada's lone Congressman, Walter S. Baring (D.), hired his sister, Marjorie, as his Capitol Hill secretary years ago. Then he lost his House seat. When he returned to Congress in 1957, Marjorie had been ordained a minister of the Unity Church in Reno, where she gives sermons in a chapel and conducts a religious school.

At $368.68 a month, Mr. Baring gave her the additional duty of maintaining his "home office" in her chapel. An aide to the Congressman explained: "She keeps us posted on what's going on."

There is a tremendous amount of behind-the-scenes nepotism on Capitol Hill. It isn't difficult to trace relationships where workers have the same family name as a Senator or Representative.

But it could take weeks to ferret out the tie-ins of the countless in-laws stashed away on committee staff payrolls, or in Government departments where lawmakers have powerful influence.

That would be time wasted. The kinfolk parade is not going to be stopped.

Reprinted with permission of Scripps Howard Newspapers.

26.   The Perils of Used-Car Buying

Pulitzer Prizes for news writing have been awarded more often for subject matter and results than for exceptional writing. Some winning articles, however, have combined outstanding investigative reporting with superior writing. Such is Miriam Ottenberg's "Buyer Beware" series, which brought about widespread action to curtail unethical practices of used-car dealers. The following story is told simply and clearly in a first-person narrative. *(Pulitzer Prize for Reporting, No Edition Time, 1960)*

Car Contracts Hook Even Wary Shopper
Miriam Ottenberg
Washington *Star*
November 3, 1959

With a dollar for a down payment, I posed as a used car buyer.

This was the answer I was seeking: Why do so many buyers complain that they thought they were to pay a certain sum for a used car and somehow got finagled into a much larger sum?

To find the answer, a fellow reporter and I chose a lot advertising repossessed cars and $1 down for any car on the lot. Obviously, we did not intend to identify ourselves as reporters. We were posing as a low-paid worker and friend.

As we reached the sidewalk outside the lot, a salesman reached us.

"You folks interested in buying a car?"

I pulled out a newspaper (not The Star) and pointed to the first car on the list—a 1959 Chevrolet, "balance due" $1,235.

He said he didn't have that one. (The newspaper with the ad had then been on the street less than 15 minutes.) He ran his finger down the list of "repossessions" to the fifth car—a 1958 Chevrolet for $1,070.

"We have that," he said, "but you wouldn't want it. It's no good. It used to be a police car."

When I waved the list again and asked to see some other repossessed cars, he took us around to the side and showed us a collection of junk—crumpled fenders, flat tires, missing headlights.

"All these reposssessed cars are like that," he said. "Even if they look all right on the outside, you can't tell. A man can ruin an engine in 20 minutes—driving without oil. It would cost more to repair one of these repossessed cars than to buy one of our good cars. Here, let me show you something you'd like."

I was playing dumb, but I thought I could risk one question.

Pointing again to the ad where it said "assume balance due," I asked, "Doesn't this mean on that Chevy, for instance, that the man had already paid maybe $2,000?"

No, he said, it didn't mean that at all.

"All repossessed cars," he said with authority, "are no good."

He tried to interest us in a shiny blue 1959 Chevrolet which, he said, was a bargain at $1,895. I admired the color but didn't think I could afford it.

We settled on a 1956 Mercury for $1,495, and he offered to drive us around in it. My companion took the wheel and told me later that the brakes were so poor that the car halted only after prolonged pressure.

Complains of price

As we drove, I worried aloud about paying for the car since it was more expensive than what I had come to see.

"I'm not worried about the terms," he assured us expansively. "We can arrange those. That's no problem. All I'm interested in is that you get the car you want."

Before we completed our spin around the block he said I could drive the car home in 10 or 15 minutes. I told him that would be nice.

When we returned to the lot he immediately ushered us into an office with a front and back room, divided by a folding plastic curtain.

He pulled out a data sheet and started asking me questions about my credit. I protested that I didn't want him to write anything down until I had learned how much I had to pay.

"This doesn't mean anything," he said. "We do it all the time. After I get this down we can talk terms."

The credit picture I painted for him didn't make me the sort of risk a bank would rush to finance. But it was good enough for him. He went off and got another man.

We were now in the presence of what is called in the trade the "close-out man."

I told him I wanted to find out how much I would have to pay a month.

Fills out forms

He immediately started filling out forms in a rapid scrawl. I protested that I wanted to know what it would cost me before we went on. He said he could explain easier when it was on paper.

To forestall more questions before he was ready, he kept up a running stream of chatter.

Apparently the salesman had told him I had pressed for a repossessed car.

"The kind of people who buy repossessed cars," he said, "carry a tool box in their car with them; and when the car stops, they just get out and fix it. It's a hobby with them. They enjoy the sense of accomplishment. But you wouldn't want that."

The loud sound of a woman's voice came from the next room. Through the partially closed doors, we could hear her: "I'll go back to the District Building. You tell me one thing, then it's another. You're not going to cheat me. I'm going back and tell them at the District Building."

The close-out man began tapping rapidly with his pen on the glass-topped desk to obscure the voices. When that didn't work, he got up and closed the curtain more firmly.

When he had the papers finished, he asked me about a down payment.

"Well," I said, "your ad says $1 down. I have it with me."

"Of course," he said, "that's only where people's credit is good. Now, I'm sure yours is good, but can't you make a down payment? Don't you have anything?"

$100 in bank

I pointed out that his ad said no payments until 1960. He brushed that aside. Under persistent questioning, I admitted I had $100 in a savings account. He wanted to know how soon I could bring it in. I told him I'd get it when the bank opened.

Now he was ready to show me what he had written on the documents. He had filled out a conditional sales agreement and a car order and bill of sale—complete with his own signature and an X to show where I was to sign.

He had written a cash price of $1,495 and a down payment of $1. In the margin, he had scrawled "pickup payment, $100," with the date I had promised to bring in the money. That would leave $1,394, and that was the amount shown as the balance due.

"Is that all I have to pay?" I asked.

He assured me it was.

Under terms of payment he had written one payment of $394 and a final payment of $1,000—both due the next week.

I was beginning to catch on, but I decided to play dumb a little longer.

"I can't pay $1,394 in a week," I protested. "I don't have all that money."

"Oh, we'll arrange that," he said. "We get you a second mortgage, just like on a house and that takes care of the $394. Then we get the $1,000 financed through a bank."

I asked about finance charges—calling them "interest," which they're not—and insurance charges.

"That's all arranged by the bank," he said. "We have nothing to do with that."

"Well, can you explain how much I have to pay a month?" I asked.

"How much can you pay?"

I told him $55.

He said that was all right and that the payment would be reduced in six or seven months. He said the $55 payment would cover both loans.

"Could you just give me an idea of how much it will all be?"

He rapidly calculated on another sheet of paper. He figured the "interest at 6 per cent" would be $90 a year or $180 for two years. When I reminded him about insurance, he figured that at $44 a year or $88 for two years. Then I did some arithmetic of my own—dividing the total by $55 a month. When it became apparent that I would have to pay longer than two years—particularly if as he said, my payments would be lowered—he hastily moved up the term of payment to 30 months. Then he threw that sheet of calculations away.

Now, I had the answer to my question. I knew why people think they are paying one amount and actually see the contract for that amount—but wind up by paying close to twice as much as they originally bargained for. The answer: Two contracts.

Trap still unsprung

I had asked more questions than the more trusting customers, but on the basis of his answers I could still have gotten trapped. Where had he led me astray?

He knew I couldn't get bank financing, and he never intended to arrange it for me.

He knew he would wind up by arranging the financing through a finance company closely associated with his lot and that the finance charges alone would be closer to 20 per cent than the 6 per cent he had figured out for me.

He knew that once the finance company had my note, the payments would not be lowered in "six or seven months," as he had promised me.

He knew that the insurance coverage would include credit life and probably health and accident insurance along with physical damage insurance and that those combined charges alone would run into hundreds of dollars.

He knew that my combined payments on my small loan and the big note could never be as low as $55 a month for even 30 months as he had represented.

But the contract he offered for my signature showed I would owe $1,494 — the cash price of the car minus a $1 down payment.

None of the charges we had been discussing was on the contract.

Suppose I signed. I knew and he knew that I couldn't fork up $1,494 in a week.

Definite pattern

Dozens of complaints I had been studying presented a definite pattern for the next step.

The used car dealer knows when he accepts a $1 down payment that no finance company will finance the entire balance. A "pick-up payment" of $100 won't satisfy the finance company either.

Usually, the finance company demands a down payment of one-third of the value of the car before it will finance the balance. This may vary from 20 to 40 per cent depending on the car buyer's credit — how good a risk he is.

So money has to be raised to bring the down payment up to the point where the finance company will be willing to finance it.

When the buyer comes in with his $100 pickup payment — as I had said I would do — a salesman drives him to a small loan establishment, usually in Maryland. That is what the close-out man meant when he said he would arrange a "second mortgage like on a house" for me.

(While the handful of unscrupulous used car dealers in the District choose Maryland small loan companies for this phase of their operation, Maryland used car dealers operate under the restrictive Maryland law which controls the amount of financing that may be charged.)

As soon as the car buyer drives away from the small loan place, the salesman demands that he endorse the small loan check over to the used car dealer.

Now, the salesman takes the buyer back to the lot.

The close-out man informs the buyer that he can't get a bank to finance the balance but he can get a finance company to do it. He prepares a new contract.

Earlier figures fade

This time, he spells out the insurance, finance charges and terms of payment. None of the charges bears any resemblance to the earlier verbal assurances.

On my $1,495 car, for instance, the way he had added the additional charges on the piece of paper he destroyed, my total cost would amount to about $1,662. He hadn't put that figure on a contract because it wasn't true.

The new contract would have given me credit for the $100 pick-up payment and the $394 small loan—leaving me a balance of $1,000 to be financed. I would be lucky if I escaped with a debt of less than $1,700—figuring finances and insurance charges. My total cost would now amount to about $2,196.

My down payment would be wiped out. I would be stuck with separate payments on the small loan. If I wanted to keep my monthly payments on the big loan within bounds, I would wind up with a lump sum and that part would be refinanced with more finance and insurance charges.

If I signed the first contract. I would be "hooked." Suppose I refused to sign the second contract. I would lose my $100 "pick-up payment." I would still have to pay off the small loan company for what I had borrowed. And I would be liable to a suit for the difference between my down payment and the total unpaid balance.

Needless to say, I didn't sign the first contract.

Stopped at next lot

In our day of shopping, that was the nearest I got to a contract.

As we approached the second lot and a salesman approached us, a man shouted: "Hold it, Sam!"

The man ran across the lot.

"This little lady is from The Star," he panted. "She wants to write a story. She's an investigator."

When I insisted that I really did want to buy a car—and thanked my stars that he had interrupted before I could go into my masquerade— he chided:

"Look honey, I know you. You're not going to get anything but straight answers from me because I know who you are."

It wasn't the first time I had run into him on a story. He was a former policeman.

© The Washington *Star*.

27.   *A Victim of Mistaken Identity*

A crusading reporter sometimes can make an enormous difference. Such was the case with the Tampa *Tribune's* John Frasca, who investigated the suspicious robbery conviction of twenty-four-year-old Robert Watson. Frasca's dogged reporting ultimately resulted in the release of Watson, sentenced to ten years in prison for a crime he did not commit. Frasca painstakingly interviewed numerous witnesses and put together a series that convinced the state that Watson was innocent. His extensive use of quotes and precise detail makes the following story seem as if it is telling itself and intensifies the impact. *(Pulitzer Prize for Local Investigative Specialized Reporting, 1966)*

Innocent Convict Argues His Case
John Frasca
Tampa *Tribune*
(publication date uncertain) 1965

The young convict leaned forward in his chair and stabbed the reporter with his piercing blue eyes. Where were you at 11 o'clock last night?" he asked.

"Home watching the news on television," the man said.

"Can you prove it?" he said.

"My wife was there," was the answer.

"You're guilty," said the convict. "What the family says doesn't count. You should have had a policeman in the house with you."

Robert Lamar Watson, 24, of Sanford, was making the point that a victim of mistaken identity—which he claims he was—cannot depend on the testimony of loved ones to save him from the accusation of a crime.

He is serving 10 years for robbery of the Kwik Serve store in Mulberry. He said he was in bed at the time of the holdup. His wife, Willadean, so testified in court at Bartow. His mother, Mrs. Grace Burton, who lives next door to the Watsons in Sanford, said she was in the house and saw him go to bed.

Watson was interviewed in the office of the prison road camp in DeLand.

"I just didn't do it," he said. "I never left Sanford that night."

Watson was convicted on the testimony of the two victims of the Kwik Serve robbery—Mrs. Emogene Conley, now living in Lake City, and Mrs. Mary Ann Caveney, of Mulberry. Mrs. Conley was assistant manager of the store the night of March 11 when a tall, blue-eyed gunman entered the building shortly after 11 p.m. and took $900 in cash. Mrs. Caveney, now working in a Mulberry grocery store, was working as a clerk.

"I've learned since that that store always has police protection at closing time," said Watson. "Why would I drive 35 to 90 miles from Sanford to hold up a store that has police protection?"

(The exact mileage from the Watson home in Sanford to the Kwik Serve store in Mulberry is 97 miles, and this reporter made the trip by automobile at night, driving just within the speed limits in an hour and 58 minutes.)

On the night of the robbery, Mulberry Patrolman Dale Kelley stopped by the store at closing time. It was his duty to wait until the receipts were tallied and then he was to escort the women to the bank for a night deposit.

Earlier, about 10 o'clock, both the Mulberry police department and the sheriff's office in Bartow received a report of a disturbance in Bradley. A deputy investigated and reported it was a false alarm. Officials theorize that the call was made in order to reduce the police strength in Mulberry during the time of the theft.

While the women were preparing to lock up, Patrolman Kelley announced he was going to investigate a car that had passed the store in a manner to arouse his suspicion. Minutes after he left, the gunman walked in. The robbery was over in from five to eight minutes, police said.

"How was I supposed to know that on this one night, the policeman would be away from the store for a few minutes?" asked Watson. "You mean, I drove all the way from Sanford on the chance that the officer would not be there?"

The two victims said the bandit had a blue rag around his neck and that he pulled it to eye-level shortly after he jerked out his pistol. They said he had "very blue eyes."

Mrs. Conley and Mrs. Caveney were shown photographs in the county's "rogues' gallery" but did not find the man who robbed them. Several days later, they identified Watson separately from two photographs which a deputy took to their homes.

The two pictures came from a file in the sheriff's office. Watson had been placed on probation for 10 years as a youth after he pleaded guilty—without representation by an attorney—to three charges following a 10-day spree with several teen-age companions in Bartow in February 1961. He had been charged with auto theft and arson. The other young man also had previous difficulty with the police.

The photographs were hauled out after a deputy sheriff asked a police informer if he knew anybody who was "tall, blond and had very blue eyes." The informer reportedly said "It sounds like it could be the Watson boy."

Officials in both Polk and Seminole counties reported, incidently, that Watson had steered free of trouble since his 1961 misadventures. Only two minor traffic violations were charged to his account.

Although the women were positive on the stand that Watson was the armed robber, they testified they did not know which had held the gun. Also, they said they didn't know whether or not he wore gloves.

"I just wasn't in Mulberry that night," said Watson. "I was doing all right. I was getting by."

"I used to cash his paychecks," said Albert C. Mims, Sanford filling station operator. "He averaged from $130 to $200 a week on his construction job. He had some checks that went over $200."

"If he needed money, he could have come to me," said R.A. McIntosh, his uncle, also of Sanford. "He was over at my house all the time. The fact is, he was getting along just fine. He was paying his bills and he was making a nice life for his family."

"I finished my work early that day, March 11," said Watson, "and I did some work in the garden that evening."

"He was working out there until after dark," said R.W. Wheatland, a neighbor. "I remember it because he was setting out some plants with his wife, mother and two little boys. He was spreading manure from his pick-up truck. That's how I remember it was March 11. He went after the manure on that day."

"After working around the yard, I went to the gas station," said Watson.

"That's right," said Mims. "He used to come around about 7:30 every night to buy gas for his car or his pickup truck. He used to get it on credit. That's why I know he was here on March 11. We had a ticket for that day. He got $2 worth of gasoline. If he was planning to go to rob a place in Mulberry, why wouldn't he have filled the tank?

"Besides, why should anybody from Sanford go to Mulberry to steal anything? They have all kinds of places around here that are just as easy to rob. Besides, some of them don't have all that police protection that the Mulberry store had."

Mike Morris, an attendant in Mims' station, said he remembered the time Watson had his automobile refueled "because I was checking up for the night, and I usually do this about 7:30 every night."

"He stayed around for 20 or 30 minutes," said Morris. "He was helping Mr. Mims on the rack."

"There was a Cadillac in there," said Mims, "and I wasn't feeling too well. Robert told me I shouldn't be working and he helped me grease it.

"Robert is one of the nicest boys in town, one of the finest. He wouldn't do a thing like they say he did. If he needed money—and I know how well he was doing, he could have come to me and got what he needed in a minute."

"It was between 7:30 and 8 when I left the station," said Watson, "and I drove out to uncle's house."

"He spent a lot of time with me that day," said McIntosh. "It was easy to remember the date, because that was the day my son, Bobbie, got a Corvette. Robert drove it around some when he got home from work, before he went after a load of manure for his garden."

"I left my uncle's place about 8:30 or so," said Watson, "and I went home. My wife and mother were there watching television."

"I was waiting on some customers," said his nephew, Bobbie McIntosh, 19, manager of a service station. "Jonathon Kelly, my buddy, was sitting out front. It was real dark by then. I heard a car horn and heard Jonathon say, 'Hey, Robert.' I turned around and saw Robert drive by. He waved at me."

"It was 9 o'clock or so when he got home," said his mother. "Dr. Kildaire had just started on television. Robert sat and watched it for a half-hour or so and then he went to bed.

"It was the last commercials before the last part began," said his wife. "Robert said he couldn't wait until the end because he was too tired.

"He was home all that night. How does anybody know if a man is home or not if his family doesn't? If they don't believe the family then anybody can be arrested."

Earlier, Mims asked the same question in a different way:

"The way that is, anybody can come to my house and arrest me, or anybody, and it doesn't matter what the family has to say about it. How can a man prove he's home if they won't take the word of his wife or his family.

"Who else is supposed to be home with him?"

The neighbors and friends of Robert Lamar Watson insist he was in Sanford the night of the Kwik Serve robbery. His boss, T.J. Leggett, Daytona Beach contractor, helped raise the money to hire an attorney. Watson borrowed the rest from his mother.

"He didn't have any money for any big expenses," said his mother. "He made enough to pay his bills and to live comfortably, but he couldn't lay his hands on any big amount.

"If he robbed that store in Mulberry, where is the $900?"

At his trial in Bartow, the State contended that Watson drove the 97 miles from Sanford to Mulberry to rob the Kwik Serve store—despite the fact that the store always—until that night—had police escort service. The state did not say how Watson came to be in Mulberry.

"I was taking Robert's sister, Betty, home from a date," said Terry Smith, a Sanford bank employe. "It was about 10:30 or 11 that night. She lives with his mother right next door. As you come around the corner, the headlights shine on the Watson yard.

"I saw his car, his mother's car and his pickup truck parked there."

"How could he have been in Mulberry that night?" asked McIntosh. "He was up early the next morning and worked all day at his job and then he worked with me from 7 o'clock that night to 1 the next morning. He didn't act like a man who had been up half the night driving about 200 miles and robbing a store.

"I went over to Daytona Beach to buy a welding machine. George Dangleman and I bought it together. When we got it back to Sanford, we saw it needed a lot of work. So I got Robert to help us straighten it out."

Meantime, the doubts that Watson committed the Kwik Serve crime continued to grow in Polk County. They were planted two weeks after his conviction when a similar armed robbery occurred in Mulberry. This time, a "tall, masked gunman" held up the manager of a supermarket and his police escort, Patrolman Kelley, near the night deposit box of a Mulberry bank. He got $1,600 in cash.

The thief also disappeared as quickly and as silently as the robber in the Kwik Serve case. In each incident, the bandit wore coveralls. Police and sheriff's deputies were on the road in search of the culprit within minutes, in each case—and one police theory is that the bandit never left Mulberry on the nights the crimes were committed.

"Hardly anybody is on the highway out this way that late at night," said one officer. "We had the area pretty well patrolled. We would have seen any suspicious car."

Watson said he plans to appeal the case but "right now I'm waiting and praying they catch the right man."

His mother said the reason there has been no appeal yet is "because we're out of money."

"We don't know what to do," she said. "Robert never did it, and nobody will listen to us. I borrowed everywhere I could for the trial in Bartow, and then there was all that expense of going back and forth. We don't have anything any more. If it wasn't for our friends, I don't know what we'd do.

"I'm just getting by, now, with what money the county pays me for taking care of two nursing patients. Robert's wife has applied for welfare but hasn't got it yet. The county gave her one patient to take care of."

"You can't imagine what all of this has done to that family," said Mims. "They were getting along just fine. They had everything they wanted. Now they're broke and having a terrible time trying to get along."

His mother asked the reporter how Robert was "taking it" in prison.

"He's pretty bitter," he said.

"Well," she said, shaking her head hopelessly, her hands held out imploringly, "what can we do?"

Reprinted by permission of the Tampa *Tribune.*

28. *The Innocent Freed*

Gene Miller's writing has the knack of taking the reader to the scene of the story, especially through the use of pointed, revealing direct quotation. Combined with the quotation, his use of descriptive details gives life and intimacy to stories. Following are two stories which helped Miller win the Pulitzer Prize twice for reporting which helped to free innocent people convicted of crime. *(Pulitzer Prize for Local Investigative Specialized Reporting, 1967; Local General Spot News Reporting, 1976)*

Will Mary Hampton's Real Story Be Told?
Gene Miller
Miami *Herald*
August 21, 1966

For the first time this week, the bizarre circumstances behind the conviction of Mary Katherin Hampton for murder may begin to emerge from a witness stand in a courtroom.

By law, she is presumed guilty. For 5 ½ years she has been in prison.

A habeas corpus hearing is set for 9 a.m. Thursday in the town of Plaquemine, La. It is near Baton Rouge. Never before has a single word of testimony been spoken from a witness stand.

It is the letter of the law in the United States, of course, that the accused is presumed innocent until proven guilty. The doctrine is basic.

A policeman's suspicion, or for that matter a prosecutor's belief, must withstand the objectivity of public trial.

In Louisiana in 1961, a teenage girl terrified of trial, pleaded guilty to two murders, believing this was her only escape from conviction and electrocution.

Thus, she waived her right to trial.

This is the plight of Mary Hampton, now 24 years old. Without delving here into the reasons behind her plea, there is much that can be said about a homicide investigation by sheriff deputies from the parishes of St. Charles and St. Mary.

For three days during that year of 1961, Louisiana deputies interrogated a man awaiting execution at Ralford Prison in Florida.

His name is Emmitt Monroe Spencer, and by any standard, those interrogations comprise one of the most peculiar confessions ever to come from a Death Row call in Florida, if not the nation.

Willingly, with perceptible glee upon occasion, Spencer told of murderous atrocities supposedly committed in state after state. Always he blamed Mary Hampton, depicting her a sexually depraved and utterly ruthless savage.

No newspaper could print the obscenities of his description. He seethed with hatred for Mary Hampton, who had lived with him 11 months, bore his son, and testified against him.

Yet Spencer remained oddly good natured. "If I get the chair in Louisiana on crimes committed there, then I'll walk in and try to help the gentlemen strap me in," he said.

The Louisiana deputies tape recorded all this on Feb. 5, 1961 and March 17 and 18, 1961. Publication was never their intent.

"If I have to destroy this tape, I will not give it to anyone that would give it to the newspapers," the voice of Howard Beebe declares on tape. Unknown to Deputy Beebe, a transcript from the tapes later found distribution.

In a rambling narrative, Spencer told Deputy Beebe and Deputy L.M. Grainer of more murders than they appeared to be interested in. "I'm not going up to solve any crimes not in my territory," Deputy Beebe announced.

Spencer, it seems, had provided the deputies with a few Louisiana "murders" they knew nothing about. He was good at this.

Mary Hampton, said Spencer, lifted her skirt to entice a male motorist in Louisiana. When the man stopped, she flung open the door and shot him to death with a .25 automatic and ..."oooooo, now that was wet," he said.

Because of the bloodiness, Mary Hampton, he, and "Tex," a homosexual hitchhiker accomplice, had to remove their clothing, he said. According to Spencer, they cavorted in the nude for an orgy, then "Tex" jumped on the dead man "and hollered he's Tarzan, flopping his arms up and down and making noises like Tarzan makes at the movies."

Logically, a flaw in the story might have bothered the deputies; namely, no one ever found a body. Indeed, no one had ever heard of "Tex" either.

Unchallenged, Spencer kept right on talking. Near Kaplan or Abbeville, La., he said, Mary Hampton murdered a woman "wearing a brownish gray rabbit fur" and abandoned the corpse "on the side of the road." They killed a man in New Orleans, too, he said.

And here, again, no one found any bodies; no one reported anyone missing.

Presumably, the deputies didn't concern themselves with such inconsistencies for they had two very real murders—unsolved for 15 months. To a policeman, an unsolved murder can be a keen source of frustration.

For the deputies, Spencer solved everything.

Sometime in the early morning hours of Dec. 31, 1959, someone fired a bullet into the right frontal lobe of Benjamin Yount, 48, the district supervisor of drilling for the Pan American Petroleum Corp. This occurred in the back room of a bar on U.S. 90 near the town of Boutte southwest of New Orleans. Apparently Yount had stopped at the bar on his way home from the oil fields.

The smashed lead pellet removed from the brain in autopsy weighed 25.1 grains. Ballistic examination indicated it came from a .22 caliber weapon.

When Yount, mortally wounded, was first discovered that morning by a clean-up man, the barmaid was missing. Police surmised that she had either killed Yount and fled or that someone had killed her, too.

She was Hermine Fiedler, 37, a recent immigrant from Germany, and on Jan. 4, 1960 her body was found 75 miles away in a marshy thicket near a spillway levee about six miles north of Patterson, La. She, too, had been shot once in the skull with a .22 caliber gun.

What did Spencer know about the crimes? Everything, he said.

In his tape-recorded discourse, he gave the deputies leads to 30 specific individuals who could link him and Mary Hampton to the murders or their whereabouts in the vicinity at the time.

Spencer said he saw two customers arguing and shaking their fingers at each other inside the bar. He said a drunk old man, shoving open the door, knocked down Mary Hampton, and that he cursed him and started to pull his gun. Spencer said he picked up a lady at the bar and gave her a ride to Gretna, a suburb of New Orleans.

The deputies never found any of these people.

Spencer said he had a voltage regulator taken from a jeep and put into his Renault Dauphine in the nearby town of Donaldsonville on his way to the bar. This was a specific and somewhat unusual act; if true, it should have been subject to corroboration. The deputies didn't find such a garage man.

Spencer said he bought a sports shirt in Hahnville, La. and a waitress with "very bad varicose veins" in that town served them. Two other assorted clerks saw them, he said, one of whom sold him a bottle of merthiolate in the town of Morgan City, La. He had scratches on his arms, he said, and the clerk said "Thank God, you don't have them on your face cause you'd look like an Indian."

The deputies found no one.

In Leesville, La., Spencer said he had sexual relations with two women, one a prostitute, and one a "one-armed" woman named "Peggy Bush." He played shuffle board with "Peggy's mother, Gladys Bush," at a bar there, he said.

Deputies found neither prostitute, Peggy, nor her mother.

At one juncture, Spencer claimed that he and Mary Hampton didn't commit the murders alone, but that there was a great conspiracy.

He named six accomplices: "Joe Anderson," or "Tex," a hitch-hiker; "Thelma Goins Spencer," his own lame ex-wife; a "dope fiend" from the New Orleans suburb of Westwego; the dope fiend's girl friend "who had a name like President Kennedy's wife, Jacqueline," a relative of "Tex" named "Billy," and finally "Billy's" girl friend a "notorious blonde hustler from Lake Charles."

Deputies failed to find "Tex," "Thelma," "the dope fiend," "Jacqueline," "Billy," or the hustler."

Spencer made sure, however, that they could find Mary Hampton. He drew them a map so they could find her home in Sandy Hook, Ky.

The deputies pressed for leads about the whereabouts of "Tex," and Spencer informed them that "Tex's" mother, father, and young sister, whom he said he had impregnated, all lived together in Meridian, Miss. None was located.

Spencer said that he, Mary Hampton, "Thelma," and "Tex" held the barmaid captive for three days in a motel in Morgan City, La., and that a gas station attendant in Boutte noticed his "little bitty car all the way from California."

The deputies found no motel clerk in Morgan City (pop. 13,540) who remembered the party. Spencer had indeed driven a small foreign-made car from California in December 1959. But no gas station man in Boutte remembered it. The population of Boutte in 1960 was 155.

On the public street in Morgan City Spencer had his ex-wife "Thelma" swinging her crutch at an "uppity Negro." Later, according to Spencer, "Thelma" told a waitress who inquired of her lame leg that "a Mack truck hit me."

The deputies found neither Negro nor waitress, nor for that matter, another woman in Meridian, Miss. with whom "Thelma" had another battle royal with her crutch.

On his way to mayhem in Boutte, Spencer dated a DeRidder, La. restaurant owner, he said, and they took along her 13-year-old daughter. He stood her up for a second date, he said. They too, are among the missing.

During the three taped interviews, Spencer gave the deputies the name of one man who is positively alive.

From Boutte, during the commission of the two murders, Spencer said he telephoned a well-known disc jockey named "John R" at radio station WLAC in Nashville, Tenn.

Spencer said he requested "I'll be Glad When You're Dead, You Rascal You."

John R. is John Reihbourg, and reached in Nashville by this

newspaper reporter a few days ago, he said he didn't remember such a call. Richbourg said he was positive no law enforcement officer ever inquired about the matter.

On the word of Spencer, and Spencer alone, the Louisiana deputies swore out first-degree murder charges against Mary Katherin Hampton. They took her into custody in Sandy Hook, Ky. on Feb. 26, 1961, returned to Louisiana, and jailed her in Hahnville.

For 43 days, until April 11, 1961, Mary Hampton professed innocence. On the 44th day, believing she would be convicted and electrocuted she entered a plea of "guilty without capital punishment."

Thus collapsed her legal presumption of innocence. The State of Louisiana had not found it necessary to prove a word. Spencer, quite accurately, had predicted, "All Louisiana does is throw in the cards and rake in the pot."

Reprinted with permission of the Miami *Herald.*

In 1976 Gene Miller won his second Pulitzer Prize for reporting. As with his 1967 Prize, his 1976 award was for work that helped free innocent convicts.

Pitts, Lee Walk as Free Men
Gene Miller
Miami *Herald*
September 20, 1975

FLORIDA STATE PRISON—Freddie Lee Pitts and Wilbert Lee walked away from the shadow of death at 37 minutes after noon Friday. They did not look back.

The clamorous din of men behind bars faded behind them. A wave of men behind cameras receded before them.

Unsmiling, Pitts and Lee acknowledged neither.

After 12 years and 48 days imprisonment for another man's crime, they walked into the world, free men, a Xerox copy of the governor's pardon folded in their billfolds.

"I've had enough of this hotel," Pitts said mildly. "They have very poor accommodations."

"I've got my prison clothes off and I've got my free world clothes on," said Lee, " and gee, baby, I feel like a Philadelphia lawyer."

They left with immediate plans. They did not announce them.

"I think we'll keep that to ourselves," Lee said.

Their lawyers, Irwin J. Block and Phillip A. Hubbart, drove them to Gainesville where they boarded a Boeing 727 to Miami.

Lee was apprehensive. It was his first time in the air.

"For nine years I was facing the electric chair," he said. "I guess I can face the airplane."

He did. At 29,000 feet he grinned. "The spirit's got me."

Pitts sipped on a Jack Daniel's and 7-Up. "Look at me now, Leo Jones," he said.

It was Panhandle prosecutor Jones who kept an all-white Panhandle jury from hearing the confession of another man to the 1963 murders of Mo-Jo gasoline stations attendants Jesse Burkett and Grover Floyd Jr.

Pitts and Lee had been convicted of those crimes nine years earlier. Jones' jury convicted them again.

That confession was ultimately heard by Gov. Reubin Askew, who last week initiated full pardon proceedings for the two black men.

The pardon said they were free. Freedom was a condition they came to understand only gradually Friday.

In the back seat of a rental car carrying him to the airport, Lee studied a Florida State trooper escort cruiser through the back window.

"This is the way I came in," he said. "And this is the way I'm leaving."

He raised his arms and stared at his wrists. "Look," he said. "No handcuffs."

All morning long they had waited restlessly for a telephone call from Tallahassee.

Lee had not slept much the night before. That was not unusual. He seldom does. It is Pitts who can sleep almost at will, awaking only when footsteps stop outside his cell. They slept in cells with a view of prison steel.

"It's been a long time since I've seen the moon and the stars and breathed fresh air," Lee said.

The electronic cell door had been closed behind them for the last time Thursday night by a fat and friendly guard, D.A. Spron.

"You ain't free yet, boy," he deadpanned. Then he grinned.

"My civil rights don't begin until I get into that parking lot," Pitts said agreeably.

Early Friday morning they traded prison blue for splashy sports clothes. A Miami television reporter, C.T. Taylor, had arranged the gift of clothing from a Liberty City boutique.

Bob and Mary Thomas of the Pitts-Lee Defense Committee had guessed at measurements. They guessed too long on the slacks: dark green for Lee, dark blue for Pitts, slightly flared. Mary Thomas borrowed green thread from the Holiday Inn desk clerk in Starke.

The alterations were made, however, by a civilian prison tailor, Leonard McElhenny. He handed the slacks, shortened, to Pitts and Lee and bade them farewell. He had tears in his eyes.

They wore their bright new clothes into the waxed and glistening visitors room where 81 newsmen waited for their stories. Eighteen television cameras whirred as Pitts and Lee took their place before a tangle of microphones at a blue-draped table.

They matter-of-factly fielded questions. They were not loquacious. "I've been locked up for 12 years," Lee said behind dark glasses.

"It'll take me a few days to describe what's going through my mind."

Someone asked Pitts how it felt to lose 12 years. "The past is useful as a guide to prevent future mistakes," he said. "Other than that I don't live in the past."

Was he bitter? "I think I can have a certain degree of bitterness," he nodded. "But animosity and hatred...no."

After the press conference they returned to prison classification officer Ken Snover's sterile office.

He handed each a Xerox copy of the governor's executive order of pardon. It bore the necessary four signatures of Askew, Attorney General Robert Shevin, Treasurer Philip Ashler and Education Commissioner Ralph Turlington.

Three other Cabinet officials, Comptroller Gerald Lewis, Secretary of State Bruce Smathers, and Agriculture Commissioner Doyle Conner, had decided not to sign.

"All you've got to say," Snover said, "is that you accept it."

Pitts, now 31, Lee, now 40, accepted. Each folded up his copy and put it in his billfold.

They declined the customary offer of non-negotiable bus tickets.

"No bus will go fast enough," Lee said.

They opened their last day's prison mail, a pile of letters and telegrams. One letter contained a "Free Pitts and Lee" button. Pitts pinned it to his shirt collar.

They gave Snover a temporary forwarding address: Post Office Box 872, Opa-locka, Fla., 33054.

Two telephone calls would free them. They paced nervously.

Pitts borrowed the telephone and, as promised, made a collect call to

Freemont, Calif. He asked for Chris Burkett, the eldest son of the murdered Jesse Burkett.

The son does not believe the two black men killed his father. He had intervened in their behalf.

"Yeah," said Pitts, "We're finally getting out."

Burkett invited them to stay at his California home if they ever came west. "I'll be looking forward to it," Pitts replied.

Twelve o'clock came and went without a telephone call. "When it's 12:30," Block joked, "we're leaving. It would be a terrible thing to shoot a man in the back who's been pardoned."

The word came first by teletype. The prison phone lines were tied up by newsmen.

At 12:25 p.m. a call came confirming the pardon.

"We've got it," said Block.

"Let's get the hell out of here," said Hubbart.

"What's your hurry?" said Block. "You've got your whole life ahead of you, Freddie."

Pitts grinned. "Let's go to Disney World," he said.

Steel gates opened before them as they walked down a broad and lengthy corridor.

As the gates ground closed behind them, they stepped into the sunlight and walked the last 30 feet to the last two chain-link fences.

Two guard dogs, positioned there, snoozed in the heat of the day.

Then they walked into the world.

One of their final farewells had come from another one-time Death Row inmate, convicted killer Dennis Whitney.

"You going back to Port St. Joe, Freddie?" Whitney asked.

They are not.

Reprinted with permission of the Miami *Herald.*

29.   *Behind the My Lai Massacre*

Seymour Hersh's investigative series on the murder of civilians in the Vietnam village of My Lai provides a cogent explanation within a clear narrative of the episode. Following is the first article from the multi-part series. Notable is its effective use of quotations for description, analysis, and differing points of view. In uncovering the details of the massacre, Hersh worked as a free-lance reporter; to get his articles published in newspapers, he and a friend set up their own small news service—with Hersh as its only reporter. *(Pulitzer Prize for International Reporting, 1970)*

Lieutenant Accused of Murdering 109 Civilians
Seymour M. Hersh
Dispatch News Service
November 13, 1969

FORT BENNING, Ga.—Lt. William L. Calley Jr., 26 years old, is a mild mannered, boyish-looking Vietnam combat veteran with the nickname "Rusty." The Army is completing an investigation of charges that he deliberately murdered at least 109 Vietnamese civilians in a search-and-destroy mission in March 1968 in a Viet Cong stronghold known as "Pinkville."

Calley has formally been charged with six specifications of mass murder. Each specification cites a number of dead adding up to the 109 total, and charges that Calley did "with premeditation mur-der...Oriental human beings, whose names and sex are unknown, by shooting them with a rifle."

The Army calls it murder; Calley, his counsel and others associated with the incident describe it as a case of carrying out orders.

"Pinkville" has become a widely known code word among the military and in a case that many officers and some Congressmen believe will become far more controversial than the recent murder charges against eight Green Berets.

Year's investigation

Army investigation teams spent nearly one year studying the incident before filing charges against Calley, a platoon leader of the Eleventh Brigade of the Americal Division at the time of the killings.

Calley was formally charged on or about Sept. 6, 1969, in the multiple deaths, just a few days before he was due to be released from active service.

Calley has since hired a prominent civilian attorney, former Judge George W. Latimer of the U.S. Court of Military Appeals, and is now awaiting a military determination of whether the evidence justifies a general court-martial. Pentagon officials describe the present stage of the case as the equivalent of a civilian grand jury proceeding.

Calley, meanwhile, is being detained at Fort Benning, where his movements are sharply restricted. Even his exact location on the base is a secret; neither the provost marshal nor the Army's Criminal Investigation Division knows where he is being held.

The Army has refused to comment on the case, "in order not to prejudice the continuing investigation and rights of the accused." Similarly, Calley—although agreeing to an interview—refused to discuss in detail what happened on March 16, 1968.

However, many other officers and civilian officials, some angered by Calley's action and others angered that charges of murder were filed in the case, talked freely in interviews at Fort Benning and Washington.

Facts agreed on

These facts are not in dispute:

The Pinkville area, about six miles northeast of Quang Ngai, had been a Viet Cong fortress since the Vietnam war began. In early February 1968, a company of the Eleventh Brigade, as part of Task Force Barker, pushed through the area and was severely shot up.

Calley's platoon suffered casualties. After the Communist Tet offensive in February 1968, a larger assault was mounted, again with high casualties and little success. A third attack was quickly mounted, and it was successful.

The Army claimed 128 Viet Cong were killed. Many civilians also were killed in the operation. The area was a free fire zone. Such zones are common throughout Vietman.

One man who took part in the mission with Calley said that in the earlier two attacks "we were really shot up."

"Every time we got hit it was from the rear," he said. "So the third time in there the order came down to go in and make sure no one was behind.

"We were told to just clear the area. It was a typical combat assault formation. We came in hot, with a cover of artillery in front of us, came down the line and destroyed the village.

"There are always some civilian casualties in a combat operation. He isn't guilty of murder."

The order to clear the area was relayed from the battalion commander to the company commander to Calley, the source said.

Calley's attorney said in an interview: "This is one case that should never have been brought. Whatever killing there was was in a firefight in connection with the operation.

"You can't afford to guess whether a civilian is a Viet Cong or not. Either they shoot you or you shoot them.

"This case is going to be important—to what standard do you hold a combat officer in carrying out a mission?

"There are two instances where murder is acceptable to anybody: where it is excusable and where it is justified. If Calley did shoot anybody because of the tactical situation or while in a firefight, it was either excusable or justifiable."

Adding to the complexity of the case is the fact that investigators from the Army inspector general's office, which conducted the bulk of the investigation, considered filing charges against at least six other men involved in the action March 16.

A Fort Benning infantry officer has found that the facts of the case justify Calley's trial by general court-martial on charges of premeditated murder.

Pentagon officials said that the next steps are for the case to go to Calley's brigade commander and finally to the Fort Benning post commander for findings on whether there should be a court-martial. If they so hold, final charges and specifications will be drawn up and made public at that time, the officials said.

Calley's friends in the officer corps at Fort Benning, many of them West Point graduates, were indignant. However, knowing the high stakes of the case, they expressed their outrage in private.

"They're using this as a god-damned example," one officer complained. "He is a good soldier. He followed orders.

"There weren't any friendlies in the village. The orders were to shoot anything that moved."

Another officer said, "It could happen to any of us. He had killed and seen a lot of killing....Killing becomes nothing in Vietnam. He knew that there were civilians there, but he also knew that there were VC among them."

A third officer, also familiar with the case, said: "There's this question—I think anyone who goes to Nam asks it. What's a civilian? Someone who works for us by day and puts on Vietcong pajamas at night?"

There is another side of the Calley case—one that the Army cannot disclose. Interviews have brought out the fact that the investigation into the Pinkville affair was initiated six months after the incident, only after some of the men who served under Calley complained.

The Army has photographs purported to be of the incident, although these have not been introduced in evidence in the case and may not be.

"They simply shot up this village, and (Calley) was the leader of it," said one Washington source. "When one guy refused to do it, Calley took the rifle away and did the shooting himself."

Asked about this, Calley refused to comment.

One Pentagon officer discussing the case tapped his knee with his hand and remarked, "Some of those kids he shot were this high. I don't think they were Vietcong. Do you?"

A source of amazement among all those interviewed was that the story has yet to reach the press. "Pinkville has been a word among GIs for a year," one official said. "I'll never cease to be amazed that it hasn't been written about before."

A high-ranking officer commented that he first heard talk of the Pinkville incident soon after it happened; the officer was on duty in Saigon at the time.

Why did the Army choose to prosecute this case? On what is it basing the charge that Calley acted with premeditation before killing? The court-martial should supply the answers to these questions, but some of the men already have their opinions.

"The Army knew it was going to get clobbered on this at some point," one military source commented. "If they don't prosecute somebody if this stuff comes out without the Army taking some action, it could be even worse."

War tribunals mentioned

Another view that many held was that the top level of the military was concerned about possible war crime tribunals after the Vietnam war.

As for Calley—he is smoking four packs of cigarettes daily and getting out of shape. He is 5-foot-3, slender, with expressionless gray eyes and thinning brown hair. He seems slightly bewildered and hurt by the charges against him. He says he wants nothing more than to be cleared and return to the Army.

"I know this sounds funny," he said in an interview, "but I like the Army...and I don't want to do anything to hurt it."

Friends described Calley as a "gung-ho Army man...Army all the way." Ironically, even his staunchest supporters admit, his enthusiasm may be somewhat to blame.

"Maybe he did take some order to clear out the village a little bit too literally," one friend said, "but he's a fine boy."

Had high ratings

Calley had been shipped home early from Vietnam, after the Army refused his request to extend his tour of duty. Until the incident at

Pinkville, he had received nothing but high ratings from his superior officers. He was scheduled to be awarded the Bronze and Silver Stars for his combat efforts, he said. He has heard nothing about the medals since arriving at Fort Benning.

Calley was born in Miami, Fla., and flunked out of Palm Beach Junior College before enlisting in the Army. He became a second lieutenant in September 1967, shortly after going to Vietnam. The Army lists his home of record as Waynesville, N.C.

An information sheet put out by the public affairs officer of the Americal Division the day after the March 16 engagement contained this terse mention of the incident: "The swiftness with which the units moved into the area surprised the enemy. After the battle the Eleventh Brigade moved into the village searching each hut and tunnel."

Reprinted by permission of Seymour Hersh.

30.   "Profiteers of Human Suffering"

It is important in newswriting to grab the reader's interest quickly at the beginning of an in-depth series. The following piece is the introduction to a six-part expose written by the Chicago *Tribune's* William Jones on the shabby state of ambulance service in the city. The story fits the bill for a quality intro piece. It is dramatic and informative and makes the reader want to stick with the story for more. Jones obtained a permit and worked undercover as an ambulance operator in the course of researching his story. For two months he observed first-hand the abysmal conditions in Chicago's ambulance industry. *(Pulitzer Prize for Local Investigative Specialized Reporting, 1971)*

Men of Mercy? Profit in Pain
William Jones
Chicago *Tribune*
June 7, 1970

They are the misery merchants, and they prowl the streets of our city 24 hours a day as profiteers of human suffering.

Waiting in filthy garages scattered throughout the city, they prey on families with an urgent need for transportation and medical care for a loved one.

They are the hustlers among the city's private ambulance operators, and they are waiting for your call for help.

Their business is big business in Chicago. The multimillion-dollar industry accounts for nearly 1 million dollars of Cook County's welfare fees each year.

At the same time, the misery merchants are exacting a toll in needless suffering and sadistic treatment of the ill that may never be inventoried.

Play Russian roulette

You may have to call the misery merchants this afternoon or tomorrow or next week. When you do, a member of your family may be gasping after a heart attack or screaming in agony after fracturing a hip or leg. As you frantically leaf thru the telephone directory to find an ambulance company, you unwittingly will be playing a game of Russian roulette with the person you are trying to help.

The stakes are high. If you are poor or black or on welfare, they are even higher. I know because I worked as a misery merchant, and this is how they operate:

1. A middle-aged man lies gasping from an apparent heart attack in his north side apartment. His throat makes a rasping sound as he desperately tries to continue breathing. A two-man ambulance crew stands over his body, arguing with a friend of the victim that the $40 fee must be paid before the man is placed on the stretcher. They are told the victim has only two dollars in cash. The crew shrugs, then lifts the still gasping man onto a kitchen chair where he slumps across the table. As they walk out of the apartment one of the attendants reaches across the table and pockets the two dollars.

A plea ignored

2. An elderly black man, his body wracked with cancer, pleads with a

private ambulance crew to handle him gently because even the slightest pressure causes extreme pain. The attendant in charge ignores his plea and grabs the man under the arms, drags him across the floor to the stretcher, and drops the patient. As the old man's face contorts in agony and breaks into a sweat, the attendant mutters to his fellow worker: "Next time the guy will walk to the stretcher."

3. An epileptic with a fractured hip lies in the rear of a police squad car for nearly two hours until a private ambulance firm that makes payoffs to the policemen is able to respond to the call. Instead of taking the victim to the hospital in the squad car, the police spend a dime to call a misery merchant. Then they wait until the ambulance— and the $10 payoff—arrive. When the ambulance finally responds, the victim is ordered to crawl from the squad car onto the stretcher. Hospital records later will be falsified to show that the victim was picked up at a neighbor's home.

She looks all right

4. An ambulance crew demands that a northwest side housewife with a broken leg write out a $49 check as she lies in the hospital. When she complains that the pain is making it difficult for her to perform the task, they fill out the check and hand it back to her to sign.

5. An ambulance driver hurls insults at a black woman while her daughter waits for emergency transportation after suffering a miscarriage. The daughter is screaming. "She looks all right," the ambulance driver decides. "She can walk down the stairs." The apartment is on the third floor. It is raining, and once outside the victim is ordered to crawl into the ambulance thru a side door.

These are a few of the incidents observed during a two-month investigation of the misery merchants by *The Tribune* and the Better Government association. The probe was prompted by complaints from other ambulance operators who told of payoffs to police and firemen, welfare fraud, and sadistic treatment of the ill and injured.

Feared a scandal

They feared a scandal that would damage the entire industry and volunteered their cooperation to end the activities.

Working with George Bliss, B.G.A. chief investigator, I obtained a city ambulance license. My partner in the undercover probe was William Recktenwald, one of Bliss' top investigators.

Despite warnings of what we would find as ambulance attendants, neither of us was ready for what we found in the world of misery merchants.

"It was the most sickening display of mistreatment of human beings I have ever encountered," Recktenwald reported. "I would go home completely outraged at what I had seen and heard." At one point, Recktenwald walked off the job after 31 hours on duty with only 40 minutes sleep. "I just couldn't take any more," he said.

Threatened with beating

At the same firm, several days earlier, an owner became suspicious of my credentials and threatened me with a beating if the company learned I was a private investigator. I managed to talk my way thru an interrogation by several employees and finished my 24-hour shift with the company. The owner will not know until he reads this story how correct his instincts were.

The world of the misery merchant is a life filled with 24-hour shifts stacked on top of 24-hour shifts at pay rates as low as 87 cents an hour. Much of the time is spent in filthy, rat-infested store fronts, waiting for calls from the company dispatcher. Your companions, for the most part, are people who entertain each other with bizarre stories about their treatment of the sick and suffering.

One ambulance driver recalled how he became angered at a fireman who called his firm with a heart attack case. The fireman called the company even though the ambulance had to travel across the city to answer the call, because the company deals in $10 payoffs for welfare referrals.

A chewing out

"I ran it (arrived at the victim's home) in 35 minutes," the driver said. "When I arrived the fireman was screaming at me; so I told the fireman I'll keep the $10 and you keep the patient. I got about five blocks away when they (his company) called me on the radio and told me to return.

"I got back and got the patient. As I was taking him down the stairs he had a cardiac arrest. I shot him into St. Bernard's hospital, but he was D.O.A. (dead on arrival); and (the company) chews me out for not taking him to County (Cook County hospital) because we'd get more mileage."

Ambulance companies charge one dollar a mile as part of their fee.

Another driver, who described himself as the south side manager of a large ambulance company, told Rectenwald that it was company policy "never to use sheets on welfare recipients. I don't lift them right either, unless I have to," the driver said. "I just swing them."

The licensing of these attendants and ambulance drivers as well as others, is controlled by the City Vehicle commission and the department of health. According to the city code, a prospective ambulance attendant must complete a standard and advanced first aid course before he is licensed.

Easy to qualify

The city permit is similar to those carried by cab drivers and is known in the industry as a "hard card." In practice, a "hard card" is issued after a person enrolls in the advanced course. The only other requirements are a $5 license fee, police clearance, and a tuberculosis test.

Both Rectenwald and I were working as attendants within minutes after we reported for work at several different companies. We received no instructions in the use of oxygen or the proper handling of a stretcher case before we were sent out on emergency calls. One operator hired me over the phone, and I worked for the company two days without ever showing my "hard card."

If there is one statement that speaks for all the misery merchants, perhaps it came one night after we answered a possible child food poisoning call in a south side housing project. We had taken the 12-year-old girl and her mother to County hospital about midnight and were returning to the south side. The driver, who also is a vice president and general manager of the ambulance company, was ridiculing the child's mother for calling an ambulance because "the kid burped."

"Some of the guys working for me get too close to these cases," the general manager observed. "Now take me. I can watch a nigger die right next to me and never take my eyes off the road."

Reprinted by courtesy of the Chicago *Tribune*.

31. *The End of the Line for the Mentally Ill*

Acel Moore and Wendell Rawls Jr. of the Philadelphia *Inquirer* begin their story of appalling abuses in a mental hospital with an ironic lead. It is designed to puzzle and thus to pull the reader into the story. Making use of extensive details and apt quotes, the writers then provide an account which not only presents the comprehensive findings of their investigation but also conveys the emotions and attitudes of inmates. The story is a good example of how important thorough observation and information are to good writing. *(Pulitzer Prize for Local Investigative Specialized Reporting, 1977)*

Where the State Treats Patients with Drugs, Brutality and Death

Acel Moore and Wendell Rawls Jr.
Philadelphia *Inquirer*
June 27, 1976

Farview State Hospital, in the rolling wooded countryside north of the Poconos, looks almost like what it was once intended to be—a benign circle of three-story brick buildings where the mentally ill who have committed crimes are treated and, if possible, cured.

A passerby driving through this anthracite region could almost mistake it for a small college or a resort hotel or a monastery.

It is none of those things. Over and over, those who have been patients at Farview and who have been lucky enough to get out describe it as a living hell on earth.

And there is a wealth of evidence from others—guards, administrators, scholars and even government investigators whose findings have been suppressed—that the description is chillingly accurate.

A three-month investigation by The *Inquirer* has revealed that:

Farview State Hospital is a place where men have died during or after beatings by guards and by patients egged on by guards.

It is a place where men who have died this way have been certified as victims of heart attacks.

It is a place where men have been pummeled bloody and senseless—for sport.

It is a place where an unwritten code requires all the guards present to hit a patient if one guard hits him.

It is a place where patients have been forced to commit sodomy with guards and other patients.

It is a place where men have been forced to live naked for years on end, sometimes handcuffed on icy floors.

It is a place where guards have sponsored patients in human cockfights and bet on the outcome.

It is a place where there is virtually no treatment aside from the use of mood-altering drugs, some of which other institutions abandoned a decade ago.

It is a psychiatric hospital without a board-certified psychiatrist.

It is a place where a man under a 30-day sentence for disorderly conduct can wait 30 years for his freedom.

It is a place where decades—26 years, in one case—can elapse between the time a patient is admitted and the time he gets a psychiatric evaluation.

It is a place where men have been denied such basic amenities as toilet paper.

It is a place where staff members and patients alike must live in a system based on hustles, extortion and theft.

These are some of the findings of The *Inquirer's* investigation—an investigation prompted by the complaint of an embittered former patient and based on scores of interviews and on the study of numerous documents previously not made public. Those interviewed include former and present guards, administrators and state officials, as well as patients who have been freed or transferred to prison.

The main findings—homicide, coverup, neglect, corruption, brutality, sodomy—form a pattern that spans the last three decades and possibly longer.

The current administration at Farview, interviewed last week, says it is trying and succeeding in stamping out many past abuses.

But the pattern of crime and neglect at Farview has easily survived all past attempts at reform, and two high-level staff members interviewed in recent days say that any new attempts at reform have yet to penetrate the guard structure that runs the hospital.

State law-enforcement authorities have long known about the abuses at Farview. Their files include strong evidence of crimes, including murder, and yet nothing has been done.

The files also include admissions from investigators that their work was superficial in crucial ways.

In November 1974, State Attorney General Israel Packel ordered an investigation of "allegations of threats, beatings, illegal contraband and deaths at the institution" at the request of Helene Wohlgemuth, then secretary of the Department of Public Welfare. Most of the investigating was done by the Bureau of Investigations, but the State Police also conducted inquiries about deaths at Farview.

By the time the results came in, Packel was no longer attorney general. On April 16, 1975, his successor, Robert P. Kane, wrote his conclusions on the matter to Frank S. Beal, then secretary of public welfare. He said, "...there have been a multitude of occasions where staff has used force against patients," but concluded that such force had not been "excessive or unlawful."

"There is no evidence supporting allegations of criminal violations at the hospital," Kane said, but he did conclude that "there are serious problems caused by patients' possession of money and other contraband...and that there has been a lack of administrative resolution of these problems..."

How was that conclusion reached?

By listening to guards and ignoring patients, according to an accompanying letter by Cecil H. Yates, director of the Bureau of Investigations.

Yates cited two predicaments that, he said, made his department's investigation "superficial." One problem, he said, was that the credibility of patients certified as both criminal and insane "must be viewed as questionable."

However, Robert Hammel, current acting superintendent at Farview, says that fully 30 per cent of the 453 patients at the hospital have never been convicted of a crime. And the records at Farview are filled with accounts of patients who were admitted not because they were "insane," but because they were troublemakers elsewhere or, in some instances, because a court somewhere simply made a bureaucratic error.

Yates also noted that his investigaton had perused the medical records of guards injured by patients, but not those patients who claimed to have been injured by guards. To do the latter, he said, would be "legally questionable."

Thus it was, he said, that "no attempt was made...to thoroughly analyze the problem" or to recommend "corrective actions."

The narrower, simultaneous State Police investigation into three deaths did turn up strong evidence of murder in one case—the death of Robert (Stonewall) Jackson in 1966. In two other cases there was conflicting evidence. In yet another three cases not involved in the investigation, questionable circumstances surround the deaths. In none of the cases were charges lodged or reforms proposed.

To moviegoers who saw "One Flew Over the Cuckoo's Nest," the circumstances under which "Stonewall" Jackson died at age 36 may have a familiar ring.

But Jackson died, and law-enforcement officials were told how, long before the film was made. It is a death that illustrates a pattern described by many former Farview patients—beatings, murder, incorrect records at the hospital and indifference from legal authorities.

Jackson's mother, Mrs. Alma Jackson of Southwest Philadelphia, says she visited him at Farview about three months before his death on Sept. 24, 1966.

Stonewall, she told The *Inquirer*, had acquired the nickname because of his formidable size and strength, but when she saw him at Farview his body was weak and twisted.

"He walked with a stick," she recalled. "He was all bent over. He told me that they were going to kill him, that he didn't have long to live."

She said she asked a doctor why her son was being mistreated. "He told me that my son wouldn't talk. He said that he was stubborn and that 'we are going to break him.'"

According to William, 57, who spent 22 years at Farview and now lives in Philadelphia, Jackson quarreled with guards on "D" Ward one evening on or about Sept. 21, 1966. It was near midnight, Ash says, when the guards "dragged" Jackson out.

Jackson ended up in a medical ward. A patient there, William James Wright, who is currently in prison at Dallas, Pa., awaiting sentencing for murder, was interviewed by State Police investigators 18 months ago.

"As a patient, I witnessed Robert Jackson beaten," he related. "He was cuffed by his hands and legs to a bed with leather restraints.

"It was late in the evening sometime between 10 p.m. and 6 a.m. Jackson was making a lot of noises. He was disturbed. The guard told a patient to stop Jackson from making noises.

"The patient then went out of the office and struck Jackson in the throat with the back edge of his right hand. He struck him only once, and Jackson started to gag; and about 20 minutes later he died."

Another former patient, William Franklin Sipes, 30, of Philadelphia, told the State Police he also saw a male nurse strike Jackson in the throat after Jackson knocked a tray off his bed with his knee, spilling some of the food on the nurse.

"As soon as I seen what was going on, I got away," Sipes said. "I was worried about what could happen."

Another inmate, Clayton Allen Terhune, told the investigation that he witnessed Jackson's final moments. "Jackson's arms and legs were cuffed," he said. "He was restrained to a bed...

"This is how it happened. The inmate working in the ward placed a pillow against Jackson's face while he was cuffed to the bed. The pillow was held against his face for a long time. In fact, the patient got on top of Jackson and put his weight on the pillow against (Jackson's) face. During this time the nurse was standing beside the bed. He was watching and did nothing about it."

The hospital's official paperwork on the death mentions none of this.

The cause of death entered on the death certificate by Dr. Joseph D. Moylan, a staff physician who is now dead, was acute coronary occlusion with myocardial infarction—a heart attack.

No autopsy was performed, and the body was embalmed by a guard who is also a registered mortician.

Jackson's mother recalls the condition of the body when she received it.

"His neck was crooked," she said. "His arm looked bent out of shape."

A year ago, Dr. Halbert E. Fillinger Jr., assistant Philadelphia Medical Examiner, concluded in a letter that was part of the State Police report:

"The Police investigation involving the circumstances surrounding this man's death as substantiated by several witnesses would certainly cast doubt on this diagnosis (death by heart failure). As a matter of fact, the information supplied to the police by several witnesses would strongly suggest that this man's death is of a highly suspicious nature.

"There are certainly several allegations that the deceased may well have been suffocated with a pillow and that the cause of death given on the death certificate is a totally erroneous one.

"If the allegations of these several witnesses interviewed by the State Police have any basis in fact, the only conclusion one can draw is that a felonious death had occurred and a thorough investigation must be conducted to pinpoint the person responsible for this man's death and see that he is brought to justice."

No charges have been filed in the death and no evidence has been presented to a grand jury, as far as The *Inquirer* can determine. Several years after Jackson's death the male nurse was fired for allegedly smuggling a pistol to an inmate.

Since The *Inquirer* began looking into Jackson's death, however, the State Police have shown a renewed interest. Mrs. Jackson said she was called last week.

"They asked me questions about his death," she said. "I tried so hard to get someone to listen to me back in 1966. No one would help us. I knew that whoever killed him would never have any rest, never have any peace."

The death of Calvin Bush on Oct. 11, 1973, may or may not have been murder. In either case, it says a great deal about what passes for medical care at Farview.

Bush, 32, died of a heart attack. At the time of death he was being subdued by eight guards, one of whom weighed nearly 200 pounds and was sitting on his chest.

The incident apparently began shortly after breakfast that day when Bush returned to the minimum-security ward where he had been living for about a year. A guard, who later testified before State Police investigators, said that Bush threatened to kill him, called him a "goddam white man" and then threatened to knock his "block" off.

The guard said that Bush had frequently been abusive, but that this time it was decided to transfer him to either the "N" or "D" wards, which the guard characterized as "a little rougher than the ones I have (worked on)."

But Bush refused, saying that he wasn't "going no place," the guard recounted. Bush then picked up a chair but was persuaded to put it down. When he walked out of the day room, eight guards dragged him to the floor and began fastening his arms in a leather restraining device.

While the guard, who estimated to State Police that he weighed 197 pounds at the time, sat on Bush's chest, a doctor ordered a 100-milligram injection of Sparine, a tranquilizer, to calm Bush down.

But Bush died first.

That, however, did not prevent guards from rolling him over and pulling his trousers down to allow a male nurse to administer the injection.

An autopsy by Marvin E. Aronson, Philadelphia's medical examiner, disclosed that the dose of Sparine was indeed given but remained concentrated in the left buttock near the point of injection. It was never circulated because Bush's heart was no longer beating.

The official cause of death was "cardiac arrhythmia due to hypertension aggravated by excitement."

Coroner Robert Jennings of Wayne County told The *Inquirer*: "I know he died of a heart attack, but I also feel that such things are brought about by unusual stress and that struggling with and being restrained by eight men, some sitting on his chest, could cause enough anger and stress."

The indiscriminate use of drugs was also manifest in the death of John Rank, 68.

Last March 2, Rank was given a ham sandwich by a guard. In quick succession, according to a post-mortem report, Rank "developed bizarre agitated behavior, jumped up from where he was sitting, ran head lowered, smashed into a wall and fell to the floor."

He was soon dead.

An autopsy disclosed that Rank apparently had choked to death on a part of the ham sandwich—an unremarkable fact, except for the fact that he had earlier been heavily sedated with a drug that inhibits swallowing.

When John Rank died, there was no nurse on his floor and no doctor in the hospital. Dr. Bernard J. Willis, the hospital's assistant superintendent and clinical director, told The *Inquirer*: "The doctors got tired of being here all the time."

When a nurse from another floor arrived, she tried to give aid, then telephoned Dr. Willis at home.

According to a preliminary investigation by Coroner Jennings, Dr. Willis ordered the body removed to the hospital morgue and placed on a table.

The body remained on the table for 14 hours and was never placed in refrigeration. Eventually it was picked up by the coroner's office, and an autopsy was performed.

By the end of last month—three months after his death—John Rank had yet to be officially associated with Farview State Hospital, according to the coroner.

A toxicological report on the thin, pale elderly man was performed by National Medical Services Inc. of Willow Grove, Pa. Dr. Richard D. Cohn disclosed these findings:

"The level of chlorpromazine (Thorazine) detected in this individual's blood is more than double the usual maximum therapeutic level. It is reasonably certain that at the level of (Thorazine) found to be present in the blood, pronounced central nervous system depression was obtained and that coordinated and reflex actions were significantly impaired.

"The blood level (of Thorazine) found is not inconsistent with an acutely toxic (Thorazine) concentration which in the absence of similar or more competent causes, could be competent, independent causes of death."

Thomas L. Garrett, 37, died at Farview on March 19, 1960, according to hospital records.

The cause of death, again according to hospital records, was a sudden and unexpected pulmonary embolism which Garrett suffered after spending 17 days in the medical ward with a fever.

What killed Garrett, however, according to patients who say they witnessed it, was a sustained beating by guards that took place in a Farview dining room in February of that year.

Hospital records say that Garrett was confined to the maximum-security ward in February after "attacking guards," and was transferred to the medical ward on March 2 after he came down with a fever.

Hospital records, however, are contradictory on the subject, and an autopsy said to confirm the cause of death cannot be found.

Ward notes for the day in question say that an autopsy was performed by Dr. Harry Probst of nearby Wayne County Memorial Hospital. Dr. Willis, clinical director at Farview, also told State Police who investigated the incident in 1975 that Dr. Probst performed the autopsy determining the cause of death.

Dr. Probst, however, told police that he could not recall any such autopsy.

The director of nursing at Farview told State Police that he was present, along with a lab technician and a guard, when Dr. John Perridge, at the time Wayne County coroner, performed the autopsy confirming the cause of Garrett's death. He said that copies of the autopsy report went to the county coroner, to the Department of Public Welfare, to two undertakers and to Farview itself.

However, Dr. Perridge told police that his records indicated that he had never performed any such autopsy, and all of the supposed recipients of the autopsy report told police that they had never received it.

Dr. Willis, who signed the certificate of death attributing Garrett's death to a pulmonary embolism, told State Police on Jan. 21, 1975, that he could remember nothing of the incident. Twenty-three days later, his memory had greatly improved. He told State Police that he remembered the incident "very well" and said that Garrett had appeared to be responding well to treatment for fever when, suddenly, he died.

Patients who were there remember it differently. They say that they believe Thomas Garrett died because he was brutally beaten by guards. They told State Police that one day in February 1960, Garrett asked a guard for a job in a dining hall and was refused. Then, they said, Garrett slapped the guard, whereupon a number of guards attacked him and beat him. Heyward Speaks, a Farview inmate at the time, who currently is an inmate at the State Correctional Institution at Graterford, Pa., told The *Inquirer* that he witnessed the incident. "All the guards around kicked and stomped Garrett," he said. "They stomped and kicked him in the side of the head. Broke him up real good. Then they put him on 'J' ward" (Farview's maximum-security ward).

"I was one of the last to see him alive. I went on the ward to shave and cut the inmates' hair. When I went into Garrett's cell, I saw he was busted up. His jaw was broken. He was semi-conscious. He was trying to say something, but he couldn't open his mouth. His ribs were busted up as well. I told the guards that I couldn't shave this man...Ten days to two weeks after that, Garrett died. We were told that he died."

The *Inquirer* is not the only party to whom Speaks has told his story. In 1969, he wrote to the State Department of Public Welfare, detailing the Garrett incident. The department handled the matter promptly. It mailed Speaks' letter back to Farview—namely to Dr. John Shovlin, the superintendent at the time. Later, Speaks said, he wrote to the state attorney general on the same subject. That letter, too, was referred back to Dr. Shovlin.

State Police did look into the Garrett incident in their 1975 investigation after another patient told them that he had heard the story of Garrett's death from many inmates.

Nothing came of the investigation.

Russell Sell was 46 when he died at Farview on Jan. 7, 1963. The cause of death was recorded as acute coronary occlusion. On the death notice, Dr. Willis wrote that the body had no wounds, no fractures and no dislocations.

However, an autopsy one day later by the Wayne County coroner reported that Sell in fact had three broken ribs. And 11 years later, Clayton Allen Terhune, a fellow inmate, testified to Pennsylvania State Police investigating the incident that Sell actually died of a severe beating administered by guards six days earlier in a hospital dining room.

Terhune said that Sell was beaten after he waved in the air a newspaper clipping reporting that Farview had purchased a large order of beef and complained that patients received little meat because the guards were stealing most of it.

Guards told State Police investigators that there was in fact a dining room fracas six days before Sell's supposed heart attack, and that he probably broke his ribs falling against a steam table.

The hospital ward notes of Jan. 7 tried to take a middle path. They noted that Sell "died this date following injuries received while being subdued during a disturbed period during a work assignment in K-3 dining room. Contributing cause of death: acute coronary occlusion."

Consider, lastly, the way Farview cared for Alfred E. Miller, 61, an epileptic who died of natural causes this year, a week before Rank.

Miller's name came up about 18 months ago in an investigation by the State Department of Justice. John M. Fitzgerald, director of social services at Farview, told investigators that another patient had informed him about repeated mistreatment of Miller by guards.

Miller was known as "Jughead." According to the testimony, the guards on the second shift in his ward "would get Jughead to strip and they would taunt him verbally until he would scream and carry on. The guards did this as amusement."

"Jughead" died in bed during a seizure. According to Coroner Jennings, this is how Farview handled his death:

"Mr. Miller's death was reported to me by Dr. Hobart Owens, who was scheduled to have been the officer of the day and should have been on duty. But instead he called me from his home in Hawley, Pa., approximately 20 miles from the institution.

"Dr. Owens reported Mr. Miller's death to my office without examining him or determining that he was, in fact, deceased."

"Being the doctor on duty does not require my being at the hospital," Dr. Owens said in a telephone interview with The *Inquirer*. "Sure, I am supposed to check the body before he is pronounced dead, but when they (the hospital) called me he was already dead.

"How did I know he was dead? A nurse told me he was dead. A nurse pronounced him dead. But it's true, I am supposed to check the body."

The patient's plight is one side of the story, the guards say. The other is the attacks on guards, and indeed there is ample evidence of guards being injured.

One guard was shot and paralyzed from the waist down by a former inmate who returned seeking one of the doctors. Another guard was bitten by an inmate and lost part of a finger. There are many other instances.

It is a fact that some of the patients at Farview are among the most vicious criminals Pennsylvania has ever produced. And it is also a fact that nearly half of them are blacks from the ghetto streets of Philadelphia and Pittsburgh, while the guards who deal with them are, almost without exception, whites from the rural area around Waymart.

Those facts and others have led several officials who have studied Farview to recommend, in private reports, that the facility be closed down altogether. But every time the suggestion has even been hinted at, both the guards' union and much of the local populace, who consider Farview a main industry, have objected.

Consequently, Farview continues—although it does shrink. Its current inmate population of 354 is down from a peak of 1,410 in 1962, largely because of court rulings on mental patients' rights. Even given those cases, however, Farview still harbors a surprising number of inmates with no evident criminal record and some with no documented classification of mental instability.

Farview officials say that as many as 100 inmates have never been convicted of a crime but are men who have proved difficult to control at other mental hospitals. And about 10 inmates have been committed voluntarily, either by themselves or their families.

The officials also say, as noted earlier, that they are doing their best to stamp out the worst abuses of the past, and they assert that what goes on at Farview today bears no resemblance to what went on earlier.

It is impossible to either confirm or altogether call into question that assertion, for news of conditions, abuse and even violent deaths seeps out of Farview slowly, carried by the handful of patients released each year who are brave enough and lucid enough to talk. The *Inquirer*, in its investigation, has been told of murders alleged to have taken place in 1946, 1950, 1954, 1958, 1960, 1962, 1963, 1967, 1968 and 1972. What goes on at Farview today cannot be accurately assessed until possibly a year or more from now.

According to the patients violent deaths tend to happen in the same basic way. The victim, sometimes baited, gets into a fight with a guard or another patient. The guards respond by forcibly subduing the patient. A short time later the patient is pronounced dead. Usually the cause is listed as a heart attack.

But this is only what former patients, say, and, as noted by Cecil Yates, Farview alumni have had a hard time persuading those in positions of authority to take them seriously. The very fact that they have been at Farview means that, whether they are or not, at one time they were branded as both criminal and insane.

That is one problem in plumbing the depths of the Farview swamp. Another is the shoddiness of the records.

Many records were lost, officials say, when a basement at the hospital flooded in 1968. Some former officials add that the surviving records are not to be believed. And indeed in some cases, such as that of "Stonewall" Jackson's supposed heart attack, there is every reason to suspect that the records are misleading.

But there can be no question that inmates at Farview are, and have been treated with extraordinary brutality, of which the recurring deaths are only a symptom.

In 1975, Joseph Jacoby, a criminologist working on a study sponsored by the National Institute of Mental Health, gave a committee of the State Legislature a strong indication of the widespread cruelty.

He and his fellow researchers interviewed 269 former Farview patients who had been released or transferred to other mental institutions between 1969 and 1971 as a result of a federal court suit.

The patients were asked what they liked most and least about Farview and its staff. With no prompting at all, Jacoby reported, 45 per cent of those who gave "recordable responses" cited brutality at Farview. In contrast, less than 2 per cent cited brutality in the hospitals or prisons to which they had been transferred.

Here are some of the responses, each from a different former Farview patient:

"The guards would knock you down and kick you if you talked."

"The way they beat them and kill them—I seen it done."

"They once beat up a guy so bad his mother couldn't recognize him. They said a patient beat him up."

"Beatings and stompings of the patients."

"Beatings they gave to the men. They beat me up about once a month or so."

"It's a butcher house—house of no return."

"Too brutal and cruel to you at Farview. They don't beat you here (the patient's current hospital)."

"At my present hospital they have good guards who don't resort to brutality. At Farview, your life is in danger from the minute you arrive until you leave."

"The guards and attendants beat me up and didn't treat me like a human being."

"Sadistic guards terrorizing and beating up on patients."

"Beating guys for no reason. My friend was beaten, had his jaw broken, and was robbed. My face was busted. I been beaten up on every ward I been on."

And so on.

Jacoby said that the percentage of those citing brutality might have been even higher had not some patients still been in fear of their former guards.

"We have reason to believe," Jacoby said, "that a number of subjects refused to answer questions about Farview candidly because they feared retaliation if they complained about conditions and their identity were discovered. One patient confided, 'They, the guards, used to tell us we'd better not talk about Farview or else. But I ain't afraid.' This fear could have been a real factor in the way some patients fashioned their replies..."

Another view of the violence was given to The *Inquirer* by John Naughton, who retired as a guard and secretary of the guards' union in December 1974 after eight years at Farview.

Naughton, now the assistant manager of a restaurant in Scranton, confirms the claim of former patients that the guards had a code that compelled them to join in on the beating of inmates.

He said that there "absolutely was a code, an unwritten but well understood rule among the guards, that when a guard hit a patient you had to jump in. If you didn't, you were pulled off that ward immediately. You were branded as a coward, or just branded, period.

"I've seen the guards come to work and start out the shift picking on a patient and put him in 'peanut' (a tiny room) for punishment—all for no reason, except that the guard could do it.

"There are guards there that just like to kick and stomp patients. There were people there that I just would spend all night pulling them off the patients."

Those who were kicked and stomped undoubtedly have even more vivid recollections.

Rayford Smith, who was a Farview patient from 1959 to 1964 and is now a prisoner at Graterford, told The *Inquirer* that he was kicked so hard in the genitals "that they ruptured my scrotum and I urinated blood for three months after the beating.

"They kicked me so hard in the stomach that I actually had a bowel movement right there. My intestines hurt for five years after that..."

Arthur Pitts, 49, served two terms at Farview, one from 1963 to 1964 and the other from 1966 to 1968, and is now at Western State Correctional Institution in Pittsburgh. During his second stay he attempted to escape but was caught hiding in a recreation area.

"The guards beat me and kicked me and stomped me," he said in an interview. "Then they stomped and jumped on my shin bones until they broke both of them. They kicked me in the face and kicked one tooth out."

Heyward Speaks, 55, a convicted rapist currently serving a sentence at Graterford, says he learned an important lesson in the first hour of his first term in Farview in 1956.

"The first night I got to Farview from Eastern State Penitentiary I was met by a guard who told me I had to take a shower first," Speaks recalls. "There was only one nozzle in the shower stall. I turned it on, and the water was ice cold. I started to step out and complain, but I could see from out the side of my eyes that about seven guards were coming towards me into the stall.

"I sensed that I had better not complain. I held my breath and stayed under the shower until I got used to the cold water. Then I was given a nightshirt and told to sit on the bench outside the shower stall.

"I watched from the bench what happened to the next inmate, a white man who came up in the same car as me. The man turned on the water, and it was cold. He jumped out and complained. They beat and stomped and kicked...him.

"When they finished beating him, his naked body looked like a piece of raw meat. I knew then I wasn't going to give anybody any trouble here."

Reprinted by permission of the Philadelphia *Inquirer.*

32. *A New Religion Sneaks into Town*

When the Church of Scientology moved into nearby Clearwater, Florida, the St. Petersburg *Times* assigned reporters Charles Stafford and Bette Orsini to investigate the serious allegations made against the organization. The reporters uncovered the theft of government documents, intimidation of local citizens and officials, and an attempt by church leaders to misrepresent themselves to the city. Stafford, Orsini, and the newspaper management were threatened repeatedly by the cult, but nevertheless published a fourteen-part expose on the group. The following story was the first in the series. It is a particularly effective introduction piece contrasting accepted religious tenets with the actions of the Church of Scientology. Stafford weaves together background information and breaking news to make a comprehensive and interesting summation of the cult's activities. *(Pulitzer Prize for National Reporting, 1980)*

Scientology Brings Four Years of Discord
Charles Stafford
St. Petersburg *Times*
December 16, 1979

It was this time four years ago—this time of year when the old-time religion celebrates the birth of a child—that the new religion came to Clearwater.

It came sneaking into town: a religion with beliefs and practices so alien to the teachings of Jesus that are preached in Clearwater's Christian churches, so different from the law of the prophets that is taught in the city's synagogues.

This is the law of the God of Israel: Thou shalt not steal.

On Nov. 9, 1975—the Sabbath—an agent of the new religion with the code name "Silver" entered Internal Revenue Service (IRS) headquarters on Constitution Avenue in Washington, and made his way to the office of Charles Zuravin, an attorney in the disclosure division of the chief counsel's office. "Silver" found the file he wanted and began copying documents. When he left late that Sunday, he took with him a stack of copies of confidential IRS documents one foot thick. That was theft.

On Dec. 5, 1975, the hierarchy of new religion issued this directive:

"Power Project 3: Normandy.

"Major Target: To fully investigate the Clearwater city and county area so we can distinguish our friends from our enemies and handle as needed."

Neighborly?

This is law of the God of Israel: Thou shalt not bear false witness against thy neighbor.

On Jan 26, 1976, a day when Scientology was still masquerading in Clearwater as the United Churches of Florida, a church official named Joe Lisa informed another church leader that he had devised a scheme to get reporter Mark Sableman fired by the Clearwater *Sun*. This was his plan: "Have a woman (elderly) go into the office and in grief and misemotion (sic) start screaming she wants to see Sableman's boss. She goes in and sees this man and screams and cries about Sableman sexually assaulting her son, or grandson. The woman takes a magazine which is lurid and perverted and throws it into the face of the man-woman and screams 'Look what he gave my son, not to mention what the pervert did...sob, sob, to my Johnny.' I'm going to the police. If you can't do something about that pervert Sableman I will see they do something to you."

Two days later citizens of Pinellas County learned that their new neighbors in the Fort Harrison Hotel in Clearwater were practitioners of a new religion, Scientology, founded just 29 years ago by a science fiction writer named L. Ron Hubbard.

It was 19 months before the government of the United States discovered that agents of the Church of Scientology had been systematically rifling files of government agencies for more than two years.

Discovery of the true nature of Scientology began on July 8, 1977—to Scientologists a day that will live in infamy—when FBI agents pounded down the doors of church offices in Los Angeles and Washington and carted away 48,149 documents. Many of these were copies of government documents that agents like "Silver" stole after infiltrating government agencies. Others were files of private organizations, like the American Medical Associaton and The St. Petersburg *Times.*

Still others were internal documents of the Church of Scientology, and these would reveal myriad dark secrets.

But knowledge of what the documents contained came slowly to the public.

On Aug. 15, 1978, a federal grand jury in Washington indicted 11 Scientologists, nine of whom held high positions in the church's Guardian Office. That office had this mandate: "To sweep aside opposition sufficiently to create a vacuum into which Scientology can expand." The 28-count indictment charged them with conspiring to steal government documents, theft of government documents, and conspiring to obstruct justice.

The 11 included Mary Sue Hubbard, world traveler, wife of the founder of Scientology, a second-ranking officer of the church; Jane Kember of England, the head of the worldwide church's Guardian Office, and these other Scientologists: Morris "Mo" Budlong of England; Henning Heldt, Los Angeles; Duke Snider (no relation to the baseball player), Hollywood, Calif.; Richard Weigand, Van Nuys, Calif.; Gregory Willardson, Beverly Hills, Calif.; Mitchell Hermann, also known as Mike Cooper, Hollywood, Calif.; Cindy Raymond, Hollywood, Calif.; Gerald Bennett Wolfe, Areleta, Calif., and Sharon Thomas, Los Angeles.

All were officials of the Guardian Office except Wolfe and Miss Thomas. Wolfe was "Silver," the agent who infiltrated the IRS, while Miss Thomas was the church's secret agent in the Justice Department.

On Aug. 29, 1978, nine of the indicted Scientologists stood before the bench of U.S. District Judge George L. Hart Jr. in the federal courthouse at the foot of Capitol Hill and pleaded innocent. Two were missing. Jane Kember and Mo Budlong were in England.

For the next 14 months a platoon of attorneys fought to prevent a trial and to keep the seized documents from the public eye. They claimed the FBI raids on church offices were illegal, that the search warrant was too general. One U.S. District Court judge upheld their claim. But two other District Court judges—one in Washington and one in California—rejected their claim. The Scientologists' appeals to higher courts also failed.

Trial was scheduled for Sept. 24 in Washington before U.S. District Judge Charles R. Richey. It did not begin. For two weeks attorneys for the government and the Scientologists argued and bargained, and on Oct. 8 Judge Richey ruled that an agreement had been reached.

As a result of that agreement, Mary Sue Hubbard and her eight colleagues appeared before Judge Richey on Oct. 26. The team of prosecutors headed by Assistant U.S. Attorney Raymond Banoun presented a written statement of the government's case backed up by three folders of documents. The defense attorneys stipulated that this was the evidence the government would have presented had the case gone to trial. Judge Richey then found the nine Scientologists guilty of one count each of the indictment.

This scenario left the defendants free to appeal. They will claim that the convictions should be overturned because the evidence used against them was seized illegally. But they will not claim they are innocent of plotting to infiltrate government agencies and steal government documents. They never have.

Having found the Scientologists guilty, Judge Richey lifted the seal from the documents seized in the FBI raids. Six boxes were made public before attorneys for the defendants and the church could appeal to the U.S. Court of Appeals for the District of Columbia. The appellate court upheld Judge Richey and on Nov. 23, the day after Thanksgiving, the court began releasing the remaining documents.

The number had been trimmed down. Certain documents seized in the raids were returned to the church, apparently because they had no bearing on the government's case. Others were removed to prevent injury to innocent people mentioned in them.

But 20 boxes—roughly half of the documents seized in the raids—were made public.

Examining them is like seeing the dark side of the moon, or stepping through a looking glass.

They were taken from church offices in Los Angeles and Washington. But there is so much in them about Scientology's plans and programs for a quiet city in Florida.

The documents reveal that the Church of Scientology came to Clearwater with a written plan to establish its program headquarters—its school of theology, so to speak—in the old Fort Harrison Hotel and to take control of the city. They show that United Churches of Florida was created as a front to protect church assets from seizure by the government.

They show that church officials conceived and carried out plots to discredit their "enemies"—the mayor who questioned their secrecy, reporters who investigated and wrote about Scientology, editor and owner of the areas's largest newspaper, even local police departments.

They show that covert agents of the church took jobs with local newspapers, community agencies, and law firms in order to spy.

They underscore what a spokesman for the Church of Scientology told a group of Clearwater High School students recently: "We step on a lot of toes. We don't turn the other cheek."

Government prosecutors, in a memorandum to Judge Richey urging maximum sentences, delivered this judgment:

"That these defendants were willing to frame their critics to the point of giving false testimony under oath against them and having them arrested and indicted speaks legion for their disdain for the rule of law. Indeed, they arrogantly placed themselves above the law, meting out their personal brand of punishment to those 'guilty' of opposing their selfish aims.

"The crime committed by these defendants is of a breadth and scope previously unheard of. No building, office, desk, or file was safe from their snooping and prying. No individual or organization was free from their despicable conspiratorial minds. The tools of their trade were miniature transmitters, lock picks, secret codes, forged credentials, and any other device they found necessary to carry out their conspiratorial schemes. It is interesting to note that the founder of their organization, unindicted co-conspirator L. Ron Hubbard, wrote in his dictionary entitled *Modern Management Technology Defined*...that 'truth is what is true for you.' Thus, with the founder's blessings they could wantonly commit perjury as long as it was in the interest of Scientology. The defendants rewarded criminal activities that ended in success and sternly rebuked those that failed. The standards of human conduct embodied in such practices represent no less than the absolute perversion of any known ethical value system.

"In view of this, it defies the imagination that these defendants have

RELIGION SNEAKS INTO TOWN 201

the unmitigated audacity to seek to defend their actions in the name of 'religion.' That these defendants now attempt to hide behind the sacred principles of freedom of religion, freedom of speech and the right to privacy—which principles they repeatedly demonstrated a willingness to violate with impunity—adds insult to the injuries which they have inflicted on every element of society."

As he prepared to sentence Mary Sue Hubbard, Judge Richey told her "we have a precious system of government in the United States...For anyone to use the benefits of those laws or to seek under the guise of those laws to destroy the very foundation of the government is totally wrong and cannot be condoned by any responsible citizen."

The judge imposed maximum sentences on Mrs. Hubbard and two other defendants: five years in prison and $10,000 fines—though he said he would reconsider Mrs. Hubbard's sentence after she has spent three months in prison. He sentenced five other defendants to four years in prison and $10,000 fines, and the remaining defendant to one year in prison—six months of it suspended—and a $1,000 fine.

There, in capsule form, you have the story of Scientology since it came to Clearwater four years ago. The details are intriguing, and they will come. But first it is necessary to understand the creation of Scientology and its creator.

Reprinted by permission of the St. Petersburg *Times*.

Part III.

PROFILE WRITING

A well-written personality profile should provide some illumination into the human character through its focus on an interesting person or persons. The techniques used by the writer may vary from a single source interview with the story's subject to a multi-source story that includes no direct quotes from the person being profiled.

The personality profile may be the most challenging of all journalistic story forms to master. While the careful selection of quotes is critical to a personality profile, there is also a need for including much descriptive detail. It is important to give the reader a feeling for the real nature of the individual, including details of surroundings, mannerisms, and quirks.

33.   A Portrait of a Pope

Anne O'Hare McCormick's 1935 profile of Pope Pius XI displays a thorough knowledge of its subjects, of Catholicism, Pius XI himself, history, and contemporary conditions. Such familiarity is a must for good news writing. While presenting a tangible picture of Pope Pius, however, the article is not so much a characterization of him as it is a comment on the turbulent world affairs just preceding World War II. It is so ably done that still, more than half a century later, the reader is able to sense the tension and drama surrounding the papacy of Pius XI. *(Pulitzer Prize for Correspondence, 1937)*

Pope Pius Steers a Course Amid Storms
Anne O'Hare McCormick
New York *Times*
December 15, 1935

Pope Pius XI assisted recently at the memorial mass celebrated annually in the Sistine Chapel for the Cardinals who have died during the year. Around him that morning were grouped most of the living Cardinals of the Curla. Beyond the lovely marble screen of Mino da Fiesole they sat in two rows facing one another, their bent white heads and crimson capes overshadowed by Michelangelo's "Last Judgment"—in a world of dark signs perhaps still the greatest handwriting on the wall. The Pope himself sat apart, on a throne beside the altar, a heirarchic figure that nothing overshadowed. In his stiff, bell-like cope, his tall miter, he looked rigid and symbolic as the rock of Peter.

At public functions Pius XI has his quality of immobility that makes every one around him appear fidgety and nervous. His vigor is extraordinary for a man of 78. His strong-featured face is still bronzed after a summer spent at his villa on the terraced hills above Lake Albano. His black hair is only sprinkled with gray. As he intones the benediction his voice is firm and resonant. His step is heavier but as decisive as on the June day in 1921 when he entered the nearby Hall of the Consistory to receive the red hat.

Even more extraordinary than the Pope's vigor is his quietness. It is not the quiet of serenity; there is too much iron in it for that. In the Vatican they speak of him as "a born Pope," meaning that his character is as papal as his office. In a period so overwhelmed by shouting rulers, he is the only one I have seen who suggests force in repose.

Those who know the Sistine Chapel remember it for the splendor of its frescoes. There the greatest artists of the Renaissance outpainted one another in the procession of masterpieces running like a frieze around the side walls. From the ceiling Michelangelo's prophets and sybils brood over the ineluctable mystery of man; and on the end wall he left that blackened judgment and revelation which must have startled his time as much as the indictments of Rivera shock ours. To recall in that place the murals of the Detroit Museum, of Dartmouth College, of the just-opened Aula Magna of Rome's new University City, is to wonder if the moderns of today will remain after 400 years as timely, or as timeless as these.

— — —

Really to see the Sistine frescoes, however, they must be seen as the back-drop of the pageant for which they were painted. When the officers of the mass moved before the altar, when the Supreme Pontiff and the princes of the church, the Swiss Guard, the papal chamberlains, files of clerics in purple and scarlet, people the choir, then the sober-colored walls and the scene below become part of one picture, blurred alike by incense and the sense of crowding centuries. And really to hear the Sistine Choir one must listen to the disembodied voices issuing from the little gallery and filling like one ineffable voice the space for which the choir was created.

But though choral and spectacle help, they do not of themselves produce the atmosphere which struck one observer most that morning. I had hardly realized how tense and troubled and super-heated is the air of Rome when suddenly, here in the heart of Mussolini's straining capital, I found myself in a place where everthing was slow and calm. It was not peace exactly—this strange relaxation. If any spot is seismological, sensitive to every spiritual tremor that shakes the earth, it is the Vatican. It was not detachment, for the Holy See, and particularly its present occupant, is intensely interested in the events and movements of the time. After a time, one perceived that it was perspective; mounting the Scala Region out of St. Peter's Square, out of the Rome of sanctions and militant resistance, one passed out of the short into the long view of things.

Everything presses on the Vatican that presses anywhere, but the very walls repeat that everything passes, too. Mussolini must do what he has planned to do this year, this hour, so he believes, or it will be forever too late. Combinations alter so quickly that no political ruler today can count on tomorrow. In the Vatican there is not only all the time there is, but a kind of continuum which makes the interval called Now both longer and less important than it is in the Fascist era, the Roosevelt adminstration, the life of a British Government.

— — —

The reigning Pontiff is the 260th of his line. Beholding him surrounded by the old Cardinals who will choose his successor, one saw not only that the Holy Father himself is always venerable but that he is an old man elected by old men. Most Popes are well over 60 before they begin their pontificates; Pius XI was 65 when he assumed office in 1922, the year the Fascists marched on Rome. The See of Peter will never be stormed by a youth movement, and there is something oddly steadying even in the hierarchical fact—at least, if you have traveled over Europe surveying the effects of youth movements and revaluing the ripeness and tolerance of age as a guarantee against the violent reaction of adolescence.

Individually the Pope is seasoned by a lifetime of priestly experience before he becomes chief pastor of his worldwide flock; officially he is one link in a lengthy chain. The attitude toward current problems of the most contemporary of pontiffs is thus in a sense non-contemporary. He comes from further back in time and looks further ahead than other rulers. His authority and responsibility are of an order so different that even when he pronounces on the same questions he speaks with another accent and another purpose.

This contrast between the secular and ecclesiastical measure was perceptible to the dullest observer present on successive days at the celebration of the Italian Armistice Day at the Altar of the Country and at this memorial service in the Sistine Chapel. At one commemoration, seventeen years ago was "the dead past"; at the other, time merges into eternity; a hundred years are reckoned as a day.

That is a truth to remember first in interpreting papal policies. They change and evolve with the times more rapidly than any one would guess who has not followed the story of the Holy See since 1870, a comparatively brief interval; but the mind of the church never loses the perspective of an old institution which has survived a good many world upheavals by refusing to be stampeded by any passing crisis.

— — —

Nothing illustrates this point more clearly than the stand of the present Pope on the raging question of competence and power of international law to preserve peace by punishing the aggressor. From all over the world, day after day, in public exhortations and private appeals, Pius XI is passionately urged to intervene in the conflict that has broken out at the very doors of the Vatican.

The Archbishop of Canterbury and the prelates of the Church of England have been especially insistent on the Pope's duty as the head of the Catholic Church to condemn Italy for wantonly breaking the peace. The least the Bishop of Rome should do, declare the most zealous, is to uphold the efforts of the League of Nations by invoking against the invader nation the powerful spiritual sanction of the church—the sentence of excommunication.

Now it is evident that peace is a paramount interest of a universal church as truly as it is the essential interest of the British Empire, which all Britons consciously or unconsciously serve. And for somewhat similar reasons. It is fact that the outbreak of the World War literally broke the heart of Pius X, because of threatened disaster in terms of spiritual empire, also—cutting communications, interrupting normal life, crippling missions, upsetting the whole existing order. More, a universal war, in which worshipers at the same altar slaughtered one another, was a kind of indictment of a universal church. Beyond the human tragedy stalked the moral failure represented by this reversion to the law of the jungle.

— — —

The war was over when Pius XI became the Keeper of the Keys, but his pontificate has covered a period of social and spiritual turbulence almost darker than the war years. From the beginning, recognizing how strained and fragile was the armistice in which the exhausted nations lived, his chief preoccupation has been to widen the bases of peace. Years before the present crisis developed, the Pope warned the statesmen of the world that their policies were heading straight for war.

During these years the Holy See itself has been immersed in a many-sided struggle. Benedict XV played the ungrateful role of neutral between two battle lines; the present Pontiff has had to steer the ancient bark of Peter through whirling cross-currents of change and revolution. He has seen the collapse of a great established church in Russia and was the first to recognize that the essential significance of the Soviet experiments is as much religious as social.

He has watched a ferocious persecution of the Catholic Church in Mexico and the now cohering fight for independence on the part of all religious confessions in Germany. He has frequently crossed swords with Mussolini in a long and successful campaign against the extreme claims of fascism in Italy. From the viewpoint of a dogmatic church, no more dangerous heresy has ever arisen than the arrogant assumptions of the totalitarian State, whether it is with God, without God or against God, to paraphrase a famous dictum.

Pius XI is intensely interested in the events and movements of his time. He reads widely, catechizes all his visitors, dips into thousands of letters. You would not believe how many people write directly to the Pope if you did not see the baskets of letters carried into his study every morning, there to be opened in his presence by four secretaries. Still less would you imagine the scope and character of these epistles.

Obviously, it occurs to people of all persuasions, all over the world, to confide to the Supreme Pontiff their family difficulties, their material needs. As many advise him what to do as ask his advice. A large proportion ask for money. The Pope does not answer these letters personally, but on hundreds he draws a line in red pencil opposite the main point of the letter and sends it off to be dealt with by his Nuncio in the country whence it comes or the Bishop of some distant diocese.

— — —

A recent visitor found him with a pile of letters from England on one hand, a book describing the new political tendencies of France on the other, and in front of him The London Times, which he reads every morning. After a perfunctory inquiry as to the visitor's health—and Pius XI has little concern for the ills of the flesh, in himself or others— he plunged without preliminaries into a keen discussion of world affairs.

In character he is not so much austere as habitually serious. He seldom smiles or relaxes. His thoroughness and tirelessness are proverbial at the Vatican. He knows the dioceses under his charge as well as he knew the books on his shelves when he was librarian of two of the great libraries of Italy. He has organized the administration of his handkerchief-size kingdom to the last detail with the most businesslike precision.

The Vatican has been completely modernized during his reign, and many of its great art collections have been rehoused. He has built enormously, for use rather than beauty, in the space at his disposal since Vatican City became the smallest independent State in the world. It is to him that it is so small; he deliberately cut out of the final settlement the adjoining Villa Doria and its park which Mussolini wished to cede. "The Church wants independence," he said, "not territory."

"Everything this Pope touches he tidies up," remarked an old monsignore rather somberly, and you can see his passion for order and system in the arrangements of Vatican City and in the model dairy farm he has constructed at his country villa at Castel Gandolfo, where the scrubbed "papal briefs," as the dairymen call the newest calves, swagger in blue-tiled stalls that are the marvel of the countryside.

Stronger still is his passion for order in the world. Political order, social order, moral order. The Pope is terribly anxious as he looks out upon the gloomy confusion of the secular scene. Through his thick spectacles the policies of contemporary statesmen seem above all discordant and short-sighted, concentrated only on the immediate.

In the effort to chart a Christian course for the social revolution, he resurrected and brought up to date a famous encyclical of Leo XIII, "Rerum Novarum," and embodied its principles in his own encyclical, "Quadragesimo Anno." Last year the sociologists seeking to reform the Swiss Confederation were studying this document. The late Chancellor Dolifuss drew on it in planning the Austrian Guild State he did not live to inaugurate. Father Coughlin asserts that he found there the inspiration for his Union for Social Justice.

Above everything Pius XI has worked for peace. In 1933, seeing the thickening clouds on the horizon, he proclaimed a "Holy Year," inviting to Rome the faithful of all nations to form a spiritual union for peace. Ever since, his every public utterance has been an appeal and a warning. Before the Italian military concentration in Africa became war—supposing it is war—the Pope spoke out strongly on at least three occasions, condemning unprovoked aggression as a crime against the moral law.

On Aug. 27, in addressing an international congress of Catholic nurses, he said, in words since frequently quoted, that a war of conquest is "an unjust war, something inexpressibly sad and horrible." Referring to the Italian argument that the war was justifiable as a defense of frontiers against incessant dangers, and necessary for the expansion of a population increasing day by day, the Pontiff declared it should and must be possible to reach a solution of such difficulties by means which do not involve war.

"One thing seems to us certain," he concluded. "If the need of expansion is a fact of which account must be taken, the right of defense itself has certain limits which must be observed if defense is not to become guilty. In any case we pray to God that He may second the activities and the efforts of men of clear vision who understand the exigencies of the true happiness of the peoples and of social justice; that He may bless the efforts of all who do their best, not by means of threats, which do nothing but irritate the spirit and aggravate the situation, rendering it every day more difficult for those who work for pacification with the sincere intention of avoiding war."

Since the war began the Pope has made every effort to bring hostilities to an end. He has had, it is reported, one of his few interviews with Premier Mussolini, whom Pius XI never met until after the accord settling the Roman Question was signed. It would be interesting to know what took place at this meeting, for both Pope and Duce are men of iron will, used to command, equally direct and forthright, equally sure they are right.

There is no doubt they understood each other; the head of the church does not mince words with the head of the Fascist State. And Mussolini has shown himself wiser than Hitler in avoiding unnecessary clashes on the home front. His attitude toward the church is conciliatory. Recently, in reply to a sharp protest from the Pope when the civil authorities decreed work on Sunday to make up for Fascist holidays during the week, the government immediately rescinded the order.

For the first time since 1870 the Pope has the status of a temporal sovereign; for the first time in sixty years relations are normal between the Italian Government and the Holy See. Many think the international position of the Vatican is not so strong with the Pope as a sovereign in an enclosed State as it was when he was the "prisoner" of Italy. Against that view must be placed the improved status of the church inside Italy; the greater freedom of the Holy See, which not only controls its own communications system but publishes the one uncensored newspaper in Italy; and now, at the first test of war, its complete immunity from the operation of sanctions.

— — —

Nevertheless, sanctions make a problem for the Vatican as well as for the Italian State. You can't function in the midst of a blockade and remain untouched by its restrictions. But it is not for that reason that the Pope takes the gravest view of the League measures to stop war. It is because sanctions are war—and one form of war leads inevitably to another.

The single thought of the Vatican is not preventive war but peace. Pius XI has not been asked to intervene in the conflict, but it is no secret that he is doing his utmost, unofficially, to speed the work of conciliation. The chance to come to terms before the application of sanctions was lost, but the Holy Father has repeatedly declared that the situation seems to him so full of danger that no responsible authority dare miss any opportunity of using influence to avert catastrophe.

Why, then, one asks, has the "peace Pope" not condemned Italy? Why has he not fulminated directly against this war? Why has he not used his moral authority to back the stand of the League of Nations against the aggressor nation? Because, say theologians, the province of the Holy See is to enunciate the moral law but not to apply it in specific secular disputes. For one who might blame the Pope for not intervening in a "moral issue," thousands would criticize him for interfering in what to them is a "political issue." His mission is to teach, to interpret the doctrine of the church; he does not pass judgment in conflicts of national interests, even when one side affronts the conscience of the world.

It happens that Pope Pius is on peculiarly friendly terms with the three principal parties in the present dispute. He has been twice to England on missions and is known to have a special tenderness for the country and the people, as well as a real respect for the British Government. Since the war, for the first time since Henry VIII, the British Government has a Minister to the Papal Court, sent at the direct instance of the King. Despite its inevitable clashes with the Fascist regime, the Vatican owes to Mussolini the historic reconciliation which put an end to an abnormal estrangement between church and State and is perhaps the most important of all factors in uniting a long-divided country.

Add to this the special interest the present Pontiff takes in the Ethiopians. The only college within the confines of Vatican City has been built for students from Ethiopia, forty of whom now study in peace and safety in the heart of the enemy country, under the direct protection of the Pope. Pius XI has been on cordial terms with the Negus ever since, as Ras Tafari, the present Emperor of Ethiopia, visited the Vatican ten years ago.

— — —

Thus personal predilections, the Pope's duty as head of an international communion, and the policy of the Holy See combine to prevent Pius XI from taking sides in this dispute. There is something more. Every utterance of Pius XI proves to the attentive reader that in the perspective of the Vatican the moral issue does not appear so simple as it does to members, say, of the League of Nations Union. Freely interpreted, it is clear that Pope Pius holds that judgment cannot be passed on one set of facts without weighing all the facts.

Italy is clearly wrong in her method of seizing by force what she needs, he seems to say; but what right means has the society of nations devised to deal with a problem like Italy's? Birth control, it goes without saying, would not seem a moral solution to the Pope; and even if the population remained static the Italian peninsula cannot support 44,000,000 people or even contain them without an explosion somewhere.

The League unquestionably is right in taking action against a breaker of the convenant; but is it right in making its first strong stand on the punitive side, enforcing Article XVI while ignoring Article XIX, which provides for revision of treaties and correction of injustices? Moreover, in defending the weak against the strong with one hand, is the other using the peace principle as an instrument to preserve great powers in their possessions? As to Ethiopia, whose moral rightness on all counts no one has questioned, the issue doesn't seem to be too clear. As the empire disintegrates before the invaders' walk-in, how much of it can be called an independent nation?

— — —

In a fog of moral issues, a tribune of morals might well hesitate to pick out one sin for punishment. No thoughtful observer in the world today can define the uneasy peace we labor to save as a just, even a possible peace. It is a peace established by war and designed to keep the world forever as the war left it.

This peace is itself so hideous a proof of the futility of armed conflict that it explains the dread and hatred of war and war-makers sweeping over the world. Nothing better or more stable can be established by more war, that is certain; but in the long view it is equally certain that there must be war — not all the sanctions in the world can stop it — until there is a league not to enforce but to create peace by working for a true equipoise, political and economic, and giving all nations instead of a favored few a vested interest in the status quo. If the Pope condemned, where would the condemnation fall?

34. *Stalin as Described by His Mother*

In 1930 H. R. Knickerbocker set out to explain the Soviet economic system and its ramifications in a series of twenty-four articles. Included was the first-ever interview with Joseph Stalin's mother — a reporting scoop of major proportions. Although the piece is an interview of his mother, it is actually as much, if not more, a profile of Stalin himself. Knickerbocker outlines the known facts of the Soviet leader's rise to power and contrasts him with his mother's story. The precise descriptions of the woman, her mannerisms, and her surroundings add much to the story's impact. It is a masterful job of humanizing a shadowy, yet incredibly powerful world figure. *(Pulitzer Prize for Correspondence, 1931)*

Stalin Mystery Man Even to His Mother, Post Interviewer Finds

H. R. Knickerbocker
New York *Evening Post*
December 1, 1930

TIFLIS—A Georgian schoolboy was asked to name the foremost rulers in his country's history.

"Vachtang the Brave," he answered, "David the Restorer, Queen Tamara and Soso the Great."

"Why 'Soso the Great'?" asked his teacher.

"Because Soso was the first to annex Russia to Georgia."

The anecdote tells volumes, but not of course until one knows who Soso is. He is the ruler of 150,000,000 though his party calls him merely "the most trustworthy interpreter of Lenin's doctrines," and his title is only Secretary General of the Central Committee. His picture hangs in every shop, factory and office in the Soviet Union. It peers out from newspaper front pages at regular intervals all over the world. He is probably the most powerful political leader in any nation. In Russia his name is a cult, a promise and a threat.

It is none of these things to his mother. To Ekaterina Djugashvili, Joseph Djugashvili, known as Koba to the Czar's police, as Stalin to the world, is simply Soso, the son whose career, astounding, improbable, has not yet fully reconciled her to the disappointment she suffered when he failed to become a priest.

Never interviewed

No member of Stalin's family except himself had been interviewed until today. His friends will not speak of his private life. There is no man of equal prominince in the world about whose person is woven so impenetrable a veil of secrecy as that which surrounds the chieftain of the All Union Communist Party. Power allures. Power from a source mysterious terrifies. Mystery about his person is one of the effective reasons why Stalin in Russia is synonymous with power unlimited.

Stalin's mother was the first of his family to break the spell of silence about him.

It was in the palace of the former Viceroy of Georgia that we met. Not in the drawing room that might have served as salon for a queen-mother at another age, but in one of her two commodious but simple living rooms.

The palace, luxuriously situated in the midst of a great sub-tropical garden, sprawls at the foot of one of the highest chain of hills that overlook Tiflis. The Viceroys of the Czar had good living here, but few enjoyed it long. Assassinations and attempted assassinations on the part of the fiercely independent Georgians kept a succession of incumbents moving in and out of the vice-regal apartments.

Stalin's will dominant

At their doors today stand uniformed sentries of the G.P.U. In the reception hall the walls are plastered with announcements pertaining to the business of the Council of People's Commissars of the Trans-Caucasian Republic, whose headquarters are here. Revolutionary posters and the eternal appeal for harder work on the Five-Year Plan remind one that all the way from Siberia to the edge of Persia the Soviet Union is dominated today by a single purpose and a single will.

It was the maternal source of that will, which today is incorporated fully in the person of Joseph Stalin, that I was seeking. Ten minutes of wandering through leafy courts, winding corridors, up and down stairs, brought me to her rooms, on the first floor.

A middle-aged woman answered our knock, asked what we wanted. She looked mistrustfully at the foreigner but consented to ask Mrs. Djugashvili if she would exchange a few words about her son. Fortunately there are very few occupations so entirely agreeable to Ekaterina Djugashvili as that of talking about Joseph Djugashvili.

The mother of Russia's man of steel looked very small when she came through the big double doors leading from her bedroom. Gray-haired, slender, dressed in gray woolen Georgian peasant costume, she peered at us pleasantly through silver-rimmed spectacles. She listened a moment as I explained my desires, her firm smile expanding at the mention of Stalin.

Stalins were anti-Russian

To my Georgian interpreter she said: "I'm sorry I speak so little Russian."

Stalin, master of the territories that once were called all the Russias, grew up in a family whose distaste for Russia was too great to admit the Russian language. The son learned it as a necessary instrument for the revolution. Today he uses it in pronouncements that determine the course of the nation, and seventy-two million Russians listen. To his mother it is still a foreign tongue.

With simple courtesy she asked us to be seated. We drew up chairs to a big table covered with a worn red cloth. She apologized for having no coffee or tea to offer us.

"Always a good boy"

Characteristically, she began, "Soso was always a good boy."

"Excuse me—who is Soso?"

"Soso? Why that's my son Joseph. Soso is our Georgian pet name for Joseph. Yes, he was always a good boy. I never had to punish him. He studied hard, was always reading or talking and trying to find out about everything. He started to school when he was eight years, in Gori."

At the mention of the name Gori, a village about three hours from Tiflis, her tone became insistent, and with vehemence she declared:

"I want to correct one thing. They talk a lot about Soso's being born in Lilo, but that's entirely wrong. Lilo was only the place where his grandfather was born. Soso was born in Gori. I could show you the place. I know he was born there. I'm his mother, and I ought to know."

She became quite excited about this.

"It was fifty years ago. Soso will be fifty-one eight days after Christmas old style. I don't know what date it would be by this new way of reckoning. I never could learn it. I only know I was twenty years old then and Soso was my fourth son.

"But all the others died before he was born. And Soso was my only son. Of course, I treasured him. Above everything in the world."

"And now," we interceded, "you are very proud of him. But did you ever dream he would become what he is today?"

His father a cobbler

She smiled a bit nervously, turned and smiled again at the middle-aged woman, a neighbor friend, and said:

"Well, no! You must know that we had planned quite other things for Soso. His father, Vissarion—well, if his father had lived he might have made a cobbler of Soso. You see, my husband was a cobbler, and his father and his father's father, and as far back as we could remember, all his folks had been cobblers. Peasant cobblers. And his father said he would make a good cobbler out of Soso. But his father died when Soso was eleven years old.

"And then"—she paused and cast another smile at her friend, who smiled back—"and then, you see, I didn't want him to be a cobbler. I didn't want him to be anything but"—she paused again—"a priest.

"Yes," she declared, more firmly, "I did dream that one day Soso would finish his studies and become a priest. That's what I dreamed."

Visions of the anti-religious institute in the Strastnoi Monastery in Moscow, the flamboyant posters of the League of the Godless, numerous church buildings in various stages of dismantlement and of the whole significance of the Communist Party's attitude toward the church came to mind.

"But," we asked, "are you still religious?"

"Well," she hesitated, "I'm afraid—I'm afraid I'm not as religious as I used to be. My son has told me so much." She peered a little harder through her spectacles.

Stalin, the seminarian

"See!" she exclaimed in a more animated tone, pointing to a picture on the wall. "That's how he looked when he was in the theological seminary."

It was Joseph, an adolescent, in the coarse, straight-collared jacket of a seminarist. Already in the youth, the eyes, mouth and facial expression bore promise of that strength of will that one day was to win him a new and meaningful name.

Another picture, quite recent, showed Stalin in a white roubashka, seated. It was inscribed, "To my mother." A much larger portrait of Lenin hung on the opposite wall, and facing the windows was a reproduction of the scene, famous in Soviet history, of the shooting by White troops of the twenty-six Baku commissars. It too, was inscribed by the artist. "To comrade Ekaterina Djugashvili."

"But there's so much to correct," she resumed. "It is not true that Soso was expelled from the Theological Seminary in Tiflis. I took him out on account of his health."

This was news indeed. All of the official biographical sketches of Stalin declared that he was a student at the Theological Seminary in Tiflis, that the religious instuction there "did not correspond to the needs of the young Djugashvili," that he became interested in revolutionary ideas and was expelled for being "unreliable."

Denies son was expelled

It is a point that will be recognized as important by any one acquainted with the psychology of the Communist Party. I probed deeper.

"No, I tell you," she insisted, "he was not expelled. I took him out on account of his health. When he went up to Tiflis from Gori and entered the seminary he was fifteen years old and he was one of the strongest boys you every saw. But then he studied too hard in the seminary, and by the time he was nineteen he was so run down that the doctors said he might get tuberculosis. So I took him out of school. He did not want to go. I took him out. He was my only son."

She finished firmly. There was no very effective answer to that. But I risked a last attempt.

"But everybody says, and all the books say that he was expelled."

"Nonsense," she exclaimed. "I took him out."

Possible that this time the official records are correct. Not only possible but certain that Stalin's mother believes she is rendering a correct account of what must have been one of the most painful episodes of her life. To his mother, a devout woman, expulsion was something that simply had to be explained away. One couldn't admit that one's son, so soon to become a priest, had been cast out for "unreliability." To the neighbors, to the family, to everybody who asked, one had to say it was his health.

All that was thirty-two years ago, twenty years before the revolution that put such a new light on expulsion from a theological seminary. Twenty years of repeating the same story imbeds it irretrievably in one's mind. After twenty years it is too late to make amendments. Stalin's mother is positive of her facts—so are the official records.

Jail, exile and revolt

For Ekaterina Djugashvili those twenty years were too full of worry to be lightly touched upon.

"I am seventy-one," she said, "but I'd be a much younger woman if it hadn't been for those years. The worst of it was when I never knew where he was. Always, in jail, in exile, in Siberia, even at the last in the Arctic."

One could appreciate her feelings. The record of those years is an extraordinary one. It explains a good many things—why they called young Djugashvili hard, why Lenin said of him that he would be a cook who'd brew hot broth, why they say in Moscow now that he is brewing it, and why his mother worried. It is a far more interesting and instructive record than that of most heads of a great state.

Highlights of Stalin's career

The mere table of dates tells the story:

1898—Aged eighteen, joined Social-Democratic organization, Tiflis.

1901 — Put under police surveillance, fled to Baku, helped found first illegal Marxist group.

1902 — Arrested.

1902-03 — Imprisoned, Kutalsk and Batum.

1903 — Exiled to Eastern Siberia for three years.

1903 — Escaped.

1908 — Arrested, exiled to Vologodsky Gubernia for three years.

1909 — Escaped.

1909 — Arrested, exiled to Solvichevodsk for six years.

1910 — Escaped.

1910 — Arrested, jailed, exiled to Vologodsky Gubernia for three years.

December, 1911 — Escaped.

April, 1912 — Arrested, exiled to Narimsky Krai, Northern Siberia.

September, 1912 — Escaped.

March, 1913 — Arrested, exiled to Turukhansky Krai, village of Kureyka, within the Artic Circle.

February, 1917 — Released by the Kerensky revolution.

Exiled six times

Nothing could hold him but the Arctic Circle. In the nineteen years from 1898 to 1917, he was arrested, jailed and exiled six times, escaped five times, spent a total of about eight years behind bars or in confinement camps. They say of Stalin that he of all exiles was least affected by their hardships. Robust, he thrived under conditions that killed his comrades.

The mere mention of those times sent a shudder of painful memories over his mother. It has been most difficult for her to realize the full significance of the change that has taken place in the status of her son.

"I visited the Kremlin once," she said. "Just once I've been in Moscow. I lived with my son there. I didn't like it. The trip is too far, and it's not like Georgia. But he seldom gets further than Sochi, over there on the coast. I think he is there now.

"Soso came to see me once in 1921 and once three years ago."

Mystery to mother, too

There was a touch of wistfulness in her voice. To his own mother, too, Stalin had elements that were mysterious. She looked around the room, and there was a long pause. The room seemed to grow bigger and Mrs. Djugashvili smaller. It was a big room, and it contained a great deal of furniture, seven chairs, all different, two plain wardrobes, three sofas, a small table in one corner and the big one where we were sitting. All this furniture seemed scanty. Outside a breeze stirred the fig-tree in the court. The breeze moved a wisp of Mrs. Djugashvili's gray hair.

"Moscow is very far.

"See," she exclaimed, and hurried over to the corner table, piled high with newspapers and periodicals. She pointed at the pile of publications every one of them containing an article, speech or picture of Stalin.

"See how he works. All this he has done. He works too hard.

"And, too, he has a family of his own, but he's much too busy for any family. There's my grandson, Yasha, Soso's boy by his first wife. Yasha is twenty-four. His mother, Katherine, died of pneumonia before the revolution.

"And now I've two more grandchildren. Soso's boy Vassily. He's eight. And the little girl, Svetlana. She's five. Both of them are by Soso's second wofe, Nadezhda Alleluja. Alleluja was a great Communist, a friend of Lenin's. Nadezhda is his daughter."

Lenin called him steel

The mention of Lenin reminded her of something. "You know," she said, "it was Lenin that gave Soso the name of Stalin. Lenin said he was like steel. It was a good name."

It was past noon. I asked if we could take her picture. She demurred. She had a headache. It would be impossible.

"Perhaps later in the day?"

"Well, perhaps. Come about 5 o'clock, and I'll see."

At 5 we were there. Ekaterina Djugashvili had been ready for us an hour. This time her costume was not the plain house dress of the Georgian peasant woman. It was the ceremonial black and white, the tasteful and effective native dress for state occasions.

We walked in the garden. Around us the magnolias and cape jasmines, the dark foliage of sub-tropical plants, the flaming red of late autumn flowers made Russia fade to a remote memory. Ekaterina Djugashvili said good-by. In the cordial Georgia manner she took my hand in both of hers and said: "I want to ask one thing. Will you send one of those pictures to Soso?"

I promised I would.

Reprinted by permission of the New York *Post.*

35.   *The Death of Captain Waskow*

Ernie Pyle wrote the following story while serving in Italy as a correspondent during World War II. The best-known frontline reporter of the war, Pyle wrote hardly anything about the bigger issues involved in the conflict. His stories instead were of courage and anger, of men who did not want to die but who faced death constantly. In the following story, as in most others he wrote, Pyle tells of those people and events he witnessed and had known. By use of theme, concrete detail, and direct, brief quotation, he captures the emotion of a company of soldiers on the death of their captain. *(Pulitzer Prize for Correspondence, 1944)*

Soldier Dies on a Moonlit Night
Ernie Pyle
Scripps Howard Newspaper Alliance
January 10, 1944

In this war I have known a lot of officers who were loved and respected by the soldiers under them. But never have I crossed the trail of any man as beloved as Captain Henry T. Waskow, of Belton, Texas.

Captain Waskow was a company commander in the Thirty-sixth Division. He had led his company since long before it left the States. He was very young, only in his middle twenties, but he carried in him a sincerity and a gentleness that made people want to be guided by him.

"After my father, he came next," a sergeant told me.

"He always looked after us," a soldier said. "He'd go to bat for us every time."

"I've never known him to do anything unfair," another said.

I was at the foot of a mule trail the night they brought Captain Waskow down. The moon was nearly full, and you could see far up the trail, and even part way across the valley below.

Dead men had been coming down the mountain all evening, lashed onto the backs of mules. They came lying belly-down across the wooden pack-saddles, their heads hanging down on one side, their stiffened legs sticking out awkwardly from the other, bobbing up and down as the mules walked.

The Italian mule skinners were afraid to walk beside the dead men, so Americans had to lead the mules down at night.

Even the Americans were reluctant to unlash and lift off the bodies when they got to the bottom, so an officer had to do it himself and ask others to help.

I don't know who that first one was. You feel small in the presence of dead men, and you don't ask silly questions. They slid him down from the mule and stood him on his feet for a moment. In the halflight he might have been merely a sick man standing there leaning on others. Then they laid him on the ground in the shadow of the low stone wall beside the road. We left him there beside the road, that first one, and we all went back into the cowshed and sat on water cans or lay on the straw, waiting for the next batch of mules.

Somebody said the dead soldier had been dead for four days, and then nobody said anything more about it. We talked soldier talk for an hour or more; the dead man lay all alone, outside in the shadow of the wall.

Then a soldier came into the cowshed and said there were some more bodies ouside. We went out into the road. Four mules stood there in the moonlight, in the road where the trail came down off the mountain. The soldiers who led them stood there waiting.

"This one is Captain Waskow," one of them said quietly.

Two men unlashed his body from the mule and lifted it off and laid it in the shadow beside the stone wall. Other men took the other bodies off. Finally, there were five lying end to end in a long row. You don't cover up dead men in the combat zones. They just lie there in the shadows until someone comes after them.

The unburdened mules moved off to their olive grove. The men in the road seemed reluctant to leave. They stood around, and gradually I could sense them moving, one by one, close to Captain Waskow's body. Not so much to look, I think, as to say something in finality to him, and to themselves. I stood close by and I could hear.

One soldier came and looked down, and said out loud, "God damn it!" That's all he said, and then he walked away.

Another one came, and said, "God damn it, to hell, anyway!" He looked down for a few last moments and then turned and left.

Another man came. I think he was an officer. It was hard to tell officers from men in the dim light, for everybody was bearded and grimy. The man looked down into the dead captain's face and then spoke directly to him, as though he were alive, "I'm sorry, old man."

Then a soldier came and stood beside the officer and bent over, and he too spoke to his dead captain, not in a whisper but awfully tenderly, and he said, "I sure am sorry, sir."

Then the first man squatted down, and he reached down and took the captain's hand and he sat there for a full five minutes holding the dead hand in his own and looking intently into the dead face. And he never uttered a sound all the time he sat there.

Finally he put the hand down. He reached over and gently straightened the points of the captain's shirt collar, and then he sort of rearranged the tattered edges of the uniform around the wound, and then he got up and walked away down the road in the moonlight, all alone.

The rest of us went back into the cowshed, leaving the five dead men lying in a line, end to end, in the shadow of the low stone wall. We lay down on the straw in the cowshed, and pretty soon we were all asleep.

Reprinted by permission of Scripps Howard.

36.   *The Death of Sgt. Shorty Plotnick*

It is often difficult for a reporter to cover a major event such as a war, day after day, and still manage to make the distant events seem relevant for readers. Hal Boyle, who covered World War II for the Associated Press, had to turn out stories on a steady basis but kept them fresh by constantly looking for new angles. The following story, which focuses on the death of a gritty sergeant, demonstrates Boyle's ability to weave detail and emotion into a tightly written piece with emotional impact. The story uses less than 700 words to give a vivid picture of a man's life and death. So skillfully done is the portrayal that the reader feels he knows the soldier even though the sergeant's real name isn't revealed until the last paragraph. *(Pulitzer Prize for Correspondence, 1945)*

"'Shorty' Plotnick Came a Long Way to Die"
Harold V. Boyle
Associated Press
September 1, 1944

WITH AMERICAN TROOPS IN FRANCE—Shorty came a long way to die—and he came against the will of the Army he had served for twenty-seven years.

"Leave me tell you," he used to say, "I'll get those Germans."

That was back in the United States. Shorty had what most soldiers regard as a soft touch, a master sergeant's rating on the operations staff of an armored outfit's headquarters.

He had the reputation of eating young "shavetails" for breakfast, and every man in the unit was fond of this sawed-off, gray-haired little man with the salty voice and the tough manner.

He was a good poker player and after twenty-seven years of selective competition with cards he had put away enough buck privates' pay so that he and his wife could afford more than C rations any time he wanted to hang up his uniform.

But although his health was poor, Shorty had no wish to get out of the Army. He was only five feet four and he was all soldier.

When he learned his outfit was going overseas Shorty had to fight a personal campaign to go along. He was the oldest man in the unit, and his friends didn't think his health would stand up under the strain of field duty.

"He had 111 things wrong with him, from varicose veins to arteriosclerosis," said Lieutenant Edward Sasson, Los Angeles, "but he wasn't looking for a way out."

Shorty was Russian and hated Germans. He hated them in the last war, too, and won the Purple Heart and three wound stripes fighting them in France. He waved those wound stripes to clinch his point—that he had earned a chance for a return at the enemy.

"Leave me tell you," he said with a deeply serious look on his gnomelike face, "I'll get those Germans."

Today a small group of officers who knew and loved the lionhearted little man stood around a jeep near the front lines and talked sadly of how the Germans finally got Shorty.

"We'd just taken a town," said his company commander, Captain James Kuhns, Greensburg, Pennsylvania, "and Shorty and two other men heard there still was a German machine-gun nest giving us trouble in one of the buildings.

"It wasn't the concern of the operations sergeant to knock it out, but you couldn't keep Shorty from going after those Germans. He was armed only with a pistol, but the two men with him had carbines. Shorty told them 'OK, I'll go out and draw their fire, and then you boys give it to them.'

"He edged out, but the Germans caught him with the first burst and mowed him down. He died before he knew he had located and wiped out that machine-gun nest. That was like Shorty—sticking his own neck out."

"Poor old Shorty," one officer said. There was silence for a minute, then another officer laughed reminiscently.

"Remember the time that young lieutenant walked up to Shorty and told him to take his hands out of his pockets, and Shorty just looked at him and said, 'Listen, recruit — — — —'?"

For a quarter of an hour they stood there within a few hundred yards of the front lines, telling legends of Shorty. He never knew his own age because he had no birth record.

"He was the best damned soldier in this division," said Major Nathan M. Quinn, Spencer, Massachusetts.

Shorty would rather have had that sentence over his grave than his own nameplate—Sergeant Joe L. Plotnick, Baltimore, Maryland—because when he was alive he proudly thought so, too. He knew he was "the best damned soldier" in any division. He wouldn't have been Shorty if he didn't think so.

Reprinted by permission of the Associated Press.

37. *An Interview with Gandhi*

While in New Delhi gathering material for a series on India, Price Day obtained an interview with Mohandas K. Gandhi. It was one of the last Gandhi granted to a reporter before being killed. In the following article, Day does an excellent job of capturing and portraying the personality of Gandhi. He uses an unconventional lead to lure the reader into the story. Writing with a light and breezy style, he does not clutter the story with insignificant details. By including

touches on Gandhi's personality—his interests, habits, and activities—he makes the interview vibrant; and by using quotes, incidents, background, and Gandhi's views, he makes Gandhi real to the
reader. *(Pulitzer Prize for International Reporting, 1949)*

Thin Thread In Gandhi's Hand – Symbol of India
Price Day
Baltimore *Sun*
January 19, 1948

"A good thread," said the Mahatma, "is a thing of beauty and a joy
forever."

With the fingers of one hand he maintained the proper delicate
tension on the cotton thread he was spinning. With the other hand he
turned the small, flat *charkha*—spinning wheel—at his side on the
white mattress.

Broken threads, he explained, could be repaired, but should not be.
He held up a little ball of broken threads. They were valuable as lamp
wicks, he said, and in many other ways such as for stuffing pin
cushions, like the blue one on the low table in front of his mattress.

Bottle of water

Also on the table sat a porcelain group of three monkeys: hear, see,
speak no evil.

A few papers, a bottle of ink, a penpoint in a stained holder, a quart
bottle two-thirds full of water and his famous dollar watch made up
the rest of the homely furnishings of his immediate establishment.

At the moment he was staying in one of the richest houses in New
Delhi, though normally he lives there in the colony of the sweepers,
among the lowest of the untouchables. In either place, the mattress
and the objects on and before it are the same.

Hand-spinning, of course, is a token of Mohandas Karamchand
Gandhi's identification of himself with the depressed millions of India,
and of his belief in village industries. It also appears to assist him in
his processes of thought.

Furthermore, at this particular time the thin white thread, held out
in his fingers, seemed to symbolize India.

The time was that of the Delhi riots, when fear had arisen that the
least bit too much strain might snap the new thread of government in
the Indian Dominion and prevent the fabrication of the potentially

strong *khadi*, home-woven cloth, of full and effective Indian self-rule.

Gandhi, after his 73-hour fast in Calcutta, had arrived in Delhi on the worst day of the riots, and had at once announced his intention of remaining until they ended.

Another campaign

His real task, however, was much wider than the stopping of the Delhi troubles. By the time of his arrival at New Delhi, it had become plain that the mass flight of Hindus and Sikhs from Pakistan, and of Moslems from India, threatened both dominions with economic disaster unless it was halted.

Less dramatically than by fasting, but with no less concentration, he went to work on a campaign which, if successful, might well be recorded by history as the greatest of all his achievements.

In brief, innumerable conferences, in his evening talks, in writing, he pursued the task hour by hour, changing his approach with each change in the situation.

"I no longer have plans," he said when interviewed. "I may hold a prayer meeting tonight, but I may not be alive."

Left shoes at door

"Whenever I make plans, something—call it God, call it Nature—intervenes. I had planned to go to the Punjab at once, but now I must stay in Delhi.

"A man going to a fire with a bucket of water must put out any fires he finds along his way. If I do this here, I will still have water to spare for the conflagration ahead."

The interview, in fact, amounted to just that, though the visit lasted longer. For the past two years, Gandhi has received few individual members of the press, and Robert Stimson, of the British Broadcasting Corporation, and I were completely surprised when several days of waiting were rewarded with our being led to his door, where we left our shoes, and into his presence.

It is not that Gandhi makes himself inaccessible. As to the press, however, his position is that he speaks in public every evening, except on his days of silence, and writes steadily, and thus says all he has to say.

Not vague on strife

To the outside observer, his prayer-meeting speeches and his writings appear occasionally diffuse, but he was not vague on the question of communal strife.

During the riots in the Punjab and New Delhi, as hatred grew between Hindu and Sikh on the one side and Moslem on the other, Gandhi's was the most potent Indian voice to declare flatly that "both sides are crazy.

"There are no data by which to measure the guilt on either side," he said, at a moment when each was trying to deny guilt, or at least insist that the other was infinitely the more guilty. "It is sufficient to know that both are guilty."

On another day, while the troubles were at their height, he said that unless the wrongdoing ceased, war between India and Pakistan would result; but even without war, he foresaw other serious consequences.

Acid, incisive accents

"If Hindus felt that there was no room in India for non-Hindus, except as slaves," he declared, "they would kill Hinduism. If Moslems felt that there was no room in Pakistan for non-Moslems, except as slaves, they would kill Islam."

These may seem simple and obvious statements, but in India at the time, with its wild and involved passions, they had the acid, incisive accents of the thing needed above all else, a dispassionate viewpoint.

Behind them, as behind most of Gandhi's words, lay more than mere reasonableness and insistence on justice. He also saw the political and economic dangers ahead.

No official position

He could speak more plainly, to be sure, than could the members of the Government, for he holds no official position.

To precisely what extent he nevertheless spoke for the Government is difficult to say. He was constantly visited by its leaders, from Governor General Viscount Mountbatten, Prime Minister Vallabhbhai Patel on down.

Indeed, this question of just how much of Gandhi's power is spiritual, and how much is political, touches what must be called the real enigma that makes each professional observer who comes to India feel that, whatever else he does, he must try to make up his mind about the Mahatma.

Wisest man on earth?

Is he, as millions of India and not a few elsewhere believe, the greatest human being produced by the generations now alive, the wisest man on earth?

He has shown, it is said, in his teaching that worthy ends can be achieved only by worthy means, a simple yet magnificent way by which one can hope to survive.

One can argue that he is, on the other hand, the greatest charlatan of our time, the most astute opportunist of the age. And one can ask whether his influence actually has been an influence for progress, or for darkest reaction.

Nehru admires Gandhi

At times, without explanation, he has called off popular movements at the very brink of success; he has been accused of being a servant of vested power.

It has been charged that his championship of the untouchables whom he renamed *harijans*, chosen of God, is not a war on the caste system at all, but merely an attempt to create a fifth major caste.

Yet, Nehru, who is irrevokably opposed to all distinctions of caste and is known to disagree with Gandhi's economic theories, admires Gandhi with a kind of sober idolatry.

So do hundreds of others of an open, skeptical temper of mind, similar to Nehru's. To them, and to millions upon millions of lesser Indians, "Gandhiji" is the great man of India, and of the world.

Unable to make up minds

With all this conflict of opinion it is no surprise to find that most observers are unable fully to make up their minds, and this correspondent now places himself in their company.

It might be added that a good many Indians also find him totally inexplicable.

That he is a great figure, however, cannot be seriously questioned. If he had done nothing else, his doctrine of *satyagraha*, "insistence on truth," nonviolent resistance, has proved to be a political weapon of tremendous effectiveness.

His struggle against the British was a struggle requiring courage, intelligence and imagination, and in India he is given credit for having done most to force the British to go. He is the father of Indian independence.

Denotes deep respect

As has been noted, the cry in the hall of the Constituent Assembly in New Delhi at the moment of independence was not "Jai Hind" but "Gandhiji."

(The suffix "ji" denotes deep respect. Gandhi's is also "Mahatmaji.")

While he has certainly worked assiduously behind the scenes of Indian politics, and continues to do so, Gandhi's real strength may be remembered as an open strength, a moral one.

It is moral in an ethical, not in a strictly religious sense, though some say that despite the mass of evidence Gandhi's thinking is drawn from all religions and philosophies. However, he remains fundamentally Hindu.

This could still be true, since Hinduism is not itself a religion, in the formal sense of a fixed creed and a fixed ritual. It is widely receptive, or has been in the past, except in its most prominent manifestation, the existence of caste.

The rioting subsided

Even when Gandhi speaks of "God," he is not talking in Hindu terms, or in Christian, or in the terms of any one religion.

"We are toys in the hands of God," he said in the early days of September. "He makes us dance to His tune. The utmost therefore that a man can do is to refrain from interfering with the dance and to tender full obedience to the Maker's will."

The people of Calcutta, to whom this was addressed, may not quite have understood it; but they did understand that Gandhi was fasting, and intended to fast until the rioting subsided, or until he died. The rioting subsided.

He did not fast during the Delhi riots later in the month, and the easing of the situation here could be traced more to military force than to his influence; but after it had eased there were Hindus who said that they were waiting only until Gandhi's departure to renew their war on Moslems.

Recovered quickly from fast

At that time, many sobering persons were hoping that Gandhi would not decide to go to the Punjab, or, if he did, that he would not fast there.

In Calcutta, they pointed out, he was fasting "against" Hindus. In the Punjab he would have to fast against Hindus, Sikhs and Moslems. They feared it would not work.

Despite his age—by Hindu reckoning, he is 79, by Western 78— Gandhi recovered quickly from the Calcutta fast.

He is, in fact, not a frail man, rather, a wiry one. When he walks he supports himself with one hand on a shoulder of one of his followers, often his granddaughter Many, but in his step there is a definite, if deliberate, spring.

Make him appear small

Also, he is tall rather than short, though when he is seated on his mattress the thin, naked torso, the squarish bald skull and the large ears make him appear smaller than he is.

His voice is no longer strong, but is quick and definite. His hands are small and steady.

Surrounded by adoration, he is still relaxed, at times dryly witty, occasionally almost gay. Behind his glasses—or over their upper rims—his eyes are alert and lively

His personal needs go little beyond pen, paper, transportation, umbrella, sandals, enough *khadi* for a peasant loincloth and the rice, vegetables, goat's cheese and curds on which he exists.

Expense of poverty

His entourage, however, consisting as it does of secretaries, cooks, physicians and followers, is elaborate enough to have elicited the remark from an admirer, that no one would ever know how much it had cost to keep Mahatmaji in poverty.

Expenses are paid by wealthy Indians, among them some of the country's leading industrialists, who have supported the struggle of the Indian National Congress.

It might be noted that few men of Gandhi's importance do their work with a smaller group of assistants.

Busy as he is, the atmosphere around Gandhi is one of calm and cleanliness—a rare atmosphere in India in the stormy weeks after Independence.

Reprinted by permission of the Baltimore *Sun.*

38.   An Interview with Khrushchev

Walter Lippmann doesn't begin the report of his interviews in 1961 with Russian leader Nikita Khrushchev by discussing the serious international issues of the day. American journalism's great intellect begins by describing the atmosphere and setting of his visits. After giving the reader a glimpse of the social life of Soviet dignitaries,

Lippmann then approaches the purpose of his interviews: to discover Khrushchev's views on the great East-West issues. Writing clearly and succinctly, yet almost casually, he wastes no words while providing detailed information and clear explanations to increase reader understanding of various matters. *(Pulitzer Prize for International Reporting, 1962)*

Khrushchev to Lippmann – Face to Face No. 1
Walter Lippmann
New York *Herald Tribune*
April 17, 1961

On this, our second visit, my wife and I were taken on a long journey by plane and auto to Mr. Khrushchev's country place in Sochi on the Black Sea. Before we left Moscow, accompanied by two interpreters and an official of the Press Department, there was much mystery about all the details of the coming visit, such as when and where we were to see the great man. In fact, as it turned out, he had no other appointments after half past eleven in the morning, when he met us in the pinewoods near the entrance of his place. Eight hours later, a bit worn by much talk and two large meals, we insisted on leaving in order to go to bed.

I would not like to leave the impression that all eight hours were devoted to great affairs of the world. Perhaps, all told, three and a half hours were spent in serious talk. The rest of the time went into the two prolonged meals at which Mr. Khruschev, who is on what appears to be a non-fattening diet, broke the rules, saying joyously that the doctor had gone to Moscow for a day or two. The talk was largely banter between Mr. Khrushchev and Mikoyan (First Deputy Premier), who joined us for lunch, and the banter turned chiefly on Armenian food and Armenian wine and Armenian customs, which include the compulsion to drink all glasses to the end at each toast. Though we all drank a bit more than we wanted, Mikoyan chose to regard us as American ascetics who only sipped their wine. Finally Mr. Khrushchev took pity on us by providing a bowl into which we could pour the wine as fast as Mikoyan filled our glasses.

Between this heroic eating and drinking we walked around the place, which is large, met Mr. Khrushchev's grandson and Mikoyan's granddaughter, inspected the new and very gadgety swimming pool and, believe it or not, played badminton with Mr. Khrushchev.

In the serious talks, I might say that my wife made fairly full notes, I made a few jottings, but there was no transcript and the translating was done very ably by Mr. Victor M. Sukhodrev, who is an official in the Foreign Ministry. It was understood that I was free to write what I liked when I had left Russia and to quote Mr. Khrushchev or not to quote him as seemed desirable. I shall set down my own understanding and interpretation of the most important and interesting points that he made.

For an opening I reminded him that we had last seen him in October 1958, nearly a year before his visit to the United States. Much has happened in these two and a half years and would he tell me what seemed to him the most important events for good or evil?

After a moment or two of hesitation, he replied that during this period the two main forces in the world—the Capitalist, and the Socialist—have concluded that it was useless to "test" the backing of their political aims by the threat of war.

In contrast with 1958 when he professed to believe that the United States and Germany might attack him, he spoke with confidence that, because of the growing strength of the Communist orbit, the threat of war from our side was dying down. As a result, the United States was abandoning the "Dulles doctrine" that the neutrality of small states is "immoral." He himself welcomed President Kennedy's proposals for a neutral Laos.

You think then, I asked him, that there has been a change in United States policy? To this he replied that while there were some signs of a change, as for example in Laos, it was not a "radical" change, as could be seen in the United States attitude toward disarmament. What, I asked him, is wrong with the United States attitude? We cannot see, he replied, that any change is imminent when the subject of disarmament is put in the hands of such a believer in armaments as Mr. McCloy. We think well of Mr. McCloy and during his time in Germany we had good relations with him. But asking him to deal with disarmament is a case of asking the goat to look after the cabbage patch.

I interjected the remark that the final decisions would be made by the President. But Mr. Khrushchev insisted that the forces behind the President would determine his policy. These forces behind the Kennedy administration he summed up in the one word "Rockefeller." The view that he is running the Kennedy administration will be news to Gov. Rockefeller. I should add that Mr. Khrushchev considers me a Republican, which will be news to Mr. Nixon.

Then we got onto the subject of nuclear testing. He said that the Western powers were not ready to conclude an agreement and that this was shown, among other things, by the demand for twenty-one or perhaps nineteen inspections a year.

He had been led personally to believe that the West would be satisfied with about three "symbolic" inspections. Nineteen inspections, our present demand, were nothing but a demand for the right to conduct complete reconnaisance of the Soviet Union.

I asked him about his attitude towards underground testing. He replied that the U.S.S.R. has never done any underground testing and never will. I asked why? Because, he said, we do not see any value in small, tactical atomic weapons. If it comes to war, we shall use only the biggest weapons. The smaller ones are very expensive and they can decide nothing. The fact that they are expensive doesn't bother you because you don't care what you spend and what is more many of your generals are connected with big business. But in the U.S.S.R. we have to economize, and tactical weapons are a waste. I report this without having the technical expertise to comment on it.

Then he went on to say that the second reason why he had no great hopes of an agreement was that the French are now testing and are unlikely to sign the agreement. It is obvious, he said, that if the French are not in the agreement, they will do the testing for the Americans. To which, I said, and the Chinese will do the testing for you. He paused and then said that this was a fair remark. But, he added, while China is moving in the direction where she will be able to make tests, she is not yet able to make them. When the time comes that she can, there will be a new problem. We would like all states to sign a nuclear agreement.

Finally, he came to his third reason why an agreement may not be possible. It turns on the problem of the administrator of the agreement. Here, he was vehement and unqualified. He would never accept a single neutral administrator. Why? Because, he said, while there are neutral countries, there are no neutral men. You would not accept a Communist administrator and I cannot accept a non-Communist administrator. I will never entrust the security of the Soviet Union to any foreigner. We cannot have another Hammarskjold, no matter where he comes from among the neutral countries.

I found this enlightening. It was plain to me that here is a new dogma, that there are no neutral men. After all the Soviet Union had accepted Trygve Lie and Hammarskjold. The Soviet Government has now come to the conclusion that there can be no such thing as an impartial civil servant in this deeply divided world and that the kind of political celibacy which the British theory of the civil service calls for is in international affairs a fiction. This new dogma has long consequences. It means that there can be international co-operation only if, in the administration as well as in the policy-making, the Soviet Union has a veto.

© I.H.T. Corporation. Reprinted by permission.

39.   The Two Faces of a Terrorist

UPI reporters Lucinda Franks and Thomas Powers faced a complex story when they decided to write about the life and death of a Bryn Mawr graduate-turned-terrorist. By talking with Diana Oughton's family and friends, they put together a 12,000-word portrait of the woman no one had really known. Their story is one of contrasts and contradictions. Through thorough reporting and descriptive writing they draw the reader into the story and maintain interest. The following story, the first in a series, sets the scene and provides important background information. *(Pulitzer Prize for National Reporting, 1971)*

The Making of a Terrorist
Lucinda Franks and Thomas Powers
United Press International
September 15, 1970

When Diana Oughton, dead at 28, was buried in Dwight, Ill., on Tuesday, March 24, 1970, the family and friends gathered at her grave did not really know who she was.

The minister who led the mourners in prayer explained Diana's death as part of the violent history of the times, but the full truth was not so simple.

The newspapers provided a skeleton of facts. Diana Oughton and two young men were killed March 6 in a bomb explosion which destroyed a Greenwich Village townhouse. Two young women had run from the crumbling house and disappeared. It had taken police four days to find Diana's body at the bottom of the rubble and another week to identify it.

Diana and the others were members of the violent revolutionary group known as the Weathermen. They had turned the townhouse into what police described as a "bomb factory." Months later, they were all to be cited in an indictment as part of a conspiracy to bomb police, military, and other buildings in their campaign to destroy American society.

The facts were clear but the townspeople of Dwight (pop. 3,086) could not relate them to the Diana they remembered. Her family, too, had its own memories.

Diana had never stopped loving her family, but the bomb which accidentally killed her had been designed ultimately to kill them and their kind. The revolution she died for would have stripped her father of his vast farmlands, blown his bank to pieces, and destroyed in a moment the name and position it had taken a century to build.

The world that Diana Oughton grew up in was a world of spacious, elegant homes, sweeping lawns, the best schools and an ancestry of distinguished and monied men.

One of Diana's great grandfathers had founded the Boy Scouts of America. Another built the Keeley Institute, the first home for alcoholics to treat the condition as a disease. Her father, James Oughton, a graduate of Dartmouth, served in the Illinois Legislature from 1964 to 1966. His holdings, which make him one of the wealthiest men in the state, include 6,000 acres of corn and soybeans, 100 head of cattle, several farmhouses, a restaurant and part ownership of the family bank in Dwight.

Diana was born Jan. 26, 1942, in a town where her family had been prominent for decades. The Oughtons paved the streets of Dwight, built the waterworks and furnished land for schools.

Diana grew up as a farm girl, huntress and horsewoman. She was the best shot in the family, drove a tractor at harvest time, was an active member of the local 4-H club and once, as a child, cried for hours when she found a dead bird and was told it could not be brought back to life.

She was close to her three younger sisters—Carol, now 26 and a television writer; Pamela, a 24-year-old housewife; and Deborah, 17, a senior at the Madeira School, a finishing school Diana also attended in Greenway, Va.

Her father, a handsome, well-read gentleman who is nearly blind from a hereditary ailment, and her mother, Jane, tall and gracious, liked to keep the dinner conversation lively and encouraged their children to discuss at home what they learned in school.

As a child, Diana was easygoing and helpful. "She never fussed or demanded this and that like most kids," said Ruth Morehart, the family cook and nanny for 21 years. "She just did what she was told."

Diana's childhood was sheltered and her upbringing strict.

"The Oughtons never let the kids run around," Ruth said. "Diana was not allowed to do a lot of things other children were. If she went someplace it was usually with her mother and father."

Her family's multi-million-dollar fortune made Diana feel a bit different from her schoolmates. They used to call her "Miss Moneybags"—a hurt which she remembered, and sometimes mentioned to friends, until her death.

Once, when only 6, she came to her nanny and said: "Ruthie, why do we have to be rich?"

A few years later, a school friend who lived in a poor section of Dwight was sent away by her family to live with a grandmother. Diana came to her father in tears. "Why can't we be ordinary like them?" she asked.

As Diana grew older she took a dislike for frilly clothes, for dressing up and going to parties. She was not a child who often asked for new things and she never made out birthday lists. Sometimes, she gave her allowance to her sisters; although they all got the same amount, Diana always seemed to have some left at the end of the week.

Diana's parents are Episcopalian but since Dwight had no Episcopal church Ruth Morehart took Diana to the Congregational church. She was confirmed but later grew away from religion altogether.

At 14, Diana left Dwight for the first time, to finish high school at the Madeira School. There she mixed with daughters of rich and prominent families and happily did all the things a Madeira girl did. In her senior year, she was accepted by all of the Seven Sister colleges and decided on Bryn Mawr.

When Diana arrived at Bryn Mawr in the fall of 1959 she was a tall, bony girl with short blonde hair and long aristocratic hands. A Midwestern Republican, she was against everything which smacked of "liberalism" or "big government." In 1960, she supported Richard Nixon against John Kennedy. She ardently defended her father's ownership of tenant farms in Alabama, since sold, arguing that he treated his tenants well and fairly.

During her first year, Diana was known as a light-hearted girl, always clowning around, and the kind of person you came to if you wanted to be cheered up. She was never scholarly and studied reluctantly, but still managed to get A's and B's. At examination time, she would entertain with caviar and sour cream and then memorize her notes on the way to the test.

If there was a Princeton or Yale weekend, Diana was always on the bus, sometimes having arranged dates with two different boys.

In 1961, when she was 19, Diana went to Germany to spend her junior year at the University of Munich. Living with a German family, she immersed herself in the culture and picked up the language quickly.

Diana made close frienships with German students and would sometimes remain late into the night at student cafes, discussing over cigarettes and coffee the social problems in the United States which she later was to feel could be solved only by violence.

She wrote to her parents of conversations with a German boy, Peter: "He said something which made sense. He said the trouble with America was it had lost its pioneer spirit...it put women in the wrong place and they were becoming neuter. Hurrah for Socialism!"

Politics were still incidental to Diana's life, however.She was still a fun loving college girl—gay and confident. She refused to wear glasses out of admitted vanity and had trouble spotting people more than a few yards away. She was casual and scatterbrained.

Diana's senior year at Bryn Mawr in 1962-63 was a year of change for young people throughout the country. The silence of the fifties had ended and young people began to think about America and found it fell short of what they had always been taught to believe it was.

During the same period, a kind of genteel bohemianism was becoming fashionable in the colleges. Diana was among the small advanced class of students, inspired by the beatniks of the 1950s, who grew their hair long and traded their shirtwaists and circle pins for sandals and suede jackets.

A book which made a deep impression on thousands of white students was John Howard Griffin's "Black Like Me," an account of a trip the author made through the South disguised as a Negro. Diana was strongly affected by it and joined a project in Philadelphia to tutor black ghetto children.

Although tutors were supposed to be limited to one child each, Diana soon had three. Inevitably, the Philadelphia ghettos began to show Diana that the prosperous tranquility of Dwight was not the rule in America.

On one occasion, she told her sister Carol how amazed she was that seventh grade children could not read.

Like thousands of other students touched by the mood in the country, Diana often spent long evenings discussing what was wrong and how to make it right. She began going out with what one friend called "sad-souled men" and showed less interest in the Princeton football players who still came to see her. She shunned college mixers and proms and listened to Joan Baez albums by the hour.

At graduation, she was listless about commencement activities and more embarrassed than pleased by the elaborate party given by her parents in a Philadelphia hotel.

The message beneath Diana's picture in her college yearbook read: "The milkmaid from Dwight who's always on a diet...traveler far and wide but never knows where she's been...loves Bryn Mawr but has never spent a weekend here."

Those who knew her best saw qualities emerge in Diana during those four years which were not described in the yearbook. Beneath the frothy exterior there was an increasingly serious, somewhat troubled young woman who was gradually growing away from the protected and privileged world of her childhood.

Reprinted by permission of United Press International.

40.   "...Who Lived in the House that Bertha Built"

When covering social issues such as the problems of the aging, reporters often overlook the human aspects of the story. Frequently it is difficult to find subjects willing to talk, expensive to spend time tracking down all the angles, and many times just too depressing for the reporter to cope with the problem. Those reporters who keep pressing on these stories are the rare few who truly can make a difference. In reporting the following story, the Milwaukee *Journal's* Margo Huston faced all these difficulties and yet still wrote an emotionally gripping and important series. Throughout the story, her play on the children's nursery rhyme that begins "This is the house..." provides an ironic motif. The chilling and unflinching descriptions of Bertha, her husband, and her daughter add a starkly realistic quality to the story that brings it alive for the reader. The story is a fine example of what a difference masterful writing can make. *(Pulitzer Prize for Local General Spot News Reporting, 1977)*

I'll Never Leave My Home. Would You?

Margo Huston
Milwaukee *Journal*
October 31, 1976

This is the house that Bertha built: Shabby bungalow, shades drawn, dark. You've seen this house, somewhere. When you were a kid, you called it haunted and raced past, screaming.

This is the woman who lived in the house that Bertha built: Urine soaks through her wheelchair, trickles down her swollen legs, into open sores, over her bleeding bare feet and lands in a pool on the warped wood floor.

At 91, her blue eyes still twinkle, her smile beckons and she manages, ever so slowly, to raise her saggy arms and motion, come here, with her fingertips.

Her stringy hair matted, she cocks her head coyly and, smiling like a contented but shriveling babe, softly pleads to this stranger, "Come here, lady, and give Bertha a little kiss."

She puts her shaky arms around the reporter who had only been doing her job: Asking questions, listening and taking notes. She hugs and hugs, hanging on, happily. Her stomach, looking like a volleyball, peeks out of her black dress. It quivers some. Then the woman purrs, like the cat she alternately pets and paddles.

But she doesn't budge; for four years she hasn't, not under her own power. It was a fall, four years ago, but 20 years before that arthritis had been crippling her body and spirit.

Even so, Bertha is some character. A visit, if you let it, can be a trip back in time and deep into all of our human fears and frailities.

Talk is constant; it flows from lively narratives about days in old Milwaukee to latter day parables that are presented, of course, as fact.

One goes like this:

Three suave gentlemen knocked at her door, proposing that if she signed her home over to them, they would take care of her forever in a beautiful new home built by a new church in Chicago. If she got ill, she would move up to the fourth floor infirmary.

"So I said, 'Don't you think they'd be forgotten up there?' These boys, they were sharp, they said (now she raises her pitch), 'You are all alone here.'

(Natural, lower pitch.) "'So, what of it, what if I am? I have my own life to live. You go around like low-down thieves. Don't you know, that's robbing the rights of every human being?' So, they could see I was disgusted and they never came back.''

As the story goes, she had a cousin who broke her knees, couldn't stand, couldn't cook, couldn't go to the bathroom, just sat there all day, blabbing like a child. Her cousin's husband, Carl, is a man who gets disgusted easily; her cousin's daughter works, so soon her cousin was placed in this new church infirmary in Chicago.

"Now what business does a husband have to sign a wife in anywhere—like a dog?'' she asks.

As it came to pass, that was the same Chicago nursing home where fire killed 113 patients earlier this year. "So when this fire was, my cousin burned to death. Now she haunts me, and I say to her husband (now there's venom in her voice), 'You killed her. That fire that burned her is your trick.'

"Why did they make that church place? I call that a murder den. How can a new building burn like that?''

Parable ended, Bertha smiles across the dark stench between her post at the cluttered dining room table and her husband's creaky chair near the broken front door, 10 feet away. She recalls how, in his younger days, he looked exactly like J. Edgar Hoover. He smiles back, fondly, and she says of her husband, "He has a heart. He's a man. He's a human being.''

Bertha has been afraid to go to a doctor, so she hasn't gone to one since she came down with pneumonia in the 1920s. But she loves TV's "Medical Center,'' along with "The Waltons'' and "Little House on the Prairie''—programs that depict "the nice life.''

Bertha's parable has a lesson, and she states it slowly, softly, but most of all deliberately.

"Leave each one live—you want to live,'' she says. "I mean, leave each one have their life.''

This is the man who married the woman who...: Hanging on to the wall, the gas space heater, the wood burning stove, he shuffles, wearily, through this dark, dreary, smelly house that has no bathtub, no refrigerator. Since his wife's fall, he has wiped up her every bowel movement, as best he could.

This man doesn't talk much; his wife doesn't let him. She screams at him, "What are you crabbin' about?'' And he replies quietly, "I'm not crabbin.''' Then he puffs his pipe.

When he does talk, crabbin' it ain't:

"When you get married, you take a vow for better, for worse, in sickness and in health. So I try to live up to the vow as good as I can.''

He speaks in raspy spurts, politely, gentlemanly and, but for his filthy T-shirt and urine soaked trousers, has the classy demeanor of

Chief Ironside.

"I was dead in love with her when I married her, and I'm still dead in love with her," he almost shouts. "But I made up my mind, this nagging can't go on. What's the use of her sitting in that chair all night, all day, all night?"

He holds out his sad arms and laments, "They've lost their strength. I can't lift her anymore.

"When the police were here last, she said I deliberately pushed her off the chair."

His wife coughs, sputters, purses her lips then shouts, "There you go. Are you going to shut up? Are you going to let me talk to the lady?"

This time, he doesn't let her.

"You know yourself," he explains, "when you're wet, it smarts and burns. She can't stand it, so she wiggles and wiggles and gets on the edge of her chair and then she goes over. That's the God's truth, as I swear on a stack of Bibles."

Silence, a rare moment.

His wife looks up with all the dignity she can muster. "I have been all my life a self-standing person."

"And that's the trouble," concluded the husband.

These are the firemen who helped the man who...: First the fire truck, then a squad, then another squad, sirens blaring, park in front of this dying house. Some of the men run in, others wait outside.

Inside, there's Bertha indelicately plopped on the floor at the base of her wheelchair, its sides solid with dusty cobwebs, its seat rotten with human waste. Facing her is a shiny new wheelchair, having a commode instead of a seat and a foam rubber ring to make sitting on a toilet all day comfortable.

"How you doing, Bertha?" asks fireman Gerald Fink in his friendliest, liveliest, most enthusiastic manner.

"Here I am again," she says, picking up the jovial mood. "I can't help myself, but I'll not complain. You're my boys. You're so good."

Meanwhile, the husband instructs the firemen to put Bertha in the shiny new chair he has just bought.

No, no, no, insists Bertha, alternately friendly to the firemen and ferocious toward her husband.

"I'm not used to that, no, no," she shouts.

Now she screams with pain, two firemen are lifting her, as gently as possible, with pads and practice as cushions. Settling back into the old rancid chair, she whimpers quietly as she slowly regains her composure.

Fireman Fink steps out to the porch, his expression now pained, and asks the reporter, "Can't you do something? Isn't there some kind of social agency that could step in? Why should people live under conditions like that—for crying out loud?"

Sounding exasperated, he adds, "Helping her into her chair, that's as far as we can go."

Turning to a police officer standing outside, Fink asks, "Shouldn't somebody step in and see what can be done?"

With a cocky smile, the officer replies, "Anybody can step in there who wants to."

These are the neighbors who watched the firemen who...: Three widowers, in their 70s and 80s, are standing halfway down the block, chatting, watching, one wearing a straw hat, another chewing on a cigar, the third standing still as a statue.

This is what they tell a stranger about the people in the shabby bungalow:

"Ornery. That's what they are. Ornery."

"She's supposed to have 13 kids, but you never see them over there. Maybe her own children can't get along with her either."

"Something could happen to him, then they'd both sit there, who knows how long."

"Haven't seen her in 10, 11 years."

"She ain't got no funds at all. The tax man's always after them."

"The law should get after them."

"It sure don't pay to get old."

The man in the straw hat says Bertha called asking for a can opener in spring, so he took over a beer can opener. That wasn't the kind of opener they needed, Bertha's husband told the neighbor, who left in a huff, taking his possession with him, never to return, until...

After the fire truck leaves, the reporter stays in the shabby bungalow to interview its people. Time passes. Soon, there's a knock. It's that same straw hat.

"Is everything all right?" asks the neighbor.

Smiling sweetly, the old woman soaked with her own urine and caked with her own feces, replies, "Everything's all right; just me sitting in a chair and I can't help myself. You're a nice man."

"Well, I just was getting concerned about the young lady. She was in here so long, I thought something might have happened," replies the neighbor, peeking his head just far enough to see the reporter sitting there at the dining room table with Bertha.

Out on the sidewalk a little voice stage-whispers, "Is it spooky in there?"

This is the nurse who criticized the neighbors who...: "The neighbors watch everything. They watch the police and the nurse and they start asking us questions," says public health nurse Carol Szymczak. "I get very upset with neighbors like that, with the fact that nobody helped her. Where were the neighbors, like 10 years ago?

"People don't want to get involved. There must have been a time, a time before they dug themselves in there and sealed out the rest of the world."

There are more Berthas, Ms. Szymczak, is convinced. Helping or trying to help neglected adults is routine work for the bulk of the city's 126 public health nurses, says Carol Graham, superintendent of the Bureau of Public Health Nursing.

"No, this is not unusual, not really," muses nurse Szymczak, a 10 year veteran of public health nursing. "And I'm sure, if there's one case we know about, there's three or four more we don't know about. Behind all those closed shades, what's going on? I know people who haven't stepped outside in 20 years. If only, if only the community could get a little bit involved. If only the family could care a little bit. If."

This is the daughter who ignored the nurse who...: A data processor for the Job Service, at 60, she definitely is her mother's daughter. Her house, a small bungalow; her legs, ankles and feet, swollen; her propensity, to talk a lot; her social life, nil; her relationship with her own daughter, sad; her obsession, never to go on welfare; her spending habits, miserly, selfish and greedy; her personality, set in its ways.

But she's determined not to end up like her mother so she bought herself an exercise bike and two books, one on psycho-cybernetics to keep her mind active, the other on charted knitting designs to keep her fingers active. Old people are so sad and lonely; she doesn't want to become one of them.

Usually after work she starts digging in her garden. Then when it gets dark, she sits with a TV tray, eats a meal of all green beans or all of something else she harvested, watches TV without turning on any lights and soon thereafter, goes to bed. On weekends lately, she paints the trim on her house and putties the windows on her garage. She wears grubbies, T-shirts, tennies.

Though certainly not warm or emotional, she seemed to enjoy talking to a reporter, but when she spoke of her mother it was if she were talking about someone she had seen on TV long ago.

Does a daughter have some responsibility to help an aging, desperate, mother?

"If it's at all possible for a daughter, I think it's a wonderful thing," she replies, sitting back in her living room chair.

What do you mean, if it's possible?

"I mean, if you have a solution on how it can be done, I'd like to hear it," she shoots back, now leaning forward. "I've got all this painting to do. I've already used six gallons of paint and five tubes of calking and I'm still not through with the garage. And at work, we're being pushed all the time, to do more."

The next question is: What's more important, your painting or your mother?

"You can say that but if I didn't do my painting, I'd have it up to my ears and in the end I'd have nothing for my investment. I've got my car to take care of. And I have leg problems, too. We've all got problems. Do you want to see me become a county charge?"

There's only 24 hours in a day, she keeps saying, and besides, "My mother won't have any part of being helped because she's afraid. She's afraid of doctors, she's afraid of hospitals, she's afraid of nursing homes, she's afraid of anything she doesn't know about."

A few years ago, she says, she tried to help her mother. She gave her an immersible electric coil for heating a cup of water. "And I'm sorry I ever gave it to her, because she never used it." Her mother's house has no hot water heater.

Besides this, besides that: "Besides I have trouble breathing over there. I get physically sick....She just wants somebody to feel sorry for her, to sympathize for her....I don't have any money to throw away.

"Besides, she's still able to make her own choices. Nobody can make decisions about what's right for someone else. That's the trouble with these welfare workers. There has to be a point where they stop interfering."

This is the social worker who filled in for the daughter who...: Her name is Nancy Woedall, but county social workers don't talk to reporters and, anyway, it was her boss' boss who made the decision that Bertha would be Milwaukee's first person to receive emergency services under a new law.

This is the law that prompted the social worker who...: Called simply Chapter 55 in the biz, this 1973 protective services law and in particular its 1975 emergency services amendments have the potential of revolutionizing social work in Wisconsin.

The desperate person who refuses to accept help (Bertha) has long frustrated social workers and public health nurses. The new law says emergency services (including hospitalization) may be provided for not more than 72 hours where there is reason to believe that if the services are not provided, the person entitled to the services or others will incur a substantial risk of serious physical harm."

To provide such services, social workers are to get a court order, but they may go ahead without one if "the time required to obtain such an order would result in greater risk of physical harm."

This month, an eight-member Adult Protective Services team begins a concerted effort of carrying out this law.

Eugene Paykel, director of the Welfare Department's Adult Services Division, envisions "a great amount of precedent setting starting very quickly as to where are the boundaries of Chapter 55." He sees Chapter 55 as "a whole new tool—not a tool to do to people but to do for them. It's a whole new arsenal."

But, he predicts, this arsenal will not interfere with a person's right to die at home. It will focus, he says, "on people who are not committable, but whose judgment is impaired." (Bertha was Paykel's choice for a first candidate.)

Further, Paykel predicts that the very existence of the team will help the community get a handle on the extent of need—on how many Berthas live in how many dark bungalows in Milwaukee. (The Health Systems Agency speculates that as many as 150,000 persons could be in need of home care. For the sake of comparison, that represents the combined populations of Fond du Lac, Oshkosh and Appleton.)

This is the judge who interpreted the law that...: Judge Thomas O'Brien, a reserve judge from Hudson, Wis., declined to talk to a reporter. He had also declined, in an informal hearing, to hear the case seeking a court order to permit the social worker and nurse, with help from the police or fire departments, to take Bertha to County General Hospital.

Assistant county corporation counsel Frank Putz, who drew up the papers seeking the court order, said the judge explained he would not issue an order for forced entry because he believed it would violate the person's (Bertha's) constitutional rights—since no one ever claimed she was incompetent.

This is the crisis that followed the judge who...: First, as Bertha's husband sees it. "For 10 days, she wouldn't listen to no reason. She laid back in the wheelchair like this," he drops his head back, way back, as if his neck were broken, and drops his hands, limply, at his sides.

"She was right out of her mind delirious, hollering do this, do that, weird visions. Finally, the hollering got so bad, I said, 'What the devil am I going to do?'

"So I called Mr. Steve Carner, the police in the district, and he said, 'We can't do nothing for you or your wife unless she consents to go to the hospital.' But she's not about to consent. So he says there's one salvation, call in the board of health and they'll get a court order. And I say, 'For God's sake, do something.'

"So, all right it was then—to tell you the truth—served fast. I didn't know what was going on. They just picked her up and off with her. They don't monkey around. Oh, and they did a good job of it."

Did Bertha finally consent?

"Oh, no, no, no," he replies. "She didn't give her permission and my permission didn't count. Law is law. That was the court order, that was the judge."

As nurse Szymczak sees it, the husband's permission did count and Bertha's own consent came that afternoon anyway. No court order was ever issued. If Bertha had protested, the nurse had planned to acquiesce—not to evoke the new emergency protective services law. "Nobody's aware of that law—at the hospital or the police department."

Everyone was painfully aware of Bertha's condition. Because her head was hanging back, her husband had been afraid to give her anything to drink, for fear she would choke. She asked the nurse for milk, but no clean glass could be found to even give her a sip of water. They tried to lift her, but her skin had adherred to that foam rubber pad and her body was stuck through the hole in the seat of that new wheelchair she had so feared.

So through all this filth, the police picked up Bertha once again, this time chair and all. By the time she reached County General, she was quieter.

"Right when we got there she let Patty (her longtime public health nurse, from whom she previously would accept no help) give her some milk," recalls nurse Szymczak. "It was a moving experience."

Yes the rubber ring had to be peeled off. "But just imagine," the nurse says, "how good it must have felt to lie down in a clean bed."

This is the death that ended the crisis
That followed the judge
Who interpreted the law
That moved the social worker
Who filled in for the daughter
Who ignored the nurse
Who criticized the neighbors
Who watched the firemen
Who helped the man
Who married the woman
Who lived in the house that Bertha built.

Because she died within 24 hours of being admitted to County General Hospital, a report was filed with the medical examiner's office telling the basics:

Bertha, seamstress, lived with her husband, born Sept. 15, 1885, died Aug. 12, 1976, of kidney failure brought on by a blood infection, also hardening of the arteries.

At 5:45 p.m. on the afternoon after the crisis, Bertha was found dead in her hospital bed.

Now her husband sits shirtless, washing himself in a bed at the Veterans Administration—where years ago he met his bride Bertha. He puts down the washcloth, apologizes for his looks, then recalls how the phone rang for him that day at the Ambassador Hotel, where the social worker had found him a room.

"The doctor said, 'I have bad news for you. Your wife passed on this afternoon.'" The widower winces, his face flushes.

"And there I was all alone. I didn't see it. I didn't know it." He drops his head and raises a single hand to cover his eyes, and he sobs.

"So now here I am. This is the end of it." He shields his eyes again, wincing, holding back. "I loved her too much."

Reprinted by permission of the Milwaukee *Journal.*

41. An Old Man's Dream

Madeleine Blais faced a challenge when she wrote about the quest of Edward Zepp, a World War I conscientious objector, to clear his name. His was a story that was anticlimactic: he already had received a general discharge in 1952 from the Army that had sentenced him to ten years at hard labor at Ft. Leavenworth. Yet, he could not drop his cause. Blais was assigned to write about the final chapter of Zepp's odyssey: his attempt to have his military release upgraded to an honorable discharge. One of the most notable characteristics of her story is its exact detail. She uses it effectively to contrast history with the present, thus giving some perspective on what otherwise might seem like a fanatical and useless gesture on the part of Zepp. Her telling of his tale is sensitive and balanced and does justice to the old man's story. *(Pulitzer Prize for Feature Writing, 1980)*

Zepp's Last Stand
Madeleine Blais
Tropic Magazine (Miami *Herald*)
October 1979

All his life Edward Zepp has wanted nothing so much as to go to the next world with a clear conscience. So on Sept. 11 the old man, carrying a borrowed briefcase filled with papers, boarded an Amtrak train in Deerfield Beach and headed north on the Silver Meteor to our nation's capital. As the porter showed him to his roomette, Ed Zepp kept saying, "I'm 83 years old. Eighty-three."

At 9 a.m. the next day, Zepp was to appear at the Pentagon for a hearing before the Board for Correction of Military Records. This was, he said, "the supreme effort, the final fight" in the private battle of Private Zepp, Company D, 323rd Machine Gun Battalion, veteran of World War I, discharged on Nov. 9, 1919—with dishonor.

Something happens to people after a certain age, and the distinctions of youth disappear. The wrinkles conquer, like an army. In his old age, Zepp is bald. He wears fragile glasses. The shoulders are rounded. His pace is stooped and slow. It is hard, in a way, to remove 60 years, and picture him tall, lanky, a rebel.

The old man, wearing a carefully chosen business suit which he hoped would be appropriately subdued for the Pentagon, sat in the chair of his roomette as the train pulled out of Deerfield Beach. With a certain palsied eagerness he foraged his briefcase. Before the train reached full speed, he arranged on his lap the relics from his days at war. There were his dog tags and draft card, even his Department of War Risk life insurance policy. There was a letter written to his mother in 1919 in France, explaining why he was in the stockade. His fingers, curled with arthritis and in pain, attacked several documents. He unfurled the pages of a copy of the original court-martial proceedings which found him in violation of the 64th Article of War: failure to obey the command of a superior officer. There was also a copy of the rule book for Fort Leavenworth, where Zepp had been sentenced to 10 years at hard labor.

When Ed Zepp was drafted in 1917, he told his draft board he had conscientious objections to fighting overseas. The draft board told him his objections did not count; at the time only Quakers and Mennonites were routinely granted C.O. (conscientious objector) status. "As a Lutheran, I didn't cut any ice," he said. Zepp was one of 20,873 men between the ages of 21 and 31 who were classified as C.O.'s but inducted nonetheless. Of those, only 3,999 made formal claims once they were in camp. Zepp's claim occurred on June 10, 1918, at Fort Merritt, N.J., the day before his battalion was scheduled for shipment overseas. Earlier, Zepp had tried to explain his position to a commanding officer, who told him he had a "damn fool belief." On June 10, Zepp was ordered to pack his barracks bag. When he refused, a sergeant— "Sgt. Hitchcock, a real hard-boiled guy, a Regular Army man"—held a gun to his head: "Pack that bag or I'll shoot."

"Shoot," Zepp said, "you son of a bitch."

Conscientious objection has always been a difficult issue for the military, but perhaps less difficult in 1917 than in recent times. Men who refused to fight were called "slackers" and "cowards." By the time the United States entered the war, the public had been subjected to a steady onslaught of "blatant propaganda," according to Dr. Raymond O'Connor, professor of American history at the University of Miami.

The government found ways to erode the spirit of isolationism felt by many Americans, and replace it with a feeling of jubilant hostility against the Germans. It was patriotic to despise the Kaiser. It was patriotic to sing: "Over There," "Oh, I Hate To Get Up In The Morning" and "Long Way to Tiperary." A new recruiting poster pointed out that "Uncle Sam Wants You." The war's most important hero was Sgt. York, a conscientious objector who was later decorated for capturing Germans. They made a movie of Sgt. Alvin York's heroics.

They made an example of Pvt. Edward Zepp, a kid from Cleveland.

Zepp was formally released from the Army 60 years and two days ago.

But Zepp has never released the Army.

At his upcoming hearing at the Pentagon, Zepp was after a subtle distinction, two words really, "honorable discharge," meaningless to anybody but himself. It would be a victory that couldn't even be shared with the most important person in his life, his wife Christine, who died in 1977.

In 1952, Zepp appeared before the same military board. At that time the Army agreed that he was a sincere C.O. His discharge was upgraded to a "general discharge with honor." He became entitled to the same benefits as any other veteran, but he has never taken any money: "I have lived without their benefits all my life." The board refused to hear his case again; only a bureaucratic snafu and the intercession of Rep. Daniel Mica (D., Palm Beach) paved the way to the hearing scheduled for Sept. 12.

For 41 years, Zepp worked as the money raiser for The Community Chest, now called The United Way, in Cleveland. He learned how to get things done, to get things from people.

For years, he has sought his due from the Pentagon. His persistence was not only heroic, but also a touch ornery. Here is a man who refused to fight in World War I but who takes a blackjack with him to ward off potential punks every time he leaves his Margate condominium at night. He talks about how there are just wars, and maybe we should have gone all out in Vietnam, "just like we did in Hiroshima, killing the whole city" and in the next breath he talks about the problems that occur when "the Church starts waving a Flag."

It is impossible to tell how much of his fight is hobby and how much the passion of a man who says he cannot die—he literally cannot leave this earth—until his honor is fully restored.

To some, his refusal to fight meant cowardice; to Zepp, it represented heroism. It is an ethical no-man's-land. War leaves no room for subtle distinctions.

For his day in court, Ed Zepp was not taking any chances. His health is failing; he is at the age of illness and eulogy. He has an understandable preoccupation with his own debilities (proximal atrial fibrillations, coronary heart disease, pernicious anemia). Many of his references, especially his war stories, are to people now gone. At $270 for a round-trip train ticket, the plane would have been cheaper, but Zepp thought flying would be too risky; it might bring on a seizure, a blackout, or something worse.

On the train the old man talked obsessively about what happened during the war. He told his story over and over and over—clack, clack, clack, like the train on the rails. Except for this constant talk there was nothing about him that revealed his mission. As he hesitantly walked the narrow, shaking corridors, making his way from car to car, he did not have the air of a man headed for the crucial confrontation of his life. He looked like a nicely dressed elderly man who might be taking the train out of a preference for gravity or perhaps in sentimental memory of the glory days of railroading.

"This was the war to end war," Zepp said on the way to the dining car. "The war to make the world safe for democracy. *Democracy.* They gave me a kangaroo court-marital."

All his life, Zepp has believed he was denied the very freedoms he had been recruited to defend. He has nursed his grievances like an old war injury, which, on one level, is exactly what they are. "They murdered me, you know. They tried to, in a way."

His refusal to fight turned him into a fighter. "I was cursed," he said. "It made a killer out of me, almost."

He said he was seeking only one thing: "My honor. My good name. I don't see how a great nation can stigmatize as dishonorable a person who was following the dictates of his conscience. When I die, I want it said of me, 'Well done, thou good and faithful servant.'"

Ed Zepp turned to the young waiter, in his starched white mess coat, who had been patiently waiting for him to order lunch. He ordered a turkey sandwich: "I can't eat much. My doctor says I should eat lightly. I take enzyme pills to help me digest."

September 1979, Sebring, Fla.: Ed Zepp's light lunch has just been placed before him. September 1917, Cleveland, Ohio: Ed Zepp's appeals to the draft board have been rejected twice.

During any long trip, there is a distortion of landscape and time; the old man's talk echoed the feeling of suspension that comes with being on the road. The closer he got to the Pentagon, the closer he got to 1917.

Before he was drafted at the age of 21, Zepp had already earned a business degree and worked as a clerk at Johns Mansville. At the time, his native Cleveland was heavily industrialized, with much social and political unrest. Socialist Eugene Debs was a frequent visitor; Zepp says the man was "fire." He remembers listening to his speeches and once joined a Debs march, clear across town, to a large hall on the west side. Debs preached workers' rights and counseled against war. So did Zepp's pastor, who was censured by the Lutheran Church for his outspoken views against the war. "War," says Ed Zepp, "was an ocean away."

Zepp's parents were Polish immigrants, Michael and Louise Czepieus. His father was a blacksmith, "not the kind who made shoes for horses, but rather he made all the ironwork pertaining to a wagon." There were five children, and all of them were sent to business school and ended up, says Zepp, "in the office world."

"I was a top-notch office man all my life," he says. In any family there is talk about somebody's lost promise, failed opportunity, and in the Zepp family, there was talk, principally among his sisters, about how, with his meticulous mind, he would have been a great lawyer, but for the war, but for what happened over there.

The waiter removed the empty plates from Zepp's table, and the next group of hungry passengers was seated.

Three p.m., Waldo, Fla., in the club car. Ed Zepp is nursing a soda, and on the table in front of him, like a deck of marked cards, are the original court-martial proceedings.

Eighty miles an hour.

The train was moving almost as fast as Edward Zepp is old, and he seemed impressed by that. "It is," he said, "a wonderful way to see the countryside." The world passed by in a blur.

Despite his ailments, there is something energetic and alert about Zepp; for two months before the hearing, he swam every day for half an hour to build stamina. Sipping his soda, he wondered whether he had chosen the correct shoes. His suit was brown and orange. He had a color-coordinated, clip-on tie and a beige shirt. "I have another suit that my wife, Christine, picked out for me, but it has all the colors of the rainbow, and I didn't want to show up at the Pentagon looking like a sport in front of all those monkeys. Oops. I'd better be careful. They probably wouldn't like it if I called them monkeys, would they?"

This trip was partly in memory of Christine, Zepp's third wife, whom he married in 1962, shortly before he retired to Florida. His first marriage was brief; during the second marriage he had two children, a son who died in his early 30s ("He served in Korea and he was a teacher.") and a daughter, now 46 years old, a psychiatric social worker who lives near Boston.

"Christine would want me to do this. She was a fighter, she was the only one I cared about. And what happened? She died. All the guys in my condominium thought I would be the first to go, but she passed away on May 1, 1977, two days before my 81st birthday. Do you know what she said to me before she died? 'I want to be buried with my wedding ring on.' I met other women at the square dances at the senior center. One of them said, 'Ed, let's go to the Bahamas for a week. Get your mind off this. It's too much pressure.' But I couldn't go away. Christine and I are married, even in death."

When Ed Zepp speaks of his third wife, his face sometimes gets an odd look; there is a dream-like minute or so. The voice catches, the blue eyes become rheumy, his words come out in a higher pitch. Just as it seems as if he will break down and sob, composure returns. The same thing often happens when he speaks of what happened during the war.

"Anyone who reads this court-martial," said Zepp, "will acquaint himself with all the vital points of my case: how the draft board refused to listen; how the Army loused it up in Camp Sherman when they failed to inform me of General Order Number 28; how at Fort Merritt, Sgt. Hitchcock held the gun to my head and forced me to pack, and then they shanghaied me out of the country on the SS Carmania, and in France they gave me a kangaroo court-martial." General Order Number 28, issued by the War Department on March 23, 1918, was an effort by the government in mid-war to expand the definition of those who qualified for C.O. status. Men who had already been drafted, but had sought C.O. status, were supposed to be informed by a "tactful and considerate" officer of their right to choose noncombatant service.

"General Order Number 28 was never read or posted during the time I was at boot camp at Camp Sherman in Chillicothe, Ohio," Zepp maintains. "This was how it was done—gospel truth: 250 of us were lined up in retreat. Lt. Paul Herbert, went through the ranks, asking each man, 'Any objections to fighting the Germans?' Well, I thought they were looking for pro-German sympathizers. I wasn't a pro-German sympathizer. My parents were Polish. I did not speak up.

"Then at Fort Merritt, Sgt. Hitchcock, he was a hard-boiled sergeant, put the gun on me. He never told the court-martial about that. He approached me in a belligerent manner; there was no kindly and courteous officer informing me of my rights as specified in General Order Number 28.

"They shipped me overseas against my will, and for two months in France I still didn't know what action would be taken against me for defying Sgt. Hitchcock and Capt. Faxon. They kept me busy with regular military work. I helped erect a machine gun range, I had rifle practice, I learned how to break a person's arm in close combat.

"During that time, Lt. Herbert propositioned me with a nice soft easy job. He came to me and said, 'Zepp, how about calling the whole thing off. I'll get you a nice soft easy job in the quartermaster.'" Zepp repeated Herbert's words in the buttery tone of voice he always uses when he repeats Herbert's words. "He tried to make a deal. But I had no confidence. I smelled a rat. And to prove to you beyond a shadow of a doubt it was not a sincere offer, find one word of it in the court-martial proceedings that he offered me a job. He was trying to make a deal. It was a trap."

"And then they shanghaied me out of the country and gave me a kangaroo court-martial. I wasn't even allowed to face my accusers." During Zepp's court-martial many of the basic facts which are part of his litany are mentioned. The sergeant who held a gun to his head testified, but no mention was made of that action. Capt. C.W. Faxon said he believed Zepp had "sincere religious objections." Sgt. Steve Kozman admitted to giving the defendant "a few kicks in the behind" on the way to the SS Carmania.

In his testimony, Zepp told about how, the same evening he refused to pack his barracks bag, "Lt. Paul Herbert came up to me and spoke in a general way about my views and called them pro-German. He also asked me if I had a mother and I said 'Yes', and he asked me if I had a sister and I said 'Yes', and he said, 'Would you disgrace them by having your picture in the paper?'"

Zepp argued that in light of General Order Number 28 the Army had no right to ship him overseas without first offering noncombatant service. The heart of Zepp's case, as he spoke it before that tribunal long ago, showed his instinct for fine, if quizotic distinctions:

"I did not willfully disobey two lawful orders, but I was compelled to willfully disobey two alleged lawful orders."

Savannah, Ga., 7 p.m. The train had crossed state lines, and Zepp had just entered the dining car for an evening meal of fish and vegetables. His conversation once again crossed the borders of geography and time.

Even at dinner, it was impossible for him to abandon his topic.

"Let me tell you about what happened after the court-martial. They put me in a dungeon; there were rats running over me, the floor was wet, it was just a place to throw potatoes, except they'd all rot. It was later condemned as unfit for human habitation by the psychiatrists who interviewed me. That was a perfect opportunity to act crazy and get out of the whole thing. But I stuck by my conscience. I was not a coward. It's easier to take a chance with a bullet than stand up on your own two feet and defy."

He talked about how the Army discovered he had "office skills" and he spent much of his time as a clerk—"sergeant's work, or at least a corporal's."

He said he was transferred to Army bases all over France during the year 1919; the best time was under Capt. John Evans: "I had my own desk, and Captain Evans put a box of chocolates on it, which he shouldn't have, because it turned me into a 250-pounder. I had the liberty of the city, and Capt. Evans gave me an unsolicited recommendation." Zepp quoted it by heart: "Private Zepp has worked for me since Jan. 3, 1919. During this time he has been my personal clerk, and anyone desiring a stenographer will find him trustworthy and with no mean ability."

In August of 1919, as part of his clerical duties, Zepp was "making out service records for boys to return home to the United States, and finally the time came for me to make one out for myself."

In September he arrived in Fort Levenworth where once again he served as a clerk: "They made me secretary to the chaplain, and I taught the boys how to operate a typewriter.

"Finally on Nov. 9, 1919, they released me. I still don't know why I didn't serve the complete sentence. I never asked for their mercy. I think it must have been my mother, she must have gone to our pastor, and he intervened."

Zepp paused, and his look became distant. There was that catch in his voice; he cried without tears.

Dinner was over.

Ten p.m., Florence, S.C. After nursing one beer in the club car, Zepp decided it was time to get some sleep. As he prepared to leave for his roomette, he said, "They tried to make Martin Luther recant, but he wouldn't. Remember: 'If they put you to shame or call you faithless, it is better that God call you faithful and honorable than that the world call you faithful and honorable.' Those are Luther's own words. 1526."

It was hard to sleep on the train; it rocked at high speeds and it made a number of jerking stops and churning starts in the middle of the night in small towns in North Carolina.

Ed Zepp asked the porter to wake him an hour before the 6 a.m. arrival in Washington, but his sleep was light and he awoke on his own at 4. He shaved, dressed, and then sat in the roomette, briefcase beside him. The train pulled in on time, before sunrise.

Wandering the almost-empty station, Zepp had a tall dignity, eyeglasses adding to his air of alertness. He sat by himself on a bench, waiting for his lawyer who was due at 7. Zepp's lawyer was a young fellow who had read about his client in Liberty Magazine. Thirty-four years old, John St. Landau works at the Center for Conscientious Objection in Philadelphia. Landau called the old man in Florida and volunteered his services. They made plans to meet at Union Station, and Zepp told the lawyer, "Don't worry. You'll recognize me. I'll be the decrepit old man creeping down the platform."

Landau, himself a C.O. during the Vietnam War, arrived at the appointed hour. The two men found an empty coffee shop where they huddled at a table for about an hour. Zepp told his lawyer he had not brought his blackjack to Washington, and the lawyer said, smiling, "I take it you are no longer a C.O."

At 8:30 they left to take Metro, Washington's eerily modern subway system with computerized "farecards," to the Pentagon.

Zepp was easily the oldest person on the commuter-filled subway. He did not try to speak above the roar. His was a vigil of silence. When the doors sliced open at the "Pentagon" stop, the hour of judgement was upon him.

"The gates of hell," he said, "shall not prevail."

It would be hard to surmise, given the enthusiasm of his recital, that Zepp was in Washington on not much more than a wing and a prayer. In April, the Pentagon had mistakenly promised him a hearing; it was a bureaucratic bungle. On May 9, he was told there had been an error; there was no new evidence in his case; therefore there should be no new hearing. On May 31, Rep. Mica wrote to the review board requesting a new hearing on the strength of his office. It was granted for Sept. 12, but Zepp had been forewarned in a letter from the Pentagon that just because he was getting his hearing, he should not conclude from this concession that "the department" admits any error or injustice now...in your records."

Just before Zepp was ushered into the small hearing room at 11, he gave himself a pep talk: "I am going to be real nice. Getting even doesn't do anything, punching someone around. I want to do things the Christian way. And I'll use the oil can. When I was at the Community Chest, I called all the women 'darlings' and I would polka with them at the parties. I used the oil can profusely."

Zepp departed for the hearing room.

The fate of the World War I veteran, defended by a Vietnam era lawyer, was to be decided by a panel of five—four veterans of World War Two, one veteran of the Korean War. The chairman was Charles Woodside, who also served on the panel that heard the appeal of the widow of Pvt. Eddie Slovik, the first deserter since the Civil War to be executed. Less than a week before Zepp's hearing, newspapers carried a story about how Slovik's widow, denied a pension by the Army, had finally died, penniless, in a nursing home.

Landau stated Zepp's case, saying that the defendant accepted the findings of the 1952 hearing, the findings which concluded Zepp had in fact been sincere: "The reason we're here is that we believe the general discharge ought to be upgraded to an honorable discharge...What we see as the critical issue is the quality of (Mr. Zepp's) service."

The first witness was Martin Sovik, a member of the staff of the Office for Governmental Affairs of the Lutheran Church Council. Like Landau, Sovik had also been a C.O. during Vietnam.

He confirmed that in 1969 the Lutheran Church of America supported individual members of the church, following their consciences, to oppose participation in war. One member of the panel asked Sovik how you can determine whether a person is in fact a C.O.

"That decision is made within a person's mind—obviously you can't know whether a person is a C.O. anymore than whether he is a Yankees' fan or an Orioles' fan except by his own affirmation."

Next the old man took his turn. The panel urged him to remain seated during the testimony. The old man marshalled the highlights of his military experience: *Shanghaied, nice soft easy job, tactful and courteous officer, hard-boiled sergeant, gun at my head, face my accusers, unfit for human habitation, unsolicited recommendation.* The words tumbled out, a litany.

Every now and then Zepp's composure cracked, stalling the proceedings. "I'm sure it's hard to recall," said Woodside.

"It's not all that," said the defendant. "I'm just living it. This was indelibly impressed, it is vivid on my mind, like something that happened yesterday."

At 1, a luncheon recess was called. Woodside promised that he would continue to listen with sympathy when the hearing resumed.

"Govern yourself by the facts," said Zepp. "Then we'll both be happy."

As they were leaving the hearing room, Zepp turned to Landau and Sovik and apologized for breaking down. "You're doing all right, you're doing just fine," said Sovik.

"I can't help it. Every now and then my voice breaks," said Zepp. "It touches me."

Sovik, putting his hand on the old man's arm, said: "It touches us all."

The afternoon was more of the same: *Lt. Herbert was not making me a sincere offer, German sympathizer, disgrace your sisters, sincere religious objections.*

Finally the executive secretary of the Correction Board, Ray Williams, the man most familiar with Zepp's case, asked the defendant:

"Mr. Zepp, since you received your general discharge under honorable conditions back in 1952 as a result of a recommendation of this board, have you ever applied to the V.A. for any benefits?"

Zepp: "No I haven't."

Williams: "You understand you are entitled to all the benefits of an honorably discharged soldier."

Zepp: "That's right. The one thing that bothers me is my conscience, my allegiance to the Almighty. I have to see this thing through....I don't think that a person who follows the dictates of his conscience and is a true Christian, should be stigmatized as a dishonorable person. And I think he shouldn't even get a second-rate discharge."

Williams: "...In all good conscience you can say that your discharge is under honorable conditions."

Zepp: "I personally feel it would behoove the United States of America, who believes in freedom of conscience, religion or the Bill of Rights, that a person who follows, truthfully follows, the dictates of his conscience, and you are obligated to follow that because you've got a relationship with God, and I don't think that we should stigmatize anybody like that as being a dishonorable person.

"And the reason I'm here at my advanced age—83, arthritis and all that—my inner self, my conscience, says, 'Now here. You go to the board and make one last effort.'" Zepp paused. He hunched forward and made ready to sling one final arrow: "In view of the fact, Mr. Williams, that there's not much difference, then why not make it honorable? There isn't much difference. Let's make it honorable and we'll all be happy."

Zepp's lawyer closed with this plea:

"The military has come a long way since 1918 in their dealing with these individuals who have religious scruples about continued military service....I would contend that it's in part because of individuals like Mr. Zepp who were willing to put their principles on the line many years ago...that it took individuals like that to finally work out a good system of dealing with conscientious objection. And that's what the military has now after many, many years. That, in its own right, is a very important service to the military."

The panel closed the proceedings. A decision was promised sometime within the next month.

Back at Union Station, waiting for the return trip: gone now the derelict emptiness of the early morning hours. In the evening the station was smart with purpose: well-dressed men and women, toting briefcases and newspapers, in long lines waiting for trains. The old man sat on a chair and reviewed the day. He smiled and his eyes were bright.

"I feel very confident. I sensed victory. I put all my cards on the table and I called a spade a spade. Did you see how I went up afterwards and I shook all their hands, just like they were my friends. I even shook the hands of Williams, my enemy, and I leaned over and I said to him, 'I love you, darling.' I acted as if I expected victory and I did not accept defeat. I used the oil can profusely."

He paused. Zepp looked up, seeming to study the ceiling. He cupped his chin with his left hand. The old man was silent. A college girl across from him watched him in his reverie, and she smiled a young smile.

Finally, the old man spoke. He seemed shaken. His voice was soft, filled with fear, the earlier confidence gone. The thought had come, like a traitor, jabbing him in the heart:

"What next?"

"I'll be lonesome without this. Here's my problem. Now that I don't have anything to battle for, what will I do? There's nothing I know of on the horizon to compete with that."

He paused. His face brightened. "Well, I can go on swimming. And I can keep square dancing. Something happens to me when I square dance; its the—what do they call it?—the adrenalin. I am a top form dancer. Maybe I can go back to being the treasurer of the Broward Community Senior Center. I did that before my wife became sick, but I quit to take care of her. I always was a fine office man. Maybe I'll become active in the Hope Lutheran Church. In other words, keep moving. Keep moving. That's the secret."

"All I know is that I could not face my departure from this earth if I failed to put up this fight."

At 7:20, there came the boom of an announcememt over the loudspeaker; the voice was anonymous and businesslike.:

"The Silver Meteor, bound for Miami, Florida, scheduled to depart at 7:40, is ready for boarding. All passengers may now board the Silver Meteor, which stops in Alexandria ... Richmond ... Petersburg ... Fayetteville ... Florence ... Charleston ... Savannah ... Jacksonville ... Waldo ... Ocala ... Wildwood ... Winter Haven ... Sebring ... West Palm Beach ... Deerfield Beach ... Fort Lauderdale ... Hollywood ... Miami."

Edward Zepp boarded the train, located his roomette and departed for home. Within minutes of leaving the station, exhaused by the day's excitement, he fell asleep.

On Tuesday, Oct. 2, 1979, the Pentagon issued the following statement:

"Having considered the additional findings, conclusions and recommendations of the Army Board for Correction of Military Records and under the provisions of 10 U.S.C. 1552, the action of the Secretary of the Army on 4 December 1952 is hereby ammended insofar as the character of discharge is concerned, and it is directed: (1) That all Department of the Army records of Edward Zepp be corrected to show that he was separated from the Army of the United States on a Certificate of Honorable Discharge on November 1919. (2) That the Department of the Army issue to Edward Zepp a Certificate of Honorable Discharge from the Army of the United States dated 9 November 1919 in lieu of the General Discharge Certificate of the same date now held by him."

"In other words," said Edward Zepp, "I was right all along."

A week later, a copy of the Pentagon's decision arrived at Zepp's Margate condominium. He discovered the decision was not unanimous. One member, James Hise, had voted against him.

"I'm so mad I could kick the hell out of him. A guy like that shouldn't be sitting on the Board. I am going to write to the Pentagon and tell them he should be thrown off the panel. It would be better to have just a head up there loaded with concrete or sawdust than this guy Hise, who doesn't know the first thing about justice. If he can't judge better than that, he should be kicked off. He's a menace to justice in this world.

"I'd like to go up there and bust his head wide open."

Reprinted with permission of The Miami *Herald*.

Part IV.
DESCRIPTIVE WRITING

Descriptive stories, as the name implies, primarily focus on describing scenes or events that have some journalistic importance. Frequently a number of related occurrences are put together to give the reader a better understanding of the overall situation.

As demonstrated by the stories in the following chapter, the critical element in writing a successful descriptive piece is weaving together numerous separate facts and scenes into a vivid story with a cohesive theme. Good descriptive writing is made possible by keen observation and the use of exact concrete details.

42.   The Biggest Shadow on Earth

In writing about a solar eclipse in 1923, Magner White turned what could have been an ordinary story into a masterpiece. The surprise lead grabs the reader's attention and pulls him into the story. Throughout the narrative, White does a masterful job of providing a moment-by-moment report of the progression of the eclipse, using good descriptive prose to convey the majestic scene. The vividness of the descriptions makes it easy for the reader to draw a mental picture of the rare event, and the detailed accounts of the reactions of animals as well as people add to the grandeur of the picture. *(Pulitzer Prize for Reporting, 1924)*

When the Moon Covered the Earth
Magner White
Scripps Howard
September 10, 1923

The biggest shadow in the world—235,000 miles high, 105 miles wide, and 75 miles thick in its densest part—fell across San Diego today, the shadow of the moon as it crossed the face of the sun.

The heavenly appointment was carried out as predicted, 120 years since the last time, 120 years until the next time.

One hundred and twenty years ago, scared Indians fled over hills at the sight, or the more civilized ones knelt before shrines in the comparatively new San Diego mission and received the comfort of padres, wise in the mysteries of the heavens.

Today, white successors to the Indians gazed from housetops, land points, and from airplanes at the sight. Some, calm in the meager knowledge of science, were unafraid; others trembled like the Indians of old as the earth's satellite blotted out the sun, leaving only its pearly corona flashing through the blackness like a halo in the sky.

Indian ceremonies of yesterday on the hills found their counterpart in a "Fete of the Sun" at Coronado, where five hundred actors dramatized the awe of the multitude during the eventful moments of the midnight that came at noon.

Smoked glasses and exposed films by the thousands were turned toward the phenomenon. Scientists strained every eye nerve, keenly aware of the tremendous possibilities for discovery that attended the fleeting moments.

Clouds and fog of the early morning added five hundred per cent to the inky depth of the shadow. Whatever was lost to science by the meanness of weather conditions was gained in impressiveness for the lay spectator.

Traveling twenty-five miles a minute, the shadow came.

The moon, which had been unseen in the morning fog, began to encroach on the sun's apparent rim. The contact was signaled immediately by a sudden "turning down" of the sun's light, more sensed than visualized.

Behind its prepared glasses, San Diego presented its composite face to the fiery convergence.

Toward the gazing city, at the top of the 235,000-mile shadow, was the greatest mystery in the neighboring heavens, something the eye of mortal man has never looked upon—the "other side" of the moon, the coldest and deadest side of one of the solar system's coldest and deadest orbs.

Steadily the moon moved on, obscuring more of the sun's face, and the shadows deepened ominously.

Nervous scientists twisted thumbscrews and made final adjustments of their costly instruments all along the coast, from Point Loma to Ensenada.

Airplanes laden with scientific instruments whirred overhead, exploring the outskirts of the speeding shadow, tiny spots that grew dimmer as the moon continued her encroachment on the sun's blazing rim.

Sudden cool gusts of wind, released from the command of solar energy, swept in from the sea as darkness fell.

In the residential districts and on suburban farms chickens, puzzled by the abrupt night, took to their roosts; and cattle stirred restlessly in the yards, the routine of their lives distorted by the happening in the sky.

Animals in the Ringling Brothers circus, waiting for the afternoon performance, paced their cages and roared and whined, disturbed by this sudden lighting up within a few hours of morning.

Noon whistles sounded—the first time a noon whistle ever sounded in San Diego during an eclipse of the sun. Midnight at midday! Paradox of 120 years.

The black pattern weaves, from lacy dimness to deeper gloom. Imaginative forebodings becoming deeper, shaking at the foundations of the security the human being feels in ordinary times; suggesting, in the thought which we hide from each other through sheer bravado, that perhaps this time something may happen that never happened before, something disastrous, something gigantic and overwhelming that will take no account of mankind's limited past experience.

And now still darker. The Mistress Moon moves on in her eternal path, prompt in her appointment. Tiny humans on the globe below, the Earth—how inconsequential before this relentless, dogged power of the solar bodies moving in their orbits.

Darker! The real shadow is coming! Incredible speed. It bursts in from the sea, going twenty-five miles a minute.

Night is upon us.

What is this fear we can't keep down? The hint of the infinite night—a world with no sun!

Our friends give us ghastly smiles, pale lilies they are. Shadow bands stripe the earth; quivering crescents of light flit on the sides of buildings.

The city glows in puny artificial light.

The blot in the sky is now complete. The sun is gone!

A tiny streak shoots out from behind the blot—a solar prominence. A scientist tells us that "tiny streak" is 80,000 miles long! Blazing and glowing at a heat beyond human imagination. It is a real hell-fire. One lick of its tongue across this earth——!

Oh, war—thou feeble destructionist!

And yet this is a small demonstration we are witnessing. The Indians of Pala in 1806 and we mental aborigines of 1923 are all together as much less than nothing before this sight of the heavens—and yet it is nothing in the universe. The burning of vast stars, such as the giant sun that exploded last winter and consumed itself in a space thousands of times greater than our solar system, was a greater characteristic of the magnitude of the universe than is this temporary darkening of a small strip of our planet.

But this terrible awe. Children on the doorstep catch it and cry out at the darkness.

Why is everything else so still? We realize it all of a sudden—there is not a laugh in the city!

By telephone we get a picture of "Quaint Tijuana" during these three minutes. There is no wickedness there now.

The saloons have no customers during this sample of absolute night. Painted women stand in their doorways and look out on the heavens for the first time, perhaps, in years with wondering minds. Before the spectacle they are moved inwardly with misgivings. The background of childhood superstition and those years, long ago, of contact with churches comes to the front.

Their poor souls, dormant and obscured by the fast life, begin to scratch inside their broken bodies—and the pain of that passing experience is sweet, because it is so rare.

"What makes it? What makes it?"

The universe has played a dark card—and that card is a trump card, for Tijuana, quick with arguments for wordly ways, has no answer to the riddle of the universe.

Ah, it's lighter now. The gloom is passing. It lifts, speeds by, and again the shadows are lacy.

The crescents are back on the sides of buildings.

The sun shoots a glaring signal from around the edge of the moon. The sun is escaping from the interloper. The inexorable laws of space that forced this illusion are now destroying it.

Boundaries of the densest portions of the black night are fleeing eastward and to the south, across Mexico.

Breezes slowly die as the sun's rays resume control of the terrestrial temperature.

Soon it is morning of the "night that came in the day."

Puzzled chickens flock down from their roosts. Cows go back to their grazing. Street lights are turned off. Frightened children are reassured.

San Diego drifts back into its marts and households.

Tijuana shakes its languor.

The spell is gone, gone for 120 years.

When the shadow returns, we shall not see it. We shall be with the Pala Indians of 1806.

And the event will be the all-absorbing topic then to those strange creatures whom we may never meet except in our imaginations—our children's grandchildren.

Reprinted by permission of Scripps Howard.

43.   *On Top of the Bottom of the World*

Detail and color permeate Russell Owen's story of the most

dramatic part of man's first flight across the South Pole. Mixed with direct quotation from the expedition's members, they transport the reader from the living room to the Antarctic. Written under difficult reporting circumstances, Owen's eyewitness account and concrete narrative language imbue the story with excitement, life, and a sense of intimacy. *(Pulitzer Prize for Reporting, 1930)*

Byrd Flies over South Pole
Russell Owen
New York *Times*
November 29, 1929

LITTLE AMERICA, Antarctica—Conqueror of two Poles by air, Commander Richard E. Byrd flew into camp at 1:10 o'clock this morning, having been gone eighteen hours and fifty-nine minutes. An hour of this time was spent at the mountain base, refueling.

The first man to fly over the North and South Poles and the only man to fly over the South Pole stepped from his plane and was swept up on the arms of the men in camp who for more than an hour had been anxiously watching the southern horizon for a sight of the plane.

Deaf from the roar of the motors, tired from the continual strain of the flight and the long period of navigation under difficulties, Commander Byrd was still smiling and happy. He had reached the South Pole after as hazardous and as difficult a flight as had ever been made in an airplane, tossed by gusts of wind, climbing desperately up the slopes of glaciers a few hundred feet above the surface.

His companions on the flight stumbled out stiff and weary also, but so happy that they forgot their cramped muscles. They were also tossed aloft, pounded on the back, and carried to the entrance of the mess hall.

Bernt Balchen, the calm-eyed pilot who first met Commander Byrd in Spitzbergen and who was with him on the transatlantic flight, came out first. There was a little smudge of soot under the nose, but the infectious smile, which has endeared him to those who know him, was radiant.

He was carried away, and then came Harold June, who between intervals of helping Balchen and attending to fuel tanks and lines and taking pictures, found time to send the radio bulletins which told of the plane's progress.

And after him Captain Ashley McKinley was lifted from the

doorway, beaming like the Cheshire cat because his surveying camera had carried on its work all the way.

Men crowded about them, eager for the story of what they had been through, catching fragments of sentences. It had evidently been a terrific battle to get up through the mountains and the plateau.

"We had to dump a month and a half of food to do it," said Commander Byrd. "I am glad it wasn't gas. It was nip and tuck all the way."

"Yes," chuckled Balchen. "Do you remember when we were sliding around those knolls, picking the wind currents to help us, and there wasn't more than three hundred feet under us at times? We were just staggering along, with drift and clouds and all sorts of things around us."

When the plane approached the mountains on the way south, Commander Byrd picked out the Livingston Glacier, a large glacier somewhat to the west of the Axel Heiberg Glacier, as the best passageway.

The high mountains shut them in all around as they forced their way upwards, Byrd conserving his fuel to the utmost, coaxing his engines, picking up the upcurrents of air as best he could to help the plane ride upward.

Clouds swirled about them at times, puffballs of mist driven down the glacier; drift scurried beneath them; it was a wicked place for an airplane to be, hemmed in by a wall of the towering peaks on either side.

This was the time when they had to lighten ship, and Byrd, looking around for what could be spared, decided to dump some food. There was a dump valve in the fuselage tank, but he had determined to go through and did not know what winds he might face at the top of the glacier. So food was thrown overboard, scattered over the ridged and broken surface of the Livingston Glacier.

"It is an awful-looking place," Commander Byrd said.

They finally reached the hump at an elevation of 11,500 feet, as indicated by the barometer, although it might have been a little more, because of the difference in pressure inland.

But there was little space under the staggering plane, buffeted by the winds that eddied through the gigantic gorge. Once at the top, Byrd could level off for a time and then gain altitude.

Then there came into view the long sweep of the mountains of the Queen Maud range, stretching to the southeast, and the magnificant panorama of the entire bulwark of mountains along the edge of the Polar Plateau.

"It was the most magnificent sight I have ever seen," Commander Byrd said. "I never dreamed there were so many mountains in the world. They shone under the sun, wonderfully tinted in color, and in the sea a bank of clouds hung over the mountains, making a scene I shall never forget."

Over the plateau the Commander set his course for the Pole. They had had a beautiful wind all the way into the mountains which held them up, but the fight to get over the edge of the plateau had used a lot of gasoline and there was some doubt as to whether there was enough to get back.

But Commander Byrd determined to go on. If they had favorable winds, coming back they would be all right, but if as much time was consumed coming in as going out, they would run out of gasoline.

He took the chance and won. Flying over the plateau with long sweeping slopes leading up to the mountains, with wind drifting snow from them along the surface, it was very difficult to estimate the drift of the plane.

But by constant attention to the drift meter Commander Byrd was able to get enough sights on the surface below to keep the plane on its course and correct the inevitable tendency in all long-distance flights of swerving to one side or the other.

Between the mountains and the Pole at one point he saw a new range of mountains, apparently between the trails followed by Captain Roald Amundsen and Captain Robert F. Scott. But the mountains far to the west, the continuation of the range running up the western side of the Barrier, were, as Commander Byrd described them, "simply magnificent."

Everyone rather hoped that mountains would be seen at the other side of the Pole from Little America, but there was nothing in sight there.

When Commander Byrd's calculations showed that he had reached the vicinity of the Pole he ran along a line at an angle to his course and then swung in a wide circle, as he did at the North Pole, to make sure of coming within striking distance of that infinitesimal spot on the earth's surface.

Some time was spent in that maneuver, and then the plane was again set on a course for Little America.

The accuracy of the navigation was strikingly shown on this part of the flight, as it was necessary to navigate the entire distance home. By means of the sun compass, the Commander hit the Axel Heiberg Glacier exactly and slid down that to the Barrier.

To understand what that means, try to realize being over a vast plain, nearly four hundred miles from the place where the mountains were entered, with an encircling rim of majestic peaks all looking different from the south from what they had looked on the way in. Captain Amundsen remarked on this vastly different aspect on his return journey.

But the course, as laid, brought the plane flying high over the Polar Plateau to the mouth of the Axel Heiberg Glacier, and Bernt Balchen kept a good elevation on the way down.

Even so, it was a rough ride, for in the narrow gorge of this glacier, which Captain Amundsen ascended on his way to the Pole, the wind eddies tossed the pland around "like a cork in a washtub," as Balchen said, the high peaks sticking up all around them. It was the hardest part of the trip from the flying point of view.

When the Barrier was reached the plane headed for the base laid down on a previous flight, and a landing there was made at five o'clock this morning (noon, New York time).

June landed the plane here because he had been here on the previous flight, and also took off and made a splendid job of it. More gasoline was put into the tanks, and, when the plane was in the air again, Commander Byrd headed to the east toward Carmen Land.

What he had seen there on the previous flight interested him, and his interest was repaid. He not only traced out more definitely the course of Charles Bob Mountains, but he also saw another range far to the east.

The camp had been out of touch with the plane for some time after the Pole was reached, although the signals from the locked radio key came in and showed that it was in the air.

Men had waited up all night in the mess hall, clustering about the radio room to get the news of the progress of the flight.

As the reports indicated the slow time the plane was making on the way in there was some anxiety, and mechanics checked and rechecked figures to estimate the amount of flying time the plane had with the gasoline in the tanks when it left and what ground speed it was making.

There was some gloom as the slow progress inland was recorded and then, as a long interval came between messages before the Pole was reached, everyone wondered what was keeping June so busy.

Finally came the message that the plane was in the vicinity of the Pole, and there was a sigh of relief and men lay down on their bunks and tried to get a little sleep.

The whine of the plane's transmitter for the loud-speakers in each house was a reassurance rather than an annoyance, and if the sound had ceased probably everyone would have started up instantly.

As it was, the fluctuations in the signals made sleep almost impossible.

The other two expert pilots in camp, Captain Alton U. Parker and Dean Smith, were "flying the plane" all the way, showing by their tense expressions how they were linked with men in the cockpit of the *Floyd Bennett*, fighting their way through the mountains.

One man lay down on the wooden bench in front of the loud-speaker and went to sleep, and when the signal strength died down at one time he jumped up as if pricked with a pin. It was an anxious night in camp, for everyone here realized what those men in the plane were facing in the climb through the rifts in the mountains.

There was a pleasant omen in the weather, however. It had been somewhat overcast to the north when the plane took off and there was a strong wind, but William C. (Cyclone) Haines and Henry Harrison, the meterologists, after taking balloon runs and receiving word from the geological party inland as to the conditions near the mountains, decided that the flight could be made.

After the plane started, the conditions steadily grew better and there was a dead calm at Little America and a clear sky with only a thin line of sea smoke to the north over the sea. Better landing conditions could not have been asked for.

In the meantime the plane had taken off at the mountains, and Commander Byrd flew east for a time so as to see over into Carmen Land. Then he set a course for Little America, and, in addition to navigating all the way, flew the plane himself for a time.

By starting so far east of the course for the camp, he placed himself out of reach of any aid from the flags laid down by the geological and supporting parties of the dog-team trail.

There was a constant tendency to fly to the east, but Commander Byrd was sure that his course lay further west and held the plane in that direction.

He hit the trail about forty miles north of Little America, in a direct course for the camp, and word was sent in from the plane that they would arrive in a short time.

Everybody here tumbled out of the houses and clustered on the snow near the Fairchild plane, where two deep trenches marked the resting places of the *Floyd Bennett's* skis.

They watched the horizon. After what seemed to be hours a thin line appeared in the southern sky and grew rapidly to the size where it could be identified as the plane.

With a tail wind it came booming in, flying high and then sliding down rapidly to a few hundred feet over the camp. The men below waved their hats and cheered, jumping up and down and yelling with joy.

The plane crossed the camp at eight minutes past ten o'clock and two minutes later had made a wide circle over the bay and landed. It taxied up to its resting place, mechanics beckoning to Balchen and June in the cockpit to steer them, and slid into its hole.

One of the most difficult flights in the history of aviation had ended, and the conquest of both Poles by air had been accomplished.

The adventurous thought born in the mind of a young Virginian several years ago had been fulfilled—the North Atlantic had been spanned and the North and South Poles encircled by airplanes.

44. Veterans March in Color and Glory

The American parade—what other subject could lend itself so easily to routine coverage? In 1931 Legionnaires numbering 85,000, all veterans of World War I, paraded in Detroit for eight hours. The *Free Press* team sent out to cover the parade produced thirteen columns of type. Sidebars filled in pieces of information, but the main story took up eleven columns describing the parade itself. The fact that the writers could sustain reader interest for that much copy is a feat in itself. The story relies on describing action and color and evoking memories of the heroism displayed by the soldiers during the war. The descriptions of the Legionnaires are not elaborate, primarily noting the colors of uniforms; yet the reader gets a sense of the grandeur of the parade. Small incidents in the crowds of spectators help the reader visualize the parade scene. Bouts between the crowds and policemen trying to keep the parade path clear provide a parallel with the war action faced by the veteran. Recollections of particular units' battles and the recall of the lyrics of songs from the Great War create a sense of history and glory. *(Pulitzer Prize for Reporting, 1932)*

Million Watch Legion Veterans March for Hours
William C. Richards, Douglas D. Martin,
James S. Pooler, Frank D. Webb, and John N.W. Sloan
Detroit *Free Press*
September 23, 1931

The Legion marched.

The Yanks came—thousands upon thousands of them who have been sung about always as coming. Pulses quickened. Tempo moved up. The pendulum flew faster. And those who thought they had lain away the World War in a cobwebby file felt again a familiar throbbing.

The crowd that watched was estimated at a million. The number of marchers was put at 85,000 by the National Commander Ralph T. O'Neill. Other estimates, among them that of Maj. Gen. Guy Wilson, field marshal, were as high as 100,000.

Still, this was nothing new. Men have marched so down the ages. They marched in Athens and Nineveh and Marathon fighting their various Armageddons; and, when these were over, they marched behind their Hannibals and Alexanders and Caesars before those they had fought for.

Hour after hour they marched on and on

They, like these, fared off to wars inspired by ideals and buoyed by ladies' prayers and kudos. Men of war the length of time differ only in quests and instruments.

Up Woodward Avenue they swept, the men of our civilization, in lush impressiveness. They came out, hour after hour, a part of the force which barged out in '17 when folly took the world by the hand and led it out on a sanguinary holiday to fill the meadows of France with dead.

All kinds of men, and the women they left behind them, filled the prideful, clicking columns. There were men who saw none of it and there were men who saw it all and played the string out. There were men too late at the final push, and men who made, in America, household names and tourist spots of tiny French villages previously unknown, unvisited, unhonored, unawakened.

There were men who never reached an outbound gang-plank and men who knew full well the green fumes rising off the long stretches of mustard, the bitterness of Archangel and the streaked sky of Belleau, clipped by lead and stumps standing like gallows-trees against the sky-line.

No packs on shoulders

Gay were these interminable columns. One realized that this, because of that gayness, was a censored photograph. This day they needed no khaki to blend inconspicuously into the landscape. They were not going up at night into the line and toward an unknown. This could be a lark in all a lark's pretty accouterment.

No awkward packs on the shoulders. Nothing of fear and solitude. Nothing of corruption and men crushed in mud, moaning ones masked with dust and calling to stretcher-bearers, men living and dying in dirty trenches—and away off beyond a broad sea, a quaint commingling of preachment about mercy, in one breath, and the glorificatons of barbarity, in the next.

Thousands upon thousands

So the thousands upon thousands marched, swinging down E. Jefferson Avenue and turning North at Woodward into the roaring canyon. It was only occasionally one could forget the magnificence of helmets, the tranquility of faces, the hilarity of bugles, and tailor for the paraders the garb in which they journeyed shipward more than a decade ago and finally, on some star-lit night when clover scented the air, heard for the first time the whine of shell and saw, perhaps, no house where one had been only a second before.

But it was no effort at times, for all we know that guns no longer grumble from the Alps to the Channel, to throw around this host its war-day aura and see its units vividly—the sappers and bombers, tank men and machine gunners, signal men, fliers, brass hats, artillerymen and all the myriad others the war casts for its shows.

Old songs strengthened old memories. Band after band blared the whistled airs of war; men came singing the tunes that lightened their packs a bit 13 years ago when their boots dragged:

Oh, Mademoiselle from Armentieres.
You might forget the gas and shell.
You'll never forget the Mademoiselle.

Up past the reviewers they came. "It's a Long, Long Trail A-Winding," the pipes of kilties skirling, drums pounding, fifes shrill and martial. Kipling's boots, boots, boots. Men from every state, every territory, every distant island, generals, top-sergeants and buck-privates.

Grand stand glitters

Pageants such as this must have epaulettes, of course, and the reviewing stand sparkled with celebrities, but it was the doughboy's show; and the high stand, after all, was just a place where hands came up briskly to salute and came down again to continue their work of making it a grand, care-free holiday as well as display of might.

Those who looked on, packing themselves into the smallest of spaces, began to gather shortly after 7 o'clock; and when the Legion entered Woodward Avenue at Jefferson at 12:10 p.m. o'clock in all its display of man power, downtown Detroit held room only for those with endurance and stout shoulders. Campus ropes, the police and volunteer gendarmes had all they could do to restrain the surging crowds, and the skyscrapers forming the perpendicular sides of the picture framed at their windows an additional army of watchers.

Shortly after noon, a sudden hush fell. Away in the distance rolled the drums. Police lines strained more than they had before. Hundreds of police struggled in efforts to control the pressing thousands. The Yanks were coming.

The marching Yanks

And around the corner they did—those marching men who after reading history went out for themselves in 1917 and wrote some.

With mounted police and four companies of U.S. regulars from Fort Wayne, the Second Infantry, and Company I, of the 106th Cavalry, U.S.A., before them, the Yanks came with Ralph T. O'Neil, their national commander; Newton D. Baker, secretary of war for America in Woodrow Wilson's cabinet; Theodore Roosevelt, the son of a famous father and swinging along on foot; Gen. Charles S. Summerall, former chief of staff, and numerous envoys of foreign governments in the van.

Twenty-seven planes from Selfridge roared overhead filling the air with the clamorous stacatto of their engines as the Regular Army men ushered in the Legion.

Behind the infantry rolled three floats of rare beauty—one wholly covered with oak leaves and pretty girls depicting a French village, another with a mammoth Liberty Bell accompanied by a battalion of girls, and a third on which were massed young women in the dress of the various nations of the world.

Many envoys present

Automobiles stopped at the reviewing stands to unload many guests, among them being Capt. Louis Sable, of the French embassy at Washington; Admiral Baron Alfredo Acton, who was in full command of the Italian war fleet when hostilities ceased; Gen. Gustav Orliez-Dreszer, of Poland; Col. Hanford C. MacNider, American minister to Canada; Col. Jack Mullen, Australia; Lieut. Col. Milton Foreman, former national commander; Mrs. Robert L. Hoyal, commander of the Legion Auxiliary's 30,000 women; Frederick Huff Payne, assistant secretary of war; Col. Baron Gaston de Bethune, of the Belgian embassy, Washington; Maj. Gen. B.H. Fuller, commanding the United States Marine Corps; L.A. Robb, state president of the New South Wales branch of the Sailors and Soldiers' League of Australia; Brig. Gen Frank T. Hines, head of the Veterans' Bureau at Washington; Maj. George R. Parker, commander of the Medal of Honor men; Frederick M. Alger, president of the American Legion Convention Corp.; and Lieut. Col. R.A. La Fleche, past president of the Canadian Legion.

Other cars dropped William D. Lyons, Minneapolis, Chef de Chemin de Fer of Forty and Eight; Mrs. Ethel Murphy, Le Chapeau National of Eight and Forty; Maj. Edward L. White, president of Fidac, the international soldiers' organization.

Mr. Roosevelt, in duck, headed the Porto Rico delegation and was wildy acclaimed as he smiled broadly and waved his hand to repeated greetings. Gov. Wilber M. Brucker and Mayor Frank Murphy, in the uniform of their World War outfits rode horseback in company with Maj. Gen. Guy M. Wilson, chairman of the parade committee. Like a roll-call of the Republic, the states and every possession of America followed in the wake of the Legion champion band of Electric Post 228, Milwaukee, gorgeous in blue and gold and playing the song of the football field, "On, Wisconsin!"

The Yanks had arrived!

They gave the place of honor, behind the distinguished guests, to the Canadian Legion, to Hawaii, the Philippines and Porto Rico, and a single Alaskan trudging along magnificently with his shirt-tail out.

Burro from Phoenix

They came from Arizona, proud leader of all state departments. By virtue of their championship standing in percentage of membership gains, the men from the land of buttes and deserts marched first. The Phoenix Post band in silver helmets and blouses of horizon blue set the cadence. Their mascot was a shambling burro.

Next came Mississippi. Then the orange trench caps of Florida waved down the avenue. North Dakota, swinging close behind, mustered half a hundred in her first contingent of Legionnaires. Flashing scarlet and white, the uniform colors of the Grand Forks

Drum Corps drew a burst of applause from the grand stands.

From the Golden West, 20 standards were sent to lead the men of California. Their black bear mascot lolled in a broiling sun. White was the costume, appropriate to the day and circumstances.

Nebraska followed its band in rapid tempo. Vermont, led by the Montpelier Post band, forced a path in the same avenue. The crowd, over anxious to glimpse the columns yet to come, had closed in toward the car tracks. No longer could 16 men march abreast. Police waged a losing battle.

Oklahoma heads Seventh

The Seventh division of the parade brought Oklahoma in the van. They were headed by the Bartleville Post band in field gray coats, scarlet trousers and silver helmets. A girls' drum corps, representing Chickasha, kept the beat for the post.

Another state department — Iowa passed the stand. The Fort Dodge Post band of 50 pieces raised its voice for the throng. Those in line were obviously feeling the heat. Official temperatures had been given by Norman Conger, government meteorologist, at 85 degrees. It was much warmer on the pavement where the line of march passed through a narrow canyon formed by the crowd. The Iowa men marched by in shirt sleeves.

Out came the old marching song, full throated:

I-O-Way, I-O-Way,
That's where the tall corn grows.

Ambulances at intervals along the route were doing their bit in first aid work. Few fell out of the parade, but onlookers, in many cases, lacked stamina for the ordeal.

Madison City, Cherokee, Muscatine, and Sioux City vied with one another in brilliant uniforms for their bands and drum corps. Dubuque, striking an individual note, sent a band dressed in brown and tan.

Kansas, the national commander's home State, was introduced by the massed flags of 10 posts. The sunflower decoration was distinctive. Robert Heitzel Post, home outfit of Commander O'Neil, named after his war buddy who was the first to fall in France, was led by Emporia Band and Winfield Band, well drilled. They halted the parade at the reviewing stand to pay respects to their chief and execute a few fancy maneuvers.

Memphis Post No. 1, one of the largest in America, introduced the

Tennessee detachment, followed closely by New Hampshire with three post standards, and Gov. John C. Winant as its distinguished guest.

Bulging human walls gave the line of march a snake-like appearance. Just beyond the reviewing stand, the Michigan Ave. mass resisted even efforts of the mounted policemen to drive them back. Near the Soldier's Monument reviewing stand for notables, there was another bulge which gave the line a twist. East of Woodward, at State, there was another indentation from the side lines.

Rainbow of color

Winston-Salem, N.C., Band and Greensboro Band, with red berets and blue coats, introduced the Greensboro Women's Marching Corps. The massed colors of this State, with several foreign flags intermingled with Old Glory, were a rainbow of color. The marching ranks were well filled.

Police officers still wrestled with the Michigan Avenue bulge which closed in to the street car tracks.

Indiana, the Eighth Division of the parade, led by a 60-piece band, in grass green, entered the picture with more than 20 massed standards, and women's drum corps with red capes over white. The Indiana boys in solid lines were the most numerous so far, with at least 1,000 marchers.

New Albany Band in Persian blue coats and white trousers, with plenty of gold lace, marched 30 men.

Elkhart wears scarlet

Fort Wayne's 80-piece band, in blue uniform, was followed by Elkhart's bearing a six-foot drum. The Elkhart group wore scarlet uniforms and scarlet tunics. Gary's band turned to black uniforms.

At 1:40 p.m., the crowd broke through police lines at Fort Street, holding up the marchers nearly five minutes while the lines were reestablished. At the Campus and Woodward, the crowd forged half way out into Woodward and stayed there—another zigzag in the line.

La Porte, with a drum and bugle corps of 40 men, was followed by Lafayette, led by its 40 and 8 locomotive firing intermittently. An old gray mare trailed them. Logansport, Ind., in bright blue, came along with Michigan City in gorgeous purple.

Force line back

The Indianapolis outfit was headed by its crack drum and bugle corps followed by a host of Legionnaires, from the National Headquarters city. It was succeeded in the line of march by Columbus,

Ind., veterans and the brass band of Valparaiso, whose deployed drummers and buglers were forced to close in as the crowds pressed farther out into Woodward Avenue. As this contingent of the parade passed, police made a concerted "attack" on the crowd, forcing the line back.

Richmond, Ind., represented by a band which has been seen many times on the streets of Detroit, preceded in the line of march the huge Polar Bear Float of Gimco Post 87 of Alexandria, Ind. Airplanes continued to roar overhead as the parade neared its second hour.

Post 46 of Tipton, Ind., representing themselves as farmers and as such, made a favorable showing which was applauded by the agriculturally minded of the crowd. They were followed by a float representing a huge ear of corn.

South Carolina gay

Bands, bugle corps and the shrill of police whistles heralded the arrival at the reviewing stand of the South Carolina Division, heading the Ninth Division of the parade.

Oregon Legionnaires, who are looking for next year's convention, followed the Carolinas in the Twelfth Division. A bugle and drum corps from Salem, Ore., was attired in uniforms consisting of white silk polo shirts and bright blue trousers.

Portland, Ore., Post No. 1, with a drum corps of 25 men with silver helmets and Sam Bowie belts over scarlet coats, was another feature of the Oregon Division.

Tableau heads Wisconsin

Massed flags of the Wisconsin State Department headed a tableau float representing the "Spirit of '76" and the "Spirit of 1917." This feature drew cheers from the crowd. It was done in bronze, the figures being posed by Legionnaires.

"On Wisconsin" was the march played by the band of the Waukesha, Wis., veterans, who supported their musicians 200 strong, in one of their largest parade representations from that State. In their contingent was a nurse corps, nattily attired in red uniforms with overseas caps of the same color.

Some of Michigan's sister state in the Red Arrow division were unrestrainable. It was the Legionnaires from Milwaukee who sang as they marched:

"The Old Gray Hearse goes rolling by;
"You don't know whether to laugh or cry;

"For you know some day it'll get you, too,
"And the hearse's next load may consist of—You."

They sang with a gusto that was infectious; and those vets among the spectators, to whom it had a familiar ring, took up the refrain.

Fur hats for Fond du Lac

There was a gap in the parade as this division passed which was a signal for the crowds to press still farther toward the center of the street, only to be thrown back as the fur-hatted drum and bugle corps of Fond du Lac, Wis., post, swung past the reviewing stand.

The second "steam engine" of the parade made its appearance as a feature of Voiture 410 of the Forty and Eighth, Kenosha. Other comedy features marked this section of Wisconsin's marchers, one a man on a high old-fashioned high-wheeled bicycle.

Marinette, Wis., in silver helmets and blue uniforms, preceded a huge turtle-like float of Louisiana Legionnaires, whose State department, with that of Nevada, completed the Ninth Division of the parade.

The crowd virtually closed in around this odd vehicle, halting the procession temporarily. The first Louisiana group passed the reviewing stand at 12:23 o'clock.

It was a great day for T.H. Nichols, 83 years old, of Jackson, who served with the Second Massachussetts Infantry in the Civil War. Proudly wearing a badge of General Sherman, he refused to ride in the parade.

"I didn't ride in our war," he said. "I was in the Infantry and am still in it. I march."

He recalled parading in Detroit in 1890. He fell in with the Louisiana delegation.

Especially during gaps in the parade were the crowds unrestrainable. They continued converging at the center of the streets, and at several places in the vicinity of the Campus the two sides came together. Police, however, were able to re-establish lines, using the street car tracks as their "line of defense."

Original police lines long since had been abandoned under the pressure of the mobs. A desperate effort was being made at 2:30 o'clock to re-establish them and push the onlookers back to the sidewalks. During this period, the parade was completely halted.

At 2:30 o'clock a motorcycle corp of the Detroit Police Department pushed up Woodward Avenue past the reviewing stand in an effort to open the way for resumption of the parade. More than 40 motorcycle men were in the squad that charged the converging lines of spectators.

Illinois marches proudly

Then came Illinois, leading the 10th Division. Illinois represents the largest of all American Legion State divisions.

They were the boys who formed the Prairie Division. They fought with the British at Chipilly Woods, and left their dead at the Meuse. They were the pivot of the Third Army Corps in the Argonne and faced the German shellfire at St. Mihiel.

They marched proudly—with reason. Among them were eight Congressional Medals of Honor, 110 Distinguished Service Crosses, 51 British crosses and 47 French decorations.

A lot they cared. They went by singing "Illinois, My Illinois," with massed flags and a business looking color guard of a dozen rifles at right shoulder and looking neither right nor left.

As far as the eye could see the street was filled with Illinois Legionnaires. Two hours and a half had passed since the parade opened and still the waves of color rolled up Woodward Avenue to be lost in the black mobs along the line of march.

A note of music spoke of the changing pace of the day. A band from Illinois struck up "America," the first time other than old army airs had crashed out.

The tempo of the crowd changed. The carnival spirit had struck a deeper note. The measured tread of thousands, pounding on interminably, the beat, beat, beat of thousands of drums, echoing and re-echoing through the deep canyons of the city street, fostered a realization that back of the color and the play and the music, there was the strongest organization in America.

The crowds sweltered under a pitiless sun; yet, they stood patiently, fascinated by the unfolding panorama.

And always there was the dull beat of drums. As one drum corps passed and the sound faded, another picked it up until it seemed as if the whole city throbbed and pulsed.

Cermak heads Illinois

Mayor Anton Cermak headed the Illinois delegation. He rode with a beauteous person symbolizing Miss Chicago. Batavia, Ill., passed with another drum and bugle corps under flashing silver helmets. Enough steel hats were shown to equip another A.E.F.

A squadron of mounted police was called to push back the crowd before the Majestic Building. They rode their horses into the press and turned them deftly about.

Chicago in force

Chicago was here in force. Sharvin Post, with another drum and bugle corps, went by, playing what sounded like:

Some day I'm going to murder the bugler,
Some day they're going to find him dead.
I'll step up on his reville and amputate it heavily.
And spend the rest of my life in bed.

Some stalwart swain proved his love. He held his sweetheart on his shoulders for a full 15 minutes that she might view the passing parade.

The Hooligans, of Morris, Ill., dressed in clown costumes, added a touch of merriment. They were unique in their dress, since most of the units were in trim uniforms and marched in perfect line, eyes front.

Crowds peril police

For a full hour, between 2 and 3 o'clock, it seemed certain that the police would lose control of the crowd at any minute. Fully 50,000 people were massed in the circle before the City Hall and backed up on Monroe, Michigan and Fort. They broke rope after rope strung by the police and swayed out so far into Woodward that the passage way remaining was not more than 30 feet wide.

A pickpocket chose this minute to go to work, and a shrill cry went up from his victim. A policeman dove for the suspected one; the crowd rushed out to see the cause of the disturbance; and before the street could be cleared again, mounted officers from the 106th Cavalry were called on to sweep the pavements clear.

Every window in the Majestic, Ford, Penobscot, Union Guardian Trust and First National Buildings that gave on the scene of the parade, framed a dozen faces.

Evanston draws cheer

Evanston, Ill., bugle corps, in peacock blue with gold instruments, swept up the street playing

I can't get 'em up, I can't get 'em up in the morning.
I can't get 'em up, I can't get 'em up, I can't get 'em up at all.

The crowds howled. The interval in the parade between the Spokane outfit and veterans leading the Minnesota state department saw clowning by the proverbial model T., which is capable of acrobatics. Up on the toe, down on the heel, and charges into the crowd, characterized the antics of this piece of machinery which was driven by members of the Spokane post.

"Who won the war? Spookum!" was the inscription emblazoned on the side of a dilapidated looking automobile in this section of the parade.

Gray Lakes, Minn., was represented by a one-man band. Blowing lustily on a big bugle and beating a snare drum, James Catalano, the only Gray Lakes Legionnaire, had a part all his own; and he played it to the great amusement of the crowd.

A warning to followers of the University of Michigan football team was displayed by the Minnesota department. Marching under a banner of "The Gopher Gang," they carried another banner with the words, "Michigan, we are after the Little Brown Jug."

Garbed as jockeys

Man O' War Post, Lexington, Ky., called attention of the crowd to the favorite sport of the Blue Grass State. Its drum major was in hunting garb of red, the drummers and buglers in jockey uniforms.

Zachery Taylor Post produced a calliope.

Portsmouth, Va., brought another touch of the Southland, and its float presented historical Colonial figures.

The press of the crowds had disappeared largely, and the ever coming Legion moved more briskly toward its destination as the clock turned into the early evening hours. Six and one-half hours had satisfied many of the spectators. They wandered away.

The Michigan units were still to come, and that held thousands on the sidelines.

As the New Jersey outfits passed the reviewing stand at 6:30 the lengthening shadows of the day grew deeper and dusk began to creep down the city's concrete valleys. In the early twilight the 18 massed standards of the New Jersey boys gleamed like brilliant jewels.

The crowd began to flow back. Almost imperceptibly, but steadily the open spaces filled, and once again the police took up the task of keeping the street car tracks clear.

Cheer wildly for New York

A shout went up from the crowd about the reviewing stand as a large drum and bugle corps dressed in gray and marching like cadets, swung into view. It was the vanguard of New York. Just as their colors passed the stand and the Legion standards dipped, the street lamps flashed on through their veils of red and yellow decorations, lending a touch of fresh beauty to the scene.

The crowd was cheering wildly for almost the first time as the Buffalo Drum and Fife Corps walked on at a quick step. Here was a sight to remember.

There were silver bands on the regimental flags of some of those units, and the crowd knew it. Who could forget the old 27th Division of the National Guard—the Yankee Division? Thrown into battle with strange comrades in arms—beside the British—they fought their fight for freedom. Their Armageddon was a bitter place known as Vier-standt Ridge, one of those ridges that the Germans swept with killing fire. Read the roll call of their dead and injured if you would know the stuff of which these men were made. Eleven thousand casualties. That's the record.

Some of them had been with the Yankee Division. They had shared the glory of that body of troops which, thrown into battle unprepared and untrained, to save the cause of the Allies, had stood like an iron brigade at Soudaine and then, re-attacking, had driven the enemy back 15 kilometers for good Yankee measure.

Overhead the red aerial beacon of the Penobscot Tower became a brilliant ball of light. The windows in the great office buildings which had been black all day, began to turn yellow, and momentarily the street lights glowed brighter as the darkness deepened.

Corps after corps of the boys from New York came swinging up the street. The roll call of the drums was punctuated minute by minute by exploding bombs.

Here comes Michigan

At 7 o'clock came Michigan, led by Gov. Brucker and Mayor Murphy. Marching behind the color guard came the State's standards—50 beautiful American flags, followed by an equal number of Legion banners in blue and gold.

One thought of the words "Like an Army with Banners," as they swept up the street. And of an Army which has earned its banners, if any ever won its standards in battle!

Gay and brave and colorful they looked last night and, in the kindly light, very young. They might have been the National Guard of old marching away for Waco. Surely they were not the hard-bitten veterans of the fighting Red Arrow Division which came back to Detroit loaded with citations and medals of honor.

What a record

Yet their record runs that way. These are the home boys who went over and smashed the Hindenburg line at the Aisne-Marne, making a total advance of 19 kilometers.

They fought with the French at Soissons and outflanked the Germans at Chemin des Dames. The French gave them a love term for that. They called them Les Terribles. These boys! Out there in tricky uniforms, and with the smiles of youth on their faces!

Nor was that all. They swept over to the Meuse-Argonne front; and for three weeks, they attacked and attacked again. Three weeks of hell, that was. Then east to the Meuse; and when the Armistice came, they were still in the front-line shock troops of the Nation, ready for the attack.

Three thousand eight hundred and ninety-eight dead they left in France. Eleven thousand wounded.

They marched again in the Big Parade and received an ovation. Virtually in close order formation, the men of this state swung between the lines of spectators, the most imposing in number, of the entire procession.

Crowds begin to shift

As day slipped over into night the crowd began to change. Many who had lined the streets since early in the day surrendered to hunger and went home to eat. Their places were taken by Legionnaires who had been near the head of the parade and who came back to watch their buddies. The Michigan detachment marched through rows in which the uniforms of their fellow Legionnaires were well sprinkled.

Michigan bands were given to the gay reckless tunes of the war. "Hinkey Dinkey Parley Vous." "You're in the Army Now." The crowd lost its weariness, and voices which they thought were gone came back. They could cheer. Those who could not applauded.

"Hail, hail, the gang's all here. What the hell do we care?"

The 23rd Engineers went by. A roar went up from the crowds that would have done well on Armistice Day.

Applaud polar bears

Silence fell, and then applause came from the crowd as the white form of a huge polar bear, mounted on a float, rolled through the lighted streets.

Behind the symbol of the strangest war ever fought by American troops marched a pitiful handful of that glorious regiment, the 339th Infantry, known as "Detroit's Own." First of the men in the national draft, they were. They came from the benches, the lathes, the counters and the offices of the city.

How they fought and died is an epic which needed no retelling Tuesday night and needs none now.

There were no great gaps between the Michigan units. Grand Rapids was only a few steps removed from Sault Ste. Marie. All moved at a lively tempo, bolstered by the gay airs. The crowd grew merrier and merrier. The Mardi Gras spirit seemed to emanate from the Michigan troops. Their comedians seemed just a little funnier, possibly because of their anticipation that the long day was nearing an end.

As the Michigan march proceeded and the skyline signs of the city blazed out overhead, it became evident that something of the Mardi Gras spirit was creeping back over the crowd and the marchers.

Strict for home boys

The Michigan Legionnaires, being at home, where parades mean nothing to them, showed less military discipline than those of the preceding states. In fact, discipline would have been impossible with groups along the line of march shrieking wildly for "Jerry" or "Bill" or "Hank."

After the Polar Bears came the Second Division. The crowd, which had thinned shortly after 6:30, again swelled until there no longer was walking room on the sidewalks. The pedestrians who attempted to cross Woodward Avenue were entirely isolated. The Michigan sections came so close at the heels of each other that there was no crossing from the east to the west side of the street.

Each distinct group could be recognized, however, by the ripple of cheering that accompanied it. The flag which marked the head of each unit was the signal for greetings.

Carry Bunyan's ax

There was something new every minute. A huge load of logging wheels, wheels on which the hubs were as high as the tallest man in the crowd, rolled by. On it was a huge ax sticking from a stump. That ax, the Grayling Post would have you understand, once was Paul Bunyan's, that legendary logging man.

A man and woman drum major led a lively band. The applause was spontaneous. Neither of the drum majors ever knew who was the favorite. Toward the close of the parade, the bands came closer and closer together. Their tunes merged. Sometimes their tempos clashed. But it was a case of who cares. The spirit of pageantry was in the crowd. Everything was grand.

Michigan's floats: Doughboys in a dugout and pretty Miss Liberty, on a pedestal behind her protectors. Another float—this one carried a queen, Michigan's peach queen.

For the first time since the Michigan posts swept into Woodward Avenue, there was a distraction. The crowd took its eyes from the parade. An airplane, whirring loudly, swung low until its wings were perpendicular with the earth and cut past the Penobscot Building. How the pilot missed it was a mystery that the crowd forgot in a burst of applause that greeted the Michigan company of Zouaves which widened into a company front as it passed the reviewing stand.

The maneuver of the Zouaves, intentional or otherwise, forced the crowd back again, widening a lane, comfortable for marching.

Darkness set in

At 7:45 o'clock it was impossible to distinguish numerals on the Legion banners or to read the names of their posts. The crowd, assured that Michigan was passing, cheered every unit without impartiality.

The Fifth Division was headed by a "German" band. Weird musicians dressed in ill-fitting uniforms! Their tunes did not fit any horn. It made little difference, for their music was lost in the laughter their antics earned.

The laugh was followed by a louder one. A boxcar passed; and on its roof was, of all things, a hula dancer going through gyrations.

The clock in the City Hall tower struck eight just as the last of the parade passed the reviewing stand. The parade lacked 12 minutes of being as long as the Boston parade. It was exactly eight hours long.

A day of drama

It was a day that none who saw it will forget. Yet it was a day that memory can never reconstruct. One will not forget the rolling thunder of drums, beating, beating, until they seemed to shake the brick and granite walls of the city's canyons. None will forget that steady tread of marching feet, going on hour after hour, nor the shrill, brass calls of the bugles. But these are only highlights. The picture itself can never be adequately redrawn.

The sheer drama of it! The patient, pleasant but determined throng. The flashing waves of color rolling up the avenue hour after hour, like the endless wash of some mighty human stream.

The blue sky, across which drifted white streamers like "the trailing robes of God." A glorious sun throwing each flash of color into bold brilliance.

The endless passing of the hours with the crowd growing larger each minute. The inexorable forward movement which defeated every effort to hold it in check.

The encroachment on the street, the imperceptible movement which finally filled the pavements until the Legion marched a path no wider than the car tracks.

Quiet but determined

The quiet, so unlike that of other throngs Detroit has seen. There were no fears, no flaunted grief. There were no long continued, uncontrolled bursts of enthusiasm. The crowds were determined to see the faces of the marching Legionnaires, and having seen them, they were satisfied.

Long shadows creeping across the streets. Early dusk—the coming of the first lights. Great red signs bursting into permanent explosion and throwing their crimson over the passing columns.

Marching into the dusk the great parade rolled on. And then came the change which turned the campus into a great bowl. Every downtown light went on, and the whole scene was transformed.

Each member of the division carried a football, tucked in his arm, much after the manner of Herb Joesting.

Girl leads Corps

The girl drum major of the Duluth Drum and Bugle Corps was a high stepper. She wore a beautiful red uniform which matched her complexion. She kicked even with her head in directing her musicians.

The drum and bugle corps marched on. There seemed no end of this particular form of martial music, despite the 150 bands.

It was too much for one Negro drummer from Charles Young Post of Charlotte, N.C. Swinging his drum to his shoulder, he dropped out of line, mopping a wet brow. He craned his neck at the Selfridge Field plans and, with a sigh, sank to a resting position on his instrument. The crowd swallowed him.

The crowd throughout the early afternoon was noticeably quiet. Occasionally scattering applause greeted bands or bugle corps of special distinction, or a particular funny float or Legionnaire-actor would elicit a laugh or hand clap.

Cheers in most cases were reserved for outfits.

"Yoo Hoo Charlie" frequently brought eyes right from "Charlie." Other than this, the crowd made no recognition of special outfits or men.

Marched in solid rank

The Massachusetts men marched in solid rank; and for the first time since the parade started, the marching Legionnaires could be seen coming north from Jefferson Avenue in extended rank.

No wonder these men marched well. They are remnants of the old Yankee Brigade. They had bitter training and discipline over there on the Western Front. They were at St. Mihiel, the Aisne-Marne and Chemin Des Dames. Fifteen thousand casualties was the price they paid for their valor and their victories.

Not until 3:30 o'clock did the parade really open up and march in anything resembling a quick step. The sun, sinking behind the skyscrapers, threw shadows grateful alike to marchers and crowd over Woodward Avenue.

It is a ditty they sung in the old days, revived for Detroit's carnival. They sung it well, in the Massachusetts parade, the boys from Lynn.

Like a corps of British grenadiers, whom their forefathers beat back at Bunker Hill, the Westboro, Mass., Drum and Bugle Corps swept up the streets at a typical British tempo.

This was their song:

> *Oh, I don't have to fight like the Infantry,*
> *Fight like the Calvary,*
> *Fight like the Artillry,*
> *Oh, I don't have to fly over Germany,*
> *For I'm a Q.M.C. —*

Revere, without horse

Paul Revere—without his horse—swaggered up the avenue in the Massachusetts line. Malden, Mass., sent greetings to the citizens of Detroit on a banner so wide that the standard-bearers had to walk sideways to get through the lane between the crowds.

Lexington, Lowell, Watertown, Boston, Concord, all names inseparably linked with another day in American history, were blazoned for the parade. It was a wordless testimonial that Massachusetts keeps the faith.

South Boston's Auxiliaries, rejecting the Princess Eugenia styles of the day, went back to the three-cornered hats of early times and wore them with a jauntiness which set women in the crowd a-twitter.

Mrs. Edith Nourse Rogers, congresswoman from Massachusetts, rode in the state commander's car in the Massachusetts Division.

The Jamaica Plains, Mass., drum and bugle corps evidently grew hungry along about 4 o'clock. It gave vent to its sentiments by playing the mess call all the way up Woodward Avenue. The words ran:

Porky, porky, porky, without a single bean.
Soupy, soupy, soupy, the weakest ever seen.

Massachusetts Legionnaires staged what was heralded as a "tea party" behind the grilled panels of a yellow patrol wagon.

Shadows crept over the street, and a freshening breeze unfurled decorative banners fixed to lamp posts and buildings. Drum majors seemed to revive as the sun was slipping in the West. The crowd was quiet.

Wear yellow slickers

Cape Cod went by wearing yellow oilskin slickers. It was followed by a Gloucester outfit in a large lifeboat.

Salem was represented by a delegation of Legionnaires dressed as witches and carrying brooms. East Lynn proved it had not forgotten how to drill.

To late afternoon arrivals on Woodward Avenue, it seemed like a Massachusetts parade, the column of troops from the Bay State continuing for nearly two hours.

The first of the Massachusetts Legionnaires passed the reviewing stand at 3:20. Their last marchers trailed up Woodward at 4:45 o'clock.

Some humorous spectator in a window high up in the Majestic Building thought to give Legionnaires some of their own hotel medicine and a shower of water, whipped by the wind into a fine mist, floated down on the paraders.

Shower paper on parade

Unusual detachments were greeted from this building by showers of paper as they swung up the avenue. Fragments revealed there will be a shortage of telephone books in the building today.

Texans went in for hand organs in their musical presentation to Detroiters. The buddies from Port Arthur, Tex., put such an instrument at the head of their paraders. A milk-white horse led another Texas contingent.

Roar welcome to Ohio

Ohio swung into view. These were neighbor boys. The Michigan crowd felt it knew them, and it gave them a roaring welcome.

Not so many years ago it seemed that homes in Michigan were reading of these boys, members of the 37th Division (National Guard), fighting in the trenches of France, even as Michigan's own sons in the 32nd Division fought there.

It was not too long to remember that the Buckeyes, who marched in such gay panoply, in purple and gold and red and silver, and who cheered back at the crowd with youthful abandon, won their service stripes in some of the most severe fighting American troops have ever seen.

They threw themselves into the Argonne to hold the line—and they held it. Pershing rushed them across country to Belgium, where the Buckeyes stormed across the Escaut River and ripped the German defense to bits. The white crosses which mark the graves of their comrades are to be found in every American cemetery from Roumain to Flanders Field. They were soldiers over there, and they stepped like soldiers Tuesday.

Martial airs catch

Their total advances in the face of enemy resistance totaled 31 kilometers, but great as that progress was in war-time, they outdistanced it Tuesday in their march into the hearts of their neighbors of Michigan.

Perhaps it was the fact that the men from the first state south marched to the strains of particularly martial music, an abundance of bands having accompanied the 12,000 Legionnaires from this state.

> *Put your head down, Fritzie boy,*
> *Put your head down, Fritzie boy,*
> *We were out last night in the pale moonlight,*
> *We saw you—.*

The crowd was exuberant as the strains of the war song came from a 60-piece band in the line of the march.

Display 'Legion Heirs'

One Ohio post made a play on the name of Legionnaires. On a well-decorated float they placed a dozen small boys in uniform and surmounted them all with a giant sign which read: "Legion-Heirs." It got a hand and a shower of confetti from the crowd.

The first Boy Scout band in the parade followed the banner of Cleveland. More than 50 boys were in the organization.

As the Ohio organizations passed, crowd scenes were being enacted. Tired spectators ambled off to side streets for rest and refreshment, only to return to a new point of vantage. The crowd had moved so far into the streets that room was available on Woodward Avenue sidewalks and pedestrian traffic moved north and south without much difficulty. It was harder for the Legionnaires, however, who were confined to the narrow lane bounded by Woodward Avenue street car tracks.

The drum and bugle corps of Galion, O., was the 100th to have passed in the parade while 44 bands had completed the line of march. This was at 5:15 o'clock.

Line speeds up

The Columbus, O., band swung past the reviewing stand playing something that sounded much like "Beautiful Katy" but swung into a military march of quick beat. The parade moved at an accelerated pace.

It was followed, however, by a hearse of the Lorraine Post, which failed to give the exact number of "hommes" accommodated. "Worst Aid Station" was the name given this vehicle. It was occupied by Lorraine Legionnaires.

Paper water-bags thrown from an eight-story window of the First National garage at E. Congress and Bates Streets became a counter attraction at this point. Groups gathered at the corner, waiting to see someone hit.

Colorado units follow

The Ohio state department was followed in the line of march by Colorado, whose Victory Post No. 4 led the contingent.

Notwithstanding that boys had climbed to their barrelled lenses, traffic lights along Woodward Avenue continued to operate as though the Legion's Big Parade were a thousand miles away. It was one-way traffic.

The Department of Pennsylvania, headed by a distinctive drum and bugle corps from Uniontown, stopped at the reviewing stand to pay its respects to officialdom. The throng cheered this unusually military outfit, dressed after the manner of Pennsylvania State Troopers, when they saluted the Governor and the National Commander.

Pennsylvania stirs crowd

The boys of the Keystone state aroused exceptional enthusiasm.

> "Keep away from the engineers,
> "Keep away from the engineers,
>   "They'll break your back —
>   "With a shovel and pack —
> "Keep away from the engineers."

Perhaps it was a veteran of the Second engineers from Marne 12 years ago, who shouted the verse from among the Pennsylvanians. He sang it alone but with the courage that made him an engineer, as he marched forward with his companions.

One of the most striking outfits was the green-clad marchers of Greensburg, Pa., in Trojan uniform of green, topped with a black-plumed broad-brimmed hat. Jeanette, Pa., bore out their reputation of "Red Devils."

Greensville, Pa., another snappy unit in powder blue uniform, clicked with the crowd. The brassy helmets and cardinal uniforms of James Zindell Post, of Mt. Pleasant, Pa., were distinctive.

Tarentum Post No. 85, of Tarentum, Pa., in white, proceeded floats with the inevitable locomotive of Forty and Eight. Quite a large detachment preferred riding in Pennsylvania buses to stepping off the long line of march.

The Quaker State was followed by Connecticut, arriving at the reviewing stand at 6 o'clock with a Police Post from New Haven at its head in uniform with black clubs.

Silk hats grace Danbury

Hartford, New London, and New Haven were numerically strong. Danbury produced a float and a silk-hatted contingent. All alone at Danbury's rear came a still spry veteran in a G.A.R. uniform who asked no odds on the tiring march and received a tremendous hand from his buddies of 1917.

Two bands of Detroit Citadel of the Salvation Army reminded the veterans of its war work.

Georgia Department stepped snappily into line in their shirt-sleeves and wearing blue field hats behind the Georgia Peach float bearing Peach Queens as well. There were four posts.

Jefferson Post, Louisville, Ky., introduced the Kentucky contingent to the spectators. In blue hats, red coats and white cross belts, the precision and rhythm of the marching bugle corps won generous attention.

The strains of "Old Kentucky Home" floated out from the band as Jesse M. Dykes Post, of Richmond, marched by.

Colors become radiant

Groups of American and Legion colors became moving clusters of jewels. Radiant colors of the marchers uniforms were whipped into a riotous rainbow, through which unreal lines of moving men kept pressing.

Out of the yellow mist far down the street came the last of the Legionnaires. And out of the black night skies overhead there echoed the last roll of the fading drums. With one movement the tremendous crowd surged free.

For nine hours, all through the day and into the night, the police had battled them back. Trucks, motorcycles, cavalry and men afoot had charged against the pressure of the crowding thousands. Inch by inch they had been forced back. Then with the last tap of the last drum, the gates swung open.

The long thin line of open space that had been so valiantly fought for by the guards through nine long hours was obliterated in a second. A swarming mass of humanity swirled under the dancing lights of the night.

Many fought their way to waiting cars and buses to go home to eat after a day in which hunger had been forgotten. But the greater number, like children released at recess, turned to play.

Gone was the martial spirit of discipline. King Carnival reigned, and far into the night the revelry ran.

The Legion had marched.

Its day was done.

Reprinted by permission of the Detroit *Free Press*.

45.   *Addis Ababa Waits for War*

Although news stories generally are thought of in conventional terms as accounts of significant events, such is not always the case. In the following story, Will Barber sews together descriptions of several common scenes in Addis Ababa, Ethiopia. None of the scenes is, by itself, significant in the conventional news sense. The story has no official sources and no attribution; yet it tells the reader a great deal. Barber's stories from Ethiopia, which portrayed the natives' valiant efforts against Mussolini's modern troops, were the first by an American correspondent. Barber was only thirty-one when he died in an Ethiopian hospital from the malaria he contracted while covering the war. *(Pulitzer Prize for Correspondence, 1936)*

Here Is a Picture of a Squalid City
Built for a King

Will Barber

Chicago *Daily Tribune*

August 4, 1935

Typewriters are clicking in the rooms next door and beyond in the darkness hyenas are howling. There is the answering bark of a dog—a friendly, homely bark—and the screech of a house cat. It is an unearthly screech—the sort of screech that used to send shivers down your back when you were a boy hunting wild cats and you raised one. Someone whistles softly. It is the corporal of the night watch of the Hotel Imperial. From a cabin down the hill within the big compound comes a voice. A late comer is returning home. To his greeting the bearded, brown skinned guard huddled in a blanketlike poncho and carrying an old Russo-Japanese war rifle that couldn't shoot on a bet, replies in Ethiopian: "Thank you—may God give you as much."

The gasoline engine that supplies electricity for this hotel—it is one of the half dozen houses having electricity—has stopped puttering. Another hyena howls. More hyenas take up the wail, and soon, if old residents can be believed, the animals will sneak into the streets of the Ethiopian capital of Addis Ababa—the new flower—to make their nightly pickings of refuse. The typewriters are only accidental—there is a mail tomorrow and stories must be sent out "on the situation," for down here in Africa, half way round the world from Chicago, people are waiting for war with Italy—but the hyenas are there every night. They are out there in the pitch darkness, where there is no light.

Darkness! As you walk abroad wth the hope of getting some news or after a visit to a movie, your flashlight bores a forlorn little hole in the darkness and up behind you comes, suddenly, eerily, a pair of bare feet and a flash of white cloak as an Ethiopian scuds for home. "Good evening" to you—"May God give you as much!" A mule patters by on unshod feet. A horse trots into the small circle of your flashlight and out again. Darkness from 7 p.m. till 6 a.m. Almost no one is out, for Ethiopians go to bed early and most of them need special permission to be out at all after nightfall. All servants, for instance, must have both day and night permits and at night must carry lanterns. It is not that crime is feared, though anything may happen here, but simply a means of raising city taxes. Then, toward morning, comes the rain, for it is summer in Addis Ababa. You draw your blankets a little closer, shiver and wish the hyenas would get on with their meal and sneak off home. Addis Ababa at night.

In the morning the city wakes early and poorly dressed men and women, who, despite the cold, wear only cotton, begin their day's toil. Slave women sling huge crockery jugs for water on their backs, the bottom resting on their bulging hips and the neck passing their stooped shoulders. Gerawkis—general name for all porters but the real name of men from a certain district—begin their long round of carrying anything that their fellowmen can think of. Beds, three or four weighty saplings for housing timbers, huge sacks of coffee each weighing 188 pounds, crates, boxes—all carried on their heads. Here comes one with a live ram slung round his shoulders; he's carrying it easily as you would wear a jacket or a feather boa. It is no unusual sight.

Donkeys, angry mules and nondescript pack horses fill the streets all day long. They dodge in and out of the foot traffic, scrambling everywhere. Cows, sheep, goats, horses, donkeys, mules, men, women, and children walk wherever they can get a footing. Down the road, if you can call a rock strewn trail a road, comes a roaring, rushing Dodge, Chevrolet, or Ford, driven breakneck and to "hell with the others." A klaxon shrieks—it is less offensive than the hyena—only because you know what it is and you know that, if the driver doesn't blow it, somebody of the vast throng of men, women, and children who fill the roadway will be killed.

The morning is old now and down the main street, threading his way through humans and animals, comes a tribal chief astride a mule, ambling proudly in the single footed fashion so much valued here. In front and behind the chieftain's mule marches or trots a crowd of retainers, half of them carrying ancient rifles, with the chief's favorite gun carried in a leather case. Only a six gun fellow!

Here now comes someone with style—a big chief, a twenty gun man. He is bound for the palace to ask a favor. Behind him comes, like the same sort of men used to follow patricians in the days of Rome's greatness, a crowd of clients. Each hope the chief will be able to intercede in his behalf against some offense or win him audience with his imperial majesty, Haile Selassie, "king of kings of Ethiopia, conquering lion of the tribe of Judah," undisputed ruler of 12,000,000 people, whom he is trying to bring into modern ways without exasperating them by sudden western innovations. A slave boy, happily bearing a rifle slung haphazardly over his shoulder, hangs onto the tail leather of the chieftan's mule. He is smiling and proud. Slave women, forever toting their heavy jugs of water, look up from their tasks. Khaki clad but barefooted soldiers salute. The traffic officer cracks his whip at a flock of sheep obstructing the road or whacks a beggar over the rump, Europeans stare, the proud chieftain raises his hat and bows deeply to an equal, nods politely to an inferior, and passes.

Over there, midway on the great, paved road (O marvels!) that leads from the old to the new palace, a crowd of shabby persons are washing their feet and ankles in a stream of brown muddy water. Opposite them is a row of butcher shops, where cattle are sold with no more dressing than having the hides ripped off—hides are more precious than animals and in the old days perhaps you wore shoes made of a hide from Ethiopia. Flies and fleas and mosquitos—even at more than 8,000 feet up in the mountains—swarm; one little black boy has two on his right eyelid and three at the corner of his mouth, but flies don't bother him. It isn't much of a town.

All the stores, except perhaps half a dozen, are one story shacks, consisting of a few boards crowned with the eternal corrugated iron roof. The houses are no better. Most of them are tokols—round, mud and lath houses with conical thatched roofs, windowless. In the daytime you get a glimpse of a family at work, and at night there is a sputtering little flame from a fire that serves as "central heating plant" as well.

Over the dark valley, where a murky, muddy stream rushes after rain, stands the old palace, looking rather eastern, a bit like the Arabian Nights. You get a fine view of it, something like the view of Chicago from the lake, or Avignon from the hills across the Rhone. You wish you were in either place as soon as you see the palace. Bare boards creak as you enter the ministry of finance next to the emperor's old home, and bare walls stare at you. It is dark inside, but the clink of big cartwheel Maria Theresa dollars is amusing. The new palace is ever so much better; simple, spotless, and well kept—about as big as a suburban mansion in the United States. The rest of the ministries and the schools stand criticism no better; their walls and floors are bare— the floors downstairs are unusable because of the damp. The schools stand in gardens—or fields. The flowers are there, but they are poorly kept; in Ethiopia nature should do most of the work and does.

The markets? One is a great muddy plain enclosed by a picket fence beyond which is a vast collection of shanties. Another covers several streets on the side of a hill of red-brown mud, down which the rain rushes. Here the stores are tiny, dirty booths crowned with thatch or corrugated iron. Inside each is a little platform on which goods are displayed. The vender squats, cross-legged, flicking away flies with a horsehair whip. You can buy anything there, but mostly Japanese stuff—"best Nippon cotton sheeting" is the word. It is cheaper than Manchester's sheets, and so the Japanese have acquired, so it is said, 90 per cent of the trade.

Your horizon is limited by a ring of mountains on which clouds damply squat. Flies and fleas and lice. You are bitten. Typhoid and typhus are endemic, doctors say, and right now they are both epidemic. No one knows how many cases there are in Addis Ababa, for vital statistics are never kept. It's a wise Ethiopian who knows his own age.

Addis Ababa is a mistake, of course, from the point of view of climate. It is too high in the mountains and it rains three months a year. The high altitude is difficult for the lowland Ethiopians, but old Emperor Menelik, who brought his empire back toward its old boundaries and whipped the Italians at Adowa, knew his highland soldiers couldn't stand the heat of the lowlands. They didn't know how to protect themselves against fever and that is why, it is said, he turned back into his mountains after beating the Italians. The whole town is on a hill and everywhere eucalyptus grows. The trees smell good, but their thick foliage prevents the sun from reaching the houses clustered under them and so all is damp. Not much of a town!

Here come a couple of Gerawki, carrying a piano on their heads. Marvelously strong fellows, though thin as bean poles. A cow town if there ever was one. It is easy to laugh—to laugh at the town, the thinly and shabbily dressed people, the chieftains with their armed bands, the women with covered faces, the traffic cops and that other touch of modernity, the American taxis.

It is easy to laugh, but what is wrong is simply that these are not a city people. They are a farming and pastoral people, used to open spaces and clearer skies. If you saw them in the country—here a sturdy farmer and there a shepherd boy, standing naked with his cloak thrown over his arm as he indolently leans on his staff, as shepherd boys do on old Greek vases—you would find them a proud, industrious, self-respecting, and independent people, anxious to keep what they have and let the world go on without them.

Reprinted by courtesy of the Chicago *Tribune*.

46.   The Liberation of Paris

Mark Watson witnessed the liberation of Paris from the German army in 1944. In the following story he provides a coherent, absorbing narrative of the Germans' last stand. Giving a firsthand account, he includes enough details and background information in the story to make the liberation fully understandable to the reader. The story's quality presents a good lesson on the value of eyewitness observation by a reporter. *(Pulitzer Prize for Telegraphic Reporting, International, 1945)*

Paris Still Lively, Happy
Mark S. Watson
Baltimore *Sun*
August 27, 1944

PARIS, Aug. 25—One of the greatest goals in the Allies' Western front campaign and certainly the principal goal of every GI Joe was entered today in force by French and American troops.

French reconnaissance elements were given the honor of making the first entry last night. As soon as this courtesy had been taken care of, American columns roared down the roads to the south and southwest of the city and headed through town straight toward the Eiffel Tower.

Fourth Division in lead

This landmark my particular column sighted through the haze shortly before noon as we sped up the highway leading through Villejuif to Port D'Italie. At dawn we had made an early start to gain contact with the Fourth Division of the American army, which at the last moment drew the right to lead the Yanks into the city.

We raced past every variety of army elements through cheering throngs of French, who seemed to line every foot of the highway. All through the suburbs the citizenry waved flags, tossed flowers and swarmed over every truck and jeep that stopped, deluging non-reluctant soldiers with enraptured kisses.

As we came through the more thickly settled suburbs, Lieut. Col. Charles Jackson, who headed our particular column, began making inquiries as to the security of the routes ahead. It was understood that the Germans had left resistance groups at various points in the city.

Placed in leading car

The French civilians were eager to give advice, but only in French which none in the colonel's jeep could understand. I was called forward so often to interpret that the affair wound up with me being placed in a French civilian's car to lead the way for our particular column. That is the sort of a thing a newspaper correspondent dreams of but usually encounters only in the movies.

In that formation we moved on, up the Avenue D'Italie with quite hysterical ladies, gentlemen and little children clamoring to touch us and the French driver beside me so excited I had to make occasional clutches for the steering wheel to save the lives of excited civilians.

We no longer saw burned out vehicles along the way which had marked most of our previous route. Here and there were German strong points from which the muzzles of now useless cannon projected. In the streets were barricades of paving blocks and upturned carts used by the French resistance troops last week just as their grandfathers and fathers had in the past Parisian revolts. Great bomb and mine holes were being filled to facilitate our passage but there was no other evidence of war damage.

Surpassed Naples reception

Never have I seen such exultation in mass. The nearest approach to it was our Fifth Army's entry into Naples almost eleven months ago, but even that was surpassed today. The fact that the smoke is rising in a few distant parts of the city and that an explosion a short distance away from us rattled the department a few minutes ago do not seem to have discouraged the public's delight in our being here.

Even the water system is working and the electical connections seem all right, although we are informed that the low fuel supply has permitted the use of current only a few hours every evening.

One encountered odd exceptions, as in the case of beautiful kid gloves. The price of these are not particularly high but the outgoing Germans had totally exhausted the supply of all large sizes into which the paws of German women can be crammed and, thereafter, the whole supply of medium sizes as well. Hence the glove shops are bursting with small and very small sizes only.

Silk scarfs expensive

Silk scarfs and fabric materials are available, but again at prices that make one's hair curl. Doubtless they will rise higher as soon as the

American soldiery comes to town and Parisian shopkeepers discover "forgotten" stocks of goods and also the GI Joes' eagerness to pay too much for souvenirs.

It's surprising to see the excellent stocks in several bookstores and the moderate prices, as long as you don't ask to have purchases wrapped, for there is a total absence of wrapping paper or other paper of any merit.

French appreciative

There is a natural pride in such French troops as have appeared, but the French people are well aware of who has chiefly effected the liberation of their soil thus far and are deeply appreciative.

I have harldy seen a frown in all Paris. Passersby listen with the deepest interest to an American's effort to make inquiries in what he regards as the French language and then go to great pains to help out in French and English gestures or, in a last resort, by taking the American by the hand and leading him to the spot he's looking for. I have had an old woman rush up, sieze my hand, and cry out thank you, thank you, American, with tears of joy streaming from her eyes, and then hastily back away in embarrassment over her own emotion.

Kisses of welcome

There's a good deal of the cheek-to-cheek kissing in the French manner—so much that one of my handsomer colleagues says he's getting cauliflower ears and another says he never was so woman handled in all his life—and the Paris welcome is not yet near exhausted.

Most of the fine hotels were used by the Germans in one way or another—the Crillion by headquarters, which brought upon that fine building a good deal of fire; the Continental by the Luftwaffe, from which trucks today are still hauling out great stores of German equipment. The Ritz had been limited to German officers of high rank and is in perfect condition.

Our own hotel is as neat and well furnished as ever, but it is wholly dependent on our army rations for food and the staff is much depleted. There is no hot water, of course, no soap, few towels but everything is so clean and well-kept in spite of the handicaps that it would be easy for the troops to spend their available leave in such a paradise of cleanliness and repose.

German's behavior good

It must be recognized that the German's behavior in Paris as far as the treatment of private property was concerned was generally wholly correct. Most of the quarters occupied were taken for military reasons only and the damage done to them was not beyond reason. This, of course, is due to the admirable discipline which the German army habitually maintains. If there is looting, it is done officially and on a colossal scale, but if looting is officially forbidden, as apparently it was in this case, there is extremely little of it.

One of my companions who lived in Paris until 1940 found his apartment wholly unhurt and even his goods in storage still sealed. Another found his apartment almost intact and his fine library undisturbed—until his American friends arrived.

After dinner he glared at one of his colleagues sprawled in an easy chair reading one book and with a dozen others which he had sampled lying on the various tables, the chairs and the floor.

"In four hours that idiot has done more to upset my library than the whole German army did in four years," snarled our irate host.

Gets 1940 letters

Another colleague found his apartment leaking and minus many things he had left there, but he had barely opened the door when the concierge bounded in, carrying four letters still unopened which the postman of 1940 had delivered there on the day after the owner's hasty departure for a Channel port.

These evidences of continuity in French life are not surprising, to be sure, for even after a much longer absence one finds many things precisely as in 1918, with new faces exactly like the old ones, and Paris once radiant as long ago, her voice as gay, her heart as warm.

Same as 1918

These must be the same bicycles one used to see even if it be another generation of riders. "The more they change the more completely they are the same." How many times one has seen that same youth on his bicycle with the laughing girl perched on the handlebars, or that middle-aged woman pedaling off to pay a call with a sedate dog riding pillion behind her, or that dignified-looking old fellow with the scholarly brow and the superb spade beard apparently working out the 98th problem of Euclid in time with his methodical pumping of his bicycle, but more likely he's wondering what it was his wife told him to do before returning home.

What elegant beards they are and what glorious mustaches on part of the old French soldiers—or even the retired English officer who wears the Victoria Cross and never bothered to flee from his Paris hotel in 1940. With the singular chivalry which one real soldier shows to another, the German command ordered that the wearer of the Victoria Cross stay undisturbed.

Perhaps it could not happen, save in Paris, which in centuries has taken to her arms all peoples of all creeds, molded them into one and has been herself molded by them. Paris is hard to change. There was great excitement when we came in, but the next day fishermen again were fishing in the Seine for the same fish that no one ever catches.

Reprinted by permission of the Baltimore *Sun.*

47. *A "Cargo of Liquid Life"*

In 1944 the U.S. Navy announced a new program of flying blood from San Francisco to the Pacific where G.I.s were in dire need. Reporter Jack McDowell of the San Francisco *Call-Bulletin* donated a pint of blood and flew in the plane with the shipment containing his donation. Upon arrival in the Pacific he watched the blood transferred into the veins of casualties in the combat zones. The *Call-Bulletin* published a five-day series of illustrated stories. The following article is one example of how McDowell integrated the two worlds of San Francisco and the Pacific to make San Franciscans aware of the suffering G.I.s. Using a personal approach, he connects the two by capitalizing on details such as names, ages, and addresses for a personal touch. He also makes the appeal stronger through a good use of quotes from blood donors and recipients. To give readers an even clearer perspective of the situation of G.I.s, he describes the conditions of soldiers, as well as giving them the opportunity to tell their own stories. *(Pulitzer Prize for Reporting, 1945)*

Call-Bulletin Man Takes
Own, Others' Blood To Islands

Jack S. McDowell
San Francisco *Call-Bulletin*
December 4, 1944

The maps say the sick and wounded GI's lying in the steaming jungles of the Marianas are more than 6,000 miles away—a quarter of the way around the world.

But the maps must be wrong—because just 48 hours after flying over the Red Cross Blood Donor Center on Jones street, where more than 100 other San Franciscans and I put blood from our veins into little pint bottles, I stepped with this cargo of liquid life to the airstrip of an advance American base within 1,500 miles of Tokyo.

Real thrill at base hospital

With the speed and ingenuity of the Naval Air Transport Service I was able to make Jules Verne look like a crawling piker, but the real thrill came in a forward area hospital as I watched color return to the paled face of a critically-burned Sea Bee.

In the bottle suspended above his hospital cot was part of 22 year old Chesla O'Brien of 3309 California street, the blood I saw drained from her arm as she lay on a cot adjacent to mine in the blood center at 2415 Jones street.

My own pint was in the hopper somewhere else, but I was able to follow that of Miss O'Brien all the way across the Pacific to the advance blood bank at Guam and ultimately to the veins of Painter Second Class Willie R. Boyter, 34 year old Navy Sea Bee from Pine Bluff, Ark.

Sailor hero saves plane

Boyter, a veteran of the D-day fighting in the Marianas, was thin and pale. He had charged up the beach of this particular island through the hell of Japanese mortar and artillery fire. His buddies dropped, dead or wounded, beside him as his outfit pushed through the withering fire. But Boyter came through the battle unhurt—only to fall victim to the accidental explosion of a drum of turpentine.

Medical officers at the base paid tribute to the sailor as a real hero.

"The drum of turpentine exploded and caught fire right near a plane," one officer said.

"Boyter was intent on saving the plane, and he ran toward the burning drum with a stick. He stuck the stick into the drum and carried it away before it could ignite the plane.

"But when he lifted the drum, the flaming turpentine spilled all over his back, sides and legs. He suffered first, second and third degree burns."

Tells story to Boyter

As the Navy doctors rigged tubing from the bottle of Miss O'Brien's blood to Boyter's arm, I sat beside his cot. He turned a pair of brave blue eyes toward me and asked if I knew the donor.

"I saw her at the blood center in San Francisco a couple of days ago," I told him. "She was in there at the same time I was."

Boyter wanted to know more about the girl who had sent him part of herself to help him back to health — and the United States.

She had donated blood three times, I told him. She just recently moved to San Francisco from Boston, and one of the first things she did was call the Blood Donor Center to make an appointment. She said that made her "feel like she really belonged to the community." She had just gone to work for the Pacific Telephone and Telegraph Company as a teletype operator.

"When she was giving her blood, she told us she was happy to do it, that she wanted it to go to some man overseas, and you're the man," I told Boyter.

A touch of color was coming back to the sailor's cheeks now and those clear blue eyes seemed to send more messages than words from his lips.

'I can't believe it'

"You don't know how thankful I am," Boyter said, licking his dry lips in the tropical heat.

"Will you take a message back to that little girl in San Francisco for me?

"Tell her something to make her feel good — tell her how much I appreciate her sending part of her own blood all the way over here to me."

Those sky-blue eyes looked beyond me now — and beyond the long rows of white cots in the Quonset hut hospital ward.

You could see they were focused on a thought — not on one of the grim reminders of war and suffering in the forward area hospital.

"San Francisco...couple of days ago..." he spoke, shaking his head slightly. "I can't believe it.

"Say, will you tell that girl in San Francisco something else for me, too? Tell her I hope her blood gets me home to my wife quicker.

"I haven't seen her in twenty-two months."

His wife, he said, is named Caroline, and she manages the coffee shop of the Hotel Pines back in Arkansas.

Not long ago Sea Bee Boyter was on the critical list of the huge base hospital where I found him. Now, according to medical officers, he definitely is on the mend.

The dramatic operation of giving blood transfusions by remote control is as daring and ingenious as any story to come from the battlefronts of World War II.

Blood plasma—the processed portion of human blood which may be kept indefinitely—has performed thousands upon thousands of miracles. Wounded men, suffering shock so severely that pulse and breathing are hardly discernible, are sitting up smoking cigarettes an hour and a half after a dressing station plasma injection at the front.

And the need for plasma is still great. Thousands of gallons of it must continue to flow into the laboratories if the Army and Navy medical men are to save the lives of these lads who fell fighting for us just forty-eight hours west of Jones street.

But, because the tissue-building red corpuscles have been removed from the plasma, another need was discovered. Whole blood from the veins of another human must be introduced into the body of the casualty.

The call for volunteers

The problem was partially solved when service doctors called for volunteers. Medical officers, hospital corpsmen, soldiers, sailors and marines—even some wounded men themselves—reclined beside casualties in forward hospitals to send a pint of their blood through a small rubber tube into the arm of a wounded man.

But the Pacific war grew larger and larger.

There was the Coral Sea, Midway and Guadalcanal, Attu, Bouganville and New Guinea, Tarawa, Kwajalein, Guam, Tinian and Saipan.

More young Americans fell under the hail of shrapnel, torpedoes and bullets thrown by the retreating but fighting enemy. More men in the field gave their blood to another who had a greater need for it. But to the medical experts in the field and in Washington, the picture was becoming all too clear. You couldn't fight a winning war by draining blood from the fighting men beyond the point of safety.

There was no shortage of volunteers, however. But every transfusion tied up men and hospital space.

The Army and Navy medical chiefs knew the only solution was to send whole blood from the veins of people at home. But blood would spoil before it ever got near the battlefronts—even in ships containing modern refrigeration equipment.

They called in experts of the Naval Medical Research Institute at Bethesda, Md., and tossed the problem into their laps.

The institute had licked knotty problems before, and soon the answer was delivered. The experts devised an inexpensive plywood box, lined with insulating fiberglass and containing aluminum bottle racks and an ice cylinder which will accommodate 19 pounds of ordinary ice.

At the same time, across the world was being blazed one of the most vast and efficient air services in the world. It's official name is the Naval Air Transportation Service, but to millions of men in uniform it is affectionately known as "NATS."

Shipments leave every day

The institute provided the container, NATS promised the transportation, and the remaining question was:

"Where is the blood coming from?"

To cut the danger of spoilage to a minimum, the West Coast was chosen as the supply point, and a hurry up call came across the nation from the surgeons general of the Army and Navy to the Red Cross blood donor centers at San Francisco, Oakland and Los Angeles.

Every day shipments of whole blood are leaving here by air. They are landing at forward area hospitals two days later. The ingenious plan is working, but the demand is for more, more, more.

The realization that the man at the front is receiving the blood from San Francisco a scant 48 hours after the donor leaves the blood center here was challenging to the imagination. I thought that other San Franciscans, too, might have trouble placing Guam and Leyte, Saipan and Tinian as close to their homes—on a basis of time—as Portland.

So, along with dozens of others—most of them women and service men—I went to the blood donor center, contributed a pint of my blood into the batch that was to leave that night. Then I followed the shipment to the sick and wounded men who receive it.

Reprinted by permission of the Hearst Corporation.

48.   *Hiroshima After the Bomb*

Covering World War II for the New York *Herald Tribune* gave Homer Bigart the chance to see first-hand the effects of the atomic bomb dropped on Hiroshima, Japan. He wrote the following story following the surrender of Japan, a month after the atomic blast. It is a detailed and interesting story of an event that is just as important today as when it occurred. Bigart does a good job in weaving together a description of the destruction with an account of the bomb victims' reactions. In doing so, he wrote not just another casualty story, but one with important insights into a historically significant event. *(Pulitzer Prize for Telegraphic Reporting, International, 1945)*

A Month after the Atom Bomb – Hiroshima Still Can't Believe It
Homer Bigart
New York *Herald Tribune*
September 5, 1945

We walked today through Hiroshima, where survivors of the first atomic-bomb explosion four weeks ago are still dying at the rate of about one hundred daily from burns and infections which the Japanese doctors seem unable to cure. The toll from the most terrible weapon ever devised now stands at 53,000 counted dead, 30,000 missing and presumed dead, 13,960 severely wounded and likely to die, and 43,000 wounded. The figures come from Hirokuni Dadai, who, as "chief of thought control" of Hiroshima Prefecture, is supposed to police subversive thinking.

On the morning of Aug. 6 the 340,000 inhabitants of Hiroshima were awakened by the familiar howl of air-raid sirens. The city had never been bombed—it had little industrial importance. The Kure naval base lay only twelve miles to the southeast and American bombers had often gone there to blast the remnants of the imperial navy, or had flown mine-laying or strafing missions over Shimonoseki Strait to the west. Almost daily enemy planes had flown over Hiroshima, but so far the city had been spared. At 8 A.M. the "all clear" sounded. Crowds emerged from the shallow raid shelters in Military Park and hurried to their jobs in the score of tall, modern earthquake-proof buildings along the broad Hattchobori, the main business street of the city. Breakfast fires still smoldered in thousands of tiny ovens—presently they were to help to kindle a conflagration.

Very few persons saw the Superfortress when it first appeared more than five miles above the city. Some thought they saw a black object swinging down on a parachute from the plane, but for the most part Hiroshima never know what hit it. A Japanese naval officer, Vice-Admiral Masso Kanazawa, at the Kure base said the concussion from the blast twelve miles away was "like the great wind that made the trees sway." His aide, a senior lieutenant who was to accompany us into the city, volunteered that the flash was so bright even in Kure that he was awakened from his sleep. So loud was the explosion that many thought the bomb had landed within Kure.

When Lieutenant Taira Ake, a naval surgeon, reached the city at 2:30 P.M., he found hundreds of wounded still dying unattended in the wrecks and fields on the northern edge of the city. "They didn't look like human beings," he said. "The flesh was burned from their faces and hands, and many were blinded and deaf." Dadai was standing in the doorway of his house nearly two miles from the center of impact. He had just returned from Tokyo. "The first thing I saw was a brilliant flash," he said. "Then after a second or two came a shock like an earthquake. I knew immediately it was a new type of bomb. The house capsized on top of us and I was hit with falling timbers. I found my wife lying unconscious in the debris, and I dragged her to safety. My two children suffered cuts and for the next hour or so I was too busy to think of what was happening in the city."

Doctors rushed from the Kure naval base—including Lieutenant Ake—were prevented from entering the city until six hours after the blast because of the searing heat of the explosion. City officials said that many indoors who were burned under collapsing walls and roofs subsequently were burned to death in the fires that broke out within a few minutes after the blast. The first impression in the minds of the survivors was that a great fleet of Superfortresses flying at great height had somehow sneaked past the defenses and dropped thousands of fire bombs. Even today there are many who refuse to believe that a single bomb wiped out the city.

A party of newspaper men led by Colonel John McCrary was the first group of Americans to reach Hiroshima. We flew in today in a B-17, our pilot, Captain Mark Magnan, finding a hole in the clouds over Kure and setting the plane down on the tiny runway of the naval air base there with about seventy feet to spare. The admiral in charge of the base, after telling us what he had seen and knew of the bombing, gave us two sedans and a truck, and we drove down a mountain, through ruined Kure and past the navy yard. A tall fence set up along the road to block the view of the yard had been removed, and we could see ten destroyers, two submarines and some gunboats anchored in the harbor.

Across the bay, beached on an island and listing to port so that the waves broke over her deck, was the battleship Haruna. Farther on we passed close to another beached warship, an old three-stacker that flaunted the silhouettes of ten American planes on her mid-stack. A four-engine bomber was among the planes the destroyer claimed to have shot down. Several tunnels and deep cuts along the highway to Hiroshima were stacked with airplane motors and other vital equipment, leaving only a narrow lane for passage. Our driver, speeding at fifty miles an hour along the concrete highway, slammed into one crated engine and swerved across the road and struck another, shearing the rear fender. Three miles outside Hiroshima we saw the first signs of blast damage—loose tiles torn from roofs and an occasional broken window. At the edge of town there were houses with roofs blown off, while the walls facing the center of the city had caved inward.

Finally we came to the river and saw the Island of Hiro, which holds, or rather held, the main districts of Hiroshima, which means "Hiro Island." In the part of the town east of the river the destruction had looked no different from a typical bomb-torn city in Europe. Many buildings were only partly demolished, and the streets were still choked with debris. But across the river there was only flat, appalling desolation, the starkness accentuated by bare, blackened tree trunks and the occasional shell of a reinforced concrete building.

We drove to Military Park and made a walking tour of the ruins. By all accounts the bomb seemed to have exploded directly over Military Park. We saw no crater there. Apparently the full force of the explosion was expended laterally. Aerial photographs had shown no evidence of rubble, leading to the belief that everything in the immediate area of impact had been literally pulverized into dust. But on the ground we saw this was not true. There was rubble everywhere, but much smaller in size than normal.

Approaching the Hattchobori, we passed what had been a block of small shops. We could tell that only because of office safes that lay at regular intervals on sites that retained little else except small bits of iron and tin. Sometimes the safes were blown in. The steel door of a huge vault in the four-story Geibi Bank was flung open, and the management had installed a temporary padlocked door. All three banking houses—Geibi, Mitsubishi and Bank of Japan—were conducting business in the sturdy concrete building of the Bank of Japan, which was less damaged than the rest.

Since the bank and the police station were the only buildings open for business, we asked our naval lieutenant guide if we could enter. He disappeared and was gone for several minutes. We stood uneasily at the corner of the bank building, feeling very much like a youth walking down Main Street in his first long pants. There weren't many people abroad—a thin trickle of shabbily dressed men and women—but all of them stared at us. There was hatred in some glances, but generally more curiosity than hatred. We were representatives of an enemy power that had employed a weapon far more terrible and deadly than poison gas, yet in the four hours we spent in Hiroshima none so much as spat at us, nor threw a stone.

We later asked the naval lieutenant, who once lived in Sacramento, to halt some pedestrians and obtain eyewitness accounts of the blast. He was very reluctant to do so. "They may not want to talk to you," he said. But finally he stopped an old man, who bared his gold teeth in an apparent gesture of friendship. "I am a Christian," said the old man, making the sign of the cross. He pointed to his ears, indicating deafness, and the lieutenant, after futile attempts to make him hear, told us that the old man, like many others, apparently had suffered permanent loss of his hearing when the crashing blast of the atomic bomb shattered his ear drums. The lieutenant stopped a few more middle-aged civilians, but they backed off, bowing and grinning. They said they were not in Hiroshima on Aug. 6.

Two boys walking barefoot through the rubble displayed no fear of infection, although no doctor could say positively that the danger had ended. They boys said they had been brought in from the countryside to help clean up the city. The cloying stench of death was still very noticeable in the street, and we were glad when the lieutenant finally motioned us inside the bank.

Except for broken windows and chipped cornices, the Bank of Japan presented an intact facade outside. Inside, however, we saw that the concussion had smashed the frail stalls and reduced the furnishings to matchwood. Under the lofty vaulted roof spaces had been roped off, and skeleton staffs of the three banking institutions sat behind crude wooden tables handing the government's new yen currency to waiting lines. Several persons showed bad burns about their necks and faces and nearly half the population seemed to be wearing gauze bandages over noses and mouths to protect them from germs. Those who entered Hiroshima and stayed only a few hours appeared to suffer no ill effects, doctors said, but many who attempted to live in the ruins developed infections that reacted on the blood cells as destructively as leukemia, except that the white blood corpuscles and not the red were consumed. Victims became completely bald; they lost all appetite; they vomited blood.

A few of the main streets of Hiroshima have been cleared. Trolleys ran through the blighted areas down to the waterfront. But the public is forbidded to drink from wells, and water has to be brought in from the countryside. Down one street was the ruined wall of a Christian church, and near it the site of the Japanese 2d Army headquarters. Hiroshima was an embarkation point for the invasion which threatened Kyushu, and the city had been filled with soldiers when the bomb fell. How many of them perished no one knows, for all records were destroyed by fire. Among the army staff members killed was the chief of military police.

The city and the prefectural (provincial) government had moved to a motorcycle plant in the outskirts of town, and there we met Dadai. He was introduced at first as "a high governmental official," but later admitted he was Chief of Thought Control. Dadai's appearance fitted his role. He looked like a man who could not only suppress a thought, but could torture it. He wore a white bandage across his brow, tied in back of his head, and the face beneath it was sallow and repressive. His tight, grim mouth hardly opened as he answered questions put to him through the naval interpreter.

He told us that the wounded were doomed by the disintegrating effects of the uranium on the white blood corpuscles. This statement, however, was not substantiated by doctors, who said they knew so little about the strange disorders that it was useless to speculate on how high the death toll would run. They cited the case of the woman who suffered only a slight cut in the explosion, yet died eighteen days later.

Neither Dadai nor local correspondents who asked for an interview seemed to believe that the atomic bomb would end the war. One of the first questions asked by Japanese newspaper men was: "What effect will the bomb have on future wars?" They also asked whether Hiroshima "would be dangerous for seventy years." We told them we didn't know.

49.   *Town Of War*

Writing about the Korean Conflict presented unique problems to
reporters because of the stalemated action that dominated much of the
war. In this story, Scripps Howard reporter Jim Lucas gave his
readers a sense of what that stalemate meant to the soldiers on the
front. Lucas' use of descriptions of the men and camp give readers a
clear sense of the nature of the conflict. The inclusion of Col. Seymour
Goldberg adds an important element of color to the story. Although
fairly short, the piece vividly captures the flavor of the events.
(Pulitzer Prize for International Reporting, 1954)

'Our Town' a World of Its Own
Jim Lucas
Scripps Howard
January 3, 1953

PORK CHOP HILL, KOREA—Our Town atop Pork Chop Hill is in
a world of its own.

Its contacts with the outside world are few—but imperative. Its
immediate concern is the enemy on the next ridge. That's "His Town."
Our Town gives grudging respect. But, if possible, "His Town" is
going to be wiped out.

Our Town's business is war. It produces nothing but death. To exist,
therefore, it must rely on others. Food, mail, clothing—even the
weapons of destruction—are shipped in.

These items are sent in from that part of the outside world which the
men of Our Town call "rear." As often—and far more passionately—
they are at war with "rear" as they are with the enemy. "Rear," which
includes anything beyond the foot of Pork Chop, is populated, Our
Town is convinced, by idiots and stumblebums.

Physically, Our Town—while hardly attractive—is not un-
comfortable. Much municipal planning went into it.

The streets are six to eight feet deep. At times after dark, Our
Town's streets are invaded by men from His Town. The citizens of Our
Town invariably expel these interlopers. To assist in maintaining law
and order on such occasions, the shelves along the streets of Our Town
are liberally stocked with hand grenades.

There are thirty to fifty houses in Our Town. They are referred to as bunkers. Each street and each bunker is numbered. After a few days it's comparatively easy to find one's way.

Half of Our Town's bunkers are living quarters. The others are stores—storage bunkers, that is. From these you can obtain a wide assortment of ammunition, sandbags, candles, charcoal, or canned rations.

Our Town's buildings are sturdy. The typical building is at least six feet underground. It is made of four-by-ten-inch logs to which are added many sandbags. It's almost impervious to enemy shelling.

Our Town is not without its social life. I went visiting this morning at 19 Third Street in Our Town. Entering No. 19, one gets down on his hands and knees. The front door is low.

My hosts were First Lieutenant Pat Smith of Hollywood, California, Corporal Joe Siena of Portland, Connecticut, Private First Class Eddie Williams of Brooklyn, and Private Don Coan of Anadarko, Oklahoma.

Don had coffee brewing in an old ration can. He opened a can of sardines. Eddie was heading for the rear on a shopping trip. His list included candles, a coffeepot (which he's had on order for a month already), and a reel of communications wire. He also was taking a field telephone for repairs.

Our Town, like others, enjoys small talk. Over coffee, the group discussed what a man should do if a grenade-wielding Chinese suddenly appeared at the door. There was no unanimous decision.

Our Town has its own banker—Warrant Officer James W. Cherry of Jackson, Tennessee. He came up the other afternoon. Within three hundred yards of the enemy, he distributed $23,411.

Many men didn't want their money, really. Money is an almost valueless commodity up here. Three days from now, the postal officer will come up the hill, selling money orders.

If money has no value, other things do. Things like candles, fuel, toilet tissue. There's never enough charcoal for the stoves which heat the bunkers. To stay warm you can climb into your sleeping bag—if you're a fool. The men refer to sleeping bags as "coffins." Too many soldiers have been killed before they could unzip their sleeping bags.

Our Town's Mayor is a tall, gangling Texan—Captain Jack Conn of Houston. He's company commander. The Vice Mayor is his executive officer—First Lieutenant Bill Gerald, also of Houston. Bill Gerald is a Negro.

The battalion commander, Lieutenant Colonel Seymour Goldberg of Washington, D.C., is convinced Our Town's residents think Colonel Goldberg is a martinet.

Colonel Goldberg always arrives in a foul mood, to be expected, since high-up officials usually are blind to local problems. The Colonel expects miracles overnight. (Privately, he concedes this is an act—"If I didn't raise hell, they wouldn't take me seriously.")

Our Town endures this outsider stoically. The Colonel says the men need haircuts. "When would they have time to get haircuts?" say Our Town's citizens. He says the bunkers need cleaning. "They look all right to us," fume Our Towners. "We live here." He says ammunition isn't stored properly. "Let up on these all-night patrols and we'll store it right," retorts Our Town—not to the Colonel's face, of course.

Invariably the Colonel corrals a hapless private and demands he be court-martialed for one thing or another. Our Town's Mayor dutifully notes the boy's name and then throws away the notes when the Colonel leaves.

But the Colonel expects this.

There was much glee the other day when the Colonel issued an order that any man found outside a bunker without bulletproof vest be punished. A moment later, the Colonel left the bunker—and forgot his vest.

There's method in the Colonel's madness. He deliberately sets out to make Our Town hate him. "If I didn't," he says, "it would go to pot."

You see, the Colonel once was a company commander who hated "rear." He knows he must prod the men up front, so that their outfit will remain—despite the presence of death itself—a proud, disciplined, organized Army fighting unit.

Reprinted by permission of Scripps Howard.

50.   *In the Trail of a Tornado*

When a tornado hit Fargo, North Dakota, on the evening of June 20, 1957, the Fargo *Forum* jumped into action. The staff put together a special edition that hit the streets six hours after the twister swept through the town, killing ten people and damaging sixty-six blocks in the city. Reporter Tom Lucier's story is a first-person account of weathering the storm. His detailed description of the tornado is a gripping reminder that the first-person point of view, frequently discouraged today, sometimes can be the most effective way to tell a story. *(Pulitzer Prize for Reporting, Edition Time, 1958)*

A Chill Sensation of Danger
Tom Lucier
Fargo *Forum*
June 21, 1957

As though threatened by an A-bomb attack, hundreds—perhaps thousands—of Fargo-Moorhead residents evacuated the two cities as tornado funnels appeared over the western horizon Thursday night.

With my wife and baby, I joined a stream of nervous motorists that sped north out of Moorhead along Highway 75. There were scores of cars parked along the highway and congested knots of vehicles at every crossroad and intersection.

Shortly after 7:30 p.m., we left our south Moorhead home. To the west, seemingly directly over Fargo, we saw the massive funnel forming and revolving. Great gulps of ragged clouds were being sucked from all directions into the vortex as the gigantic funnel moved toward us.

From under the terrible blue-black storm head, small funnels dangled like teats from an udder. Then two solid, almost perpendicular funnel columns formed side by side, seemingly reaching to the ground. We said a silent prayer for anyone who might be under these black brooms of potential sudden death and moved on to the north.

By this time traffic was converging onto Highway 75 from all avenues and we joined the caravan. Many of the evacuees had stopped along the highway and gotten out of their cars to watch the huge formation move over the city with deadly majesty.

The wind seemed to be coming from all directions; and as we watched with the rest, the great column began to veer toward the northeast—straight in our direction.

With a chill sensation of danger, I joined the cars that began now to move north at increasing speed.

Suddenly the countryside was swept with a pounding, blinding rain. The wind howled, lightning ripped the sky and hailstones—some nearly as big as ping-pong balls—pelted the car. Traffic came to a stop.

When it was over, we saw the thunderhead moving west over Dilworth. Although still funnel-shaped, it did not look so dangerous as before and did not touch down. It seemed to be breaking up.

As we waited to start back to Moorhead, a long gray-white tube snaked down from the swirling skies and touched down on the momentarily flooded fields east of the highway about 500 yards away.

This tube, of relatively small diameter, seemed to curl thousands of feet into the air. Moments later, it was sucked up into the atmosphere and disintegrated.

Reprinted by permission of the Fargo *Forum.*

51.   *A Numbing Visit to a Death Camp*

The structural concept behind the following story by A.M. Rosenthal is simple. It is told as a guided tour through a World War II Nazi extermination camp. Yet it has a forcefulness rarely matched by news stories. Mood and images, created by the writer's use of selective and concrete details, pervade the article, forcing the reader to imagine himself as one of the camp's visitors. Combined with the irony and paradox of details, these characteristics leave the reader with a sense of numbness in the presence of the memories of history and the awfulness of Nazi inhumanity. *(Pulitzer Prize for International Reporting, 1960)*

There Is No News From Auschwitz
A.M. Rosenthal
New York *Times*
August 31, 1958

BRZEZINKA, Poland—The most terrible thing of all, somehow, was that at Brzezinka the sun was bright and warm, the rows of graceful poplars were lovely to look upon, and on the grass near the gates children played.

It all seemed frighteningly wrong, as in a nightmare, that at Brzezinka the sun should ever shine or that there should be light and greenness and the sound of young laughter. It would be fitting if at Brzezinka the sun never shone and the grass withered, because this is a place of unutterable terror.

And yet, every day, from all over the world, people come to Brzezinka, quite possibly the most grisly tourist center on earth. They come for a variety of reasons—to see if it could really have been true, to remind themselves not to forget, to pay homage to the dead by the simple act of looking upon their place of suffering.

Brzezinka is a couple of miles from the better-known southern town of Oswiecim. Oswiecim has about 12,000 inhabitants, is situated about 171 miles from Warsaw, and lies in a damp, marshy area at the eastern end of the pass called the Moravian Gate.

Brzezinka and Oswiecim together formed part of that minutely organized factory of torture and death that the Nazis called Konzentrationslager Auschwitz.

By now, 14 years after the last batch of prisoners was herded naked into the gas chamber by dogs and guards, the story of Auschwitz has been told a great many times. Some of the inmates have written of those memories of which sane men cannot conceive. Rudolf Franz Ferdinand Hoss, the superintendent of the camp, before he was executed wrote his detailed memoirs of mass exterminations and the experiments on living bodies. Four million people died here, the Poles say.

And so there is no news to report about Auschwitz. There is merely the compulsion to write something about it, a compulsion that grows out of a restless feeling that to have visited Auschwitz and then turned away without having said or written anything would somehow be a most grievous act of discourtesy to those who died here.

Brzezinka and Oswiecim are very quiet places now; the screams can no longer be heard. The tourist walks silently, quickly at first to get it over with and then, as his mind peoples the barracks and the chambers and the dungeons and the flogging posts, he walks draggingly. The guide does not say much either, because there is nothing much for him to say after he has pointed.

For every visitor, there is one particular bit of horror that he knows he will never forget. For some it is seeing the rebuilt gas chamber at Oswiecim and being told that this is the "small one." For others it is the fact that at Brzezinka, in the ruins of the gas chambers, and the crematoria the Germans blew up as they retreated, there are daisies growing.

There are visitors who gaze blankly at the gas chambers and the furnaces because their minds simply cannot encompass them, but stand shivering before the great mounds of human hair behind the plate glass window or the piles of babies' shoes or the brick cells where men sentenced to death by suffocation were walled up.

One visitor opened his mouth in a silent scream simply at the sight of boxes—great stretches of three-tiered wooden boxes in the women's barracks. They were about six feet wide, about three feet high, and into them from five to ten prisoners were shoved for the night. The guide walks quickly through the barracks. Nothing more to see.

A brick building where sterilization experiments were carried out on women prisoners. The guide tries the door—it's locked. The visitor is grateful that he does not have to go in, and then flushes with shame.

A long corridor where rows of faces stare from the walls. Thousands of pictures, the photographs of prisoners. They are all dead now, the men and women who stood before the cameras, and they all knew they were to die.

They all stare blank-faced, but one picture, in the middle of a row, seizes the eye and wrenches the mind. A girl, 22 years old, plumply pretty, blonde. She is smiling gently, as at a sweet, treasured thought. What was the thought that passed through her young mind and is now her memorial on the wall of the dead at Auschwitz?

Into the suffocation dungeons the visitor is taken for a moment and feels himself strangling. Another visitor goes in, stumbles out, and crosses herself. There is no place to pray at Auschwitz.

The visitors look pleadingly at each other and say to the guide, "Enough."

There is nothing new to report about Auschwitz. It was a sunny day and the trees were green and at the gates the children played.

52. *An American City Put to the Torch*

On Aug. 15, 1965, the Los Angeles *Times* made the unconventional decision to send an ad salesman to report a story. However, the story—the five-day riots in the mostly black area of Watts—demanded unconventionality. Robert Richardson, a 24-year-old black salesman, was chosen presumably because the *Times* thought he would be less of a target during the rioting. By virtue of the following story, Richardson became part of the 1966 Pulitzer Prize-winning team. Richardson's piece is loaded with graphic detail. He takes the reader with him, painstakingly describing the nearly $200 million worth of destruction. The story is an example of the power of a well-written but simple descriptive piece. (*Pulitzer Prize for Local General Spot News Reporting, 1966*)

'Burn Baby Burn' Slogan
Used as Firebugs Put Area to Torch
Robert Richardson
Los Angeles *Times*
August 15, 1965

Negro arsonists raced autos through otherwise deserted Los Angeles streets, flinging Molotov cocktails into store after store and shouting a hep slogan borrowed from a radio disc jockey:
"Burn, baby, burn!"
It was an eerie scene Friday night. Streets crowded with hundreds of rioters Thursday night were debris-littered but empty. Lighted windows were few. It was almost like a ghost town.
But new flames continued to shoot up. Speeding cars criss-crossed the area. Occupants exchanged the now familiar one, two and three finger salute and shouted the grim slogan "Burn, baby, burn!"
(One finger meant he was a Watts man, two meant a Compton man and three fingers meant a man from a Willowbrook area.)
The rioters were burning their city now, as the insane sometimes mutilate themselves.
A great section of Los Angeles was burning, and anyone who didn't return the crazy password was in danger.
I, too, learned to shout "Burn, baby, burn" after several shots were

fired at me. Luckily none of the bullets hit my car, and luckier still, none hit me.

At Holmes Ave. and Imperial Highway I saw a looted Safeway Store all but destroyed by fire.

At 120th St. and Central Ave., a Shoprite Market was burning.

Other stores were burning near Manchester Ave. and Broadway, burning alone, with no one apparently paying the least attention. I saw nobody near them.

Near Vernon and Central Aves. several stores were burning over a six-block area from north to south. All had been looted. People had carried off everything, even such commonplace articles as mops, brooms and soap powders.

Firemen here were struggling to combat the flames.

In some spots helmeted police armed with shotguns seemed to have the upper hand.

Looters arrested

At Avalon Blvd. and 120th St., I saw five patrol cars converge on a smashed-open liquor store full of looters.

Police arrested nine suspects in the place, five women and four men, and lined them against a wall outside.

For the first time that evening I saw a crowd begin to gather. Half a dozen cars halted and parked. A knot of people gathered on the opposite corner and a few jeered.

But none attempted to throw a rock or interfere with the officers.

In all that area I saw only two businesses open and operating. Both were service stations, one operated by Negroes, the other by whites.

'Where is everybody?'

Neither had been disturbed by rioters, and there seemed no explanation for their charmed existences, except both were familiar in their neighborhoods.

I asked whoever I met, "Where is everybody?" and some said, "Over on Broadway—all up and down Broadway—moving toward the West Side."

They were right. You could follow them by the burning stores.

At 81st St. and Avalon Blvd. a looted liquor store was burning, but there was no crowd. At 76th St. and Central Ave., the White Front Store was pillaged and burning out of control, but still no crowd.

At Manchester Ave. and Central Ave., I found a crowd burning a hotdog stand and a taco place. Teenagers stood around yelling "Burn, baby, burn."

I was being shot at again, and it was time to go. Two fire trucks came by with sirens going and I took off right behind them, west on Manchester and north on Broadway.

We passed a furniture store burning out of control and arrived at 48th St. and Broadway. Two furniture stores and a clothing store were burning. They had been cleaned out of everything movable. There were 16 fire trucks on the scene.

I had a flat tire now. One tire had been shot out, and the spare I put on was wiped out by broken glass.

I had to do all of my telephoning from a street-corner booth in a gas station. You have no idea how naked you can feel in an exposed, lighted telephone booth.

But I was hep by that time. Whenever a group of Negroes approached to look me over I knew what to do.

You open the door, stick your head out, and shout, "Burn, baby, burn." Then you are safe.

53.   *A Fatally Tangled Life*

Anthony Lukas' article on the last few weeks of Linda Fitzpatrick's life makes effective use of a structure rarely employed in news writing. It juxtaposes contrasting and contradictory points, effectively carrying out the underlying theme: Miss Fitzpatrick was living two contrasting lives. By telling the story from several people's points of view, Lukas is able to capture the tension and contradictions that marked the ten weeks before the end of her life. As with most good news stories, Lukas' is based on thorough research and includes concrete details that reconstruct scenes in a way to allow the reader to visualize the story. *(Pulitzer Prize for Local Investigative Specialized Reporting, 1968)*

The Two Worlds of Linda Fitzpatrick
J. Anthony Lukas
New York *Times*
October 16, 1967

The windows of Dr. Irving Sklar's reception room at 2 Fifth Avenue look out across Washington Square. A patient waiting uneasily for the dentist's drill can watch the pigeons circling Stanford White's dignified Washington Arch, the children playing hopscotch on the square's wide walkways and the students walking hand in hand beneath the American elms.

"Certainly we knew the Village; our family dentist is at 2 Fifth Avenue," said Irving Fitzpatrick, the wealthy Greenwich, Conn., spice importer whose daughter, Linda, was found murdered with a hippie friend in an East Village boiler room a week ago yesterday.

Mr. Fitzpatrick spoke during a three-hour interview with his family around the fireplace in the library of their 30-room home a mile from the Greenwich Country Club.

For the Fitzpatricks, "the Village" was the Henry James scene they saw out Dr. Sklar's windows and "those dear little shops" that Mrs. Fitzpatrick and her daughters occasionally visited. ("I didn't even know there was an East Village," Mr. Fitzpatrick said. "I've heard of the Lower East Side, but the East Village?")

But for 18-year-old Linda—at least in the last 10 weeks of her life— the Village was a different scene whose ingredients included crash pads, acid trips, freaking out, psychedelic art, witches and warlocks.

If the Fitzpatricks' knowledge of the Village stopped at Washington Square, their knowledge of their daughter stopped at the unsettling but familiar image of a young, talented girl overly impatient to taste the joys of life.

Reality in both cases went far beyond the Fitzpatricks' wildest fears—so far, in fact, that they are still unable to believe what their daughter was going through in her last weeks.

It is perhaps futile to ask which was "the real Linda"—the Linda of Greenwich, Conn., or the Linda of Greenwich Village. For, as The New York Times investigated the two Lindas last week through interviews with her family and with her friends and acquaintances in the Village, it found her a strange mixture so tangled that Linda probably did not know in which she belonged.

The last weeks of Linda's life are a source of profound anguish for her parents. The forces at work on young people like Linda are the source of puzzlement for many other parents and of studies by social workers and psychologists, as they seek to understand the thousands of youths who are leaving middle-class homes throughout the country for the "mind expanding drug" scene in places like Greenwich Village.

Until a few months ago, Linda—or "Fitzpoo," as she was known to her family and friends—seemed to be a happy, well-adjusted product of wealthy American suburbia.

"Linda is a well-rounded, fine, healthy girl," her mother, a well-groomed blonde in a high-collared chocolate brown dress, said during the interview in Greenwich. Throughout the interview Mrs. Fitzpatrick used the present tense in talking of her daughter.

Attended good schools

Born in Greenwich, Linda attended the Greenwich Country Day School, where she excelled in athletics. She won a place as center forward on the "Stuyvesant Team," the all-Fairfield County field hockey team, and also gained swimming and riding awards. She went on to the Oldfields School, a four-year college preparatory school in Glencoe, Md.

A blonde tending to pudginess, she never quite matched the striking good looks of her mother, who as Dorothy Ann Rush was a leading model and cover girl in the thirties, or of her elder sister, Cindy.

At country club dances, Linda often sat in the corner and talked with one of her half-brothers; but, apparently more interested in sports and painting than dancing, she never seemed to mind very much.

According to her family, Linda's last summer began normally. In mid-June she returned from Oldfields after an active year during which she was elected art editor of the yearbook. She spent several weeks in Greenwich, then left with the family for a month in Bermuda.

Vacations in Bermuda

"The family always takes its summer vacations together; we always do things as a family," said Mr. Fitzpatrick, a tall, athletic-looking man in a well-tailored gray suit, blue tie and gold tie-clip. "Sometimes we went to Florida, sometimes to the Antibes, but for the past few summers we've rented a house in Bermuda. This time it was at Paget."

The family included seven children—Linda and 9-year-old Melissa ("Missy") from this marriage; Perry, 32, Robert, 30, Carol, 27, and David, 25, from Mr. Fitzpatrick's first marriage, which ended in divorce; and Cindy from Mrs. Fitzpatrick's first marriage, which also ended in divorce. But this time only Linda and Missy accompanied their parents to Bermuda, while Cindy and her husband joined them later for 10 days.

As the Fitzpatricks remember it, Linda spent "a typical Bermuda vacation"—swimming in the crystal ocean; beach parties on the white sands; hours of painting; occasional shopping expeditions to town.

'The girl we knew'

On July 31 the family returned to Greenwich, where Linda spent most of August. Again the family insists she was "the girl we knew and loved."

They say she spent most of her time painting in the studio in the back of the house. But she found plenty of time for swimming with friends in the large robin's-egg-blue pool, playing the piano, and sitting with Missy.

"Linda and Missy were terribly close," their mother said, biting her lip. "Just as close as Cindy and Linda were when they were younger."

If Linda went to New York during August, the family said, it was "just a quick trip in and out—just for the day."

The Village version

Friends in the Village have a different version of Linda's summer.

"Linda told me she took LSD and smoked grass (marijuana) many times during her stay in Bermuda," recalls Susan Robinson, a small, shy hippie who ran away last May from her home on Cape Cod. "She talked a lot about a fellow who gave her a capsule of acid (LSD) down there and how she was going to send him one."

Susan and her husband, David, who live with two cats and posters of Bob Dylan, Timothy Leary, Allen Ginsberg and D.H. Lawrence in a two-room apartment at 537 East 13th Street, first met Linda when she showed up there some time early in August.

The Robinson apartment served this summer as a "crash pad"—a place where homeless hippies could spend the night or part of the night. Scrawled in pencil on the tin door to the apartment is a sign that reads: "No visitors after midnight unless by appointment please." It is signed with a flower.

"Linda just showed up one evening with a guy named Pigeon," Susan recalls. "She'd just bought Pigeon some acid. We were fooling around and everything. She stayed maybe a couple of hours and then took off."

Flying on acid

"But we liked each other, and she came back a few nights later with

a kid from Boston. She turned him on, too (gave him some LSD). She was always doing that. She'd come into the city on weekends with $30 or $40 and would buy acid for people who needed some."

David Robinson, a gentle young man with a black D.H. Lawrence beard who works in a brassiere factory, recalls how Linda turned him on on Aug. 22. "We went to this guy who sold us three capsules for $10 apiece," he said. "She put one away to send to the guy in Bermuda, gave me one and took one herself. She was always getting burned (purchasing fake LSD) and that night she kept saying, 'God, I just hope this is good.' We were out in the Square (Tompkins Park) and we dropped it (swallowed it) right there. Forty-five minutes later—around midnight—we were off.

"We walked over to a pad on 11th Street just feeling the surge, then over to Tompkins Park, then to Cooper Union Square, where we had a very good discussion with a drunk. By then we were really flying. She was very, very groovy. At 8 a.m. I came back to the pad to sleep, and Linda took the subway up to Grand Central and got on the train to Greenwich. She must have still been flying when she got home."

That weekend in Greenwich, Mrs. Fitzpatrick was getting Linda ready for school. "We bought her an almost entire new wardrobe," she recalled, "and Linda even agreed to get her hair cut."

For months Mr. Fitzpatrick had complained about Linda's hair, which flowed down over her shoulders, but Linda didn't want to change it. Then at the end of August she agreed. "We went to Saks Fifth Avenue, and the hairdresser gave her a kind of Sasoon blunt cut, short and fun. She looked so cute and smart. Hardly a hippie thing to do," Mrs. Fitpatrick said.

The first day of school was only 11 days off when Linda went to New York on Sept. 1. When she returned to Greenwich the next day, she told her mother she didn't want to go back to Oldfields. She wanted to live and paint in the Village.

A surprise for family

"We couldn't have been more surprised," Mrs. Fitzpatrick said, fingering her eyeglasses, which hung from a gold pin at her left shoulder.

"Linda said her favorite teacher, who taught English, and his wife, who taught art, weren't coming back. She just adored them—when they went to Europe she just had to send champagne and fruit to the boat—and she couldn't face going back to school if they weren't there.

"What's more, she said there wasn't anything else she could learn about art at Oldfields. They'd already offered to set up a special course for her there, but she didn't want more courses. She just wanted to paint. She thought she'd be wasting her time at school."

Mother and daughter talked for nearly two hours that Saturday morning of the Labor Day weekend. Then Mrs. Fitzpatrick told her husband, who at first was determined that Linda should finish school.

Reluctant consent given

"But we talked about it with all the family and with friends all through the weekend," Mr. Fitzpatrick recalls. "Finally, on Sunday night, we gave Linda our reluctant permission, though not our approval." Linda left for New York the next morning, and the family never saw her again.

"After all," her mother put in, "Linda's whole life was art. She had a burning desire to be something in the art world. I knew how she felt. I wanted to be a dancer or an artist when I was young, too."

The Fitzpatricks' minds were eased when Linda assured them she had already made respectable living arrangements. "She told us that she was going to live at the Village Plaza Hotel, a very nice hotel on Washington Place, near the university, you know," her mother said.

"'I'll be pefectly safe, mother,' she kept saying. 'It's a perfectly nice place with a doorman and television.' She said she'd be rooming with a girl named Paula Bush, a 22-year-old receptionist from a good family. That made us feel a lot better."

A room at 'The Plaza'

The Village Plaza, 79 Washington Place, has no doorman. A flaking sign by the tiny reception desk announces "Television for Rental" amidst a forest of other signs: "No Refunds." "All Rents Must be Paid in Advance." "No Checks Cashed." "No Outgoing Calls for Transients."

"Sure, I remember Linda," said the stooped desk clerk. "But Paula Bush? There wasn't no Paula Bush. It was Paul Bush."

Ruffling through a pile of stained and thumb-marked cards, he came up with one that had Linda Fitzpatrick's name inked at the top in neat Greenwich County Day School penmanship. Below it in pencil was written: "Paul Bush. Bob Brumberger."

"Yeh," the clerk said. "She moved in here on Sept. 4, Labor Day, with those two hippie guys, Bush and Brumberger. They had Room 504. She paid the full month's rent—$120—in advance. Of course, she had lots of other men up there all the time. Anybody off the street—the dirtiest, bearded hippies she could find."

'She was different'

"*I kept telling her she hadn't ought to act like that. She didn't pay me any attention. But you know she never answered back real snappy like some of the other girls. She was different. She had something—I don't know, class. The day she checked out—oh, it was about Sept. 20—I was out on the steps, and as she left she said, 'I guess I caused you a lot of trouble,' and I said, 'Oh, it wasn't any trouble, really.'*"

"*You want to see the room? Well, there are some people up there now, but I think it'll be O.K.*"

The elevator was out of order. The stairs were dark and narrow, heavy with the sweet reek of marijuana. A knock, and the door to 504 swung open. A bearded young man took his place again on the sway-backed double bed that filled half the room. The young man and three girls were plucking chocolates out of a box.

Against one of the light green walls was a peeling gray dresser, with the upper left drawer missing. Scrawled on the mirror above the dresser in what looked like eyebrow pencil was "Tea Heads Forever" (a tea head is a marijuana smoker) and in lighter pencil, "War Is Hell." Red plastic flowers hung from an overhead light fixture. The bathroom, directly across the hall, was shared with four other rooms.

"Would you like to see Linda's room?" her mother asked, leading the way up the thickly carpeted stairway. "That used to be her room," she said, pointing into an airy bedroom with a white, canopied bed, "until she began playing all those records teen-agers play these days and she asked to move upstairs so she could make all the noise she wanted."

On the third floor Mrs. Fitzpatrick opened the red curtains in the large room. "Red and white are Linda's favorite colors; she thinks they're gay," Mrs. Fitzpatrick said, taking in the red and white striped wallpaper, the twin beds wth red bedspreads, the red pillow with white lettering: Decisions, Decisions, Decisions.

Orange flashed here and there—in the orange and black tiger on the bed ("that's for her father's college, Princeton; we're a Princeton family") and in the orange "Gs" framed on the wall, athletic awards from Greenwich Country Day School.

On the shelves, between a ceramic collie and a glass Bambi, were Edith Hamilton's "The Greek Way" and Agatha Christie's "Murder at Hazelmoor." Nearby were a stack of records, among them Eddie Fisher's "Tonight" and Joey Dee's "Peppermint Twist." In the bright bathroom hung blue and red ribbons from the Oldfields Horse Show and the Greenwich Riding Association Show.

"As you can see, she was such a nice, outgoing, happy girl," her mother said. "If anything's changed, it's changed awfully fast."

Downstairs again, over ginger ale and brownies that Cindy brought in from the kitchen, the Fitzpatricks said they had been reassured about Linda's life in the Village because she said she had a job making posters for "Poster Bazaar" at $80 a week.

"Later she called and said she'd switched to a place called Imports, Ltd., for $85 a week and was making posters on weekends. She sounded so excited and happy," Mrs. Fitzpatrick recalled.

Nobody The Times interviewed had heard of a store called Poster Bazaar. At 177 Macdougal Street is a shop called Fred Leighton's Mexican Imports, Ltd., where, the records show, Linda worked for $2 an hour selling dresses for three days—Sept. 11, 12 and 13. On the third day she was discharged.

"She was always coming in late, and they just got fed up with her," a salesgirl said. Although Linda was given a week's notice, she left on Sept. 14 for a "doctor's appointment" and never came back.

A try at panhandling

Before she left, she asked the manager not to tell her parents she had been discharged, if they called. The manager said the parents did not call after Linda had left, although there had been one call while she was working there.

David Robinson said Linda supported herself from then on by "panhandling" on Washington Square. "She was pretty good at it," he said. "She always got enough to eat."

Linda may have had some money left over from what her mother gave her before she left ("I gave her something," Mrs. Fitzpatrick said, "I thought she was going to be a career girl"), although she never had very much those last weeks.

Yet, David recalls, Linda frequently talked about making big money. "She had a thing about money. Once she told me she wanted to get a job with Hallmark cards drawing those little cartoons. She said she'd make $40,000 a year, rent a big apartment on the Upper East Side and then invite all her hippie friends up there."

Experimenting with art

"We're a great card-exchanging family," Cindy said. "Whenever the occasion arose—birthdays, holidays, illnesses—Linda would make up her own cards and illustrate them with cute little pictures of people and animals."

From a pile on the hall table, Cindy picked out a card with a picture of a girl and an inked inscription, "Please get well 'cause I miss ya, love Linda XOX." In the same pile was a Paris street scene in pastels, two forest scenes made with oils rolled with a Coke bottle, several other gentle landscapes. "Linda was experimenting with all sorts of paints and techniques," Cindy said.

"You want to see some of the paintings she did down here?" asked Susan Robinson, as she went to a pile of papers in the corner and came back with five ink drawings on big white sheets from a sketching pad.

The drawings were in the surrealistic style of modern psychedelic art: distorted womens' faces, particularly heavily lidded eyes, dragons, devils, all hidden in a thick jungle of flowers, leaves and vines, interspersed with phrases in psychedelic script like, "Forever the Mind," "Flying High," "Tomorrow Will Come."

"Linda was never terribly boy crazy," her mother said. "She was very shy. When a boy got interested in her, she'd almost always lose interest in him. She got a proposal in August from a very nice boy from Arizona. She told me, 'He's very nice and I like him, but he's just too anxious.' The boy sent flowers for the funeral. That was thoughtful."

The Robinsons and her other friends in the Village said there were always men in Linda's life there: first Pigeon, then the boy from Boston, then Paul Bush.

Bush, the 19-year-old son of a Holly, Mich., television repairman, is described by those who knew him there as "a real drifter, a way-out hippie." He carried a live lizard on a string around his neck. Bush, who says he left New York on Oct. 4, was interviewed by telephone yesterday.

The nonexistent 'Paula'

"I met Linda at the Robinsons about Aug. 18—a few days after I got to town," he recalls. "We wandered around together. She said her parents bugged her, always hollered at her....So I said I'd get a pad with her and Brumberger, this kid from New Jersey.

"She said she'd tell her parents she was living with a girl named Paula Bush because she didn't want them to know she was living with a man. That was O.K. with me. I only stayed about a week anyway and Brumberger even less. Then she brought in some other guy. I don't know who he was, except he was tall with long hair and a beard."

This may have been Ed, a tall hippie whom the Robinsons saw with Linda several times in mid-September. Later came James L. (Groovy)

Hutchinson, the man with whom she was killed last week.

Toward the end of September, Susan Robinson says Linda told her she feared she was pregnant. "She was very worried about the effect of LSD on the baby, and since I was pregnant, too, we talked about it for quite a while."

Father inclined to doubt

"I don't believe Linda really had anything to do with the hippies," her father said. "I remember during August we were in this room watching a C.B.S. special about the San Francisco hippies. I expressed my abhorrence for the whole thing, and her comments were much like mine. I don't believe she was attracted to them."

However, Linda's half-brother, Perry, recalls that during August Mr. Fitzpatrick also read a story about Galahad, a New York hippie leader, and expressed his "disdain" for him. Linda mentioned casually that she had met Galahad and that she understood he was "helping people," but her father let the remark pass, apparently considering it of no significance.

Her friends say Linda was fascinated by the scene in the Haight-Ashbury section of San Francisco. In late September she apparently visited there.

Susan Robinson recalls that she did not see Linda for some time in late September and that suddenly, on Oct. 1, Linda turned up at her pad and said she had been to Haight-Ashbury. "She said she stayed out there only two days and was very disappointed; that it was a really bad scene; that everybody was on speed (a powerful drug called methadrine). She said she got out and drove back."

In the first week of October, the Fitzpatricks got a postcard postmarked Knightstown, Ind., a small town 30 miles east of Indianapolis. Mrs. Fitzpatrick did not want to show the card to a visitor because "it was the last thing I've got which Linda touched." But she said it read roughly: "I'm on my way to see Bob (her brother, who is a Los Angeles lawyer). Offered a good job painting posters in Berkeley. I love you. I will send you a poster. Love, Linda."

Also in the first week of October a girl who identified herself as Linda telephoned her brother's office in Los Angeles but was told he was in San Francisco. She never called back.

When Linda saw Susan on Oct. 1 she told her she had met two warlocks, or male witches, in California and had driven back with them.

"This didn't surprise me," Susan said. "Linda told me several times she was a witch. She said she had discovered this one day when she was sitting on a beach and thought how empty it was and wished there was someone there. She said a man suddenly appeared. She was always talking about her supernatural powers. Once she was walking on a street in the Village with this girl Judy, and she stumbled over a broom. 'Oh,' she told Judy, 'this is my lucky day. Now I can fly away.'"

"Linda told me she met these two warlocks out there and that they could snap their fingers and make light bulbs pop. She said one of the warlocks took her mind apart and scattered it all over the room and then put it together again. Ever since, she said, she felt the warlock owned her."

'That's not true'

"One of the newspapers said Linda was interested in Buddhism and Hinduism and all that supernatural stuff," Cindy said. "That's not true at all. I don't think she ever even knew what it was."

Last Friday a self-styled warlock who said he was one of the two who drove Linda back to New York was interviewed in the Village. The warlock, who called himself "Pepsi," is in his late 20's with long, sandy hair, a scruffy beard, heavily tattooed forearms, wire-rim glasses and long suede Indian boots.

"My buddy and I ran into Linda in a club in Indianapolis called the Glory Hole," Pepsi said. "We took Linda along. You could see right away she was a real meth monster—that's my name for a speed freak, somebody hooked on speed.

"We were two days driving back. We got in on Oct. 1, and she put up with me and my buddy in this pad on Avenue B. She was supposed to keep it clean, but all she ever did was sit around. She had this real weird imagination, but she was like talking in smaller and smaller circles. She was supposed to be this great artist, but it wasn't much good. It was just teeny bopper stuff—drawing one curving line, then embellishing it.

A lot of potential

"It sounds like I'm knocking her. I'm not. She was a good kid, if she hadn't been so freaked out on meth. She had a lot of, what do you call it—potential. Sometimes she was a lot of fun to be with. We took her on a couple of spiritual seances, and we went out on the Staten Island

Ferry one day at dawn and surfing once on Long Island."

Pepsi saw Linda at 10 p.m. Saturday Oct. 8 standing in front of the Cave on Avenue A with Groovy. She said she'd taken a grain and a half of speed and was "high." Three hours later she and Groovy were dead—their nude bodies stretched out on the boiler room floor, their heads shattered by bricks. The police have charged two men with the murders and are continuing their investigation.

"It's too late for the whole thing to do us much good," her brother Perry said on Saturday after he had been told of her life in the Village. "But maybe somebody else can learn something from it."

Copyright © 1967 by The New York Times Company. Reprinted by permission.

54.   *Four Days of Rage*

Nothing is quite as dramatic as an eyewitness story written by a skilled reporter. Tom Fitzpatrick encountered a truly explosive story on Oct. 8, 1969, with the beginning of the Weathermen's Four Days of Rage in Chicago. Through vivid imagery, he captured the tension of the evening for the reader. The opening description of Bad Marvin, the swaggering protester, is the foundation on which Fitzpatrick built the story. He returns to Bad Marvin when Marvin's torch has been extinguished, offering a memorable contrast. As Marvin's fate goes, so goes the protest. Fitzpatrick also effectively uses the word "you" to bring a sense of immediacy to his readers. Instead of relying on first person or the more traditional third-person, Fitzpatrick chose to involve his readers directly in the narrative. That approach makes for an exciting and well-crafted story. *(Pulitzer Prize for Local General Spot News Reporting, 1970)*

A Wild Night's Ride With SDS

Tom Fitzpatrick

Chicago *Sun-Times*

October 9, 1969

Bad Marvin had been standing in front of the fire he had made of a Lincoln Park bench for about 30 minutes, shouting to everyone in the crowd and warning them how bad he was.

It was 10:25 p.m....and now about 200 kids began racing out of the park, heading toward the Chicago Historical Society. Bad Marvin started running, too, brandishing a long piece of burning board in his right hand.

"Viva Che," he kept shouting as he ran. "Viva Cuba."

"Bring the war home now," screamed a girl running alongside him.

She was so caught up with running in the dark that she ran right into a large tree outside the Historical Society and collapsed in a lump, the first casualty of the night.

By now the main force of the group had reached North Federal Savings, at the northwest corner of North and Clark. It's a big, impressive building with large plate glass windows and here's where the tide turned.

A tall skinny kid in a white helmet ran a little in front of the crowd and tossed a rock through one of the large windows. The first rock was soon followed by a second and a third, and then cheering.

Now everyone is shouting at the top of his lungs and it's amazing how many of them have come out of the park with rocks in their hands.

"Ho, Ho, Ho Chi Minh!" they're shouting. A blond in the front row is waving the Viet Cong flag.

Once on Clark Street and heading south, the kids have taken over the entire street. The street is narrow enough to create an echo as the windows start exploding on each side.

Three rocks go through the windows of the Red Star Inn and apartment windows on all sides are falling.

The sound of shattering glass hits everyone in the group like an electric shock. You are not alone when you are in a group like this. From now on, it was going to have to be a wild ride. And if you were going to find out what happened, you had to go along with it.

By this time you have already learned one important rule about running with mobs who are tossing rocks. You have to stay up front and stay right on the street with them.

If you get on the sidewalk, you'll never see the rock that hits you instead of an apartment window. There is risk in this, too, because you must time your moves so that you get away from the whole outfit as soon as you see the line of police forming ahead of you.

The police weren't in sight and the wild march went on all the way to within 50 yards of Division Street. And there the police were waiting.

They were lined up across the street and they weren't saying a word. It was a sight so formidable that you didn't blame the kids when they turned and ran back on Clark and then turned east on Goethe to escape.

Goethe was where it really got bad. Every car window for a two-block stretch was smashed and so were the lobby windows of a high-rise apartment on the corner of Dearborn and Goethe.

The kids knew it was all over for them but they kept on the attack.

And now, as we're heading into the eye of the storm on Division Street, I see a beautiful thing happen. It's Bad Marvin, the guy with the flaming stock who was bragging to everyone how bad he was going to be. Bad Marvin is running away and his torch has burned out.

It always makes you feel good when the tough-talking guys cave in, but now what does happen is not good. All the kids who have been wound up so tight from listening to the inflammatory speeches in the park are going to take it in the head.

"Charge!" one little kid screams as he runs for the police line. "Charge!" the cry comes back as about a dozen more follow him.

The squad cars are at the intersection and the kids are being thrown into them as quickly as possible. One policeman is leaning over a squad car holding his head. He's been hit by a rock and he's bleeding and he's mad.

But the kids aren't stopped yet. Some of them head east to Lake Shore Drive. Another group turns back and races west along Division.

This is the first confrontation. You will see three more at different intersections before it ends at Crilly Court on North, just west of Wells. There are only about 50 kids left and this is the time it scares you.

Walking in the middle of the street, you're amazed to see cars heading toward you as if they mean to run you over. The cars are filled with policemen, some in plain clothes, some in uniform.

As they leap out, you can see at least three of them have their revolvers drawn. The others are wielding clubs.

The kids run but they don't have a chance. They have been asking all night for a confrontation and now they get one.

Within minutes the street is cleared and Deputy Supt. James Rochford is walking toward Sgt. James Clark to get a final report. But there is no smile of triumph on Rochford's face. He was through this same thing during the Democratic National Convention of 1968 and he didn't take any delight in it then, either.

"All right," Rochford says to Clark. "Get the men to clear the street. Let's all just get out of here."

Reprinted by permission of the Chicago *Sun-Times*.

55. *A Destructive Force Broken Loose*

Gaylord Shaw of the Los Angeles *Times* had been investigating the issue of dam safety for more than a year when the Laurel Run Dam in Johnstown, Pennsylvania, broke, killing scores of people in 1977. Although Shaw had uncovered serious deficiencies in the maintenance of the nation's dams, his series had received little attention until the Johnstown disaster. The story below, written two days after the dam break, describes the destruction caused by the rushing water and looks at the causes. It is a well-researched and written spot news story, combining descriptive prose with the effective use of background information. *(Pulitzer Prize for National Reporting, 1978)*

Johnstown Dams Called 'Time Bombs'
Gaylord D. Shaw
Los Angeles *Times*
July 23, 1977

JOHNSTOWN, Pa.—The helicopter swooped low through the ugly gap in Laurel Run Dam, then hovered over an expanse of mud and rock where two days earlier a reservoir had contained 100 million gallons of water.

Joseph Ellam, Pennsylvania state dam safety engineer, surveyed the scene and said with frustration: "For 19 years, I've been trying to tell people they had time bombs up every one of these hollows. They didn't believe me."

By "time bombs," Ellam was referring to scores of aging dams that dot the narrow valleys of southwestern Pennsylvania—some of them clearly inadequate to cope with torrential rainstorms that periodically strike the region.

One of those storms dumped a dozen inches of rain during last Wednesday's early morning darkness and caused about one-third of the 400-foot-wide dam to collapse, releasing a wall of water that fed a flood now blamed for at least 55 deaths and $250 million in damage.

Laurel Run Dam, built 60 years ago to supply water to Johnstown, suddenly became an instrument of disaster. And it became the latest tragic symbol of a national problem disclosed earlier this year in a month-long Times investigation; hundreds of aging, defective dams pose the potential for catastrophe because they are unable to hold back severe floods.

Engineers like Ellam have known for years that hazards lurk in some of the nation's 50,000 large dams, but their warnings and pleas usually have fallen on deaf ears of politicians and other officials who must pass the laws and appropriate the money to deal with the problem.

Thus, frustration seemed to surround Ellam as he made a helicopter inspection Friday of Laurel Run Dam and a smaller dam several miles away that also collapsed in Wednesday's storm.

Ironically, this second dam, which had held about 8 million gallons of water, is just a short distance upstream from the remnants of a 70-foot-high dam that failed in 1889 and killed 2,200 people—the nation's worst dam disaster. "I stop there every year," he said of the 1889 disaster scene. "It's a sobering reminder..."

The valley downstream from Laurel Run Dam offers a new sobering reminder of the destructive force held in check by America's dams.

Once it was the community of Tanneryville, the tranquil home of middle-class steelworkers, carpenters and truck drivers, of families named Dragovich, Felix, Peskorich and Thomas.

Now it is a valley of death, destruction and despair.

The shattered remnants of houses are piled atop one another. Cars and trucks are submerged in mountains of mud. Telephone poles and other debris are strewn about like toothpicks. And the people, some with tears, some with stoic silence, are searching for friends and relatives.

Charles Kramer, 39, a home remodeler, found the body of a fishing companion partly buried in the mud beneath three uprooted trees. "His trailer washed away when the dam went down," Kramer said. "Nobody knows what happened to his wife and children...I know of at least 30 persons missing."

William Rayha and his wife said eight of their neighbors were missing. They scrambled to safety themselves, but their home, two cars and all of their clothing and furniture were swept away. All that's left is the red concrete floor of their garage. "This is it...all we have left in the world," Mrs. Rayha said. "Twenty years of work and struggle..."

Further downstream, in the community of Seward, Gary Henderson, 26, has spent the last two days poking in the mud for bodies. He found one, "a little boy, 9 years old," Henderson said. "I was sick..."

Henderson, the manager of an aviation company, said many of the bodies in Seward had been found in cars. "It seemed like they were trying to get away, but something must have happened real fast," he said. "It was the dam, I guess."

Some bodies were believed to have been carried for miles downstream, and authorities feared that some would never be found. The force of the water was so intense, witnesses said, that massive boulders were bouncing like pebbles.

"Rumble, rumble, rumble—you could hear the rumble, and then you could hear the houses cracking," said one witness, Harry Ashcroft.

John Beltz, a township supervisor who carried a list of 42 persons he said had died in the valley, said residents should have been given some warning about a possible dam collapse.

His neighbors agreed—and were angered by initial official comments that the dam had not caused the damage—that it simply had been the immense amount of rain that fell within a short time and had set off the flooding.

"What do they think—that a little creek did all this?" said Sammy Felix, a 30-year-old housewife, as she motioned toward the wrecked houses. "Somebody fell down on the job. Why didn't they blow the sirens and get the people out when the dam was filling up?

The dam tender, Timothy Lentz, told reporters the collapse occurred suddenly when the dam's spillway could not cope with the rapidly rising reservoir. The water surged over the top of the 42-foot-high earthen structure and soon it was breached. There was, Lentz said, "a gigantic roar louder than thunder...I thought the side of the mountain was coming down."

Ellam cited "grossly inadequate spillway capacity" as the probable cause of the overtopping and subsequent failure of the dam and said the same problem plagued many of the state's 900 other large dams.

"These dams were built 50, 60, 70 years ago," he said. "The state of the art is much different today, but what do we do about all the old dams?"

The Times reported earlier this year that only half of the states had dam safety programs and that 36,000 large dams in the country had never been inspected by state or federal engineers.

Pennsylvania's dam safety program, although limited in funds and manpower, is ranked by experts as one of the top 10 in the nation.

Ellam said Laurel Run Dam had been inspected by his office a year ago and found to be well maintained and apparently in good condition.

In addition to examining the two failed dams Friday, Ellam completed an emergency inspection of 10 other "problem dams" near Johnstown, accompanied by a Corps of Engineers expert, Stuart Long. "They look a lot better than they did yesterday—they're all OK," Ellam said of the 10 dams. "I'm relieved. Thank God it didn't rain again."

56. A Land Frozen in Time

Richard Ben Cramer knew there was a story to be told in the no-man's land of occupied Lebanon—and he encountered the same roadblocks that stopped other reporters from getting there. Cramer, however, used his ingenuity to get around the official obstacles and literally walked the last two miles through no-man's land to report the story. The following piece is an impressive example of descriptive writing, giving the reader a strong sense of the bitter emotions present on both sides of the conflict. Cramer's contrasting of the Arab and Israeli troops and his detailed imagery of the destruction caused by their fight make for an important and memorable story. *(Pulitzer Prize for International Reporting, 1979)*

A Walk Through No-Man's Land
Richard Ben Cramer
Philadelphia *Inquirer*
March 17, 1978

RAS EL BAYADA, Occupied Lebanon—It is eerily still in no-man's land, a two-mile testament to the lesson that people are as much a part of the landscape as houses and fences and fields.

Here, eight miles from Lebanaon's southern border, between the last Fatah commando checkpoint and the spearhead of the advancing Israelis, the chickens come out to meet you on the road. It has been 48 hours since grain was scattered for them in their yards.

Here, everything is frozen in time, like a Pompeii without the lava. Crates of oranges are stacked, unattended, next to empty houses. Telephone wires dangle broken and useless from their poles. An open spigot pours an endless stream of water onto a swamp that once was a garden.

Here, the mere whoosh of a breeze through the leaves can make you sprint for cover, scanning the sky for warplanes until you dive into the orange groves...only to emerge a moment later feeling foolish and shaky from the rush of adrenalin.

To be sure, there is noise to break the stillness—a child's cry, an engine or a laugh. And without man, the eeriness is unrelieved in this world between two worlds.

Behind the last Fatah checkpoint, the teenagers bearing Kalashnikov submachine guns and wearing jaunty red berets talk quietly among themselves for long, nervous hours.

The fear of the Israelis is palpable. The sky is constantly watched. For 48 hours, on the streets and in the fields, the little bands have shifted.

They move constantly—occasionally fighting, more often just moving, farther and farther back.

The latest news is passed by word of mouth, from the children who seem to be everywhere, or from passing Jeeps or cabs full of commandos.

Transport is arranged on an ad-hoc basis. A Peugeot with no muffler stops. A Lebanese is driving. A Palestinian sits by his side. The back seat is stacked with 16 captured Israeli machine guns.

This is Fatahland, as the Israelis call it, where everyone might be a commando and children of 10 know how to handle the Kalashnikov.

Fatahland has been shoved north from the border, helter-skelter, so that now it is near the ancient Mediterranean port of Tyre. Still, the welter of movement and talk is quite organized.

There are few radios and no walkie-talkies. But the movements of an outsider—every step he takes—are watched and reported.

For two days, in the face of Israel's massive assault, the Palestinian forces have had to shoot and run away.

"There is no way for us to face such heavy weapons," said a commando officer in Tyre. "It would be useless. It would be foolish."

Still, on the village streets and in the camps along the coast, the spirit among the commandos is broodingly vengeful.

"With every step, they will pay," the officer said. "They will pay a price such as Israel never has had to pay."

The Fatah command posts have been moved and re-moved to avoid the threat of Israeli artillery and bombs. Yesterday's location was unknown to 12 of 13 commandos near the front. Yet, somehow, the orders get through. The communications network is the whole population.

Everywhere, but nowhere in particular, stand the young men with the light machine guns. When the first rumble of planes is heard, they silently slip away. After the last Israeli bomb has dropped, they are suddenly, miraculously everywhere again.

Close to the last Fatah checkpoint, the fear shows on every face. No one knows whether the Israelis will push forward again.

The civilians have begun to disappear. Cars and trucks full of refugees have been leaving for the last two days. One Mercedes heading north last night was filled with 16 people—three in the front, four children between the seats, five on the back seat and four sitting in the open trunk.

In the streets and fields, there is constant movement.

"You had better go away now," said a commando at a headquarters near Tyre. "It is not good to stay too long in one place."

As the last checkpoint approaches, the taxi driver bows out. For once, it is not a matter of money.

"I am Arab," he says, and he draws a finger across his throat to indicate his fate on the other side of the line.

The commandos at the barrier are startled by footsteps. "It is impossible; don't go," they say. "The Israelis are very near. They kill for nothing."

And then, all is past, and the stillness sets in.

On the lone walk, there are monuments to the violence of 48 feral hours.

A BMW sedan with a flat tire is pulled to one side of the road. Except for the tire, the car is intact. There is no explanation for its presence, until a door is opened to reveal upholstery spattered with blood.

Farther along, five cars are burning. Their stink testifies to the accuracy of the Israeli aerial assault. The blistered hulks sit on bare wheels, tires burned off in the explosions that halted the cars.

In the back of a Mazda, a burnt skeleton of a machine gun lies in the open trunk. When the machine gun is moved, two lizards dart out of their new home for the bushes at the side of the road.

There are daisies growing in the bushes, and the air holds the scent of honeysuckle. Birds sing in the intervals between explosions on a hillside to the east.

Suddenly, around a bend, the squawk of a shortwave radio cuts through the air.

Ahead, two giant Israeli tanks stand on either side of the road, their snouts pointed toward Fatahland.

The tanks form a gate, of sorts, to a new world, one of pure geometry and punctilious organization. To the left and right, fields have been cleared of their crops and American-built personnel carriers scuttle over the raw earth on rubber treads.

There are halftracks and Jeeps, supply vehicles and trucks busy here and there.

The Israelis are settling in, bringing a new order.

A visitor causes some consternation. There is nothing in the manual.

"Go there," says a private atop one of the tanks. He points to a spot on the road, cutting off further questions.

"They don't let us talk," he says.

The Israeli equipment almost gleams. It is huge and new, as American as a baseball bat.

Communication here is by radio. There is no shouting, only the roar of machinery on the earth.

About 50 soldiers surround the machines. They pass without words. A couple of them gawk. One smiles.

In the middle of the field, a group on foot is listening to rock music on Israeli radio.

But there is worry on their faces, matching the fear on the Palestinian faces up the road.

"They are all around here," a freckled private says.

He looks west to an orange grove and the Mediterranean, only 150 yards away.

"I cannot tell you that there are not terrorists behind those trees right now."

Another complains that the personnel carriers are not armored.

"They are only aluminum," he says. "Even a regular bullet passes right through."

A third soldier cuts him off.

"Don't talk," he says.

A major pulls up in a Jeep. He has a printed itinerary taped to a band on his arm.

There is a discussion about whether the visitor should be forced to leave. No one can seem to imagine walking through the orange groves in Fatahland.

The major says the Israeli forces are going nowhere this day.

"If you ask me, I'm not the prime minister," he says, "but I'd say this is it."

Hebrew barks over the radio of his Jeep. He answers with a monosyllable and climbs back in.

"You will go back?" he asks, incredulous, with a look up the road. "You are crazy."

Reprinted by permission of the Philadelphia *Inquirer.*

57.   *The Refugee Life*
of Death and Destitution

The following story by Joel Brinkley of the Louisville *Courier-Journal* reveals the plight of refugees in Thailand in the late 1970s. Its vivid descriptions and statements from refugees and relief workers bring the distant news event closer home to the reader. While presenting his own view of conditions in refugee camps, Brinkley makes it possible for the reader to see the tragedy through the eyes of the refugees themselves. *(Pulitzer Prize for International Reporting, 1980)*

Living the Cambodian Nightmare
Joel Brinkley
Louisville *Courier-Journal*
December 2, 1979

Gaunt, glassy-eyed and possessionless, they crouch in the heat amid thousands of others, hungry and diseased. They stoop over small, dry plots of rock-hard soil. And they wait.

They wait in tight lines for hours to get today's ration of food from international relief agencies: a bowl of rice gruel, two bananas, a bucket of brown drinking water.

They wait for doctors to heal them.

Some wait for news of family, though many know their relatives are dead; they remember watching brothers and sisters, parents and children being murdered, or struggling for a final breath before starvation.

They wait for another assault by Thai soldiers who come to rape their women. Or for the Vietnamese troops to launch an all-out offensive that would drive them across the border into Thailand.

And some wait to learn where the next steps in their miserable lives will lead them. Meanwhile they sweat, swat at mosquitoes and inhale the stench of hundreds of thousands of suffering and dying countrymen.

Death and destitution.

Seven million Cambodians have been caught between the two since 1975.

About 3 million are already dead, and many who remain alive could die soon from disease or starvation.

The lucky ones are the million or so Cambodian refugees who escaped the grip of the communist Khmer Rouge, dodged gunfire from Vietnamese invaders and trekked hundreds of miles with little or no food to sanctuary in refugee camps on the Thai border.

But what kind of sanctuary is it?

For many, it's a rectangle of hard, bare ground the size of a desk top. It's a plastic sheet for cover, so low overhead that it rubs the noses of some who sleep.

It's the searing odor of sweat, defecation and death. It's the ceaseless buzzing of a million flies and the hack of 10,000 coughs.

It's row upon row of black-faced sufferers whose futures hold no promise or respite.

Life in a refugee camp is hellish, unbearable. The relief worker who ends his first day wet-eyed can't always blame the choking dust.

But compared with life in Cambodia since 1975, many refugees say their present plight doesn't seem so bad.

Talk to them.

As they tell of years of horror and misery that Westerners can barely comprehend, their faces are expressionless and dull. Their voices are flat, as if they're talking about a dull day at work.

Their tales end with a cold, nodding acknowledgement of the death of their nation and culture.

"It is very sad about my country," said Say Khol, a 30-year-old man who once taught English in Phnom Penh. He was sitting in Cambodia's Samet Meanchey refugee camp a half-mile from the Thai border, drawing in the dirt as he talked.

"Small boy, he no have anything to learn. Old man, he no have anything to eat. Cambodia is only here. This is all that is left of my country. Soon this will be gone, too."

Like many Cambodians, Say spoke English often "until Pol Pot. Since then, I scared to speak one word or I be killed. I forget so much."

Pol Pot is the communist commander whose Khmer Rouge soldiers overthrew the American-backed military government of Gen. Lon Nol in 1975. (Khmer is the Cambodian race, as Anglo-Saxon is the British race.) After the overthrow, Pol Pot's soldiers began executing everyone with any hint of wealth or education—especially those who spoke a foreign language.

The executions were supposed to purge centuries of Western influence and remake Cambodia into a self-sufficient, rural society.

Death came swiftly from machetes and bullets, or slowly from prolonged torture. More than a million Cambodians died that first year.

Some were hung upside down by their feet, their heads submerged in buckets of water. They remained alive as long as their neck muscles could hold their faces out of the water. Still others were publicly disemboweled.

Chilren were chained together, then buried alive.

Say, a handsome young man, had been a lieutenant in Lon Nol's army. But when the Khmer Rouge forces approached Phnom Penh, "I threw away my uniform, put on my clothes to look like an ordinary farmer and tried to leave the city."

The executions had already begun.

"I saw many, many people killed, hit on the back of the neck with a bamboo knife. They threw the bodies into huge, big piles in the middle of the street.

"I saw my friends in those piles."

He escaped the Khmer Rouge's notice. Then with the rest of Phnom Penh's survivors, he said, "I got pushed by Pol Pot into the country, to Kampong Speu Province" in southwestern Cambodia.

Like other survivors, Say was forced to live on a commune and work as a rice farmer for several years, conscious every minute that he'd be executed the moment he betrayed his middle-class past.

"They pushed me very, very hard. I worked every day, 4 a.m. to 11 p.m., with only two meals. No religious holidays."

At communes across the country, Khmer Rouge soldiers would, without warning or apparent provocation, grab workers and take them away. Sometimes weeks or months later, Say and other refugees said, workers would stumble upon mangled bodies in the corner of a rice field.

"Later, Pol Pot pushed me to Battambang Province (in western Cambodia), where we built a big, big water tank," Say said. "No machines or tools. Just people. We worked 24 hours a day, seven days a week until it was finished. Many people, old people and young people, they died, dropped while we worked, and we worked around them.

"We have only a little bit to eat. Seven spoons of rice a day. Seven spoons, sir. That's all. Sometimes we eat only salt and little animals and the leaf of a tree."

Millions of Cambodians in other communes suffered along with him.

"In my place many men kill themselves," said Theam Den, a refugee who used to be a medical student. "They hang themselves or slit their own throats at night."

This spring, Vietnam invaded Cambodia, driving Pol Pot and his Khmer Rouge forces to the far west, where they still skirmish today.

"Vietnamese soldiers, they first tell us they are good people," Say said. "They tell us not to be afraid of them. At first we believe them. But then they make force on the Cambodian people.

"They no give us anything to eat. They take away our rice, where I not know. I know only that we don't have anything to eat except the little bit of corn they give us."

That's a typical assessment of the Vietnamese invaders, made by refugee after refugee. Initially friendly, the Vietnamese passed themselves off as Cambodia's saviors. But later they seemed more cunning than concerned as they stole the people's food.

"We think the Vietnamese are not giving food to the Cambodian people because they know the world will feed us if they don't," said Suthoni Nginn, a 31-year-old refugee who worked for the Catholic Relief Service in Phnom Penh until 1975.

Huol Seng, a chauffeur in Phnom Penh until 1975, said, "Pol Pot, he kill by knife. The Vietnamese, they kill by rice. Our people get angrier and angrier and skinnier and skinnier."

Bong Say, who was an English and French teacher at the Lycee Siem Reap, a high school in north-central Cambodia, grew rice first for Pol Pot, whose troops killed five of his nine children. Then he farmed for the Vietnamese.

"The Vietnamese were gentle in town, but cruel in our neighborhoods," he said. "When harvest season came, they took away all our harvest knives and put mines all around the fields so we couldn't get any of our rice. They give one small can of corn per family a day. Not enough. Not enough. They send our rice to Vietnam.

"If we stop giving rice, people must die."

Say Khol, the former Englsh teacher, sneaked off one night this fall with the thin bandoleer of rice he had saved and walked to Thailand.

"I walk five days," he said, counting on his fingers. "More than 100 kilometers. I walk at night and see many, many others walking too, some fast, some very slow.

"We dive into bushes if we see Vietnamese soldiers coming. Some of us very sick. Many, many bodies lying by the road. Everywhere it smells bad from the dead."

Now Say squats with the 200,000 others in the border encampment and waits.

"My family is alive in Battambang, and they will come soon," he says with more hope than conviction. "I know they will come."

Khlot Chhvy's family will not be joining him in the Thai refugee camp. They were killed by the Khmer Rouge.

With friends, Khlot walked two months last summer from his central Cambodian commune to Thailand. "We had nothing to eat. We eat leaves and bamboo and little bugs. I think perhaps I die in the forest."

Of the 25 people who left with Khlot, 18 died either from starvation or were "shot by the gun," he said.

And at the Thai border there were new threats.

"Khmer Rouge, they dig holes in the jungle floor, by the border, and put bamboo stakes in the bottoms. They cover the holes with mats. Two of my friends, they step into one of those holes when they try to cross the border, and they scream and die on those stakes."

Khlot waited until daylight, when no troops were around, to cross the border.

Others waited weeks or months in the weeds before finding a safe moment to cross.

Chamm Peoum, 18, lay in the underbrush three months. "It was very, very difficult to live in the frontier," he said recently, only a few hours after slipping across. During his first day of "freedom," he sat quietly on the floor of a bamboo-walled holding pen in the Aranyaprathet camp for legal refugees. Being out of Cambodia made him very happy.

"There are many, many people on the frontier. Many of them die. Unless you have money or jewelry, you die."

Chamm gave the little gold or jewelry he had saved to Thai citizens who sneaked across the border to sell food. But frequently, Vietnamese soldiers would steal all the refugees' jewelry, Chamm said.

"When the Vietnamese take our gold, we no can buy food. And then we certainly die."

Once they're across the border, many refugees carry two thoughts with them.

Chamm offers the first with passion. "All the people, we want to kill Pol Pot. We want to kill him very much."

The second comes softly from Theam Den, his eyes downcast. "I can never, never go back to Cambodia. Never again."

58. *A Nation in the Grip of Fear*

The following article by John Darnton is notable for its letter format. Normal means of communicating by newspaper correspondents had been shut down in Warsaw, from where Darnton was reporting, in 1981. He therefore was required to send his dispatches by regular post. Addressed to Robert Semple Jr., the New York *Times'* foreign editor, the letter is a masterful piece of news writing. It is built around a clear thematic focus on the fear that the government had instilled in Poles. The reality of the theme is made apparent through Darnton's eyewitness account and his use of concrete scenes which the reader is able to visualize. *(Pulitzer Prize for International Reporting, 1982)*

A Letter From Warsaw:
'Fear Can Come Back
as Quickly as a Door Slamming'
John Darnton
New York *Times*
December 17, 1981

Dear Bob,

At least twice in the past 24 hours the official Polish press agency has used the word "normalization" to apply to events here. For Poles and other East Europeans this is a dreaded code word.

"Normalization" is what happened to Czechoslovakia after a Warsaw Pact invasion crushed the "Prague Spring" of 1968. In the peculiar jargon of Communist officials, in which words can mean their opposite, it is the restoration of orthodox authority. To people it is the almost unbearably painful process of watching the dismantlement, piece by piece, of freedom and liberties painstakingly won.

A major part in that process is fear, and fear, it is clear, has become of the new military Poland. *(As written.)* It is strange; perhaps the one defining trait of the Polish "renewal" of the past 16 months was the absence of fear.

A calculated campaign of intimidation

With a massive show of manpower and equipment and a calculated campaign of intimidation, the military authorities here are trying to break the spirit of resistance of the workers' movement.

Yesterday evening, a caravan of 273 police cars, trucks, water cannons and other hardware moved slowly through the city at rush hour. Thousands of onlookers were forced back on the sidewalks, dark figures waiting on dirty snow banks and trees in the cold. It seemed a parade of brute force.

This morning at an early hour three secret policemen barged into the small apartment of a Polish journalist. They insisted that he sign a document asserting that he would no longer "act in a manner to oppose socialism in Poland." He resisted and was bundled away. His wife pleaded with the policemen as they dragged him down the stairs. One of them responded, "Don't worry, we'll be back tomorrow for you to sign it."

The fear campaign is working in some respects. Already people open their doors just a crack, to inspect who is there. They play the radio loudly while talking, or set the water running—old devices from the Stalinist 1950s to foil the eavesdropper.

For someone who has lived here for almost three years, it is as if a door that was gradually opened has been suddenly shut.

'You're being observed'

"I can't see you now," whispers a Polish friend, as he answers his door and steps into the hallway, closing it behind him. "Didn't you hear? I was detained. I just got out. I'm sure you're being observed."

"We can't talk here," says another Polish friend standing in a stairwell, with a glance at a man nearby, who said he was a taxi driver waiting for a customer. He may, or may not, have been listening.

It takes a long time for fear to go away, weeks, or months even, in which people slowly learn that they can speak out or, emboldened by others, write more forcefully and honestly in the newspapers. But fear can come back as quickly as a door slamming.

Overwhelming show of force

The full extent of the strike protest to the imposition of martial law cannot be determined with all communications down all over the country. But in areas where foreign journalists have been able to reach, factories in the Warsaw region, what broke the backbone of the protest was fear. The authorities mounted an overwhelming show of force—surrounding factories with tanks and armored cars and simply waiting for darkness and curfew to unsettle the demonstrators inside.

Workers who gave up said afterwards that they felt isolated, with no idea of what was going on in other parts of the country. They were worn down, sometimes hungry, and began thinking of their children. Women among them began weeping. When the troops and policemen burst in, they were offered a chance to leave, unharmed, if they would separate themselves from their leaders.

"We really had no other choice," said one worker at the Huta Warsgawa steel mill. "They had live ammunition, and their guns were raised. They seemed as scared as we were."

In other regions, resistance is still going on and some workers are apparently determined to repel an armed attack. But what the outcome will be cannot even be guessed.

'Will have to eat their words'

"Poles always called the Czechs cowards for not resisting in '68," said one foreign visitor here who travels frequently throughout Eastern Europe. "Now they will have to eat their words. The Czechs were invaded by five armies; the Poles did it all by themselves."

A major factor in the ease with which military rule has been established so far is the Polish love and respect for the army. The army, like the flag and church, is a symbol of nationalism.

"All this time we were all looking at the army and saying that because it is mostly made up of conscripts it might not be loyal to the government," said one European diplomat. "What we didn't see was the other side of the coin. Because the army contains so many sons and brothers, people were reluctant to move against it."

The most telling scene in the capital over the past three days, perhaps, occurred yesterday morning when busloads of soldiers moved into the Polish Academy of Sciences to break up a strike by some of the country's most eminent thinkers. The crowd was sullen and angry as the troops led away men in rumpled suits and spectacles and loaded them into a bus. But no one even threw a snowball. Minutes afterward, a truckload of soldiers goes past and, surprisingly, some of them wave to the crowd, for all the world like liberating soldiers, not agents of repression.

The military decree that was promulgated the morning after the army moved in was Draconian, and it was prominently displayed on posters and the two newspapers allowed to publish. Penalties range from two years to death, for seemingly minor infractions. It simply overwhelmed people.

Soldiers posted at intersections throughout the city turned cars away and let others through, rerouting traffic without any logical rhyme or reason. It was effective psychological harassment.

'The time for true courage'

One Polish journalist, sitting at a cafe and talking to a foreign colleague with a nervous glance over his shoulder from time to time, displayed the demoralization and depression that most Poles seem to be feeling. It was, he said, the intellectuals who would feel the backlash. All his journalist friends, he said, were now out of work. One by one, he predicted, new newspapers would open up, and one by one his friends would be offered jobs, if they were judged reliable. "Now comes the time for true courage," he said. "I wonder how many will measure up. It's either that or going to the work center for a job as a street cleaner."

"We are back to 1951 and '52," he continued, referring to the Stalinist years. "It would take us 20 years to rebuild what we had here."

Solidarity, he suggested, has talked a great line, but at no time over the past 16 months did the union really prepare a plan to counter a massive display of force. It was not envisaged that things could turn around so quickly, he said. Nor was it even thought that fear could come back so quickly.

Yours sincerely,
John Darnton

59. *The Aftermath of a Flood*

Putting an important breaking story into perspective on a tight deadline is one of the real challenges of news reporting. It can be especially difficult to do when the story involves a devastating natural disaster. Dan Luzadder, columnist for the Fort Wayne (Ind.) *News-Sentinel*, wrote the following piece under such conditions. He used his own observations to offer some insight along with the fact and figure stories written by other staff members that appeared beside it. *(Pulitzer Prize for Local General Spot News Reporting, 1983)*

A Fitful Night for Those Whose Dreams
Lie Under the River
Dan Luzadder
Fort Wayne *News-Sentinel*
March 15, 1982

It is midnight Sunday, at the moment of this dispatch, and the streets are quiet. But in the heart of the city, hearts are breaking.

Homes sit under water. Cars have been swallowed up. Houses sit dark and empty of occupants as furniture floats on the floors.

The lapping, slowly rising waters make an insidious sound on clapboard walls. But otherwise the evacuated areas are quiet. And all is calm.

This is what the eye sees, the ear hears. Yet, as the city's sandbag heroes lie down to rest tonight, only turmoil greets those made refugees of the flood of '82.

They sleep tonight on lumpy, unfamiliar cots in rooms with linoleum floors. In the church centers, this thankful and restful sleep comes only when anxiety succumbs to fatigue. And hundreds more bed down in strange houses, waiting for word of more rain.

At this hour, it is said, 3,000 have been forced from their homes. Most are of the old working class neighborhoods, which lie along the west banks of the city's three rivers.

It is mainly here that the city swallowed water and spit up refugees. Boat people. Tired Marines, firefighters, and volunteers came after them, helping the cumbersome and reluctant into small aluminum crafts, ferrying them again and again to the high ground where other transportation waited.

Now, at midnight, the evacuated parts of the central city sit in the dark, their power cut, the gas off, all semblance of normality gone.

Those who made a stand in time—fighting with sandbags and hasty earthen dikes—have only to wait for the rivers to crest. Their homes are spared, for now, and their confidence returns. They sleep in their own beds tonight. But they wonder too, how much more water the city can take? And rain lurks in the night sky.

To the west of the rivers, the heartbreak is the hardest. The loss greatest. Where the Maumee and St. Joe only licked the levee-tops, residents climbed floodwalls hourly for inspections of the water's leading edge. They looked for signs of hope. Where the levees held, they found it. Where they did not, hope drowned like a rat.

A thousand stories are being told tonight by the refugees. Things they saw and heard.

One thinks of a house on Van Buren Street, where sunlight sparkled springlike off a bright yellow picket fence. An elderly couple waits in the front yard of their little yellow house. The gentleman sits on a yellow chair on the walk, a cane across his knee. His wife, her yellow hair now white, stands watching the curious walk by. They are a Rockwell print. A yellowed photograph, out of place.

A block away the water inches up the street toward them. The woman speaks only broken English. Her husband only nods. Worst flood. Ya. Worst flood. How high is it coming? A shrug. Will they have to leave? A faint, uneasy smile. Who knows? she says. Who knows?

Along the levee of the Maumee, where the river runs its widest and deepest, the whispering water rolls in the dark. Few people come and stand on the levee under the street light. It is unnecessary now. They feel safe.

In the pocketlike Lakeside neighborhood, nestled in the bend of two rivers, the waters did not win. Here there is elated relief. The sleepless anxiety of Saturday night is over. There are no cots, no anguish over flood-damaged lives. They escaped the flood. But it came so close.

Now, just after midnight, as the city slips into sleep, its 3,000 refugees housed and fed, there are still two worlds. The wet and the dry. The highlanders and the lowlanders. Two cities, separated by swollen rivers and closed bridges. Two kinds of luck. Good and bad.

Tomorrow, it is hoped, the cresting will come. The crest comes, the water recedes and the homeless return to the little sorrows of lost momentos. And to dig out, once more.

But that is tomorrow. Tonight there is still that uneasy sleep of the weary; unfamiliar beds, the strange emptiness of a battle—part lost and part won. Tonight, in the heart of the city, hearts are still breaking. But the wost is over. The streets are quiet. And all is calm.

Reprinted by permission of the Fort Wayne *News-Sentinel.*

Part V.

ANALYTICAL WRITING

The task of the analytical writer is to help the reader understand the full import of an event. The reader should not be left with questions in his mind after he reads such a work. It is the responsibility of the writer to anticipate the thinking of his reader and to provide adequate explanation and background.

Background and evaluation both are important to analytical writing. Background is important to analytical writing because it is used to tell what led up to the news event. Evaluation is used to describe its significance and to complete the context.

The purpose of the analytical story is to give the reader a better perspective of selected news events. Unless the writer has expert knowledge about the subject, he is not qualified to write such a story.

Analytical articles seek to analyze the news. They put into perspective the bare facts related in news stories. They do not merely supplement the facts, but instead explain and thereby give more meaning to the facts.

60. Why Germany Hated America in 1916

Herbert Bayard Swope, the first winner of the Pulitzer Prize for Reporting, was a master of gathering news, placing it in clear perspective, and presenting it in a logical and lucid form. In Germany during the first years of World War I, he prepared for Americans accounts of news events and explanations of German actions and attitudes. The following story examines the psychology of Germany's hatred for America in 1916, a time preceding U.S. entry into the war. It is a complex idea, but Swope handles it through a unified thematic story structure, a lucid analysis of the reasons for the hatred, a cohesive arrangement of points, and coherent, economical sentences. *(Pulitzer Prize for Reporting, 1917)*

German Hatred Aims To Crush Wilson's Policy
Herbert Bayard Swope
New York *World*
November 6, 1916

Throughout Germany today the hatred for America is bitter and deep. It is palpable and weighs you down. All the resentment, all the blind fury Germany once reserved for England alone have been expanded to include us and have been accentuated in the expansion. The Germans have an outlet for their feelings against England—they express themselves on the battlefields and through the Zeppelins and submarines; but against America they lack a method of registering their enmity. And so this bitterness that cannot be poured out has stuck in and saturated the whole empire.

The chagrin and humiliation of their failure to end the war before now through victory are visited upon America. The failure gave birth to hatred. Throughout the length and breadth of Germany the belief is certain and unqualified that had it not been for American moral and physical help to the allies the war would have been long since over. With magnificent disregard of the checks and reverses, both military and economic, Germany has suffered at the hands of the allies, her sons, from top to bottom, say that only America is to blame for the fact that the war is now well into its third year, and the more pertinent fact that as time goes on the German chances are bound to grow less.

It is a common thing to hear in Germany that America has a secret alliance with England, under which she is operating now; it is even more of a commonplace to be told that America is deliberately seeking to prolong the war and circumvent peace for the "blood money" she is making out of the struggle. Germany's fear of defeat and loss of prestige are laid at our door; we are made the sacrificial goat offered on the altar of self-glory.

Hate may have no boundaries, but it has beginnings, and it is not hard to classify the grounds from which the German hatred of America springs. There are five, possibly six. They are, as the Germans put them: First—The supply of munitions to the allies. Second—The illegal blockade, for which we are responsible since we have not stopped it. Third—The interference with neutral mails. Fourth—The allies' worldwide commercial blockade. Fifth—The submarine doctrine we have compelled Germany to accept. And the sixth may be one that is not so frequently expressed, but which is nevertheless a considerable factor—that America is out of the war and prospering: for what is more unusual than for envy to breed hate? Perhaps this sixth cause of German hatred might with equal truth be applied to the resentment said to exist against us in the other countries at war, for surely Germany is not the only one who resents our peace and prosperity.

To the list I have given I might add as one of the contributory causes our interpretation of neutrality, for this is made the object of bitter recrimination in Germany, and it is a subject on which even those placed in the highest positions speak with the utmost candor. Von Jagow, Chief Secretary of State for Foreign Affairs, and Zimmerman, the Chief Under Secretary, in discussing the American attitude, phrased the sentiments of their country when they said to me: "The American neutrality toward Germany is one of the head; toward the allies it is one of the heart. What America does for the allies she does voluntarily and gladly—what she does for Germany she does because she must."

This is a mild view compared to the popular idea. The resentment against America has been cumulative in its growth, while that against England is perhaps less today than it was at the beginning. Because her military activity is against the English, it has wrought at least a measure of satisfaction. But the very fact that America has been out of reach of a concrete demonstration of German hatred has made more serious the conditions existing in the empire today with reference to America, which are those of an actual menace. And the form it takes is the widespread and highly popular agitation for the resumption of the rucksichtslose (ruthless) Lusitania type of U-boat warfare.

Throughout Germany the agitation for this plan grows stronger day by day. The Chancellor is holding out against it, but how long he can restrain it no one can say. I left Germany convinced that only peace could prevent its resumption. And the same opinion is held by every German with whom I spoke, and it is held also by Ambassador Gerard. The possibility was so menacing that it formed the principal cause of the Ambassador's return at this time so that he might report it to Washington. The World set this point out in detail in a wireless dispatch I sent on Oct. 10 from the Frederick VIII, on which the Ambassador returned.

But while the plan of returning to the Lusitania type of submarine warfare is made more popular by the fact that it would be a blow at America, since America struck this weapon from German hands, it must not be thought that the advocates of the resumption view it merely as an offering to hate; they insist that it is an instrument of great military value, and they pretend to believe that its use will tend to shorten the war. However, the most ardent disciples of this plan can give no logical reasons for their belief, while those supporting the Chancellor in his opposition are able to demonstrate the soundness of their attitude. In normal circumstances this alignment of reason against unreason would be a guarantee against the success of the "rusichtslose" advocates, but when a nation has its back against the wall, fighting for existence, reason gives way to fury, and fury stops at nothing.

If it be impossible to indict a nation, it appears to be equally difficult to hate a whole nation without centering the hatred upon some one point or man. In the case of Germany, President Wilson personifies America, and so the German hatred is centered on Wilson. Further, because President Wilson in represented by Ambassador Gerard, that official is loaded down with responsibility for all the shortcomings the Germans are able to perceive in our attitude toward them. It is a difficult thing for a neutral to be neutral in Germany today. The best friends of Germany must admit that her demands on one's sentiments are rather harsh. In Berlin any one who is not outspokenly an advocate of German supremacy is gazed upon with coldness and suspicion.

Ambassador Gerard, seeking to interpret the principles of the President of the country he represents, has been neither pro-Ally nor pro-German, but merely pro-American, and for this he has been attacked, although the attacks have been cloaked under various and specious causes. I found that in Berlin the Government thought well of

Mr. Gerard, but that the people viewed him solely as the American Ambassador, and the adjective before his title was enough to damn him. To a considerable extent the censors are responsible for feeding this sentiment in the articles that they have permitted to be printed. They even resent the Ambassador's efforts to inform his own country of the depth of the German feeling against it. They say if he were "truly friendly" he would say nothing which might increase the tension, even though the Germans themselves, through some of their spokesmen, have deliberately sought to bring about a strained relation.

A striking illustration of this was afforded in the Tirpitz manifesto in which the Grand Admiral called upon all his followers to prepare for the certain struggle that was to come between Germany and the "Anglo-Amerikanthum." While this utterance was given circulation in Germany, the censors declined to permit it to be sent out of the country until America learned of it through the embassy, after which it was permitted to be put upon the cables, since a continued suppression would have made the effect even more serious than it was. Not long ago it might well have been doubted if Germany would have been willing to accept intermediation at the hands of the President. Now they would be happy to have it come from him, although they will not admit that either he or his Ambassador has been sincerely working to bring about peace among the belligerents. I can say on highest authority that Germany has been eager to have the President take some steps toward arranging, if nothing else, an armistice. But she has not yet shown a willingness to authorize such a proceeding officially. She wants the peace proposals to be brought to her; she will not go after them, not even to the extent of requesting the preliminary good offices of America. It is safe to say that no matter what indirect efforts she may employ in this connection, Washington will do nothing until a formal request has been made.

The campaign for the rucksichtslose U-boat warfare is regarded by one man in this country, who speaks with the highest German authority, as being in the nature of a threat intended to accelerate and force upon us a movement toward peace. The Ambassador himself had his attention drawn to this just before he left Berlin, but he declined to accept the interpretation.

America's failure to have effected a peace before now has been more of a crime in German eyes than her own failure to have forced one through military conquests. That is another count in the indictment lodged against Wilson. That is another reason why Wilson's defeat on Election Day would be regarded as a gigantic German triumph.

Everyone I spoke to in Germany believes this. It would be treated as a victory, not because the Germans feel there is certainty that Hughes is the man the Germans want, but because there is a certainty the Wilson is the man the Germans don't want.

While there may be behind Germany's interest, not to say active interference in our internal politics, a motive and hope of some gain in seeking the election of Hughes, there is an apparent and admitted motive of satisfying the German passion for reprisal—of punishing those standing against her. That is what Germany seeks, and the Germans admit it. On all hands I was told that Wilson must be humbled; that Wilson and his country must be taught a lesson. This was stated to me unequivocally, in so many words, by many Germans—officers, soldiers, Government officials, bankers, merchants; and by none of these classes was it stated more emphatically than by the women with whom I spoke. All believed that the defeat of Wilson will be in the nature of a rebuke and a warning to this country for the attitude it has assumed toward the empire.

One distinguished member of the Foreign Office in Wilhelmstrasse, who is himself rather favorably disposed toward America and the Administration, interpreted the feeling of his nation in these words: "If Germany was certain Hughes would be her enemy, still would she seek Wilson's destruction. 'Let us smash Wilson now,' the people say, 'and then if Hughes proves another Wilson we will smash him too in another four years.'"

But many Germans are by no means certain that Hughes will not prove their friend. When you ask them why they think so, they assume a wise look and finally say that the million and more "true sons and friends of Germany" in America are not entirely devoid of reason— they are supporting Hughes, and they must have substantial reasons for so doing. "Hughes," the explanation runs on, "has not driven these supporters from him, and therefore it is safe to believe that they are to get something in return for their support, and that something will be a greater friendliness to Germany."

What specific acts of "friendliness" Germany expects from Hughes in the event of his election they do not make plain except negatively in their declaration about Wilson's striking their "mightiest weapon" (submarines) from their hands. When they are asked how Hughes— even admitting that he wanted to be more friendly than Wilson, which they assume because of his hyphenate support—could set aside the will of the American people and reverse the restrictive submarine policy which they had approved, the answer is made that Hughes would have the people with him in anything he did, since the people had elected him for four years and given him full power to do as he pleased for that length of time. Because our anti-submarine attitude is so big a matter to them, they think it also of primary importance here, and I was told by many that it is an actual factor in our election, and that the choice of Hughes in German eyes would be regarded as an actual repudiation of Wilson's prohibition of the unrestricted use of the U-boats.

I can say positively that this belief is based upon so-called information that has been received from America, although the information is not credited by the more intelligent. It is fair to add that only a minority of those with whom I spoke in Germany actually has hope of political gain through the election of Hughes, but however he may turn out, all with whom I spoke desire his election in their greater desire to smash Wilson.

In my three months abroad, and in all my intercourse with representatives of the various strata that make up life in Germany— soldiers, sailors, laborers, politicians, clergymen, professors, newspaper men, business men, farmers—I did not hear one voice raised for Wilson except that of Maximilian Harden, the famous journalist, whose series on "If I Were Mr. Wilson" touched and pleased the President deeply but met scant favor in Germany. Not even Dr. Helfferich, Secretary of State for the Interior, and a vital factor in keeping the peace between the two countries, can see in the President's utterances any friendliness toward Germany. He, in common with the others, seeks to differentiate between the President and the American public, which it is believed wishes a greater friendliness to Germany and German methods than Wilson has shown.

There are those in Germany who doubt that this fancied sentiment would actually be reflected by Hughes were he to be elected. One prominent banker with whom I spoke said that it would be too much to expect that the son of a Welsh Baptist minister would be apt to do much for the Germans. But this half-formed fear is nothing to the resentment against Wilson, and so German encouragement to the opposition to his re-election goes on.

Reprinted by permission of Micro Photo Division, Bell & Howell Company.

61.   In Search of a Haven in a Foreign Land

Lauren Lyman's exclusive article on Charles Lindbergh's moving his family from America in 1935 is a good example of news writing by a reporter thoroughly familiar with his subject. Lyman was conversant with the material for the story, and his knowledge shows. The writing style is natural, almost casual, rather than mechanical and forced. The flow is smooth, blending background, present circumstances, and information known to the public with inside information to which Lyman was privy. The story provides a strong argument for the necessity of knowledgeable reporting for good news writing. *(Pulitzer Prize for Reporting, 1936)*

Threats Force Lindberghs from America

Lauren D. Lyman
New York *Times*
December 24, 1935

Colonel Charles A. Lindbergh has given up residence in the United States and is on his way to establish his home in England. With him are his wife and 3-year-old son, Jon.

Threats of kidnapping and even of death to the little lad, recurring repeatedly since his birth, caused the father and mother to make the decision. These threats have increased both in number and virulence recently.

Although they do not plan to give up their American citizenship, they are prepared to live abroad permanently, if that should be necessary. Where they will live in England when they get there not even their closest friends know, and it is probable that neither the Colonel nor his wife knows. They have many friends there and expect to visit at first until they can find a place that suits them.

They chose England as the place of refuge for a number of reasons, the most important being their belief that the English have greater regard for law and order in their own land than the people of any other nation in the world.

The Colonel has twice visited England, the first time just after his historic flight to Paris in 1927, and the second time in 1933 when with Mrs. Lindbergh he flew to England from the United States by way of Greenland and Iceland. The consideration with which they were treated by everyone then, even during the excitement that immediately followed their arrival, impressed them, and they hope that there they can find the tranquillity and security which have been denied them in their own land.

They want especially to provide for Jon a normal childhood, free from fears and with opportunities to grow and develop naturally. So far that has been denied him here.

They wish also to do some things themselves. Mrs. Lindbergh has her own studies and writing, which she enjoys. The Colonel would like time to do research and reading himself.

So far as could be learned yesterday Colonel Lindbergh does not expect to sever connections completely with either Pan American Airways or Transcontinental and Western Air. He is a technical adviser to both companies.

A year ago at his own request his salary from Transcontinental and Western Air was stopped. With the development of new planes for them he felt that there was no pressing need for his active service. Now with the clipper ships of Pan American spanning the Pacific on regular schedule and with the same great flying boats built under his eye ready to start test work on the Atlantic it is understood that he feels free to terminate his active work with this company also.

While it was only with the greatest reluctance that Colonel and Mrs. Lindbergh reached the decision to leave their home, their friends and their manifold interests here, once they had made it they acted quickly.

A week ago the Colonel obtained his passports secretly in Washington. With the cooperation of government officials as well as the representatives of Great Britain at the port from which they sailed their plans were kept secret until after their departure. The name of the steamship on which they sailed and its sailing day, together with the fact that the Lindbergh family had booked passage, was kept a secret through the cooperation of the steamship company. Even the police of the port were not informed.

When the time came for them to go they slipped quietly away from Englewood, journeyed to their port of departure and, unaccompanied by servants, went aboard. There were no goodbyes save to the immediate family. They will spend Christmas at sea and may even see the passing of the old year at sea.

The three Lindberghs are the only passengers on the ship. This arrangement was made possible, it was understood, because at this season of the year the passenger traffic on the North Atlantic is not particularly heavy.

While it may be a lonely Christmas and New Year for them, it will be free from fear such as the family has never been without since Jon was born in August 1932.

Even before that there were threats. It was recalled last night that shortly after his famous solo flight to Paris Colonel Lindbergh was threatened. The threats came for the most part from cranks, sometimes from persons definitely insane, but now and then from men who were clearly after money and nothing else.

At the insistence of friends, who thought that the famous flier should have a bodyguard—which he refused to have—the Colonel started carrying a pistol. Then after the furor over his great achievement faded somewhat the threats became less until they almost ceased.

Two years after his flight came the announcement of his engagement to Anne Spencer Morrow, the daughter of Dwight W. Morrow, then American Ambassador to Mexico. They were married on May 27, 1929, and along with congratulations from all over the world there came a resurgence of the threateners, some insane, some merely cranks and some whom the post office authorities regarded as potentially dangerous.

Here and there arrests were made, but they were accomplished unobtrusively for the most part; and when, as was often the case, writers were found to have mental twists they were turned over to institutions for treatment. These conditions were not new either to the police of the larger cities and the States, or to the government agents.

In greater or lesser volume these letters are sent to all prominent people, and knowing this the Lindberghs did not regard them as particularly important even when they poured in by the hundreds. For the most part they were stopped by the post offices and sent to Colonel Lindbergh's office in New York where they were sorted and turned over to the proper authorities for investigation.

This was the condition of affairs in the winter of 1932. Charles A. Lindbergh Jr. was approaching his second birthday. His father, flying back and forth across the country, had picked himself a forested region near Hopewell, N.J., for a home and encircling it on his flying map with his pencil had said to his friend and lawyer, Colonel Henry Breckinridge, "Please buy me that."

It was done. The land was assembled from two counties. The home was built, and little by little the family was moving into it. Here the boy would grow up in his own woods and fields without the artificial existence usually forced on a child of famous parents in the more complicated existence of towns and cities. So they dreamed and planned.

Save for the fact that the home was built and save for mention from time to time of a flying trip, the Lindberghs were obtaining the retirement from the public eye that they sought, and with this came a further drop in threatening letters, almost a cessation.

Then came the kidnapping, and all that has followed it. At once as the news was broadcast the letters climbed from tens to hundreds and then thousands. Some were merely notes of condolence. Some were well meant proffers of aid. But hundreds were from persons obviously unbalanced, and among these came the threats.

As the weeks and months passed, the tide of letters receded somewhat to rise again when in August 1932 Jon was born.

They contained a new note, a sinister note, specific threats against the new baby. There were not many at first, but there were enough to cause concern, and among them were the letters from criminals, bent on extortion. Many of these latter have been run down, and at least a dozen arrests have been made.

Once more the tide dropped until the arrest of Hauptmann. It did not rise then to any formidable extent, but since his conviction and as the date of execution approached the threats began to grow in number; not many as compared to the days just after the kidnapping, but enough to cause real concern.

It had been suggested after the kidnapping that the Lindberghs might leave the country, but from sources close to the family it was learned that they had entertained no such suggestion in their own minds. They planned to stay right in this country where the Colonel found the work he enjoyed the most—the technical side of air transport.

It had been noted that the letters from the unbalanced as well as the criminal type jumped in number with the publication of sensational stories, and so it was expected by the authorities that this would be the case when Bruno Richard Hauptmann went to trial.

The Lindberghs were pleasantly surprised when the number failed to increase as they had anticipated. There were some but not enough to cause great concern. Then the conviction of Hauptmann and his sentence to death and the publication of sensational stories brought an increase with more and more definite threats against Jon.

The looked-for recession in the wave of threats finally came although the letters did not stop, and the fear they provoked was always present.

Through all this time the State, Federal and local authorities gave the family every possible protection, acted with promptness when any especially sinister document appeared and watched over the Lindbergh family with unceasing vigilance.

Jon was entered in a nursery school and was driven there daily. But the tension that surrounded the child was bound to go with him to school and to create a fear there. It was as though the Lindbergh family were living alone on a frontier, their home surrounded by savages. In a sense it was worse, for the frontiersman could recognize the savages, but this borderland family had no such protection.

Still they saw nothing to do but to go on. They were flying in a fog, with hidden dangers all about them, but they had to keep on flying.

Then two things happened.

When the Supreme Court refused to entertain the Hauptmann appeal and it seemed that the Bronx carpenter, sentenced to die for the murder of Charles A Lindbergh Jr., was a step nearer the carrying out of the sentence imposed, the case according to many observers was suddenly made a matter of political importance.

Doubts credited to Governor Harold G. Hoffman were cast on the verdict. The Governor promptly denied he had voiced such doubts, but at the same time stated what he termed the "doubts of others" in extended interviews.

At once threats against the Lindbergh family began to show up, threats from the unbalanced and also from the merely criminal.

The rising tide came at the same time as an unfortunate and disturbing incident.

Not long ago, as Jon was being taken by automobile from his school to his home, a large car containing several men came close alongside and crowded the car containing the lad to the curb, forcing it to stop.

Men jumped down. A teacher accompanying the little lad clutched him tightly. Suddenly cameras were thrust into the child's face and clicked. Then the visitors jumped into their machine and sped away, leaving a badly frightened teacher and little boy.

Since then Jon has not been to school.

Since then the Hauptmann case, with the execution date less than a month away, has received more than a little attention, especially when it became known that the Governor had been a secret visitor to the condemned man's death-house cell.

The letters are coming once more, the demands for money, the threats of kidnapping and murder, and so the man who eight years ago hailed as an international hero and a good-will ambassador between the peoples of the world is taking his wife and son to establish, if he can, a secure haven for them in a foreign land.

62. Germany's First Blitzkrieg and the Collapse of Poland

The following story by Otto Tolischus on Germany's lightning defeat of Poland at the beginning of World War II provides a good example of what a reporter's thorough understanding of a subject can do for a story. Even though a number of characteristics of effective writing style are evident, the quality of the story is made possible primarily by Tolischus' knowledge of military strategy and history. The writing is clear, the choice of detail revealing, and the phrasing appealing, but the ease and naturalness with which Tolischus tells the story is a result of his familiarity and comfortableness with the material. Thus, he is able to carry the reader smoothly through an absorbing account of an event covering a huge geographical area and vast amounts of episodes and occurrences. *(Pulitzer Prize for Correspondence, 1940)*

German Army Crushes Poland
Otto Tolischus
New York *Times*
September 11, 1939

WITH THE GERMAN ARMIES IN POLAND—Having hurled against Poland their mighty military machine, the Germans are today crushing Poland like a soft-boiled egg.

After having broken through the shell of Polish border defenses, the Germans found inside, in comparison with their forces, little more than a soft yolk, and they have penetrated that in many directions without really determined general resistance by the Polish Army.

That is the explanation of the apparent Polish military collapse in so short a time as it was gathered on a tour of the Polish battlefields made by this correspondent in the wake of the German army, and, sometimes, in the backwash of a day's battle while scattered Polish troops and snipers were still taking potshots at motor vehicles on the theory that they must be German. But even these border defenses seem weak, and beyond them there is nothing.

It is a mystery to both Germans and neutral military experts on the tour with the writer that the Poles made no provisions for second or third lines and that in retreat they did not make any attempt to throw up earthworks or dig trenches such as helped the Germans stop the Allies after the Marne retreat in 1914.

In fact, the only tactics the Poles seemed to have pursued in the retreat were to fall back on towns from which, later, they were easily driven out by artillery fire or just as easily flanked. But presumably neither their number nor their equipment, which, judging from the remnants thrown along the road of retreat, was pitifully light as compared with the Germans', permitted them to do anything else in view of the enormous length of the border they had to defend.

Again God has been with the bigger battalions, for the beautiful, dry weather, while converting Polish roads into choking dust clouds on the passage of motor vehicles, has kept them from turning into mud as would be normal at this time of year; this has permitted the German motorized divisions to display the speed they have.

But the Germans have proceeded not only with might and speed, but with method, and this bids fair to be the first war to be decided not by infantry, "the queen of all arms," but by fast motorized divisions and, especially, by the air force.

The first effort of the Germans was concentrated on defeating the hostile air fleet, which they did not so much by air battle but by consistent bombing of airfields and destruction of the enemy's ground organization. Having accomplished this, they had obtained domination of the air, which in turn enabled them, first, to move their own vast transports ahead without danger from the air and, second, to bomb the Poles' communications to smithereens, thereby reducing their mobility to a minimum.

Today the German rule of the air is so complete that, although individual Polish planes may still be seen flying at a high altitude, the German army has actually abandoned the blackout in Poland. It is a strange sensation to come from a Germany thrown into Stygian darkness at night to a battlefront town like Lodz, as this correspondent did the night after the Germans announced its occupation, and find it illuminated although the enemy is only a few miles from the city.

With control of the air, the Germans moved forward not infantry but their tanks, armored cars and motorized artillery, which smashed any Polish resistance in the back. This is easy to understand when one has seen the methods of open warfare attempted by the Poles and an almost amateurish attempt at digging earthworks for machine-gun nests.

To German and neutral experts the Poles seem to have clung to eighteenth-century war methods, which, in view of modern firing volume and weight, are not only odd but also futile. This does not mean that the Poles have not put up a brave fight. They have, and the Germans themselves freely admit it.

As a purely military matter, the German army is the height of efficiency. It moves like clockwork, without hurry and apparently almost in a leisurely manner. Yet the army moves with inexorable exactitude. The roads into Poland are jammed but not choked with heavy vans and motor trucks carrying food and munitions, while the Poles have to depend mainly on their smashed railroads or on horse carts. Bombed bridges are soon passable for the Germans and they move forward quickly. Communications lines follow them almost automatically.

Poland may not be lost yet and may be even able to offer further resistance by withdrawing into the eastern swamp. But as long as the present disparity between the military resources and her will to fight exists she faces terrible odds.

63. *Life Behind the Iron Curtain*

The following story by Paul Ward is a distinguished example of reporting of international affairs. It was made possible by Ward's decade of specializing in international reporting and lengthy research on the Soviet Union. Clear and well-written, the story, as well as the nineteen-article series of which this one was a part, constitutes one of the best and most revealing pieces of reporting ever done on the human aspects of life in Russian. The series attracted so much attention the articles were collected after publication in the Baltimore *Sun* and published as a pamphlet. *(Pulitzer Prize for International Reporting, 1948)*

Many Risk Russian Secret Police Ire By Trying To Migrate to U.S.
Paul W. Ward
Baltimore *Sun*
April 30, 1947

The little anteroom of the American consulate in Moscow is crowded these days with men and women seeking permission to enter the United States. The scene and its dramatis personae provide as good an introduction to Soviet life as any inquiring American who gets behind the "iron curtain" is likely to find.

These men and women, who want to escape from the communist utopia to the land of the "capitalist exploitation" look like Russians but say they are not. They say they are Americans, that they were either born in the United States to Russian parents or emigrated to the United States from Russia and acquired American citizenship by naturalization.

Returned in '20s and '30s

Some of them returned to Russia in the early 1920s when revolutionary favors, combined with Communist propaganda and their own vestigial heart ties to the fatherland, made the U.S.S.R seem — at trans-Atlantic distance—truly the "promised land." Others were not drawn by that mirage until the depression of the early 1930s smashed their confidence in "the American way of life."

But whenever and however they came to the Soviet Union, they came with hopes high. Now those hopes are dead. So deep is their disillusionment that they are ready to risk the quite probable displeasure of the Kremlin's secret police by attempting to re-establish their American citizenship and shake the dust and snows of the

U.S.S.R. from their feet.

Few will succeed, for most of them surrendered their passports to the Soviet authorities when they crossed the Russian frontier years ago. The majority have slight chance of establishing their American citizenship in the fashion required to receive assistance from Washington in getting back to the United States.

Dual role not recognized

Even the few that can prove American citizenship have no easy road ahead, for the Soviet Government does not recognize dual citizenship and will not release them without a struggle. Their willingness to undertake all the risks, travail and uncertainties involved in the business of getting to America is as eloquent of the misery of life in the Soviet Union as their garb.

Most of them wear the tatter-demalion garments that are the standard costume of all save the privileged classes in what its rulers like to call "this classless state."

The women have shawls over their heads and are swathed in gray quilted cotton coats like Chinese coolies. They clomp in and out on stockingless feet, wrapped in rags and covered with *valinki*, the felt boots that are supposed to be peasant footwear but have to be favored by city folk, too, since the more urban shoes are hard to acquire.

Boots ruled "uncultured"

In a snobbish mood, the Soviet Government declared such boots "uncultured" when British, French and American delegations were about to descend on Moscow for the Big Four conference that has just ended. Wearers of *valinki* were forbidden to enter any of the hotels where the visiting foreigners were likely to see them.

In similar mood Soviet authorities also forbade display or sale to foreigners of puppet dolls whose heads—far more cleverly modeled than those of the stereotyped dolls that remained on sale—represented the Russian peasant as pleasantly stupid.

The men seeking refuge in the United States are less likely than their wives to be wearing felt boots. Most of them are clad in the remnants of Red Army uniforms, including leather boots, that serve a majority of males as civilian garb in this country where a sleazy suit of hand-me-downs costs more than a month's wages.

Men and women both are saved from the distinction of looking like beggars only by the fact that their costumes are indistinguishable from those of the great majority of Russians who cannot even hope to escape to the United States. It is not only in their garb, however, that the would-be escapists are typical.

They are representative of Soviet life in other ways. For one thing, they are not all Muscovites or even residents of the R.S.F.S.R., by far the biggest of the sixteen Soviet republics, stretching from the Baltic to the Pacific and covering three fourths of the Soviet Union.

They drift in from all parts of the U.S.S.R. — from the Ukraine, White Russia, Lithuania, Latvia, Estonia, Turkmenia, Uzbekistan, Tajikistan and Kirghizia — bringing with them their tales of misery.

British recognize value

That they are a source of valuable information on conditions in parts of the Soviet Union inaccessible to foreigners is recognized by Britain's Foreign Office, if not by America's State Department.

The British Embassy, which is similarly besieged by would-be fugitives claiming British citizenship, keeps a former chief of military intelligence in charge of its consulate and ready to quiz the applicants. The State Department, on the other hand, continues to treat the business of receiving applications for visas and passports as merely a clerical affair of rubber stamps and legalisms.

Some of the many reasons underlying the desire of these people to escape from the Soviet Union will be dealt with in greater detail in subsequent articles. It will suffice here to give two exemplary reasons, aside from the fact that, like all other residents of the U.S.S.R., except its privileged clique, they are hungry, ill clad and housed in a fashion so miserable as almost to defy description.

Most of applicants farmers

Most of the applicants are farmers. They had found life in the United States too hard for them. But in Russia they have found it harder. They have been living on collective farms, raising their families in sod houses, log cabins or similar shacks with mud floors and equivalent sanitary facilities.

They have been laboring from dawn to sunset an average of 250 days a year and getting for their labors, in the typical case, a daily wage comprising:

4 ½ pounds of grain.

9 pounds of potatoes.

6 ½ pounds of other vegetables.

2 pounds of hay.

1 to 4 cents in cash.

The industrial workers among them have fared no better.

Unions enforce "speed-up"

They have found themselves working under a system that employs all the devices which Communists, liberals and "progressives" in this country revile as "anti-labor." They have been compelled to join what are, in effect, "company unions" whose primary function is to enforce a "speed-up" system, raising production quotas and cutting production costs.

They have had to live in what are, in effect, "company houses" and trade at "company stores" for wages barely sufficient to pay their rent and buy the rationed foodstuffs and other essentials their families require.

They have to buy these things at prices inflated by heavy sales taxes which—despite the Left's traditional opposition to such levies as an unfair burden on the poor—the Soviet Government prefers to income taxes.

Tied to their jobs

They have been tied to their jobs by a "labor book" system such as the Nazis instituted in Germany. They have also been tied to them by a housing system under which if a worker quits or loses his job, he simultaneously loses the only room he and his family have found to shelter themselves from the snow and rain.

Their freedom has been further limited by a legal system and a set of "labor discipline" laws which make a worker who takes a day off to go fishing—or simply is a few minutes late to work—subject to criminal prosecution and imprisonment.

It is perhaps readily understandable why farmers or industrial workers who have memories of America are eager to desert the Soviet Union. Even those whose memories of America are mainly memories of the depression years when they were on relief.

For an unemployed man on relief under the WPA in America was so much better off than a fully employed Soviet worker is today that Russians, when the American system is explained, confess bafflement, saying: "But why should they (the relief recipients) want ever to return to work?"

What is puzzling to an American, on the other hand, is the attitude of Russians who have never had a taste of "the American way of life," who have been born since the 1917 revolution and subjected to nothing but Soviet propaganda pictures of the United States as a land of enslaved and impoverished masses.

"Such a wonderful life"

Why do they also want to go to the United States? It is unmistakable that many of them do.

It is a common experience of Americans in Moscow to be told by Russians: "You have such a wonderful life."

It is not said out of politeness; there is too much risk involved in such an utterance to make it merely a pleasantry.

Even zealous Communists betray themselves in this respect when trying to explain, for example, why the Kremlin refuses exit permits to young Russian girls who married American or British soldiers during the war.

"Most of them married only to get out of the Soviet Union," they say.

Reprinted by permission of the Baltimore *Sun.*

64. *Security, Loyalty, and Guilt by Suspicion*

Bert Andrews, Washington bureau chief for the New York *Herald Tribune* in the 1940s, had a chance to observe closely the effects government security measures were having on State Department employees. In a series of eight stories in November 1947, he outlined the issues. The last article in the series, published a little more than two weeks after the first story, detailed the changes in State Department policy enacted because of Andrews' exposes. The following story is notable primarily for its clear explanation of the various sides of the security issue. Andrews' reporting skills are combined with a clear, concise writing style that helps put the story into an understandable perspective. *(Pulitzer Prize for National Reporting, 1948)*

Federal Loyalty Check Is No. 1 Topic in Capital
Bert Andrews
New York *Herald Tribune*
November 8, 1947

In this city of Washington, where 195,000 of the 2,000,000 civilian employees of the executive branch of the Federal government work and play and talk—talk, that is, when they're not too frightened to open their mouths—the burning topic of conversation this week has been the whole problem of security and loyalty.

Always the conversation gets around to one basic question. It can be put this way:

"Is there anything to be alarmed about, as far as the 195,000 employees here and the 2,000,000 altogether and the whole population of the nation are concerned, in the fact that certain State Department employees have been dismissed without ever having been informed of the charges against them?"

There are four schools of thought.

One school, exemplified by some of the top men in the State Department, insists there is no danger that such summary procedure will ever affect the completely innocent.

A second, exemplified by many of the lesser people in the department, is that a witch hunt is on and that it behooves them to keep quiet lest State Department investigators' ears be listening. (One man who left government service after years of work in two departments told this reporter: "I have talked to at least twenty State Department people in the past few days. They are bitter, upset and scared." This reporter and others in the Washington bureau of the New York Herald Tribune have talked to many more people in the department. All agree with the words "bitter, upset and scared.")

A third is the "so what?" school—a very small one—which argues that it doesn't make much difference to the mass if a few innocent individuals get hurt and that suspicion is as good grounds for dismissal as is proof.

The fourth school is perhaps best represented by editorial writers in three Washington newspapers who are demanding, with increasing firmness, that suspicion is not enough and, in the demanding, are strongly criticizing either President Truman or Secretary of State George C. Marshall or both.

Representative opinions from all four schools will be presented here in the form of excerpts from statements, letters or editorials.

A large part of the comment resulted from the publication in last Sunday's New York *Herald Tribune* of the case history of the investigation and dismissal of a state department employee who can be described merely as Mr. Blank.

A large part of the comment will be news to President Truman and Secretary Marshall.

Here are samples of the thinking of the schools represented:

School No. 1 (The "no danger" school)—Secretary Marshall represented this. He acknowledged that eleven employees dismissed had no "true hearing." He said they could not be given the charges because the charges were based on "highly classified material" not under the department's control. He left it doubtful that they could even learn the charges, even on appeal to the new loyalty review boards or the Civil Service Commission.

School No. 2 (The "we're scared" school)—Two letters typical of many received as a result of the Mr. Blank article show some of the mental turmoil.

First letter: "There's a lot more hidden, judging by what I observed in the last year—my last with the government. I saw but few of the 'loyalty investigation' files, but I saw the effects. In agencies covering the country, the subordinate officials who always did the best jobs were the ones terrorized. Terrorized by sudden questioning, to them inexplicable, by two suddenly appearing agents demanding to know: 'Who was with you at that meeting at —Street on the afternoon of Aug. 19, 1942? We know you were there. We took your car number.' The victim later drove to that address, which he had never heard of before, and tried to ascertain who lived there. Later I read the long dossier. Since the agency cleared the man, the only inference is that a lot of fabrication went into that case. There has been so much of it that I began to wonder what newspapermen might begin to lift the lid. As you know, fifty years ago France was torn by a social conflict between the powers of government, including generals, and the rights of the governed. The implement then was hysterical anti-Semitism, just as it is now hysterical anti-Communism, and, as now, heightened by the fears of 'military machinations of a foreign power.'"

Letter No. 2: "I have read with growing horror of the situation. Nevertheless, when I sat down to write to Secretary Marshall, urging him to remedy the situation that obtains in Washington, I realized that because of my wife and children I dared not write to him. Although I am not a Communist, I could be smeared as was Mr. Blank. Has it occurred to you that what is happening in such cases is the result of the military's infiltration of our government?"

School No. 3 (The "So what?" school)—There is one letter from one advocate of this way of thinking. An excerpt: "Regardless of the exact state of Mr. Blank's innocence, the line has to be drawn somewhere, and I think the American people, especially those who lost husbands or sons in this last war, are wholeheartedly in favor of drawing it in favor of our country....We are not too worried about the Mr. Blanks. Let them get jobs where they can exercise their civil liberties all they want but in ways that won't endanger our liberties."

As for school No. 4, it was noteworthy because of the sharp language used by the Washington *Post*, the *Evening Star* and the Washington *Daily News*.

A news story in the *Post* said bluntly: "Secretary Marshall put on his five-star military manner yesterday at his first press conference since Sept. 10...The Secretary gave brusque and uninformative answers." An editorial in the same paper said: "He added to the general perturbation about the new discipline he has imposed on the State Department in the name of security....The reason for his taciturnity lies, we suppose, in his military training. Working always in private, inured to silence about the big problems he has been given to solve, he has brought the habit to the State Department and gives the impression that the prying press is simply an intrusion on his time. This is not a statesmanlike attitude....On June 5 he said that 'an essential part of any successful action on the part of the United States is an understanding on the part of the people of America of the character of the problem and the remedies to be applied.' The Secretary has fallen down on this requirement. We are left to wonder for what purpose he called yesterday's conference."

An editorial in the *Star* slapped at President Truman for criticizing the press for what he described as setting up a straw man and then knocking it down. He was referring to press attacks on "censorship" regulations set up by the Veterans' Administration and later revoked under press criticism. Said the *Star*: "If that proviso designed to protect administrative officials against 'embarrassment' was a straw man, it was conjured up not by the newspapers but by the President's own Security Advisory Board....As the American Society of Newspaper Editors recently pointed out, this ill-advised 'gag rule' is censorship in its worst form."

And the *Daily News*, criticizing generally the security situation, said:

"We believe there is urgent need for some agency that can serve as a safeguard against miscarriages of justice. It should have authority to find out whether investigations that result in decisions to discharge employees have been made fairly, and whether genuine efforts have been made to get at the facts. The American people want the disloyal ejected from Federal jobs. But they also want the utmost possible assurance of protection for the loyal."

© I.H.T. Corporation. Reprinted by permission.

65. An Ill-Conceived Plot To Take over Russia

The following story by Harrison Salisbury on events in Moscow immediately following the death of Josef Stalin provides a good example of how a reporter skillfully can weave a narrative constructed from information gathered from many sources. By carefully selecting and arranging the material, and through the use of concrete details, Salisbury leads the reader through a story which, even though lengthy, maintains interest throughout. The Pulitzer Prize commendation to Salisbury read: "The perceptive and well-written...articles made a valuable contribution to American understanding of what is going on inside Russia. This was principally due to the writer's wide range of subject matter and depth of background." *(Pulitzer Prize for International Reporting, 1955)*

Beria's Troops Held Moscow, But He Hesitated and Lost

Harrison E. Salisbury
New York *Times*
September 21, 1954

For about seventy-eight hours, in March of last year, Lavrenti Pavlovich Beria held Russia in the hollow of his pudgy hand. He was supreme. There was no one who could challenge him—not Malenkov, not Khurshchev, not Molotov, not the Army.

At any moment within those fateful hours, Beria might have

proclaimed himself dictator, all-supreme ruler of Russia, heir of Stalin.

He did not do so, and in that failure to act he sealed his own fate. The life that came to an end last Christmas Eve, probably in the blood-stained cellars of the Lubyanka Prison, was doomed from that moment when Beria did not act.

The story of the March days of 1953, just before and just after the death of Stalin, has never been publicly told. Much of it was concealed and suppressed by the Moscow censorship. Many details are not yet and possibly never will be known outside the tight little circle of men in the Kremlin who were the chief actors in one of the great dramas of modern times.

Enough is known, however, so that the factors that led to Beria's removal and execution can be traced with almost crystal clarity, in an otherwise Florentine labyrinth of intrigue and counter-intrigue, plot and counter-plot.

These factors were so obvious at the time that this correspondent could confidently note in his private correspondence that a showdown over Beria's power was inevitable.

To see why this was so it is necessary to turn back to the story of the events of Stalin's death in March, 1953—the real story, not the emasculated one that was all that fearful censors permitted correspondents to cable at that time.

The first announcement of Stalin's fatal illness was made in Moscow about 8 a.m. on March 4, 1953. It said the Generalissimo had suffered a massive cerebral hemorrhage early Monday morning, March 2, two days previously. It was apparent to everyone in Moscow that the question was how long the end would be in coming. It did not seem likely to be long.

This anticipation proved correct. At 4 a.m. on March 6, the Moscow radio, in its shortwave broadcasts overseas and to provincial newspapers within Russia, announced that Stalin had died at 9:50 the previous evening.

This correspondent was at the Central Telegraph Office in Moscow at the time the flash on Stalin's death came through. The office is in Gorky Street, just two blocks from the Kremlin. At frequent intervals that night I circled the Kremlin by car and toured central Moscow. All was quiet in the city. There were lights burning late in the Kremlin, but that was not unusual.

About 1 a.m. a number of Kremlin limousines pulled into the Kremlin garages, as if returning from taking home the participants in some midnight conference. About 3 a.m. three big limousines parked in front of the Moscow City Soviet building. This was the first indication of anything unusual. A few minutes later a woman at the Izvestia distribution desk said the papers would be "very, very" late.

Link to world severed

These details are cited to show how quiet was the center of Moscow on the night of Stalin's death. Nor was there much drama in the way the news reached the Moscow correspondents. My chauffeur, sitting at the car radio tuned to the Tass dictation-speed broadcast, heard the announcement at 4 a.m. He shambled in and whispered in my ear. I filed a bulletin I had already prepared, and within a few minutes the other correspondents had filed theirs.

But there the matter ended. An iron censorship clamped down. The cables about Stalin were not passed. Neither was a message about office accounts that this correspondent tried to file.

Not only were no messages passed, but a telegraph clerk flipped all the jack cords out of the switchboard through which international calls are placed. While the switchboard lighted up and correspondents frantically shouted to be connected with London and Paris and Stockholm, the operator sat quietly with folded hands. The censors ordered her not even to touch the board. A few minutes later a sleepy mechanic hurried in, ripped open the back of the switchboard and yanked the main cable.

It was three and a half hours before communications were resumed from Moscow. The world got its first news of Stalin's death, not from Moscow correspondents but from London pickups of the Soviet radio.

However, thanks to the hiatus imposed by the censors, this correspondent is in possession of an almost complete picture of what occurred in Moscow in the hours immediately after the official announcement of Stalin's death. And that account is the key to the Beria story.

Seeing that no copy was likely to be passed for hours, I got into my car and made several tours of the city. As late as 5 a.m. the center was absolutely quiet. Outside of the City Soviet, where obviously some arrangements connected with the death were going forward, there was no sign of unusual activity. No more militia (as the Russians call their police) were on duty. Only a few lights dimly burned in the Kremlin. Nothing extraordinary.

Beria's forces appear

But shortly before 6, a difference became apparent. Whereas before that hour traffic was sparse, possibly even sparser than is customary in those predawn hours, smooth-running, quiet convoys of trucks began converging on the center of the city. They rolled quietly down Gorky Street. They slipped noiselessly down Lubyanka Hill. More appeared from beyond the Moscow River and slowly crossed through the Red Square.

In each of these trucks, sitting silently, arms folded, on wooden cross-benches, was a detachment of twenty-two soldiers of the special battalions of the M.V.D., or to translate its initials, the Ministry of Internal Affairs, Beria's ministry.

For the first hour or so the disposition of these troops was not apparent. The truck convoys crossed and recrossed the center of the city without obvious pattern. Slowly little knots of trucks congregated at various intersections and began to accumulate in the enormous open squares that are so numerous in the heart of Moscow.

Around 7:30 a.m. the censorship on Stalin's death was lifted, and it was about 9 o'clock before I again emerged from the telegraph office. Vast changes met my eyes. By that time there were thousands of troops in the central part of the city and great lines of trucks. Columns of tanks had also made their appearance on upper Gorky Street. All the trucks, all the tanks, all the troops bore the familiar red-and-blue insignia of the Ministry of Internal Affairs. They were Beria's forces.

I went over into Red Square. The way was still open, and a curious spectacle was revealed. A thousand or two thousand persons were standing in a cigar-shaped crowd toward the main Spassky Gate of the Kremlin. The crowd was quiet and well-mannered and had not yet been interfered with by the police. Obviously these people expected (correctly, as it turned out) that Stalin's body would be brought out through this gate.

It was extraordinary to see a crowd freely collected right in the middle of Red Square. I had never seen such a thing before. While I watched, however, freedom of movement into and within Red Square gradually was brought to an end by a giant pincers operation of the M.V.D.

First, light lines were thrown across the streets giving access to the Square. Persons were allowed out, but not in. Then, rapidly growing bodies of troops were introduced into the lower end of Red Square and began to press the crowds back away from the Spassky Gate toward the State Historical Museum end.

Drifting back with the crowds, I saw that the troops intended to clear not only Red Square but Manezhny Square and Theatre Square, the big adjacent open spaces, as well. During the next hour, this great pincers operation continued and the movement of both pedestrians and traffic in the heart of the city was brought to a total halt.

Moscow is constructed like a series of expanding rings. The Kremlin is the innermost ring. About a mile out is the second ring, a tree-lined boulevard constructed on the site of an old city wall. Perhaps half a mile farther out is a second broad asphalted boulevard, the Sadovaya Circle, built on the base of another old wall. Avenues radiate through these circles, like the spokes of a wheel, giving access to the heart of the city.

Iron band on city's heart

The military movement that had occurred clamped an iron band on each of these circles and spokes. Not only were thousands of troops deployed across all these streets and along their sides to form cordons, but tens of thousands of trucks were brought into Moscow and formed bumper-to-axle and tailboard to radiator, into impenetrable barricades. At all key points the truck and troop barricades were reinforced by phalanxes of tanks drawn up three deep.

There was an iron collar around Moscow's heart; and from about 10 or 11 a.m. of March 6, 1953, until 4 p.m. on March 9 it was not removed.

During those hours not one person entered or left the center of Moscow without leave of the M.V.D. command, Beria's command.

There was literally no traffic movement in the center of the city. The New York Times offices were right in the heart of this dead area, in the Hotel Metropole. Since The Times car was operating on the morning of March 6, it was within this area; and, by one of those strange quirks of fate, it continued to operate within the closed ring during all those hours, molested and threatened repeatedly by the M.V.D., but somehow continuing to pass through the seven police lines that barred the way from the Metropole through Theatre and Manezhny Squares and the back door of Gertzen Street to the telegraph office.

This fantastic military operation had steel tentacles that rammed their way back through the city to its outskirts. Nor was this the limit of the M.V.D.'s grip on Moscow.

On Sunday, March 8, this correspondent decided to investigate rumors that thousands of persons were arriving in Moscow from all over the country to view Stalin's body, which was then lying in state. There were reports that the trains were so crowded that persons had ridden the roofs of trains all the way from Leningrad in sub-freezing weather.

There was no way of getting to the railroad stations, all of which lie at or beyond the second circle, except by walking through the count-less military barricades. The metro (subway) system was working, but not to the sealed-off center of the city.

Not long after dawn, I left the Metropole Hotel and made my way past sleepy sentry lines, past curbside campfires where some troops were whiling away the hours, playing accordians and stamping out tunes with their soft leather boots, to the Kursk railroad station. There the true state of affairs was considerably different from the rumor. Notices, hand-written, were posted at the ticket offices. All trains out of Moscow were running, but no trains into Moscow within the suburban radius or other near-by points.

Moscow was a city truly sealed off—not only on the inside, but from without as well.

Later that day, by dint of simply walking past the sentry posts with an absolute air, I strolled right into Red Square. It was a strange feeling. The huge square was deserted. Troops were on guard at all the entrances to keep everyone out. But in the center, at the famous Mausoleum, there were power cables running out from inside the Kremlin, and power chisels and hammers were busy. Fifteen or twenty workmen were busy chiseling the name of Stalin into the stone beds beside that of Lenin and making arrangements in the tomb's inner chamber.

A colonel of the M.V.D. was supervising the work, Beria's colonel. I strolled over and watched idly. No one paid any attention. It probably seemed to them that I had a right to be there, otherwise the sentries would not have admitted me.

It was deathly quiet in Red Square except for the intermittent sound of hammers and chisels. The quiet must have been noticeable to the men inside the Kremlin walls. It was then that the thought struck home so sharply.

Proof of Beria's power

What troops were these that held the city? M.V.D. troops. Were there any other troops in the city? No. Could any other troops enter the city? No. The closest military camps were all M.V.D. camps. Other troops could enter only with M.V.D. permission or by fighting their way street by street through the barricades. What of the Air Force? Perfectly useless. Even if it bombed the whole city to rubble, it could not break the grip of the M.V.D. upon every strategic position in Moscow.

And what of the Kremlin? The men who were there were there because the M.V.D. permitted them to pass through the lines. Or, if they wished to leave the Kremlin, they could leave only by M.V.D. permission.

It was not likely that the men in the Kremlin had failed to note that they were, in effect, the prisoners of the M.V.D. They were men trained to think in military terms and, particularly, in terms of civil war and street fighting. To the military leaders the realization of their position must have been even more forcible.

Because the M.V.D. was not just a group of initials. It was not just a department of the Government. It was an individual. A powerful, ruthless man of extraordinary ability named Lavrenti Pavlovich Beria. And it was Beria's troops and Beria's tanks and Beria's trucks that had accomplished this small miracle and taken over the city of Moscow while the radios were still blaring out the news of Stalin's death to the startled citizenry.

Using the basic movement plans that twice a year for many years had been employed on May Day and on Nov. 7 to control traffic movement in the center of the city, and simply extending the plan back to control the whole city and its environs, Beria had with the smoothness of clockwork put Moscow into his grasp.

It was too smooth and too complete and too good.

Strong hand overplayed

No military man could see that exhibition and feel a moment's safety—unless he trusted Beria completely or unless Beria was the top boss. It was too plain and too obvious that Beria had a machine that, before dawn any morning, could take over the Kremlin, take over Moscow and, having done this, have a crack at making Beria master of all Russia.

There is not much doubt that Beria himself was fully aware of his power at that moment. It is also likely that he had only in the final hours of Stalin's life regained full and unchallenged control over the M.V.D. He and his command of this vast police army had been one of the targets of machinations that generally are described as the so-called "doctors' plot," which had a vital role in the events leading up to Stalin's death.

But in the coalition of forces that occurred at or about the time of Stalin's death, Beria got back his M.V.D. Perhaps that is why he overplayed his hand so badly at a moment when he was not prepared to strike for full mastery of Russia. Perhaps he did not fully realize the impression he would make on his colleagues. Whatever the explanation, on the next day, Monday, when Stalin was formally laid to rest beside Lenin, Beria spoke at the funeral bier along with Georgi M. Malenkov and Vyacheslav M. Molotov. There was an undercurrent in Beria's speech that could have flowed only from his knowledge of his power.

He sounded just a little more condescending toward Mr. Molotov and Mr. Malenkov—perhaps more in his delivery than in his language. What was more interesting, he sought to convey without exactly saying so that he spoke for the Army as well as the police.

It took only three and a half months to demonstrate that condescension was not exactly called for on Beria's part and that he had shown the Army, only too plainly, the power and danger of his position. There can be no shadow of a doubt that, from the moment Beria sealed off the Kremlin and Moscow with his troops he signed his own death warrant.

He was not strong enough to rule. But he was too dangerous to any other ruler or rulers. In the unstable coalition of party, police and Army, Beria had too much sheer miltiary power that could be too quickly applied at the center. He was too big for the triumvirate, but not big enough to be dictator.

The only real surprise about Beria's end was that it came so soon. It was a measure of the real weakness of his position (once his troops were out of Moscow) that his colleagues were able to deliver the coup de grace so quickly and with hardly a ripple on the surface of the Moscow waters.

A legend has arisen in some quarters outside Russia in the months since Beria's downfall that he was a great "liberal." It is recalled that the anouncement of the exposure and reversal of the so-called "doctors' plot" was made in the name of his ministry. It is said that he advocated more liberal measures for Russia's multitudinous and usually mistreated minority nationalities.

Some color, perhaps, is lent to such tales by the fact that Beria was a minority man himself, coming from Georgia and being partly of Jewish ancestry and from the small mountain area known as Mingrelia. While he bossed Georgia before going up to Moscow in 1938 at the end of the purge period he did a good deal for the Georgian Jews, sponsoring a charitable Jewish aid society, various trade and farm schools and even opening a museum of Jewish culture, which still survives.

Liberal label belied

However, as Stalin's police chief he was the man who carried out the deportation of hundreds of thousands of minority nationals from their home places, Balts to Central Asia, Byelorussians to Siberia, Jews to the Far North, and so on. It is hard to find in his record as M.V.D. chief any trace of "liberalism." Nor did I ever hear anyone in Russia suggest that the chief of the secret police was really a kind and liberal man.

One piece of so-called evidence that was cited to bolster the case for Beria's "liberalism" was the fact that, whereas the man he installed as chief of special investigations of the M.V.D. after the reversal of the doctors' case in April, 1953, was executed along with Beria last December, the previous chief inquisitor, a man named Ryumin whom Beria had blamed for fabricating the doctors' plot evidence, had not, apparently, been punished.

Six weeks ago, however, a brief announcement in the Soviet press revealed that Ryumin had been executed for his role in the notorious conspiracy. That demolished about the only remaining pin supporting the case of "Beria the liberal."

Naturally, hardly a word of any of the foregoing was ever permitted to pass the Moscow censorship.

66. *The Vietnam Nightmare Begins*

As chief of the Associated Press' Saigon bureau in 1963, Malcolm Browne had the difficult job of coordinating coverage of the Diem family government and its clashes with various Vietnamese groups. He had to fight official censorship and the other problems in a police state to get his stories out, but he was dedicated and persistent in reporting the events leading up to and during the Vietnam War. The story below is an impressive example of a thorough and compelling wrap-up piece. It shows how several events from different locales were related and what their impact was likely to be. His descriptive yet restrained style makes the deaths of the Buddhist monks and nuns seem all the more disturbing, while placing their acts within the overall scope of events in the country. *(Pulitzer Prize for International Reporting, 1964)*

Political 'Realism' Rips Nation Apart
Malcolm W. Browne
Associated Press
September 7, 1963

In its nine years of independent existence, South Vietnam has been scourged by terror and political intrigue.

Now it is experiencing a nightmare.

The nightmare began 10 days ago, and its effects have jolted capitals around the world.

Buddhist soldiers—trained by Americans—invaded pagodas where once they had worshiped. They cracked the skulls of Buddhist monks. Shotgun blasts shattered the serenity of monastery cloisters.

Catholic joined Buddhist in fighting other Catholics and Buddhists. Families were torn apart. Friends became enemies. Blood flowed in town and city.

In the countryside, furtive Communist Viet Cong guerrillas fought on. In North Vietnam, the Communist regime gleefully broadcast the news from the south, as if anticipating an issue for rallying the population behind the drive they have relentlessly pursued since the 1930s to envelop the whole country for communism.

"Here goes eight years and $2 billion worth of American aid down the drain," remarked a U.S. official sourly as reports of violence poured into his office.

U.S. Asian policy endangered

In Washington, administration officials feared a keystone of U.S. policy in Asia might be tottering. Americans have stationed 14,000 troops on Vietnam's soil and are spending $500 million a year to shore up this little chunk of Southeast Asia against the Communist steamroller.

What motivated the violent government crackdown on the Buddhists? From remarks dropped by persons close to President Ngo Dinh Diem and his powerful brother, Ngo Dinh Nhu—who together rule the country—it seemed the plan was to crush Buddhist and political opposition, force potentially recalcitrant army leaders to support the government, and lay down a hard line to the United States, all in one sweep.

"To save a nation, radical surgery is necessary sometimes," said a ranking Vietnamese cabinet minister. "We believe history will show we were right. America disagrees. But America lost China, Laos and many other countries to the Communists. We think our methods are realistic.''

The chain of events began May 8 in the city of Hue. An angry crowd gathered at Hue's main pagoda, Tu Dam. Leading monks made speeches the like of which had not been heard in public since the Diem administration began.

The government had ordered religious flags taken down everywhere. Buddhists were angry. It was Buddha's birthday. Flying the five-colored Buddhist banner was among the traditions. They were embittered because Roman Catholic banners still flew in various communities. The president and his family are Catholics, and this also is a source of Buddhist resentment. Perhaps three quarters of the people embraced one form of Buddhism or another.

An obscure major resorts to force

From the gently rising hill where the Tu Dam pagoda is perched, thousands of persons marched behind saffron-robed monks and nuns. They trudged along Hue's main boulevard to an American-built broadcasting station. There they demanded entrance to broadcast their protests, and the first of a long series of bloody demonstrations erupted.

An obscure major named Dang Sy, the local security officer, threw his forces at the demonstrators. Troops fired in the air. Soldiers hurled tear gas gernades. Fire hoses were turned on. Two blasts went off in the crowd—grenades, said the Buddhists. Armored cars crushed several persons beneath them. Screaming girls hurled their shoes at troops and vehicles.

When it was over, eight were dead. Three more died later of wounds.

The news spread, and insurrection rumbled among the Buddhists. Men and women who had not been in pagodas for years chanted long-forgotten prayers.

In a country like Vietnam, politics is made in the cities. The countryside peasant, busy scratching out a living, knows little of the forces shaping his destiny and cares about politics only when he is directly affected. But people in cities like Hue and the coastal towns are strongly Buddhist and know what is going on.

Townspeople of Hue hardworking, tough

Hue normally is preoccupied with its own bustling affairs. The town is bisected by the Perfume River and dotted with magnificent tombs of bygone kings. Its 90,000 residents are tough, courageous, accustomed to hard work. President Diem and his ruling family come from a village near Hue, and from the Hue area come many of the regime's deadliest enemies.

Saigon is not easily aroused. A sprawling capital of 2 million, Frenchified and lovely despite teeming slums, it has seen politicians, wars and crises come and go. But many Saigonese were aroused now.

Buddhist leaders put forward "five demands." They called for an end to alleged persecution, equal rights with Christians, release of jailed demonstrators, government acknowledgement of responsibility for the bloodshed with punishment of the perpetrators, and compensation of the victims.

Saigon, where demonstrations always were strictly forbidden, saw its first public challenge to the Diem government May 30.

In front of the National Assembly building, 356 Buddhist monks and nuns leaped from buses and taxis and stood for hours on the mall, protest banners raised. In Saigon and simultaneously in Hue, 400 miles to the north, hunger strikes began.

Violence erupted again June 4. Students demonstrating in Hue ran into a blockade and sat in the streets. Troops threw glass containers of a liquid—never officially identified—on the pavement where the students squatted. About 70 were hospitalized with severe burns.

Hue's Tu Dam pagoda was blockaded. Soldiers charged with fixed bayonets on any assembly of students.

In Saigon the most violent shock of all came June 11. A demonstration had begun and police apparently expected nothing exceptional. Silently marching monks had just left a small pagoda. A grey sedan led the procession.

At 9:20 a.m. the sedan stopped abruptly. Three monks stepped out, carrying a plastic can. Several hundred marchers formed a circle at an intersection.

An aged monk, Thich Quang Duc, seated himself on a cushion, legs folded. Two other monks poured gasoline over his shaved head and stepped back. Quang Duc lighted a match and calmly folded his hands in the Buddhist lotus position. For five minutes he sat motionless while the skin was seared from his body. The charred form sprawled grotesquely.

A wail arose from the monks and nuns. They raised banners proclaiming that "A Buddhist priest burns for five demands."

Monks shed their outer robes to fashion a sling and carried the body to the Xa Loi pagoda, Buddhist national headquarters. The pagoda's great bell tolled to the accompaniment of thunder from a huge drum behind the statue of Buddha in the main hall.

A week later Quang Duc's charred body was cremated. His ashes were distributed to stupas—Buddhist reliquaries—and pagodas throughout the nation. The local Buddhist hierarchy proclaimed him a saint.

The robes that had carried the body were cut into tiny pieces and distributed. Some said each fleck of yellow cloth provided miraculous protection for the wearer. Dots of yellow appeared everywhere on dresses and lapels.

Yoga, prayer freed old monk of pain

At Saigon's Quang pagoda, a U.S. educated monk named Quang Lien said:

"Thich Quang Duc was a courageous and intelligent old man, adept at Yoga. It was Yoga and prayer that freed him of pain in his final minutes. His act has given Vietnamese Buddhism tremendous moral strength—a strength that will be able to stand even the test of bayonets and machine guns."

On Sunday, June 16, about 8,000 demonstrators moved down a wide Saigon boulevard. Combat police met them with clubs and tear gas. Young men and women struck back with stones and insults. A 15-year-old boy was killed, many were injured.

That same rainy Sunday, about 60 nuns tried to march from Giac Minh pagoda to Xa Loi temple. Halted, they sat in the street. Police herded them into vans, cuffed them about and carted them off to another pagoda.

The government that day announced it had agreed in principle to settling the "five demands," though President Diem said that the government was merely agreeing to policies always exercised. Buddhist leaders said they were ready to accept the government's word. Briefly, the struggle subsided, but behind scenes the political activity was intense.

Ngo Dinh Nhu, powerful brother of the president, distributed a document to the million-member youth corps he commands, condemning the agreement and indicating preference for a tougher line. Buddhists displayed the document as evidence of bad faith.

Many Buddhist leaders were in prison. Meetings in the stark, concrete Xa Loi monastery were conducted by Thich Tri Quang, an enigmatic young monk from Hue who reads and writes English and French but will speak neither. The government has called him a Communist, but he has said he believes Vietnam must fight the Communist from the north with all its might.

On Sunday, July 7, another brief outburst was quelled by combat police and plainclothesmen, but the nation was in for another shock that night.

Nguyen Tuong Tam, the nation's greatest living poet and author, faced trial the next day with hundreds of others accused of involvement in plots. He took poison and died, leaving an eloquent protest note.

The trials brought generally light sentences. They seemed only a show of force indicating the government would tolerate no more opposition.

But by July 13, the day of the poet's funeral, it was clear that every opposition group had made common cause with the Buddhists, even if there was no direct collaboration. The government hinted it detected the hand of communism. It said that agents at Tam's grave had arrested a Red agent who had planned to create a bloody incident among mourners.

On July 16, about 200 monks and nuns marched to the U.S. Embassy residence and stood in the street two hours, calling for American help. Ambassador Frederick Nolting Jr. was away at the time. Police did not interfere, but the government, which frequently had voiced suspicion of American plotting against it, was angered.

Next day, thousands of women and children gathered before dawn at Saigon's tiny Giac Minh pagoda for a procession. Combat police sprinted down Phan Thanh Gian Boulevard with bayonets fixed.

Police boxed in the crowd with barbed wire, pounced on marchers with clubs and rifle butts. Young girls, dresses stained with blood, tore at the barbed wire with bare hands. Police herded several hundred marchers into vans and detained them three days at the crematory where Quang Duc's body had been reduced to ashes.

Saigon's sultry air was charged with tension. There was a suicide fever in it. Monks and nuns for weeks had sent letters to Xa Loi pagoda offering themselves for immolation in flames.

Buddhist leaders ordered barbed wire strung around the wall of Xa Loi pagoda. Inside, nuns armed themselves with insecticide sprayers loaded with vinegar and pepper.

A wall separates the pagoda from the U.S. Aid Mission's parking lot. Monks asked U.S. aid officials to break an escape hole in the wall in case Buddhists might need asylum. The request was turned down.

On Sunday, Aug. 4, in the sleepy fishing town of Phan Thiet, 100 miles east of Saigon, a 20-year-old novice monk named Nguyen Huong slipped from services at a pagoda. In a small town square he poured gasoline over himself and lighted his robes.

Young novice's body was spirited away

Government authorities found the body and spirited it away to a relative. Martial law was clamped on the town whose people are mostly Buddhists.

Near midnight, on Aug. 12, an 18-year-old school girl climbed half way up the outside stairs of Xa Loi pagoda in Saigon. In the rain, she drew a hatchet from under her dress and tried to chop off her hand. The monks said that she had done it as a sacrifice to the cause.

Two days later, a 17-year-old novice monk, Thanh Tue, left a pagoda near Hue in the dead of night, set fire to himself and died in a blaze of gasoline. Monks at the pagoda, intent on a public funeral, carried the coffin toward the highway to Hue. Soldiers sailed into the crowd, using steel helmets as weapons, and laid out many monks. They seized the coffin and whisked it off to a relative in a northern village.

At times there was hope for conciliation. Buddhist leaders said they had trusted Diem's good faith, but were worried about others, including Diem's brother Nhu.

Nhu's beautiful and powerful wife poured more fuel on the flames. She declared that all the Buddhists had done for their country was to "barbecue a monk." Her father, Tran Van Chuong, then ambassador in Washington, reprimanded her and later resigned his post, along with his staff.

Hour is too late for reconciliation

Diem had named a commission, headed by the vice president, a Buddhist, to deal with the problem. Buddhists had been granted permission to fly their flag on certain occasions. The government promised that the National Assembly would look into claims of inequalities. The officer in charge during the May 8 bloodshed in Hue was fired.

But the hour was late for such measures. More and bigger trouble was in store.

On Aug. 15, Ambassador Noiting ended a stormy two-year tour in Saigon and left. Buddhist leaders said they had planned demonstrations after the arrival of the new ambassador, Henry Cabot Lodge. But privately they admitted worry.

On the day Noiting left, a 29-year-old nun became the first of her sex to join the fiery suicides. The nun, Dieu Hien, died in flames in Ninh Hoa near the northern coastal resort of Nha Trang. The provincial chief said that the nun's body had been seized by authorities and given a pauper's burial. Monks in Nha Trang were furious. Demonstrations began and the town was placed under martial law.

In Hue that night a period of eerie, unreal quiet was broken suddenly by a loudspeaker carrying the voice of Tieu Dieu, a 71-year-old monk whose son was a university professor in Saigon. He announced he would burn himself alive in support of the Buddhist cause and in protest against Mrs. Nhu's remarks. He died in flames in the pagoda courtyard a few hours later while monks and nuns chanted prayers and snapped pictures.

Hue was placed under strict martial law. On Aug. 17, with the town's death-like quiet broken only by the rumble of military vehicles, the government announced dismissal of the Catholic rector of Hue University, who had been moderate in his approach to the Buddhist problem. There was talk that he had clashed with Archbishop Ngo Dinh Thuc, another brother of President Diem. Students, both Catholic and Buddhist, promptly demonstrated.

A nationalist crisis was at hand. On Sunday, Aug. 18, Hue's Tu Dam pagoda, opened by government permission, was jammed by people listening to funeral oratory over Tieu Dieu's body. In Saigon, about 17,000 rallied at Xa Loi pagoda, chanting and cheering. In a dozen or more towns of the central highlands and coast areas, tension ran high.

Jittery jeep driver enrages the crowd

At Da Nang, a coastal city 300 miles northeast of Saigon, American eyewitnesses reported that a demonstration of about 4,000 Buddhists had begun with official permission. Troops surrounded the area, but there were no incidents until a jeep tried to drive into the crowd.

In the jeep were an army captain and his driver. According to several accounts, the driver became alarmed when shouting Buddhists surrounded the jeep, and he fired several shots. This apparently maddened the crowd. Demonstrators hauled the two men from the jeep, disarmed them, burned the vehicle and beat the officer. Buddhist Boy Scouts finally dragged the officer to safety.

In Saigon, high cabinet ministers said that it was the last straw for the palace. It was then, the ministers said, that Diem and Nhu decided on all-out force against Buddhist leaders, political opponents and what the Diem government once called American meddlers.

Da Nang was placed under military control. Monks in Nha Trang were bottled up in their pagoda. In Hue, Tu Dam pagoda monks had scheduled a huge funeral demonstration for a burned monk Aug. 22.

On Tuesday, Aug. 20, monks at Xa Lai pagoda hauled benches across staircases, evidently as barricades. At about 11 p.m. a monk named Duc Nghiep reported he had received news from a devout and important Buddhist that police had orders to mass around the pagoda.

Just after midnight the monk telephoned a correspondent and excitedly reported, "The police have come. They're at the gate. Tell the American Embassy quickly." Then the line went dead.

A few minutes later, several hundred U.S.-trained special forces troops, police and uniformed palace bodyguards blasted their way through the pagoda's iron gate with explosives. Floodlights cast a garish glare over the courtyard. A din of gongs, drums and screams was punctured by shots. In the neighboring U.S. Aid building, U.S. Marine guards were poised and ready with riot guns.

Two frightened monks scaled the concrete wall into the parking lot and told the Americans they had seen at least one monk shot and killed and many others wounded.

After 15 wild minutes, the shooting subsided. Ambulances and trucks loaded with prisoners roared away into the night. At one hospital, an eyewitness reported, at least 30 wounded monks were admitted.

Throughout Saigon and all South Vietnam, key pagodas were hit, monks and nuns were arrested and carted away in vans.

In Hue, troops invaded Tu Dam pagoda and seized the body of the dead monk. Shotgun fire was heard. At Hue's other pagoda, Dieu De, inflamed people made a stand and a pitched battle developed with attacking paratroopers. The resisters fought with sticks and fists for a bridge over the river leading to the pagoda. Hundreds were wounded. (Probably many were killed. There are no reliable casualty lists from any of the actions that night.)

Dieu De pagoda fell soon after dawn, and while troops cleared the streets, people of Hue beat gongs in protest from behind their windows.

Troops in Saigon took over all key installations and Minister of State Nguyen Din Thuan told a U.S. official that the president had declared a national state of siege. Maj. Gen. Tran Van Don was named to take charge of national security. Posters denouncing "Buddhist traitors" were slapped on buildings throughout the capital.

President Diem said he had decreed martial law to safeguard the nation's security. Arrests had run into the thousands. Ngo Dinh Nhu told correspondents later that more than 1,000 Buddhists were in jail. He denied any had been killed.

American officials denounced the violence as a broken promise to deal with the Buddhists moderately.

67. Incompetent and Callous Justice

An effective news story can evoke a mighty response from readers. The following story on incompetent and uncaring judges by Howard James proves it. With the first scene, the reader's indignation is raised, and the emotion is not forgotten when the story is finished. How does a news story create strong feeling? Not through emotion-laden adjectives, to be sure. Good evidence is provided by James' writing that the most effective approach is for the reporter to select human stories and to tell them with concrete, meaningful, realistic detail. The purpose of James' article, however, is not primarily to fire emotions but to solve problems. From the stories of worthless judges, James leads the reader into a clear explanation of the causes of the problems and possible solutions. *(Pulitzer Prize for National Reporting, 1968)*

A Robe Doesn't Make a Judge
Howard James
Christian Science Monitor
April 12, 1967

It is 11:43 a.m. on a Wednesday in late February. Spring is edging into Louisville, Ky., and on the street people have shed their coats and are nodding and smiling.

But in the courtroom of Circuit Judge R---- there are no smiles. A middle-aged barber, accused of wounding a man, is worried. His freedom and future are at stake.

On the witness stand his daughter, an attractive woman, tells the jury how the victim provoked the shooting by taunting her father and by getting youngsters to block the barbershop driveway to keep customers away.

As she testifies, an aging newsboy enters the courtroom and hawks papers.

With considerable rustling Judge R---- opens his newspaper to the comic page. After reading for several minutes he pulls the section out, folds it into a smaller square, and counts quietly to himself, apparently working the crossword puzzle.

The young woman seems nervous. She speaks rapidly.

Judge R---- looks up from his paper and tells her to slow down. There is a note of irritation in his voice when, a few minutes later, he again orders her to speak more slowly, so the court stenographer can keep up.

The stenographer, who already has put down her pen and is checking her fingernails, says, "Oh, I gave up a long time ago."

When the defendant's daughter finishes, two other witnesses take the stand briefly. Judge R---- denies the prosecution request to let a woman use the chalk board to clarify her testimony.

At 12:38 p.m., the judge adjourns court for lunch until 2 p.m.

Visitor lectured

A visitor, after buying license plates in another office, has stopped by to watch. With adjournment he rises to leave before the jury has departed. Judge R---- orders him stopped by a bailiff, brings him before the bench, and gives him a lecture on courtroom decorum.

What happened on this day in Louisville is unusual. But it is far from unique in the nation's state courts.

In criminal court in Manhattan a judge read his newspaper-sized law bulletin while holding hearings. Lowering a corner to listen now and then, he kept the paper in front of his face as defendants appeared before him. To those involved each case was an important matter—worthy of his full attention.

In Cincinnati a new Common Pleas magistrate, Judge K----, was reading, ironically enough, copies of the Journal of the American Judicature Society during a narcotics trial. (It is the Judicature Society that has pioneered in improving the administration of justice. It should be mentioned, however, that there are judges, known for their brilliance on the bench, who manage both to read and rule with perception and without lapse in rapport with the cases before them.)

Judge angered

Behind a bench in Manhattan, Judge S---- became furious with a defendant when the man's lawyer did not show up in court. The defendant said his attorney was in a higher court in another city. The judge refused to listen and raised the man's bail—putting him behind bars "until your attorney shows up." He also ordered the man to phone the lawyer, James Horan. The defendant buttonholed another attorney, Irving Unger, and asked Mr. Unger to help. When Mr. Unger, who confirmed the fact Mr. Horan was in court, tried, the judge shouted him down and stormed off the bench.

One recalls that Harry W. Jones, Cardoza professor of jurisprudence at Columbia University, once said, "Every multijudge trial court of general jurisdiction has at least one tyrant in residence."

Later that day, perhaps after thinking it over and learning that a newspaper reporter had been watching, the judge reversed himself.

In San Francisco Municipal Court, Judge F---- was hearing traffic cases. He argued with the defendants, seemed to have trouble reading police accident reports without help from aides, and made sarcastic remarks.

When a woman with a Spanish accent, who was trailed by several children, said she couldn't pay an $18 traffic fine, he asked her if her husband worked. Upon her explanation that he had left her, Judge F---- demanded: "Why don't you throw him in jail?"

Later he did show some compassion by giving her a 30-day suspended sentence—but not before he had embarrassed her before her children and a courtroom full of spectators.

When I asked others in the courthouse about Judge F----, I was told he was "a brilliant criminal lawyer who thinks he is above hearing traffic cases" but must, under the system, take a turn at it.

Courts chosen at random

Today there are some 3,700 major trial judges in the United States (courts of general jurisdiction) and roughly 5,000 judges in lower courts.

If my sampling is a fair indication (I simply sat down in courtrooms selected at random around the country and listened), perhaps half of these judges are, for one reason or another, unfit to sit on the bench. This is the same percentage given by several leading lawyers and judges interviewed.

"About half are good judges," says Joseph Harrison, a Newark, N. J., lawyer. "The others have various kinds of shortcomings."

Generalizations upset many judges. They prefer to have adverse publicity swept under the rug, for it might harm their image or professional pride.

Many with high standards find it hard to believe that other judges can falter and fall. Even today some Oklahoma judges refuse to believe that members of their state Supreme Court took bribes, even though one has confessed and another is in prison.

Some judges fear that a public airing of dirty judicial laundry will further reduce respect for law and order.

Others hold out hope

Others, like Robert C. Finley, Chief Justice of the Supreme Court of the State of Washington, take a balanced view, arguing that while courts must be criticized and improved they are not beyond hope: "Otherwise our society would have broken apart long ago."

Certainly very few lawyers or laymen have followed a path as far-reaching as that taken by this reporter, who was assigned to sit in courtrooms across the country to watch and listen. Judges seldom visit other judges' courtrooms. And only a handful of lawyers spend time in court, and that usually in a single city or section of the country.

"What qualifications should a judge have?" Opinions vary widely, and Columbia's Professor Jones points out that "no person or organization has been rash enough to offer an authoritative definition of...'qualified.'"

Vincent A. Carroll, who is chief judge in Philadelphia's Common Pleas Court, suggests that "a man doesn't have to be a genius. He does need a substantial background in the community and a good legal education."

Most judges feel experience as a trial lawyer is essential. Many contend top-flight, small-town lawyers make the best judges because they have broad experience in trying both civil and criminal cases.

The American Bar Association's canons of judicial ethics state that a judge should be, among other things, "conscientious, studious, thorough, courteous, patient, punctual, just, impartial, fearless of public clamor, regardless of public praise, and indifferent to private, political, or partisan influences...."

Professor Jones suggests that "only a man of first rate (intellectual) capacity can make sound, split-second decisions on questions of criminal law and procedure, exercise sentencing responsibilities thoughtfully and wisely under exhausting pressure of time, and improve procedures to make assembly-line law enforcement seem less cut and dried."

Incompetent judges can be classified into one or more of the following 11 categories, all too frequently observed in action by this writer since January.

1. The hacks: These men are given judgeships as a reward for long and faithful service to a political party, or to some political leader. While many make excellent judges, dozens of others do not belong on the bench.

"The most important thing, if you want to become a judge, is to have good political contacts," says one bitter New York trial lawyer. "You don't get to be a judge by practicing law. You've got to sit in the clubhouse and build your contacts.

"Almost all state judges are picked because of their experience in public life—in politics," says Geoffrey C. Hazard Jr., executive director of the American Bar Foundation.

2. The retirees: One of the largest groups, these men seek the bench as semi-retirement from the trying life of practicing law. They arrive at work late (if at all), take frequent recesses, spend two hours at lunch, and go home early. Some play golf or go fishing while men languish in jail and civil cases pile up.

3. The failures: These men were incompetent lawyers who sought judgeships because they had trouble earning a living as lawyers. They can be found in every section of the nation, but are most prevalent in states where judicial pay is low and prestige is little higher.

4. The inattentive: These men have heard it all before, find judging a bore, or simply couldn't care less. They lean back with their eyes closed, read, doodle on a legal pad, or stare out of the window. I have watched some chat on the telephone or hold whispered conversations with aides who want papers signed while witnesses testify. And this has happened in nonjury cases.

In Miami, Fla., Judge Jack M. Turner leaned back in his chair with his eyes closed, his arms up behind his head, as he tried two men for running a bookie joint. A few minutes later he admitted in open court that he "wasn't paying attention" to some of the evidence.

Both men were sentenced to a year in jail.

"It isn't just a question of a judge sitting there in a robe," says Delmar Karlan, director of the Institute of Judicial Administration in New York. "He must be putting his mind to it."

5. The misfits: Another large group, these are competent lawyers with personality quirks that keep them from living up to the canons of judicial ethics. Many are abrasive and short-tempered. Others come to court with their minds made up, refusing to acknowledge that each case is different. In each state a few men simply cannot make decisions. And some, who were skilled trial lawyers, are irritated by the unskilled men who argue cases before them.

A Pittsburgh lawyer, Gilbert Helwig, sums it up this way:

"A good judge has judicial temperament. He must give up a certain amount of vanity and be willing to listen. He cannot decide the case before he hears it. Then there is the question of discipline. Nobody tells a judge how much work he should do. And in criminal court there is a need for compassion."

6. The informal: In some cities "open court" is a misnomer. Most business takes place in the judge's chambers, with little dignity or decorum. It is an experience not unlike having to appear in the office of a political boss for favors or to be reprimanded.

7. The incapacitated: A judge, complaining of old age or ill health and unable to serve, can continue to draw full pay while preventing an active replacement from taking over. Last year only 22 of 30 common pleas judges (the court of general jurisdiction) in Philadelphia were available for regular assignments. One has been disabled for several years, but is serving a 10-year term.

8. The inexperienced: Judging is not a career in the United States, as it is in some countries. The subject is not taught at law schools. Further, "a man can have a distinguished career in the law today and yet he may have almost never appeared in court," says Professor Jones.

In terms of formal training, then, every judge who takes the bench is inexperienced. Fortunately, most begin to measure up within a few months or years. Unfortunately, too many lawyers fail to recognize the drastic differences between practicing law and sitting on the bench as an impartial judge.

9. The lazy: Dozens of judges never look up the law. They "wing it," trusting memory or the lawyers who appear before them, and usually rationalizing that they are "too busy." This group also sees little need to challenge the prosecutor or others who appear in court to see that justice really wins out.

An excellent example of how a good judge can protect justice:

Tom Daniel Grammer, a 19-year-old in Portland, Ore., with little education, pleaded guilty to first-degree arson before Judge Alfred T. Sulmonetti with the support of the district attorney and his court-appointed lawyer.

Before accepting the plea, Judge Sulmonetti questioned the boy. He learned that the boy had been working for his brother-in-law helping to demolish a condemned building. His pay: $1.25 an hour plus "all the copper wire" found. To remove the insulation from the wire he set fire to it in the basement of the building being demolished.

Leaving the fire for two or three minutes, he returned to find it out of control. He quickly called the fire department. For this the district attorney charged him with arson.

Judge Sulmonetti turned down the guilty plea, and a trial was held.

Instead of going to prison the youth returned to a state home for the mentally retarded.

10. The weak: It takes a strong man to rule against a close friend or a political sponsor, knowing that an adverse decision may end the friendship or end the support. For these and other reasons—especially fear of reversal—dozens of judges are pushed around by lawyers or let outsiders influence justice. One of the greatest offenders: the press.

Adds Mr. Karlan: "I hear constantly of judges who are afraid to try cases. Afraid they may make fools of themselves. And some judges let others—bailbondsmen, the clerk, a district attorney, or defense attorney—run their courtrooms."

11. The prejudiced: When a lawyer becomes a judge, he does not simply shed his old opinions and wiggle into a robe of objectivity. Instead he brings with him a viewpoint developed by his experiences. These include such influences as his economic, religious, and ethnic background.

A wealthy corporate lawyer, educated in the best private schools, may have little understanding of the problems of an uneducated laborer who says he cannot hold a job long enough to pay his ex-wife back alimony. A clean-cut Midwestern judge may give little justice to a dirty, long-haired teen-ager, thus making the inscription "equal justice under the law" meaningless.

And there is old-fashioned prejudice. When I asked a Miami, Fla., judge why he gave a surprisingly severe sentence to a Spanish-speaking youth, he told me: "He's only a migrant, after all."

State trial courts have these incompetent judges for many reasons. Often it is because of politics or because the system of selection is so poor. In many communities there is little or no screening of candidates. Frequently the voters pay no attention to the screening committee, or no qualified lawyer wants the job.

A candid view offered

One respected judge, Maurice A. David, of Columbus, Ind., is very candid on this point. He retired from the Marine Corps in 1964 and opened a law office. His experience had been in military law. Five months later a group of local lawyers came to his office and asked him to run for judge.

"I put this question to them," he says. "'If you have such a burning desire to find a new judge, why don't you run yourselves?' Any one of them would have been qualified.

"Their answer: 'We can't afford to run. The pay is too low. Judge ----
is an honest enough person, but he is irascible and unpleasant to deal
with."

With this urging, plus a military pension of $6,000 a year, and a
judicial salary of $18,500 in the offing, Mr. David agreed to run as a
Democrat in a county that often elects Republicans.

"I was elected by the Johnson landslide in '64," he says. "And I can
easily lose in the next election."

About 70 miles west, in Spencer, Ind., Circuit Judge Austin B.
Childress had not—when I visited him—filed court records with the
county clerk for over four years. At my request the clerk showed me
the books. The first entry was made in February 1819. The last Sept.
29, 1962.

Excess of care admitted

Judge Childress says he is unable to bring the records up to date
because he is overly concerned with commas and periods and perfect
use of words.

"I am too meticulous," he told me. "I have made it a practice to hire
inexperienced girls from business schools and train them, and I have
had two operations. Each kept me away for six weeks."

Yet only recently did the six lawyers in Spencer ask the State
Supreme Court to step in. And none apparently wants the job of judge.
Experienced lawyers in Spencer net $25,000 a year or more, one said.
The judgeship pays only $12,500.

Many judges are deeply embedded in politics, or owe allegiance to a
political boss who may be able to influence decisions.

The chief judge of the Circuit Court in Cook County, Ill., John S.
Boyle, has the reputation of being a tough, demanding administrator
as well as a close friend of the Mayor of Chicago. The day I visited him,
campaigning for the spring election was under way. On his desk was a
sign: "Daley for Mayor." Court personnel, including deputy state's
attorneys, wore Daley buttoms.

As I traveled from state to state I told judges and lawyers what I
saw—without naming Judge Boyle, Chicago, or Mayor Daley. To a
man they condemned any judge who would so blatantly violate the
judicial canons of ethics which prohibit "the public endorsement of
candidates for political office."

Threat of resignation

A highly respected New Jersey jurist added that not even wives can
mix in politics in his state. One judge, whose wife did, complained he

could not control her. The problem was quickly resolved when the judge was told to tell her she had a choice: Get out of politics or see her husband resign his judgeship.

Why this concern over mixing politics and justice?

"The need to find funds to finance a political campaign and the low pay of judges are leading reasons why we have corrupt judges," says Elvin J. Brown, a highly respected district judge from Norman, Okla.

One of the great problems facing the courts: Few states have anyone to keep watch over judges. As Bernard G. Segal, a top Philadelphia lawyer, points out, "A judge is just a lawyer elevated to the bench. He may be a poor administrator, or poor at research, or have other shortcomings."

Sometimes he is not even a lawyer. This is often the case in small-town traffic courts and in other courts that handle "minor" cases that are very important to those involved.

Some of these men with limited legal skill push their way up into higher courts.

Legal knowledge doubtful

In Ardmore, Okla., Judge Joe Thompson, who sits in five counties as a district judge, was on the bench, his robe open, his collar loose, his tie askew, and his front shirt gaping.

Although he attended law school in Oklahoma City, he admitted to me he knows little about the law. He got on the bench more than 12 years ago when his home county (he lives in Marietta) needed a county judge—a secondary post that includes presiding over county governmental meetings and probate matters. With no one else willing to serve, the two district judges asked the State Supreme Court to give him a special permit until he passed the bar exam.

A cloud hangs over his passing the exam. He failed it several times. Some say three. Others say four. Judge Thompson says he has forgotten the details, but that he passed with ease on the final try, whatever the number.

He denies reports that he cannot read and write, explaining he is left handed and "can't read my own scribbling." His clerk reads his instructions to juries, he says, because "I've got sore eyes."

After serving eight years as county judge he ran against W. J. Monroe (one of his benefactors who helped him get the initial appointment) and won the seat as district judge. It was a little more than four years ago that he was elected district judge. Last spring he won a second term.

"He's not the smartest man on the bench, but his heart is as big as a washtub," says former District Judge John Caldwell, who served as Judge Thompson's court reporter during his first four-year term in District Court, often backstopping the judge by giving him points of law.

Commenting on complaints that some of his practices raise big questions, Mr. Caldwell says, "Judge Joe lets some lawyers take advantage of him. And when he doesn't like you he lets you know it. So some people get the wrong impression."

The judge also has a reputation for helping out home county folk who get in trouble with the law. But not always.

A man accused of arson made a deal with the assistant district attorney in Judge Thompson's home town of Marietta. The two agreed that a guilty plea probably would net him "only" 25 years.

But Judge Thompson, before sentencing the man, recessed court to find Willis Choate, the young business manager of the local paper.

"He asked me what kind of sentence he should give, and I told him the people are pretty hot, and I'd sentence him to 50 years," Mr. Choate says.

Judge Thompson did. It was later reduced by the Court of Criminal Appeals.

'Court order'

In Sioux City, Iowa, Judge George Paradise made news not long ago when he became bothered by noise outside his home one evening. He went out on the street and told several young men to leave, that he was a judge, and that it was a court order. The next morning he cited them for contempt. The case was appealed to the Iowa Supreme Court, where the judge was upheld, though the punishment was reduced.

In Savannah, Ga., a woman judge is being challenged by the grand jury. Stella Akin, who has served since 1957, is said to have "repeated and protracted absences" from the bench, throwing the burden on an associate municipal judge.

From time to time charges against judges are more serious than incompetence. But corruption is hard to prove. A judge who takes bribes obviously does it in secret. And neither party involved will shout it from the housetops.

"There are many ways for a judge to be corrupt," adds Mr. Hazard. "It doesn't always mean he's going to take a satchel of money."

A Suffolk County, N. Y., judge, Floyd Sarisohn, was recently up before a five-man panel of the New York State Supreme Court's Appellate Division on charges of helping a prostitute stay in business, fixing a speeding ticket for a friend, jailing an innocent woman, setting bail at $1.5 million on a burglary suspect, and freeing three men in a case before another judge. The case is still pending.

Excellence also observed

While problems are numerous across the country, I saw many excellent judges in action. Municipal Judge Murray Goodman of Miami Beach was fair and friendly. When five men corrected violations to city building ordinances he praised them for their cooperation, reopened the cases, and set aside findings of guilty so that they would not have court records. Emphasis is on getting cooperaton and compliance. Yet he does not allow people in court in beach attire, nor can they smoke, chew gum, or read in court.

One young woman in Los Angeles, Bonnie Lee Martin, a Municipal Court commissioner, selected by the judges themselves, was without a doubt one of the finest judges I observed. She handled tough morals cases and difficult points of law with dignity and skill.

While Los Angeles judges were all among the best in the nation, I found the younger municipal judges there more alert and pleasant while on the bench than a few older men sitting in Superior Court.

Oklahoma, despite many judicial problems, also produces men of high calibre—like Elvin J. Brown, district judge in Norman.

How can the quality of judges in the United States be improved?

Many say raising salaries would help. Eugene A. Wright, one of the nation's outstanding trial judges, retired from the Superior Court of Seattle, Wash., last fall to become vice-president of a bank.

In Pittsburgh, Common Pleas Judge Ruggero J. Aldisert, an excellent judge, had a six-figure income as a successful trial lawyer.

"My wife and I have, after years, adjusted to our new budget," he says.

He makes $30,000 as a judge, but his take-home is far lower after taxes, penson payout, life insurance, and other expenses. And as a judge he is unable to write off business expenses on his income tax.

But some say pay is only part of the answer. A burning desire to see justice done, and the prestige of office helps.

The majority of states need a better system of selecting judges. Though it has its detractors, most court critics point to the merit-selection plan proposed in 1913 by Elbert M. Kales, a Northwestern University law professor, and backed since that year by the American Judicature Society.

Under the plan, an impartial committee of lawyers and laymen receives nominations and then draws up a list of qualified candidates, usually three for each vacancy. The governor then appoints new judges from this list. At regular intervals each judge's name is submitted to voters, without party designation, on a ballot that reads: "Shall Judge ----, of the ---- Court, be retained in office? Yes ---- No ----."

First adopted in St. Louis and Kansas City in 1940, it is often called the Missouri plan. Alaska included it in its constitution when admitted as a state in 1948. In 1962, Iowa and Nebraska joined. During this same era other states began to use it in selected cities or for certain courts. Interest is slowly beginning to grow 54 years after the plan was first proposed.

Appointive setups

Seven states, Connecticut, Delaware, Massachusetts, New Hampshire, New Jersey, Rhode Island, and South Carolina, have appointed judges since colonial times, while several other states have returned to the appointive system after finding popular election unsatisfactory.

Yet some 36 states continue to follow the tradition attributed to the Jacksonian era of democracy some 125 years ago under which in order to win office, judges must raise funds and give speeches to people who often couldn't care less.

Tenure, the length of appointment or elected term, is a key factor. Massachusetts judges serve for life, as in the federal system. New Jersey judges serve seven years, and then for life. Pennsylvania judges are elected for 10 years. In many states judges serve four years. These include Arizona, Arkansas, Idaho, Oklahoma, South Carolina, South Dakota, Washington, and several others.

Vermont judges are elected to two-year terms by the Legislature. However, a bill now under consideration would lengthen the term to six years.

Few top lawyers are willing to give up a successful practice for a short term on the bench. And it takes time and experience to become a good judge. Thus long terms are generally supported.

Six years is common. In five states judges serve for 8 years. In Delaware they serve 12, and in Maryland 15 years.

Coupled with tenure is the need for a good removal system. California's system is cited as an excellent solution, for it does not put judges at the mercy of politicians, but does keep a check on judges.

Los Angeles Judge William B. Neeley, former chairman of the California Committee on Judicial Qualifications, says anyone—lawyer, defendant, or citizen—is able to file a complaint against a judge. There are no forms to fill out. Only a letter to the commission is required.

To protect judges from cranks and political enemies, the complaints are kept confidential. So are the names of the complainers, to protect them from reprisals.

In California it has been found there is little need for formal action against a judge. Usually a letter asking him to respond to complaints results in reform, although the commission "sometimes gets flimsy excuses."

One judge was accused of "becoming very arbitrary and often sharp with witnesses." The judge wrote back that the "complaint is well-founded. I have had many health and family problems, and I can see how this has affected my actions in court." Although the complaining group was never notified of steps taken, they soon told the commission that "the judge is doing much better."

A few states have adopted the California system, or are considering it.

Supreme Court as overseer

In New Jersey the chief justice of the Supreme Court oversees judges, sets working hours, and generally controls the bench. A judge "can't even take a day off without reporting in," says one official. Yet a proposed system of removing unfit judges has been held up by the New Jersey Legislature for years.

Most states require impeachment proceedings which usually means it is almost impossible to remove an incompetent or corrupt judge.

Most judges have their own "kingdoms," with no one having power to make them work, keep them from becoming abusive or arbitrary, or correct other human failings. Appeals courts only rule on errors of law. Lawyers across the country say they are afraid to challenge judges because it will harm their practice and their clients. And in most cities the public doesn't know what is going on, nor does it care.

Yet many judges and lawyers point out that reform will not come from within. It will be up to laymen to make changes.

68. *A Listless Life of Numbing Hunger*

The following story by William Mullen provides a good illustration of how a reporter can present a critical issue in a clear and readable way. The problem of extensive famine is told first in the stories of two children, drawing the reader into the account through human interest. To avoid the possible problem of thematic disintegration later in the article that could be caused by the expansiveness of the topic, Mullen introduces in the lead the global scope of famine. From the early pictures of the children, he leads the story naturally into a discussion of the reasons causing famine and of the difficulties in solving the problem. Throughout, even when dealing with conditions on a world-wide scale, Mullen keeps the story readable through clear language and explanation. *(Pulitzer Prize for International Reporting, 1975)*

Famine: Slow Death of 500 Million People
William Mullen
Chicago *Tribune*
October 13, 1974

It is the same sun that rises each day over Singimarie Pachuniper, a tiny village in eastern India, and Kao, a tiny village in central Niger in the middle of Africa.

Dawn comes first to a refugee camp for farmers in Singimarie where 6-year-old Saku Barman rises unsteadily to his feet and totters out of an open lean-to into a listless day of numbing hunger.

Six hours later dawn comes to the Sahara nomad camp in Kao where a spindly 4-year-old girl named Hameda weakly gets to her feet to face the same sort of day.

Once in the sun, Saku and Hameda, though 5,500 miles apart, cast the same shadow.

They are the shadows of ghastly apparitions, of walking child-skeletons, doomed by the same natural and man-made forces to a short, unhappy existence on Earth.

"I don't think Hameda will survive much longer," a village official told Tribune photographer Ovie Carter and me when we visited on a chilly desert morning early in August.

"It will only take a cold now, or a case of diarrhea, and she will be gone."

Already too weak to stand on her own for long, Hameda's emaciated body clung spider-like to her mother's back most of the day.

Mother and child stayed close to each other and close to their skin tent. A row of tents stretched like a finger from the village into the rolling, brown desert dunes.

"There just isn't enough food coming in," the village official said. "We are losing two or three people every day now."

When we visited Singimarie several weeks later, the village teacher gave Saku Barman about the same chances for survival.

"Unless he gets some milk within a few days," the teacher said, "he will be dead. Twenty people have died already this week."

Saku and a younger sister spent their days walking like stick figures through the sweltering little town, wandering among a gaunt, ragged populace that was just as hungry as they.

Hameda is black, the child of desert nomads whose cattle and livelihod have been destroyed by a six-year African drought.

Saku is brown, the child of rice farmers killed in a devastating August flood in India.

Until this summer they were children of different worlds, separated by race, religion, culture, and way of life.

Weakened in the aftermath of flood and drought, starved by the world's inability to get food to them when they needed it most, they faced the same fate.

By the end of the summer, Saku and Hameda looked like brother and sister—dirty, naked, and dying. Their faces were no longer the faces of children, but immobile masks, deeply lined with unfilled folds of skin.

The only emotion left was the terror that sometimes silently filled their eyes while they sat quietly through the day, haunted perhaps by their own private child dreams.

By now it is likely Saku and Hameda are dead.

The thin lifeline of trucks that brought irregular food shipments to Hameda's village was stopped in the middle of August.

When we visited Saku's village, India had no food at all to deliver there. The government was just starting to ask around the world for emergency food donations.

The story of Hameda and Saku is, of course, not a new one. Famine has been a killer every year since history began.

But there is growing concern among world food, agricultural, and weather experts that the world has fallen into a situation much more serious than ever before.

They fear that the many thousands of children like Saku and

Hameda who died this year have been carried away in the first wave of what may become the greatest disaster in history.

Many experts are predicting 500 million people will perish in famine by the year 2000.

Sayed A. Marei, secretary-general of the World Food Conference which will convene in Rome next month, believes current crop failures and poor food distribution have left 460 million people "permanently hungry."

"Over the past two years it (the food shortage) has become so serious that it quite literally threatens the survival of hundreds of millions of human beings around the world," Marei said.

"Such a threat carries with it the gravest implications for the peace and security of the world."

In three months of travel through the African Sahel—the semi-desert area just south of the Sahara—and the flood-stricken northeast section of India, we saw why the experts are worried.

We saw in West Africa thousands upon thousands of acres of once productive pastureland destroyed by the growing Sahara Desert. No amount of aid or work could reclaim it—and so the entire lifestyle of nomadic cattlemen, who for centuries were able to live off the land, has been destroyed.

In Ethiopia we saw the aftermath of the drought destroy Emperor Haile Selassie's government and throw the nation into turmoil that threatens to disrupt any concentrated development effort for years.

In India we saw the intense resistance by mothers and fathers to any form of birth control. Their reasoning was simple: They must have at least six or seven children so that one or two would survive to adulthood and take care of them in their old age.

The story was the same in each of the countries we visited—Senegal, Mauritania, Malie, Upper Volta, Niger, Chad, Ethiopia, and India. Each country has more people than it has land and resources to feed them.

Though the catastrophic drought in West Africa and Ethiopia seemed to have been broken this year with a near-normal rainy season, people continue to die in the remote bush because it is impossible to get food to them.

India, which even in good years loses thousands of people to malnutrition, is quietly bracing for its worst famine since 1943.

The problem is that in recent years nearly everything that could go wrong with food production has gone wrong—and all at the same time:

—The global energy crisis has dried up the flow of fuel and fertilizer to poor developing nations which, when they began using them in the last decade, thought they were going to be self-sufficient food producers.

—World inflation and recession have forced the cutback in millions of dollars of development assistance from wealthy nations to the poor.

—Emergency food reserves held by the world's wealthy nations have been depleted to their lowest level since World War II by several years of massive crop failures and natural calamities.

—Erratic global weather patterns have wreaked havoc in the form of floods, storms, and drought on millions of acres of crops in Africa, India, Russia, and North and South America. This year experts are predicting at least 2 per cent less food will be harvested than last year.

The impact of food production in one nation on the wellbeing of people in another nation on the other side of the world is very real and immediate.

Failures of the corn crop in Illinois this summer most certainly means prices will go up and somebody, somewhere in the world for lack of money to buy the corn will go hungry.

Crop failures in Russia that two years ago forced the secret sale of 30 million tons of wheat from the U. S. had a dramatic effect on the rising price of bread for American housewives.

When Chicagoans last winter impatiently cursed their way through lines at gas rationing service stations, farmers in India could not get gasoline to operate their irrigation pumps. Nor could they get petroleum-based fertilizers for their crops.

Indian farmers, who were growing surplus crops three years ago, will harvest an estimated 10 million tons less food this year than the nation needs. That food the country can ill afford to replace through world purchases.

While American mothers complained in the supermarkets this year about the mounting prices of bread and milk, the rising prices were causing more serious problems in Africa and India.

World grain prices shot up so steeply that the government of Niger couldn't buy and deliver enough food to Hameda's village, and she began to die.

Milk became so short in supply in the U. S. that we could no longer ship it to nations dependent on our powdered milk—like India—and Saku Barman began to die.

President Ford expressed his concern when he told the United Nations on Sept. 18:

"Developing and developed countries...we are all a part of one interdependent economic system.

"The food and oil crises demonstrate the extent of our interdependence. Many developing nations need the food surplus of a few developed nations, and many industrialized nations need the oil production of a few developing nations.

"Let us not delude ourselves. Failure to cooperate on oil and food inflation could spell disaster for every nation represented in this room."

Ford pledged that the U. S. would substantially increase its development aid to projects geared to increasing food production.

When he announced the U. S. would spend $675 million on such projects compared to the $253 million spent this year, however, the nations which will be receiving the aid were disappointed.

They were expecting far more, and in fact will ask for far more from all wealthy nations at the Rome conference.

They insist the main cause of the problem is unfair distribution of the world's wealth, noting that the U. S. has 6 per cent of the world's population but consumes 30 per cent of the world's goods and services.

The poor nations argue that birth rates of Europe and America have been steadily declining in proportion to the rising standard of living and education of their populations.

The same thing would happen, they say, if the wealthy nations transfused more of their wealth into the development of poor nations.

Dr. M. S. Swaminathan, director general of the India Council for Agricultural Research, said he hopes the U. S. will be won over to that point of view by the time the Rome conference starts.

"The crucial role the U. S. must play in Rome this November is to put the political will of the developed nations to work to alter the world's food problems," he said.

"Today's food problems are too important for mere words. They need commitment and action."

At the conference, the poor nations will be asking the U. S. and Europe to buy them dam projects, irrigation systems, fertilizer, roads, and expertise.

"President Kennedy said we would wipe out hunger within our lifetime given the political will to do so," Swaminathan said.

"I think he was right, and I think he proved his point when you put a man on the moon. He wanted America to put a man there within 10 years. There was political will to do so, and it was done."

There is considerable doubt that the U. S. and Europe, reeling from inflation and recession, would be willing to foot the bill for the sort of assistance the poor nations will seek in Rome.

Rather than increasing its foreign aid, in recent years the U. S. has been cutting back in money commitments and in the scope of its aid.

"Big showcase projects—building dams and highways—just isn't our bag anymore," one U. S. official in Ethiopia told me.

No matter how large or small foreign aid becomes in scope, it may not be able to alter the vast problems confronting us in the end.

Five years ago there was great hope that the so-called "green revolution" might wipe out hunger and malnutrition.

Scientists came up with new plant varieties and irrigation and fertilization schemes that transformed several chronic food-short nations in Asia and South America into food exporting nations.

But the scientists have yet to come up with a magic formula to curb the greed and self-interest of oil and fertilizer producing nations. They have put the green revolution out of reach for most of the world's farmers by quadrupling the price of oil and fertilizer in the last two years.

Medicine has tried to help by sending cheap vaccines to the far corners of the Earth, eradicating dozens of fatal diseases, doubling the life expectancy of the people of India and Africa.

But medicine has yet to develop a vaccine that could have filled the empty stomachs of the children of Singimarie when the village ran out of food.

Nor has medicine found a pill that cures the colds or the dehydrating attacks of diarrhea that were killing the malnourished children of Kao.

Massive dosages of foreign aid could build dams and harness rivers to help the impoverished nations of the world become self-sufficient.

But no amount of money can buy a monsoon season when the rain fails and the rivers go dry and the irrigation ponds evaporate.

In the villages and camps where people have already started to die, the arguments, speculation, and expectations for man-made solutions seem far away.

In those dark, faraway places where people day by day watch hunger erode the bodies of their families and neighbors, there is a quiet almost ethereal acceptance of things.

A mother's comforting hand placed on her starving child's head replaces words.

A father's prayer gives them hope.

"It is up to Allah," a nomadic tribesman told me in Niger. "If He wants us to live, we will get rain. If He wants us to die, then we shall surely die."

Reprinted by courtesy of the Chicago *Tribune*.

69.   *The Preface to the Presidency*

Among his peers, Walter Mears has a reputation for speed and an unerring news sense in spot coverage. Along with speed, accuracy, and objectivity, he provides the reader with solid interpretation, assessment, and explanation. He tells the reader not only what is happening each instant, but gives the perspective necessary for understanding the large pattern of development. He has the ability to produce comprehensive analytical stories, paying close attention to significant details, coupled with a gift for reducing it to readable, lucid copy. His approach is evident in the following story from the 1976 presidential campaign. *(Pulitzer Prize for National Reporting, 1977)*

New Hampshire Promises Close Presidential Races
Walter R. Mears
Associated Press
1976

CONCORD, N. H.—President Ford's hairbreadth victory over Ronald Reagan in New Hampshire's keynote Republican primary points to a long struggle for the Republican presidential nomination. It signals that a quick knockout blow will be hard to land in the procession of elections to come.

Ford is a winner, and that helps, but the New Hampshire verdict also shows that, when they get to the voting booth, Republicans are closely divided between the man who is President and the man who wants to be.

Georgia's Jimmy Carter was the big winner in the first of the presidential primaries, scoring a comfortable victory that makes him the frontrunner among Democratic candidates. There are nine all told.

Carter's new mantle is one that can have drawbacks. But it is a giant step forward for the former governor who came to New Hampshire as a nobody more than a year ago and left with first prize.

"I remember when we couldn't find a microphone," said Carter. He'll find plenty now, for it is both the blessing and the curse of the frontrunning candidate that he faces intense scrutiny every step of the campaign way.

With the ballots counted after an all-night Republican tally awarded

Ford his victory, the political caravan breaks camp and moves southward, the Democrats to do battle in Massachusetts next Tuesday, Ford and Reagan to meet again in Florida on March 9.

Ford captured his first statewide political contest with 51 per cent of the vote, a margin of just over 1,300 ballots.

With 94 per cent of the vote counted, Ford had 54,051 to Reagan's 52,706.

Among the Democrats, the tally read this way:

—Carter 22,591 or 30 per cent.
—Rep. Morris K. Udall of Arizona 18,146 or 24 per cent.
—Sen Birch Bayh of Indiana 12,376 or 16 per cent.
—Former Sen. Fred Harris of Oklahoma 8,625 or 11 per cent.
—Sargent Shriver 6,500 or 9 per cent.
—Sen. Hubert H. Humphrey of Minnesota, on write-in votes, 4,180 or 6 per cent.

The New Hampshire vote was a preface, to be overtaken within days by the decisions of other voters, in bigger states. Reagan had an apt phrase for it: "One primary does not a summer make."

It will take 51 to do that, in almost weekly competition that won't end until June 8.

Reagan and his managers had tried hard to convince political opinion makers that running reasonably close to Ford was all that could be expected of them. But offstage, Reagan men clearly thought they had the lead and might win outright.

"I feel what's happened tonight is a victory," Reagan said after midnight, with the Republican verdict still in doubt.

"Hogwash," countered Rep. James Cleveland, the Ford campaign chairman. "A victory is a victory, particularly for an incumbent who is making tough decisions...against a guy who can...make promises every day of the week."

There was another phase in the primary, and Ford was winning that decisively. With the vote count nearing completion, delegates backing him for the nomination led for 19 of the 21 seats New Hampshire will have at the Republican National Convention.

Carter led for 15 of the Democratic delegates, Udall for four.

Howard R. Calloway, Ford's national campaign manager, said Reagan had been beaten in his strongest northern state. Reagan said he had done better than anyone should have expected.

They can argue about that forever—or at least until the next primary. The fact is that Ford won, in a state where Reagan enjoyed the ardent support of the dominant newspaper, the Manchester Union-Leader, the backing of Gov. Meldrim Thompson and a superior campaign organization.

Reagan was campaigning today in Illinois, which holds its primary March 16, but by nighttime, he is due in Tampa, Fla. And the New Hampshire loss may well lead him to intensify his personal campaign in Florida.

"They told us that any kind of a victory would help the President in Florida," a Ford campaign strategist said. "Well, we've given them any kind of a victory."

The Reagan ploy had been to try to hold Ford to the standard expected of elected presidents. That's what did in Lyndon B. Johnson eight years ago, when he won the New Hampshire primary but was rated a loser because he only had a seven-point margin.

But Ford is not an elected president. He holds office by appointment and succession. The New Hampshire primary was his first electoral test outside the Grand Rapids, Mich., congressional district that 15 times elected him to the House.

And Reagan, actually, has been on both sides of the argument, saying on one hand that he shouldn't be expected to beat an incumbent, and on the other that he has the background to prove he can win elections.

"I don't see how anybody could be a right wing extremist and win two elections by landslide margins in California, where it is more than three to two Democrats in registration," he said after Ford described him as too far to the right to win the White House.

He said his showing in the primary "indicates that a great percentage of the people in our party do not...feel that way."

By the same reasoning, it also shows that a greater percentage want Ford to be the nominee.

For what it's worth, there also is a bit of history on Ford's side now. There have been six previous presidential preference primaries here and, in that time, no candidate who did not win in New Hampshire has made it to the White House.

Across the ballot, Udall, the second-place Democratic finisher, was sounding a victory-in-defeat theme not unlike Reagan's. He said he has emerged "as the leader of the progressive center candidates in New Hampshire," by which he means everybody except Carter.

But Carter said his New Hampshire victory was not a matter of ideology. He said that might be the case later, in Massachusetts or in Florida. He also said that in a two-man race, he thinks he could beat Alabama Gov. George C. Wallace easily.

And he added that he had proved that being from the South wasn't the campaign handicap some people thought it would be.

Despite New Hampshire's sendoff, Florida, where Republicans are conservative by habit, remains a difficult test for President Ford. He will campaign there Saturday and Sunday. Next Tuesday, Ford will win the Vermont primary unopposed and should have no major problem in carrying Massachusetts, where Reagan has not mounted a campaign effort although his name is automatically listed on the ballot.

For Carter and the Democrats, Massachusetts is the next big test. Wallace is running there, riding Boston's bitter school busing controversy. So is Sen. Henry M. Jackson of Washington, who has been sharply critical of Carter.

As Udall told it, a good many Democrats had agreed to help Carter, particularly in southern states, to head off Wallace. But Carter isn't just a stopper now; he's a leader.

Bayh claimed his third-place New Hampshire finish was gratifying. Harris said he had hoped to do better and thinks he will in Massachusetts. Shriver said much the same thing.

And Harris had a word of explanation for his No. 4 ranking: "Our problem is that the little people were not able to reach the vote levers."

Reprinted by permission of the Associated Press.

70. *Images of War*

Thomas Friedman's lengthy story on the defeat of the Palestinian Liberation Organization in Lebanon in 1982 is a wonderful model of how a reporter can draw material from many sources and put all the pieces together in a meaningful and readable way. The success of the story is the result of a number of approaches to style and structure. Most important is the narrative form in which the story is told. Rather than using primarily explication or an "inverted pyramid" arrangement, Friedman tells a number of smaller stories, anecdotes, and episodes, all of which work together to build the larger story. The stories are made possible by his gathering of bits and pieces of information from various sources—people and news stories—and combining them with his own observations. *(Pulitzer Prize for In-*

ternational Reporting, 1983)

A Reporter's Notebook: Weeks of Siege
Thomas L. Friedman
New York *Times*
August 20, 1982

BEIRUT, Lebanon—In a sense, after July 3 it was all over but the shooting.

It was on that humid Saturday evening during the Moslem holy month of Ramadan that Yasir Arafat, the chairman of the Palestine Liberation Organization, first agreed in writing to leave Beirut.

Between then and today much blood was spilled, many speeches made and much negotiating done, but it is now clear that on July 3 the fate of the P.L.O. in Lebanon was sealed.

Sunni Moslem leaders gather

The setting for such a historic moment was a fitting one—the white, three-story palace of former Prime Minister Saeb Salam, built by his father in 1912 when he was a deputy in the Ottoman Parliament. On that Saturday afternoon the eight leading Sunni Moslem figures of west Beirut, including another former Prime Minister, Takeddin al-Solh, gathered in Mr. Salam's marble-floored dining room to discuss how to persuade the P.L.O. to leave besieged west Beirut. Mr. Arafat and his top political adviser, Hani al-Hassan, were invited to join the group at 12:30 P.M.

When Mr. Arafat arrived, wearing his tightly creased pea-green army uniform and cap, he and his aide were ushered into the dining room and seated around the long Chippendale English table lighted by an antique chandelier.

Mr. Salam, a still crafty 77-year-old politician, opened the discussion in a praising tone, reaffirming to the guerrilla leader that his men had fought the good fight against impossible odds and had performed better than anyone could have predicted. The P.L.O. had covered itself in honor, Mr. Salam said firmly, and now was the time to leave with honor.

Mr. Arafat was sitting to Mr. Salam's right with his cap removed revealing his bald head. He listened intently to the remarks of the various Moslem figures who controlled west Beirut, and responded with counterarguments of his own. The dignity and honor of the P.L.O.

was at stake, he declared. This was a question of "saving face," and he and his men would never lose face before the Israelis. They would prefer, he said, to die fighting street-to-street than quit west Beirut in disgrace.

Seeing that his soft-spoken approach was not having its intended effect, Mr. Salam began to raise his voice.

The military battle was obviously over, he shouted, and now was the time for the P.L.O. to transform itself into a purely political entity outside Lebanon, for its own sake and for the sake of west Beirut.

Clearly hurt and on the defensive, according to people who were there, Mr. Arafat began shouting back: "Do you want to push us out? Is that it?"

"With all the sacrifices we have made for you and your cause," stammered Mr. Salam in a still louder voice, "you cannot say that about us. It is better for you and for us that you go, with your honor."

The discussions continued in this tone for four and a half hours, with others occasionally interjecting remarks to cool things down. At one point a crew from the Lebanese television arrived to take some posed footage of the meeting, but even as the camera was running the talks exploded into another shouting match between Mr. Arafat and the others. One of the notables at the meeting had to use his influence to get the film casette back from the Government-run television before it could be shown on the nightly news.

At 5 P.M. Mr. Arafat agreed to study what had been discussed with his colleagues in the P.L.O. leadership and return with some kind of answer. As it was Ramadan, Mr. Salam invited Mr. Arafat to join him that evening for the "iftar" meal, the traditional breaking of the daylong Ramadan fast.

At 7:15 P.M. Mr. Arafat and Mr. Hassan returned, joining the Salam family and the other notables around the dining room table. Everyone agreed that there should be no talk of politics during the meal of ground meat, cold yogurt and eggplant. Mr. Arafat listened as the others exchanged anecdotes, eating little except for the black olives set in the middle of the long wooden table.

After dinner Mr. Arafat asked if he could be excused to perform the evening prayers alone. He went into Mr. Salam's den, faced south toward Mecca and performed the ritual prayers on the white carpet in solitude.

When he returned to the dining room table, Mr. Arafat said he had something to deliver. He removed the ever-present green notepad from his pocket and slipped out a folded piece of white P.L.O. stationery. Putting on his black glasses, Mr. Arafat began to read from the document, written in his own hand under the letterhead of the P.L.O. commander in chief.

His voice full and resonant, Mr. Arafat read, "To our brother Prime Minister Shafik al-Wazzan"—to whom the note was officially addressed—"With reference to the dicussions we have had, the Palestinian command has taken the following decision: the P.L.O. does not wish to remain in Lebanon."

Mr. Arafat then proceeded to outline in a very general fashion the security guarantees the P.L.O. was demanding for the 650,000 Palestinian refugees who would remain in Lebanon.

When he finished reading the crucial lines Mr. Arafat handed the note to Mr. Salam, who immediately had it photocopied. Mr. Arafat then took it back and delivered it later that evening in an even more emotionally charged meeting with Mr. Wazzan. The Prime Minister eventually conveyed its contents to the American special envoy, Philip C. Habib, the man for whom the note was intended all along.

The rest, as they say, is history.

The 1948 War, fought in 1982

No one ever quite got the name of this war right. The Israelis called it the Peace for Galilee operation, but it was clearly more than that. The Lebanese tended to call it the Israeli invasion of Lebanon, but that never really captured what was at stake either. In retrospect, the events of the past summer clearly have much deeper historical roots.

In talking to the Palestinian guerrillas one always gets the sense that they were fighting the war against the Jews that their fathers and grandfathers failed to fight in Palestine in 1948. The battleground may have been Lebanon, but to them this was the real Palestinian-Israeli war finally being fought 34 years later, with no Arab states getting in the way.

That feeling of a battle long-delayed came through most powerfully in an interview with Dr. George Habash, the leader of the Marxist Popular Front for the Liberation of Palestine and the founder of the Arab nationalist movement. The pediatrician-turned-guerrilla has futilely been fighting the Israelis since 1948, when he was 21. Easily the most charismatic of the Palestinian, and probably Arab, leaders, Mr. Habash met this reporter in an underground bunker at his west Beirut headquarters a few days after the Israeli Army had overrun all the guerrilla bases in southern Lebanon.

The air was stale and musty, and "Dr. George" sat erect behind a small table, surrounded by a knot of young guerrilla devotees. To him the fact that the battle in south Lebanon had been lost was totally insignificant. The most important point was that there was a battle at all.

His silver hair standing out in the dim light, Dr. Habash punctuated all of his comments by slamming his left arm down on the table, sending little puffs of dust into the air.

"I thank God," he shouted, oblivious to the irony of the great Arab Marxist appealing to the Almighty. "I thank God," he continued, bringing his fist down on the table. "I thank God that I lived to see the day that a Palestinian Army fought an Israeli Army. Now I can die. I don't need to see anymore."

Waving his arm around at his young followers, he added, "I feel sorry if anything happens to these young men, but now I can die, for we really fought them."

A deep bitterness over lack of aid

Whatever their pride in having battled the Israelis alone, there was nonetheless a deep and seething bitterness among Palestinians over the fact that not a single Arab country lifted a finger to help them militarily. The Palestinians finally gave a war and nobody came. Nobody but the Israelis.

A few weeks into the conflict, after the negotiations had begun, a reporter asked a Palestinian professor at the American University of Beirut—if he were going to give a party for all of the P.L.O.'s friends when this was over—whom would he invite?

"The French," said the professor straight away, "definitely the French. Then maybe a few Americans, some other West Europeans and maybe even some Egyptians for the help they have been in Washington. I might let the Saudis be the waiters. No Soviets allowed."

In the last days of the Beirut siege, some difficult weeks later, a reporter asked the professor the same question. This time he thought longer. Again, he said the French could come, maybe a few Americans in Washington, but no Arabs whatsoever. "Not a single one," he said. "I would not even let the Saudis clean up after the meal."

Anger expressed in graffiti

It was inevitable that this bitterness would eventually express itself in the form of graffiti, particularly as the siege wore on. Someone calling himself "Ayub" began putting up crudely written Arabic posters in shop windows on the side streets off west Beirut's main Hamra thoroughfare. Most of them were addressed to the Arabs.

"There are two kinds of Arabs today," read one sign. "The Arabs of fear and the Arabs of sheep. But we alone in west Beirut are making history. Ayub."

"Today we are in shelters," read another poster, "but tomorrow the Arab leaders will be on shish kebab skewers. Ayub."

Finally, the one that captured the truly existential sense of abandonment felt by many Palestinians and even Lebanese, read: "Tell your children what Israel has done. Tell your children what the Arabs have done. Tell your children what the world has done. Ayub."

In an interview in the first month of the war, Mr. Arafat told a reporter that the Arab inaction was only temporary. "How long," he asked, "will the Arabs remain silent?" Clearly, it was much longer than either he or the anonymous Ayub ever expected. Ayub, incidentally, is the Arabic name for Job, the biblical figure of endlessly patient suffering.

'I will not shake the hand of an occupier'

War, like politics, makes for some strange bedfellows. In the early weeks of the Israeli invasion, correspondents who had lived and worked in P.L.O.-controlled west Beirut for their entire careers suddenly found themselves nose-to-nose with Israeli soldiers and officers besieging the capital. There was a certain attractive novelty to these meetings at first. Reporters used to go for a day to Christian east Beirut or the surrounding hills just to "talk to an Israeli," and sniff them over as if they were some kind of strange beings. The favorite watering hole for these close encounters was Emille's Restaurant in Baabda.

One afternoon a group of west Beirut-based reporters trundled off to Emille's to meet some of their colleagues from Jerusalem and an Israeli officer. Included in the west Beirut contingent was a Jewish reporter from a Communist European paper, one of the very few Jewish correspondents working out of the western half of the capital.

When they arrived at Emille's, the Israeli officer went around the table introducing himself and shaking hands with each correspondent, until he got to the Communist reporter. The Communist refused to shake the Israeli officer's hand, saying "I will not shake the hand of an occupier."

The Israeli officer shrugged off the slight, and the group proceeded with its lunch. Over coffee, the west Beirut reporters began pressing the Israeli officer for his assessment of whether or not the Israeli Army would storm west Beirut, and, if it did, what would happen to all of the correspondents living there in the Commodore Hotel. The officer told them not to worry, that no harm would come to any journalists—but they kept pressing him. Finally, the exasperated officer said, "If I have to, I will personally drive my own car into west Beirut and take you all out safely.

"All except this one," he added, pointing his finger at the Communist correspondent who had snubbed him.

"But," chimed in the other reporters, "he is the only Jew among us."

Said the Israeli officer, "I should have known."

A blase attitude toward violence

The first thing one develops after living in Beirut for any length of time is a sense that all violence is localized. Because so many shooting incidents between rival gangs used to break out at any moment around town, people began taking them in stride. If it was not happening on your street, outside your door, then it might as well not be happening at all. Life would go on as usual, only a bit nosier.

This somewhat blase attitude toward violence carried over into the first weeks of the Israeli invasion, when one could find Israeli fighter jets attacking Palestinian positions on the southern outskirts of the city, while across town people were sitting in seaside coffee houses taking in the entire drama with the aplomb of spectators at the Paris air show. There was also an unspoken understanding—which later evaporated—that somehow the Israelis knew what they were doing and whom they were hitting. People actually moved about freely during the first air raids, counting on the renowned accuracy of Israeli pilots.

"I was going out one afternoon in the middle of an air attack," remembers Nawaf Salam, a university researcher, "and my parents told me, 'Stop, don't go out; the planes are everywhere.' I told them, 'Look, this is not Bashir Gemayel and the Phalangists. This is Sharon.' Right away they knew what I meant and let me go. Only later, when the Israelies started hitting everywhere, did this break down. Then, everyone felt he could be a victim."

Amid bombing, a little mouse causes fear

One of the most fascinating things one could observe during the siege, and nearly daily bombardments of some magnitude or another, was how, despite it all, people remained for the most part so very human. Just when you expected people to be paralyzed by fear, they reacted in just the opposite way—especially the Lebanese, who have a certain anarchic resistance to disorder.

The editor of a widely known Beirut newsletter tells the story of being in his apartment with his college-age daughter the night of a particularly heavy bombardment of west Beirut by Israeli artillery and gunboats. Their apartment is directly across from that of a senior P.L.O. official. Shells were whistling back and forth, and Israeli planes were crisscrossing the night sky, dropping orange flares that hung over the Palestinian refugee camps like spotlights over a boxing ring. There was no electricity, and the editor and his daughter were lodged in the middle of the apartment trying to avoid the rattling windows.

Suddenly they saw a mouse.

It had crawled out from behind a sideboard, and its two little eyes were flashing right up at them.

"Well, let me tell you something," remembered the editor. "We forgot about everything going on around us. I can stand the bombing, but cannot stand a mouse in the house. My daughter grabbed a flashlight, and I found a big fly swatter, which was the only weapon we had in the apartment, and we chased that little mouse all over, even out onto the balcony. We didn't give a damn about the planes. Fear for us came from that little mouse."

Israelis urge all civilians to flee Beirut

Ever since the last week in June the Israelis have been trying to get the estimated 500,000 civilians in west Beirut to leave so that they would not come under fire when the Israeli Army attacked the 6,000 to 9,000 guerrillas trapped in the western half of the capital. They made repeated radio broadcasts and twice dropped multi-colored leaflets warning people to flee for their lives. This, however, was easier said than done.

Many husbands sent their wives and children out, but stayed behind to protect their apartments and property from the thousands of squatters looking for shelter. Many people would leave and come back as soon as the fighting died down, because they could not afford to live in a hotel or rented apartment in east Beirut or the mountains. Almost all of the wealthy left, many of them leaving their apartments behind in the hands of Indian, Ceylonese or Eritrean maids whose passports they would take with them to insure that the servants did not abandon west Beirut.

But there was one group of people who could not leave even if they wanted to—the 200,000 civilian Palestinian refugees. The people whose houses, property and lives were the most battered by the Israeli attack could not leave, with some exceptions, because the Christian Phalangist militiamen of east Beirut would not let them through the crossing points.

One refugee's attempt to leave

After the Israeli bombardment of Sunday, Aug. 1—dubbed by the west Beirut press as "Black Sunday" because of the intensity of the shelling—the leftist Beirut daily As Safir carried the story of a 50-year-old Palestinian refugee with official papers from the Lebanese Government. The man could no longer stand life in besieged west Beirut and decided to take his chances and try to cross to the Christian eastern half of the capital, having heard that some people were being let through.

When he came to the Museum Crossing point, he first encountered an Israeli checkpoint. The Israeli soldiers examined his papers and waved him through. A few hundred feet down the road he came to a Phalangist checkpoint, the paper said. The Phalangist militiamen took one look at his documents and turned him back.

Lugging a single suitcase with all of his belongings stuffed inside, the man trudged back to the Israeli checkpoint. Just as he got there sniping broke out along the crossing point, between Palestinian and Israeli troops. The man ran for cover, leaving his suitcase sitting in the middle of the road outside the Israeli position.

When the shooting stopped, the Israeli soldiers emerged from their outpost and found the suitcase sitting there. Fearing that it was some kind of booby-trapped object, they riddled it with machine-gun fire, the paper reported. By this time the old man had returned to claim his belongings. The Israelis were apologetic. The old man bundled together his tattered luggage and shredded identity papers and shuffled back to west Beirut.

Arafat and aides disappear from public view

In the final days of the Beirut siege, the top officials and military officers of the P.L.O., including Yasir Arafat, all but disappeared from public view. Almost no interviews were being granted, and the normally gregarious Mr. Arafat was not being pictured in any papers for days at a time. Palestinian officials said the guerrilla chieftains were taking extraordinary security precautions to avoid possible Israeli "hit squads" or attempted assassination by fighter planes.

The anti-Palestinian Christian Phalangist radio took to broadcasting the names of buildings where they said Mr. Arafat was sleeping at night, as part of their own psychological war against the guerrillas.

A leading Lebanese politician, who was acting as a central intermediary between Mr. Arafat and Mr. Habib, said that even he had not seen the guerrilla leader since Aug. 1. He said Mr. Arafat would no longer communicate by telephone and sent all his messages through written notes by way of two trusted aides. Answers to his messages have to be communicated through the same aides, who can be reached at a special phone number.

Unusual security measures

Mr. Arafat is understood to sleep at a different location every night and to travel around in at least a dozen different armor-plated automobiles of various sizes and shapes.

His fears are not without some foundation. On Aug. 6 two Israeli fighter planes prowled around the central west Beirut skyline in the early afternoon and out of nowhere swooped down and blew apart a single six-story apartment bloc in the heart of the city. Scores of civilians were crushed to death in the building, and it is strongly rumored that some P.L.O. officials might have been using the apartment bloc as a type of auxiliary office. It was the only building bombed by the Israeli jets the entire day and was nowhere near the front.

Just how cautious Mr. Arafat has become was reflected in an incident that took place in late July, in the middle of the negotiations. Mr. Arafat was at the home of a distinguished Lebanese politician, holding talks in his living room while his guards and the Lebanese politician's guards stood watch in an adjacent sitting room.

Suddenly the phone rang. It was a friend of the Lebanese politician calling from Israeli-occupied east Beirut. The man was told by one of the Lebanese politician's guards that his boss was not available now because he was meeting with Mr. Arafat. As soon as those words were out of his mouth one of Mr. Arafat's guards scribbled out a note saying that his location had just been revealed to someone calling from east Beirut. The note was slipped to Mr. Arafat in the meeting; he read it, passed it on to his host and immediately asked to be excused.

Human nature at the frontier

The most fascinating aspects about reporting events in Lebanon are the insights it affords into human nature. It is only at the frontier, under extreme conditions, that you see how people are capable of behaving both positively and negatively. Lebanon today is the frontier. In besieged west Beirut you find out which one of your neighbors will share his last bottle of cooking gas with you and which gas station owner will take advantage of the shortage and charge you 10 times the price. They are all here, mixed together in the same city.

The summer in Lebanon: one vivid image

Of all the images from the summer, none stands out more vividly than the one from June 5—the day before the actual invasion began. A reporter and his assistant were driving to south Lebanon along the coastal highway running out of Beirut. A few miles south of the capital they stopped to pick up a bottle of water. While they were halted, two Israeli jets dive-bombed the highway only a few miles ahead, near Naameh, turning a 500-yard stretch of road into a field of crushed asphalt and twisted cars.

The reporter and his colleague rushed to the scene of the attack, and by the time they arrived a group of volunteer civil defense workers were already busy trying to pry people out of the mangled cars and a school bus.

One group was gathered around a half-buried Mercedes, out of which two feet were protruding. The workers pushed away the boulders covering part of the twisted wreckage and slowly began to extract the body.

It was a teen-age girl. She was wearing blue jean overalls, wih a blue and white striped T-shirt. Her head had been blown off, leaving a bloodied stump of neck.

Moaning "Allah Akbar, God is great," the civil defense workers gently placed the girl's body on a stretcher and took it away, her arms dangling limply from both sides.

The reporter could never get the picture of that girl out of his mind. She came to represent the thousands of nameless, faceless, literally headless Lebanese and Palestinian civilians who died in this war— whatever it will finally be called and whatever it will truly prove to be about. He often wondered what her name was. Where was she going? And, most importantly, what was the meaning of her death?

In reflecting on that question the reporter was always reminded of a conversation about the brutality of life in Lebanon that he had had before the war with Charles Rizk, the president of Lebanese television.

"In Lebanon," observed Mr. Rizk, "death is at its most absurd and scandalous, because when you die here you really die for nothing."

71. *How the Federal Bureaucracy Works*

Saul Pett, known for his masterful handling of a wide variety of story topics over the years, tackled a massive subject when he undertook explaining the federal bureaucracy for the Associated Press. He did it by weaving history, current events, the nameless bureaucrat, and the typical, harried citizen into a cohesive and coherent story. Nearly 10,000 words long and containing more than 100 numbers, the story is impressive for its specificity as well as for its huge scope. Pett takes common, and frequently vague, complaints (overregulation, inefficiency, reckless spending) and backs them up with stories from real people. Pett goes further, however, by explaining the conditions that led to such complaints. Despite the unusual length of the story, interest is sustained, thanks to the informational rewards Pett offers. The reader learns that the government supports sixteen glassblowers, four bicycle repairmen, and five swineherds on its vast payroll. What reader could possibly turn away from such a tale? *(Pulitzer Prize for Feature Writing, 1982)*

The Bureaucracy: How Did It Get So Big?
Saul Pett
Associated Press
1981

WASHINGTON—We begin with the sentiments of two Americans two centuries apart but joined in a symmetry of indignation.

One said this: "He has erected a multitude of new offices and sent hither swarms of officers to harass our people, and eat out their substance."

The other said this: "The government is driving me nuts. The forms are so complicated I have to call my accountant at $35 an hour or my lawyer at $125 an hour just to get a translation."

The latter opinion belongs to Roger Gregory, a carpenter and small contractor of Sandy Springs, Md., a man of otherwise genial disposition.

The first statement was made by Thomas Jefferson of Monticello,

Va., in the Declaration of Independence in the bill of particulars against the king of England that launched the American Revolution.

It is one of the ironies of history that a nation born out of a deep revulsion for large, overbearing government is now itself complaining, from sea to shining sea, about large, overbearing government.

Somewhere between Thomas Jefferson and Roger Gregory, something went awry in the American growth hormone. And now, in our 40th presidency, Ronald Reagan is trying to saddle and tame a brontosaurus of unimaginable size, appetite, ubiquity and complexity.

In designing a government, James Madison said, "The great difficulty is this: you must first enable the government to control the governed and, in the next place, oblige it to govern itself." Has it?

One is often told that in a democracy the people get the government they deserve. In the process, do they also get more government than they want? Does anybody recall voting for regulations which resulted in three years of litigation between the city of Los Angeles and the U.S. Department of Labor over whether the city was guilty of discrimination against the handicapped by refusing to hire an assistant tree-trimmer with emotional problems?

The government of the United States is so big you can't say where it begins and where it ends. It is so shapeless you can't diagram it with boxes because, after you put the president here and Congress there and the judiciary in a third place, where in the hell do you put the Ad Hoc Committee for the Implementation of PL89-306? Or the Interagency Bird Hazard Committee? Or the Interagency Task Force on Inadvertent Modifications of the Stratosphere? Or the Interdepartmental Screw Thread Committee? Or the Interglacial Panel on the Present?

The government of the United States is so unstructured it is owned by everybody and owned by nobody and run by nobody. Presidents run only a part of it. Presidents can't even find and sort out the separate parts.

Jimmy Carter tried. On the crest of promises to streamline and make sense out of the federal bureaucracy, he began by looking for the blueprint. He appointed a panel and the panel looked everywhere, in the drawers, in the closets, in the safe, but they couldn't find it.

"We were unable," the panel concluded, "to obtain a single document containing a complete and current listing of government units which are part of the federal government. We could find no established criteria to determine whether an organizational unit should be included or excluded in such a list."

President Carter never did find out what he was president of. As a candidate, he had flayed the "horrible, bloated bureaucracy." As president, he managed to reduce one or two minor horrors but added to the bloat.

Other presidents have found the bureaucracy an immovable yeast. Franklin Roosevelt ran into so much resistance from the old departments, he created a flock of new agencies around them to get action. Harry Truman complained the president can issue an order and "nothing happens." He tried to reorganize the bureaucracy with the help of Herbert Hoover but not much changed. John Kennedy said it was like dealing with a foreign power.

It was all much easier when Mr. Jefferson was president. Then the entire federal establishment throughout the nation, civilian and military, numbered fewer than 10,000. They wouldn't fill half the Pentagon today.

Since 1802, the population of the United States has multiplied 55 times while the population of government has grown 500 times. Since 1802, and most especially in the last 50 years the government has been transformed, far beyond the ken of the men who started it, in size, power and function. The capital of capitalism now subsidizes rich and poor, capital and labor.

The number of civilian personnel (2.8 million) and military personnel (2.1 million) employed by the federal government has remained fairly constant in recent years. But federal programs have brought vast increases in state and municipal personnel.

Thus, government in the United States on all levels now employs 18 million people. One out of six working Americans is on the public payroll. Government on all levels now costs more than $832 billion a year. Clearly, it is the nation's largest single business and the least businesslike.

None violates Polonius' advice to Laertes more severely than Uncle Sam. He is both a borrower and a lender. He borrows in cosmic amounts and lends on a celestial scale. He lends at less interest than he borrows. And every year, billions slip through his fingers and disappear into the sinkholes of waste, mismanagement and fraud.

But governments are rarely designed for efficiency, especially democratic governments, and most especially this one. This one has grown spectacularly as people demanded more and more of it and as politicians and bureaucrats saw or stimulated those demands. This government was designed for accommodation and consensus. It began on the docks of Boston, not the other side of town, at the Harvard business school.

Poor old Uncle. He does many essential things that only government can do. He is capable of great change, a necessity for governments that would survive. He has held the place together 205 years in more freedom and conflict than history ever knew. But he is a creature of diverse forces. He gets it on all sides and is perceived in many ways.

A big, bumbling, generous, naive, inquisitive, acquisitive, intrusive, meddlesome giant with a heart of gold and holes in his pockets, an incredible hulk, a "10-ton marshmallow" lumbering along an uncertain road of good intentions somewhere between capitalism and socialism, an implausible giant who fights wars, sends men to the moon, explores the ends of the universe, feeds the hungry, heals the sick, helps the helpless, a thumping complex of guilt trying mightily to make up for past sins to the satisfaction of nobody, a split personality who most of his life thought God helps those who help themselves and only recently concluded God needed help, a malleable, vulnerable colossus pulled every which way by everybody who wants a piece of him, which is everybody.

In one lifetime, the cost of all government in the United States has become the biggest single item in our family budgets, more than housing, food or health care. Before World War II the average man worked a month a year to pay for it; now it takes four months. Now it consumes a third of our Gross National Product. In 1929, it took a tenth.

Our federal income tax began in 1913 but it didn't begin to bite until Pearl Harbor. At that, we have been spared the irony that befell Mother England. Her income tax began as a "temporary war measure" in 1799, to fight Napoleon.

It is in the nature of government measures to achieve immortality. Few die. Governments expand in war and contract slightly in peace. They never go back to their previous size. Peacetime emergencies also have a way of becoming permanent. The Rural Electricification Program was set up in 1935 to bring electricity to American farms. Today more than 99 per cent of farms are electrified, but the REA goes on, 740 people spending $29 million a year.

When we were kids, the word trillion seemed a made-up word like zillion. Now it's for real. Last year, the federal government owed $914.3 billion. Next year it will owe $1.06 trillion. It is owed $176 billion in direct loans. It has also guaranteed loans for $253 billion. If Chrysler and the others default, the government debt would rise to nearly $1.5 trillion. Like the man said, it all mounts up.

If you would begin to visualize the physical presence of the government, you must brace yourself for more statistics. The government of the United States now owns 413,042 buildings in the 50 states and abroad, excluding military installations abroad. That costs nearly $107 billion. It also leases 227,942 square feet of space at an annual rental near $870 million. It owns 774,895,133 acres of land, one-third the land mass of the United States. Uncle is big in real estate.

The government of the United States is so big it takes more than 5,000 people and $210 million a year just to check part of its books. The government is the nation's largest user of energy. A check by a House committee found the government was saving less energy than much of the nation and the Department of Energy itself had an "abysmal" record of conservation. The government uses enough energy to heat 11 million homes. It owns 449,591 vehicles. It leases others.

Among others, the government finds it needs the service of 67,235 clerk-typists, 65,281 secretaries, 28,069 air traffic controllers, 27,504 computer specialists, 13,501 internal revenue agents, 5,771 economists, 5,479 voucher examiners, 3,208 psychologists, 16,467 general attorneys, 38 undertakers, 519 non-military chaplains, 1,757 microbiologists, 658 landscape architects, 3,300 librarians, 62 greenskeepers, 16 glassblowers, 8,092 carpenters, 66 saw sharpeners, 4 bicycle repairers, 6 tree fellers, 5 swineherds, and 15 horse wranglers.

"The government is driving me nuts," says Ruby Beha of "Ruby's Truck Stop" on U.S. 50 near Guysville, Ohio. "And the more you make, the more they take."

She complains of high taxes and government forms which require half her waking life, she says, to fill out. She couldn't agree more with Alexis DeToqueville, the 19th century French observer of governments, who said, "The nature of despotic power in democratic ages is not to be fierce and cruel but minute and meddling."

Unlike King George, King Sam sends hither swarms of officers with bundles of money and oodles of regulations. In his great urge to protect everybody from everything, from disaster and discrimination, from pestilence and pollution, he sends money with strings attached.

In this, he is damned if he does, and damned if he doesn't. If he sends money without regulation, he risks monumental larceny. If he sends it with regulation, he risks outraged citizens.

He has an outraged citizenry. More than the size of bureaucracy, Americans who complain about government complain they are up to their esophagus in indecipherable forms, choking red tape, maddening detail and over-zealous bureaucrats.

In Jamesville, Wis., an inspector from the U.S. Department of Agriculture cites a small meat packing plant for allowing the grass to grow too high outside the plant. What, one cries to the heavens, does that have to do with the meat inside?

"I guess," says Dan Wiedman, the man in charge of sanitation at the plant, "he feels that if the outside isn't neat, the inside isn't sanitized."

In New York, the president of Columbia University says that the sum he must raise is $1 million a year for government paper work.

In Sheldon, Iowa (population 4,500), the mayor has to fill out 27 feet of government forms, in quadruplicate, every year, most of them concerning minority employment. Sheldon has no minorities.

In Cambridge, Mass., the president of Harvard says that the federal government, with the strings it attaches to federal funds, tries to decide "who may teach, what may be taught, how it should be taught, and who may be admitted to study."

In Hanover, Wis. (population 200), three men operate a small junkyard called Hanover Auto Salvage. One man is the owner, but all three work 60 hours a week and all three draw equal amounts of income from the business every week. The Department of Labor says the two non-owners should be paid overtime. They did not ask for the overtime. Why, they ask, should they be paid more than the owner for the same work?

In Baltimore, Md., Stephan Graham, director of the zoo, is told by the U.S. Department of Agriculture he must do something about the high bacteria count in a pool occupied exclusively by three polar bears.

The bears have been there a long time. They have lived longer than your average polar bear. They are in good health. The man from Agriculture agrees but regulations are regulations. How, asks the zoo keeper, do you get bears to change their personal habits to keep the bacteria count down? Dunno, says Agriculture, but comply or get rid of the polar bears.

In New York, Mayor Ed Koch is told that unless he installs elevators for the handicapped in subway stations, he risks losing federal funds for mass transit. The elevator system would be so expensive, says Koch, it would mean that each subway ride by each handicapped person would cost the city $50. It would be cheaper to transport them by limousine or cab.

In North Carolina and other places in the South where blacks can now attend white colleges, the Department of Education threatens to withold federal funds unless black colleges are made more attractive to whites.

In Washington, D.C., Sen. Daniel Patrick Moynihan (D.-N.Y.) complains that for the better part of a year his staff had to negotiate with the Senate Ethics Committee over whether the senator had used the letter "I" more times than the franking privilege rules allow.

"Personally phrased references...shall not appear more than five times on a page," according to Section 3210 (a) (5) (c) of the rules. "The essence of the argument," says the senator, "was whether the term we, as in 'we New Yorkers,' implied the term I."

In Janesville, Wis., a small banker complains that since they ask the same questions every year, why can't federal and state bank examiners share the answer and eliminate one of the inspections?

In New York, a long investment prospectus from Merrill Lynch Pierce Fenner and Smith includes this cautious paragraph:

"Section 13. Masculine Pronouns. Masculine pronouns, whenever used, herein, shall be deemed to include the feminine, and the use of the masculine pronoun shall not be deemed to imply any preference for it or any subordination, disqualification or exclusion of the feminine."

God forbid anybody should think that the mighty Wall Street firm was so male chauvinist, so illegally macho, they wouldn't accept money from female investors.

The men (there were no sex discrimination laws then) who wrote the Constitution of the United States were deliberately imprecise. They left room for growth and change. Their descendants often were compulsively detailed.

Somebody in Washington gets an idea. Wouldn't it be nice, especially since there is a lobby of the handicapped, if street curbs had ramps for people in wheelchairs at intersections? Simple? No.

The word goes forth from Washington across the land, wherever federal funds are involved in road construction, that ramps be installed at intersections, each to be a specified width, length, pitch and non-slip material.

The first thing that happens is that in a heavy rain the water running along the gutter is diverted by the ramps and deposits its debris, not in sewers, but out in the street. The second thing that happens is that in the winter, snow plows rip up the protruding grades. The third thing that happens is that blind people relying on canes complain that the ramps confuse their perception of where the curb ends and the street begins.

Washington's passion for detailed regulation has its ironic inconsistencies. For example, the government asks fewer questions of a man buying a Saturday night special than it does of a man importing a salami from Italy. And the man who buys a gun is allowed to leave with his purchase before his answers are verified.

Washington was far more cautious when the city of Des Moines planned to build a viaduct over a railroad in 1971. The estimated cost then was $1.3 million and the feds would put up half in matching funds. But it took five years for the city to persuade Washington that its regulations about environment and noise would be satisfied. By then the viaduct cost $4.1 million. It would have been faster and cheaper if the city had built the viaduct itself, footing the entire bill.

The federal government is easily ridiculed for its bureaucratic excesses, its stifling regulations, its intrusive Big Brotherism. But against that, one needs to recall it was the federal government, not the states or private industry or private charity or the free marketplace, that sustained the country in the Great Depression and saved it from revolution. It was the federal government that ended slavery in the South and had to come back 100 years later with "swarms of officers" to make that liberation real.

It is the federal government that insists management pay labor overtime for overtime work, that cushions the shock of dismissal and prevents child labor. It is the federal government that keeps the poor and the aged out of county poor farms and back attics. It is the federal government that keeps Wall Street honest, makes bank deposits safer, makes the air and water cleaner, reduces deaths in the mine shafts of Pennsylvania, keeps horrors like thalidamide from disfiguring our babies, makes American airways the safest among the world's busiest, and keeps chaos out of our airwaves by controlling shares to the small Citizen Band owner and the big television networks.

It is the federal government and its loans which keep many small and large business men in business, many farmers on the family farm, many students in college. It is the federal government which injected new life into many downtown areas of the dying cities, with money for new hotels, parking garages, civic centers and open plazas. It is the federal government that gave Detroit its Renaissance Center and Baltimore a revitalized harbor.

"I have no apologies for the federal government being interested in people, in nutrition, education, health and transportation," Hubert Humphrey once said. "Who's going to take care of the environment and establish standards? You? Me? Who's going to work out our transportation problems? The B & O Railroad?"

Others ask, who would do all this with better planning and greater efficiency? Chrysler? Lockheed? The New York Central Railroad?

Elmer Staats, as head of the General Accounting Office, spent 15 years ferreting out waste, fraud and sloppy management in Washington. He found plenty. He is not naive about the bureaucracy. He says:

"Americans have come to expect more and more from government while trusting it less. Many of the same individuals who bemoan the growth of government are the first to seek its help when their own interests are involved.

"They decry the government bureaucrats but are unwilling to accept positions in government because the salaries are too low or the ethical requirements too high. They speak out at every opportunity against the encroachment of government but fail to speak up when asked to volunteer for community endeavors. They most often assert demands or speak of rights rather than duty, obligation or responsibility. They see nothing inconsistent with pleading for tax reduction yet expect public services to remain the same.

"The once prized characteristic of American society of hard work and self-reliance too often has given way to the view that 'someone else should do it' or someone else should pay the bill, that someone else being government."

The men who created our government were suspicious of government. They feared any restrictions of individual liberty. They were more interested in preventing the accumulation of power than in promoting its efficient use. Thus, they gave us a government of checks and balances and separation of powers in a design that built in tension, competition, even mutual suspicion between branches of government. It was not a blueprint for a smoothly coordinated team.

James Madison, the "father of the Constitution," said that under that document the states would be more powerful than the central government and the federal taxing powers would not be "resorted to except for supplemental purposes of revenue." He said federal powers were "few and defined" while state powers were "numerous and indefinite." Federal powers would be "exercised principally on external objects...war, peace, negotiation and foreign commerce." State powers would extend "to all the objects which...concern the lives, liberties and properties of the people."

When Mr. Jefferson was in the White House in 1802, the entire federal establishment in Washington numbered 291 officials; the entire executive branch, 132 people. Congress consisted of 32 senators and 106 representatives, all of whom had to get along with a total staff of 13 among them. (Congress has 3,500 today.) The Supreme Court had six justices, and one clerk among them.

The business of the national government then was defense, minting money, conducting foreign relations, collecting revenue, maintaining lighthouses for navigation and running the postal service, which in those days belonged to the Treasury Department and—would you believe?—turned a profit.

Almost all the things that governments do that affect the lives and fortunes of its citizens were done by the state and local governments, and that wasn't much. Then and for decades after, the national government got along on customs and excise taxes.

The chief proponents of a strong central government then were business leaders, and they wanted it only strong enough to protect commerce, provide a nation-wide free home market and a sound currency and banking system.

The public attitude toward the poor reflected the young country's sense of rugged individualism, reliance on family and a strong work ethic. The poor were thought to be poor because of personal failure.

From the Revolution to the Great Depression a century and a half later, help for the needy came mostly from family, charity or local government. Local public relief bore a stigma.

The federal government grew slowly in its first 150 years. On the expanding frontier, it was involved in territorial jurisdiction and land grants for public education, roads, flood control, drainage, canals and railroads. Until 1893, federal money largely went to pensions, public buildings and river and harbor improvements. There were short term federal deficits because of the Civil War, the recession of 1890 and World War I, but nothing like what would come later.

The first federal regulation of the private sector came in 1863 with the creation of the Office of the Comptroller of the Currency as part of the national banking system. In the next 40 years, only two regulatory agencies were added—the Interstate Commerce Commission and the Animal and Plant Health Inspection Service.

Generally, the federal government remained aloof from most domestic affairs. Generally, it was a quiet time and presidents were not overworked. Grover Cleveland could take afternoons off, riding in his Victoria drawn by a matched pair while the citizenry tipped their hats and said, "Good afternoon, Mr. President."

If it were possible to chart the American dream, you would have a steadily climbing line from 1776 to 1860, a sharp drop for the Civil War and then again a rising line with minor dips, rising, rising, rising, to a pinnacle in 1929. We were prosperous. We were buoyant. We were supremely confident.

Then the wheels fell off.

Suddenly, 12 million Americans, one out of four of the country's breadwinners, were looking for jobs that didn't exist. More than 5,000 banks failed and 86,000 businesses went out of business and, in 1932 alone, 273,000 families were evicted from their homes.

In the spreading hunger and deepening humiliation, middle-class neighbors knocked on back doors for handouts. Some people ate weeds and some people fought over leftovers in the alleys behind restaurants and rioting farmers dumped cans of milk rather than sell for two cents a quart and in many places people talked of revolution from the left or the right and across the land nobody seemed to be able to do anything about anything. With all the property foreclosures, with tax revenues way down, the state and city governments were virtually helpless to help, private charities dried up, and the whole blessed country seemed at a dead stop.

Only the federal government had the resources to help, and under Franklin Roosevelt it did. This was the watershed, the great turn in history in which laissez-faire died and the basic philosophy of American government was profoundly altered.

Federal Emergency Relief. Social Security. Unemployment compensation. The Civilian Conservation Corps. The National Labor Relations Act. The Securities and Exchange Commission. The Agriculture Adjustment Administration. The Tennessee Valley Authority. The Work Progress Administration.

The cartoons showed men leaning on shovels, but it was WPA, or a form of it, that built 10 per cent of the new roads, 35 per cent of the new hospitals, 70 per cent of the new schools. Denver was given a new water supply system; Brownsville, Tex., a port; Key West, the roads and bridges that connect it to Florida mainland.

WPA built the Lincoln Tunnel between New York and New Jersey, the Camarillo Mental Hospital in California, the canals of San Antonio, the Fort Knox gold depository in Kentucky, Dealey Plaza in Dallas and Boulder Dam in the Colorado River.

Franklin Roosevelt made the economic welfare of Americans a federal commitment. In his turn, Lyndon Johnson took the ball and ran with it—ran away with it, some say.

The '60s were a time of high unemployment and great economic growth. Every American, it was thought, could be assured a job, a minimum standard of living, adequate diet, decent housing and sufficient health care.

Everything looked possible if you threw enough money and expertise at it—the moon, Vietnam, the policing of the world in our image, the end of poverty, racial injustice, decay of the cities and the sliding quality of life. Thus, we got:

More aid to the poor. More foreign aid. Supreme court decisions to ensure the rights of minorities and the accused. Food stamps. Medicare. Affirmative Action. Job training. Child care. School lunches. Housing and rent subsidies. Corporate subsidies. Educational aid. Urban renewal. Consumer programs. Wars on poverty and cancer and pollution. Projects to combat heart disease, reduce mental illness, raise reading scores, reduce juvenile delinquency.

All of it was part of what seemed like an unquestioning national momentum to take the risk and inequity out of life, in ghettos and board rooms, in factories and farms, in schools and homes. And people voted for the candidates who made government bigger, Republican as well as Democratic, and before long Washington was into everything from the number of Hispanic teachers in Waukegan to the number of prongs in the electric plugs of a bakery in West Warwick, R.I.

The cost of domestic social programs rose from 17 to 25 per cent of the Gross National Product between 1964 and 1974. Defense outlays grew, too, but as a slice of the federal budget domestic programs became twice as large as defense.

Much was attempted, much was accomplished, much ended up a mess. Where failure resulted, it usually was attributed, in retrospect, to an excessive confidence in what government could do. The war on poverty fed and housed the poor but largely failed to make them self-sufficient. Subsidized housing provided better housing but no less crime in the disrupted neighborhoods. Federal efforts to improve student learning fell far short of their spectacular promises.

Ed Koch was a congressman who voted with the flood tide of federal largesse, a fact he now regrets as the mayor of New York swamped in federal regulations.

"The bills I voted for came to the floor in a form that compelled approval. After all, who can vote against clean air and water or better access and education for the handicapped?

"As I look back, it is hard to believe that I could have been taken in by the simplicity of what Congress was doing and by the flimsy empirical support—often no more than a carefully orchestrated hearing record or a single consultant's report offered to persuade members that the proposed solution could work throughout the country."

While the rapid growth of the federal government began in the '30s, it is since 1960 that its restrictive effects have deepened profoundly on individuals, business and lesser governments. Between 1961 and 1973, Washington sprouted 141 new agencies, more than a third of the current total, and none disappeared.

Twenty years ago, federal money going to the state and local governments was slightly more than $7 billion. Now there are regulations tied to the money. Now there are 1,260 sets of rules. Then, federal aid went almost entirely to the 50 states. Now it also goes directly to 65,000 cities, towns and wide bends in the road.

A commission appointed by Congress last year concluded that the constitutional system of shared and separate powers among federal, state and local governments is "in trouble."

"The federal government's influence," the commission said, "has become more pervasive, more intrusive, more unmanageable, more ineffective, more costly and, above all, more unaccountable. The intergovernmental system today is a bewildered and bewildering maze of complex, overlapping and, often, conflicting relationships.

Gov. Bruce Babbit of Arizona, a Democrat, aimed his shaft directly at Congress:

"It is hard to see why a national Congress, responsible for governing a continental nation, should be involved in formulating programs for rat control, humanities grants for town hall debates on capital punishment, educating displaced homemakers, training for use of the metric system, jellyfish control, bike paths and police disability grants.

"It is long past time for Congress to...ask with the shades of Jefferson and Madison, 'Is this truly a national concern?' Congress ought to be worrying about arms control and defense instead of potholes in the streets. We just might have both an increased chance of survival and better streets."

Almost since he yawned, stretched and left the cave to get organized, man has made bureaucracy part of his history.

Julius Caesar levied a 1 per cent general sales tax. He also levied an inheritance tax, which contained history's first and most picturesque tax loophole. Close relatives of the deceased were exempt.

It is because of bureaucracy that we think of Bethlehem at Christmas.

"And it came to pass in those days that there went out a decree from Caesar Augustas that all the world should be taxed. And all went to be taxed, everyone into his own city. And Joseph went up to Bethlehem...to be taxed with Mary, his espoused wife, being great with child."

Long before Ronald Reagan, there was a Roman historian, Tacitus, who viewed bureaucracy with gloom and doom. "The closer a society is to ruin," he said, "the more laws there are."

If true, we are not alone. In recent years, in most places of the world, small government has grown large, and large government has grown larger. The rising tide of paternalism from national capitals has been nearly universal.

Sweden, where someone calculated a new law or ordinance was passed every eight hours of the last decade, now spends more than half of its national income on government. Other countries which spend relatively more on government than we do include the United Kingdom, France, Belgium, Canada, West Germany, Austria, Holland, Denmark, Norway and Italy. Among the major powers, only Japan spends less than we do; it has virtually no military establishment and meets welfare needs through the private business sector.

We are not alone in our irritation.

In Italy, it took Giuseppe Grottadauria two-and-a-half years to get his residence papers switched from Messina to Rome, without which he couldn't vote, buy a car or register his son's birth.

In Italy, it can take four hours in a line at the post office to pay a phone bill. It can take years to get a phone installed and months to register in a university, by which time the new student is taking final exams.

In Sweden, the government intruded on a national pastime. It decreed that people picking and selling wild berries must be registered for income tax. The result was that for two years Sweden had to import berries while thousands of tons rotted in the forests.

In Nanking, China, the requisitioning of 1.3 acres of land took three months and the signatures of 144 officials in 17 different organizations on 46 documents.

In Japan, Mihoko Yokota returned from eight years in the United States and applied for a driver's license. She was asked for proof of residence. She tried to register her new address in Kamakura but was told she needed a form from her last address in Japan. She asked her mother in Hiroshima to send the form by special delivery, but when she went to the Kamakura post office to register her new address in order to receive the mail she was told she needed proof of residence which she could not get from the Kamakura city office until her mother in Hiroshima sent the form which could not be delivered until the post office had the form from the Kamakura city hall which finally meant that the form from Mihoko's mother had to be hand-carried by a friend traveling between the two cities. If you're wondering what yamemasho means, it is the closest the Japanese come to saying, to hell with it.

Students of sanity know there are two ways to react to the Catch 22 situations, the claustrophobic red tape, the sins, excesses and sheer idiocy of big government. One way is to react with indignation; the other, with humor. A carefully calibrated combination of both comes highly recommended for dealing with the following:

The Pentagon's XMI tank program, costing $13 billion, produces a tank which can't run in any but dust-free conditions like those in the lab.

The National Aeronautic and Space Administration asks Congress for $1.1 billion for a new telescope. Turns out NASA made a small bookkeeping error. It will cost $2.2 billion.

The Department of Health, Education and Welfare (now the Department of Health and Human Services) estimates that in fiscal 1979 it blew $2 billion in overpayments or payments to ineligibles in three major welfare programs. Ideally, it says, it hopes to reduce this slippage to 4 percent. That's still $1.1 billion.

Various federal agencies do nothing about $2.5 to 3 billion owed the government by contractors and grantees for questionable payments. Nobody knows the complete total because of poor bookkeeping. One tiny part of HEW blew $1.5 million by letting the statute of limitations expire before trying to recover improper charges.

The government has 12,000 computers. The General Accounting Office spot-checks the payroll computer at the Department of Housing and Urban Development. It feeds the computer fictitious names. Turns out the infernal machine would have paid Donald Duck.

By one estimate, the government spends $9 billion a year on outside consultants. Two-thirds of the contracts are reportedly let without bids. Many of the consultants are former officials of the agency seeking the consultation. Many of the resulting studies end up in drawers and are never used.

One consultant is paid $440 for working Sept. 31, 1978. (Thirty days hath September.) The Environmental Protection Agency pays $360,000 for a study which shows, among other things, that the average speed of trucks in Manhattan is 68 mph. (!)

The new Department of Education pays $1,500 a week for six weeks to a consultant (a former Education official) to design an office layout for its top executives. The Energy Department consults outsiders to explain an act of Congress (the Civil Service Reform Act). Another department hires a consultant to find out how many consultants it has.

A bureaucrat in the Bureau of Labor Statistics makes one mistake in computing used car prices nationally, which pushes up the Consumer Price Index by two-tenths of 1 percent, which increases benefits for millions of people getting regular checks based on the Index.

The General Accounting Office estimates that in the past five years it saved taxpayers nearly $21 billion that otherwise would have gone down the drain because of waste, bad management and uncollected bills. Since the GAO makes only special checks at the behest of Congress, that figure has to be regarded as the tip of the iceberg colored red.

Horrendous as that is, there are those who suspect that private industry is in no position to look down its corporate nose at government.

Clark Clifford, the Washington attorney who has dealt with both for years, says he has also seen "scandalous waste" in the private sector. Paul O'Neill, a former high official of the Office of Management and Budget and now a senior vice president of International Paper Co., adds, "The steel and auto industry make huge mistakes. If you put the Washington press corps on the back of industry you'd find equal stupidity."

With a couple of differences. Private industry has a bottom line: profit. A widget that saves money is highly prized and rewarded.

Government has no bottom line, and money becomes an abstraction, as if it belonged to nobody. In government, if your department spends less this year, you're apt to get less from Congress next year. A bureaucrat who finds he can get by with fewer people may find his own grade and salary reduced.

Also, private industry generally can still fire people. The government of the United States generally can't. Once in, federal employees are tough to get out, like headless nails.

An agency fired an employee for beating his supervisor with a baseball bat. The Federal Employees Appeals Authority ordered the culprit reinstated in the same job under the same supervisor with eight months back pay. Reason: the employee was given insufficient notice of dismissal.

It took a Commerce Department manager 21 months and mounds of paper work to fire a secretary who consistently failed to show up for work for reasons of health which proved phony. The manager had to devote so much time to the case his own work suffered and he received a reprimand.

In New York, a postal worker was fired for shooting another man in the stomach during a difference of opinion. The attacker went to jail but appealed his dismissal. He won reinstatement and $5,000 in back pay on the grounds that the papers were filled out wrongly. So they filled them out rightly and this time the firing stuck but the postal gunslinger kept the $5,000.

Nearly all federal employees are protected by Civil Service or other rigid umbrellas. They are also represented by 78 labor unions and associations. Civil Service was begun in 1883 to replace the old spoils system by which all federal workers could be fired every four years. Merit replaced politics as a condition of employment.

But in 1919, a congressman was complaining on the floor of the House about all the "clinkers" in government who couldn't be purged: "They are in all departments, killing time, writing answers to letters that do not answer, stupidly pretending to do work that live employees must do over again."

Fifty-nine years later, President Carter complained to Congress: "It is easier to promote and transfer incompetent employees than to get rid of them. It may take as long as three years to fire someone for just cause....You cannot run a farm that way, you cannot run a factory that way, and you certainly cannot run a government that way."

Added to the Civil Service complications were the difficulties created by equal opportunity legislation. An administrator would have to think hard about firing a member of a minority for incompetence. If the incompetent countered with a discrimination suit, the administrator would have to hire his own lawyers to defend himself. If the decision went against him, he could lose pay or position.

In 1978, out of 2.8 million people on his payroll, Uncle Sam managed to fire 119 for "inefficiency." Later that year, Carter got some civil service reform out of Congress and in the next go-round 214 employees were sacked for the same reason. Not exactly a spectacular leap forward. There remained a huge permanent core entrenched in concrete and beyond the reach of presidents to touch.

Low-level federal workers are said to be paid somewhat more than their counterparts in the private sector. Many higher levels are paid much less than they could earn on the outside.

Federal pensions are generally better than private ones; and in recent years, along with cost of living increases, 99 per cent of federal employees were given annual merit raises. Were there really that many that good?

In the Carter administration, Carol Foreman headed food inspection and consumer services in the Agriculture Department. "I have a staff of 10,000," she once said. "A few are very dedicated, a few are very talented, and then there are the others."

The goof-offs and foul-ups in government obviously get more attention than the people doing their job. Few Americans were aware of the calibre of Foreign Service officers until the hostages came back from Iran. Few were aware of the young lawyers who pass up golden offers from big firms to work in legal aid for the poor. The doctors in public health get no attention every day they prevent epidemics until the day they fail. The men and women who leave fat corporate jobs to work much harder for much less in government get no space in the papers until one of their number is caught with his hand in the till.

Most students of government agree that the trouble with government is not the bureaucrats, good, bad, or indifferent, but the chaotic system that incubates and nourishes them.

What we have is a big, implausible, ramshackle house, distorted by random additions, by corridors that go nowhere and rooms that don't connect, a house loosely expanded through the years for numberless children, most of them unexpected. There was no family planning. There was no architect.

"Congress has the power but not the incentive for coordinated control of the bureaucracy while the president has the incentive but not the power," said Morris P. Fiorina, a political scientist.

Congress can create, change or kill an agency through its funding power. Presidents can only hope to mobilize public opinion. Presidents seek re-election and a place in history. Members of Congress seek re-election but, each being one of 535, cannot count on immortality. Congressmen get re-elected, not for the broad strokes of history, but for the post offices or sewage systems or dams they bring their constituents.

And back there, everybody is for saving money in general but not in particular. The taxpayer in Colorado may not shed a tear over cuts in urban renewal funds for New York, but don't touch his water projects. And vice versa, the taxpayer in New York. And the rural congressman, who couldn't care less about a Model Cities program, votes for Model Cities in a trade for a vote for farm subsidies from the urban congressman. "A billion here, a billion there," said Everett Dirksen. "Pretty soon, you're talking about real money."

Even the pure in heart can't escape the swelling effect of politics. Two powerful Republican senators (Jesse Helms and Robert Dole) had candidates for the job of assistant agriculture secretary for governmental and public affairs. The Reagan administration solved the dilemma by splitting the job between the two choices but not the salary. Each will be paid $52,750 a year.

There is, we are told, a constituency for every dollar in the federal budget. Everyone seems to have a compelling reason, and consistency is not always the rule of the day.

The American Medical Association, which once opposed Medicare as socialized medicine, now opposes cuts in Medicare on which many doctors depend heavily for their income.

In 1978, the snow was so heavy that cities in Michigan asked for federal money to help with the snow removal. In 1979 the snow was so light that ski areas in Michigan asked for federal aid. Rain or shine, Uncle Sam often finds himself in a no-win situation.

If he insists on taking more time to examine the eligibility of people asking for welfare, does he risk causing some of them to starve or freeze? If he doesn't guarantee a loan for Chrysler will he be responsible for throwing thousands of auto workers out on the street? If he sends a mother to jail for food stamp fraud, won't he have to feed her children in a foster home at greater cost? If he cuts subsidies for the merchant marine and airlines will he have enough ships and planes in the next war?

Presidents come, presidents go, but in Washington there remains a permanent bureaucracy with its own ideas, momentum, inner resources, cozy ties with key members of Congress and ingenious ploys for survival. Nothing evokes the fancy footwork of a bureaucrat so much as a presidential attempt to cut his budget.

Ask Amtrack to cut the fat out of its operation and it comes back with a dandy plan to eliminate railroad routes going through the home districts of powerful committee chairmen in Congress who would never tolerate it. Ask Interior to save money and it proposes to close the national parks earlier or shut down the elevators in the Washington Monument, neither of which the public would take lying down.

Generals are very good at this, although lately they haven't had to be. Ask a general in the Pentagon to cut and he goes dutifully before an appropriations committee, with whose chairman he is secretely wired, and he says, loyally, yes, he can oblige the president. But on further questioning, his expression grows more pained until finally, in all candor, he lets it be known in hushed tones, that the proposed reduction would leave the entire East Coast of the United States defenseless.

Deeply embedded in the inner workings of the permanent government, like the wheels and timing mechanism of a bank vault, there are "iron triangles" of power and expertise which continue to hum, quietly and smoothly, regardless of the passing sounds of elections.

At the three corners, there are the bureaucrats running a given program, the key congressmen favoring it and the special interest groups benefiting from it. They are welded together for mutual self-interest and survival. They can defy presidents.

Bryce Harlow, who has been around Washington almost as long as the Monument, who worked on the Hill and served in high places in the Eisenhower and Nixon administrations, likens the triangles to complexes of bees.

"They form like bees around a flower, and they stroke it and milk it and make it give forth its honey. They are in all departments of the government, and they don't much care who is president or who is the Cabinet member in charge. To a large extent, America is governed by these complexes.

"Lets begin with an administrative under-secretary in say the Agriculture Department. We'll call him Jack Brown..."

Jack knows everybody. He knows the key people in his department who are dependent on him. He knows John Doe and Horace Smith in the Office of Management and Budget. They have been working together for years on agriculture budgets. They socialize together.

Jack Brown also knows Bill Gordon, a veteran member of the professional staff of the House subcommittee on farm appropriations. Jack and John and Horace and Bill and their wives go to the same conventions together, to meetings of the cotton council, the soybean council, the Grange, the Farm Bureau.

"Everybody knows everybody and they all get on well together," Harlow concludes, "and they are all milking the same flower."

More and more professional bureaucrats are people who were trained in specialized sciences and technologies and seek to apply their expertise in government. They have counterparts on the staffs of Congress and in state and local governments. They form a network of experts on which presidents, Congress, governors and mayors rely. They speak their own language. They sometimes agree more with each other than with the people they work for.

It used to be, says Sen. Daniel Moynihan, who was an assistant secretary of labor under Kennedy, that "when the Labor Department needed a policy, it sent out for one, you might say, from the AFL-CIO." Now it gets policy from in-house experts.

Samuel Beer, a professor of government at Harvard, maintains that most of the Great Society programs began with the professionals in government, not with the public demanding them.

"In the fields of health, housing, urban renewal, highways, welfare, education and poverty, it was in very many cases people in government service, acting on the basis of specialized and technical knowledge, who conceived the new programs, initially urged them on the attention of the president and Congress, and indeed, went on to lobby them through to the enactment."

Whether the programs begat the constituents or the constituents begat the programs, whichever came first, the chicken or the egg, we now have a lot of chickens in Washington. And they all know how to lobby. They all know how to bring pressure for and against.

It used to be, someone said, that politics was about a few things; now it's about everything. It used to be that the major power blocs which shaped government were business, labor and agriculture. Now power is fragmented into a thousand insistent voices, which have to be heard and reconciled.

They are highly organized for the annual fight over the federal pie and fight frequently for their slice with the help of interested bureaucrats. They have become so effective as to cause some students of government to fear that power in this country has shifted from the people and their elected representatives to organized interest groups and bureaucrats.

E Pluribus Unum is in trouble. If ever we were one out of many, we are now many out of one. John Gardner, founder of Common Cause, calls the centrifugal forces of special interest groups a "war of the parts against the whole."

The parts multiply like the denizens of a rabbit warren on New Year's Eve. Everybody, it seems, wants something or opposes something; and, in the melee, bureaucracy grows larger and more shapeless and threatens to become, in itself, a government of too many people, by too many people, for too many people.

Reprinted by permission of the Associated Press.